PRINTING TYPES
THEIR HISTORY, FORMS, AND USE

PRINTING TYPES

THEIR HISTORY, FORMS, AND USE

A STUDY IN SURVIVALS

BY

DANIEL BERKELEY UPDIKE

WITH ILLUSTRATIONS

*"Nunca han tenido, ni tienen las artes otros
enemigos que los ignorantes"*

VOLUME I

THE BELKNAP PRESS OF
HARVARD UNIVERSITY PRESS
CAMBRIDGE, MASSACHUSETTS
1966

K 5 3 4 2 0

Second Printing of the Third Edition

PUBLISHED IN GREAT BRITAIN BY

OXFORD UNIVERSITY PRESS

LONDON

PRINTED IN THE UNITED STATES OF AMERICA

PREFACE TO THE THIRD EDITION

Very soon after the Great Voyage of 1492 came further discoveries of American lands by sundry explorers. Bishop Las Casas, though recognizing the virtues of these men and the importance of their achievements, nevertheless drew a clean line of discrimination between them and Christopher Columbus. "For it was he," the Bishop wrote, "that put the thread into the hands of the rest, by which they found the clew to more distant parts." Analogy must not be carried too far. No two men can be imagined more unlike than Christopher Columbus and Daniel Berkeley Updike, but they are of one breed in that each of them in his way and in his circumstances unwound a thread which led his generation to a new world.

Printing Types is one of those happy books which immediately upon publication find that a place has been awaiting them. Readers of many sorts realized at once that this was a long-needed book, though not many of them had previously been so acute as to recognize and proclaim that need. The modestly titled *Printing Types, a Study in Survivals* did more than provide its readers with an unexampled gathering and winnowing of facts; it created in them a broadening of historical interest, and led them into new depths of social and cultural understanding. The book has never been dislodged from the place it took in 1922. Its factual data continue to be invaluable to students, and its power to move men to reflection remains unabated.

Good workman that he was, Mr. Updike built a foundation for the structure of his book in the form of several fact-filled chapters on the nature of cast metal types—what they

were, how they were made, and the alphabets from which
their faces were derived. The organization of the book as a
whole is simple, for its text thereafter grows naturally from
these foundational chapters, telling as it proceeds the story
of type faces in their employment in unbelievable variety in
western Europe through nearly five hundred years of constant change in the fortunes and ideologies of the nations.
What a realm of interest that narrative disclosed! Those
who have come after Updike in the writing of typographical history have in many instances enlarged areas with
which he was imperfectly acquainted by splendid special
studies of books and type and their makers; these and others have set him right where occasionally he went off the
course; and more than once certain of his judgments have
been questioned. But one thing remains clear: it was he
who put the thread into the hands of the new generation of
typographical historians.

Updike's thread was his perception of an evolving standard of judgment which continuously discarded the unfit and
left surviving in the printer's cases types and ornaments of
usable, practical character, adaptable to varied employment,
and of esthetic excellence. The distinction between the unfit
and the survivals is the substance of the book. Updike carried out his search for excellence, for "simplicity and proportion," through the overlapping decades of the Middle
Ages and the Renaissance with its vast enlargement of the
world's interest in the arts and letters, in geographical discovery and scientific exploration; through eighteenth-century
rationalism; through centuries of war and disaster down
to the restlessness and indecision of our own period. In his
progress he walked sure-footedly through small, dark printing houses and type foundries as well as great and spacious
establishments; he went into the conclaves of workmen

organizing themselves for resistance to their masters, and of masters protesting the exactions of government. In relating his personal adventure in this pursuit of excellence, he created a history of printing through the centuries with letter forms as its skeletal basis, with the men who made them and the men who used them as its flesh, and as its breath of life the continuous implication of a relationship between material forms and ever-changing human impulses and ideas.

The publication of *Printing Types* unloosed a force in the field of research which in this country and in England and elsewhere continues to add in book and monograph to the large body of writing upon the history and esthetics of letter design. It aroused interest also in the broader subject of the history of printing, whether general or particular as to place or period. No longer may the history of the press be discussed without reference to the forms and mode of employment of its chief accessory.

Another result of the publication of the Updike book, less easily measured, was a new awareness of the dignity of his craft and of his responsibility toward it acquired by the practical printer. "In *Printing Types*," the writer of this preface said a good many years ago, "Mr. Updike gave away the secret of his own excellence as a printer, made it clear that two things not purchasable from typefounders or press builders underlay his own success in the craft he practised, that is . . . knowledge and taste. Every American printer with ambitions beyond the completion of the day's work perceived through his reading of the book that knowledge was something which could be acquired, and that the process of acquiring it was an adventure which would broaden his field of experience and increase the number of his pleasures. The search for it sent him to a thoughtful examination of the pages of old and new books and taught him the value of tradition in the successful carrying on of his craft. That other quality, taste, he found to be another sort of thing; some have it, some have it not. It probably cannot be inculcated in those who lack it, but in those who have a little bit of it, the amount can be increased. *Printing Types* performed this service for the thoughtful American printer, acquainting him with a great tradition and providing him with a grammar of its language.''

Something fresh and pleasant came upon the American typographical scene. The reflective and ambitious printer studied with a new understanding of fundamentals the type-founders' specimen books available to him. He studied also the best employment of the types he bought and in consequence made the ordinary book of commerce—novel, thriller, or what not—easy to look at and easy to read. Those printers who were handmaidens to the advertising agencies quickly realized that there was profit in choosing thoughtfully type faces appropriate to the subject matter of their displays. In an address in honor of Mr. Updike, delivered at the Grolier Club in 1940, the late David Pottinger described as ''enormous'' the influence of *Printing Types* upon the writing of typographical history as well as upon the printing practice of the preceding eighteen years, saying of it in the latter connection: ''It stimulated the revival of sound old types that had been forgotten for more than a century. It gave impetus and direction to the movement in typography during the past two decades that makes it possible for us now to celebrate the fifth centenary of printing with a consciousness that we have not wasted our heritage.''

The influence of the book was even broader than has been indicated. It went beyond the studies of scholars and the workrooms of the printers into the home of the ordinary man. Through the aroused interest of certain book publishers the layman learned that there existed differences in type faces besides that of variation in size. On the last page of many of the books he now read was to be found a colophon which informed him of the name and origin of the type in which his book was set and the name of the printer in whose shop the pages had been composed. Here, truly, was a new rapprochement of consumer and producer, the creation of an enlargement of interest in the lives of many men of many kinds, a new and sympathetic understanding of a commonplace factor of their daily lives.

Printing Types is a serious book saved from solemnity by the style in which its matter is presented. The writing is stripped clean of excess in any form. It is effortless and fluent but precise and firm in construction, alive without "liveliness." Wit, sometimes dry and sharp in character, slips unobtrusively into the text, allusiveness is frequently there, anecdote is one of its devices, but none of these is employed for any reason except to advance understanding. One immortal anecdote may be quoted here if only by way of indulgence to the author of this preface. Mr. Updike is writing of Fournier *le jeune:*

"Fournier was a man typical of a certain class in France, who treat their work with a respect which dignifies both it and them. For he was neither a bad workman, a bad pastry-cook, nor a bad Frenchman, who, being taxed with thinking that ornamental pastry was the one Fine Art in the world, modestly replied, "No: there are *three* Fine Arts —Sculpture, Painting, and Ornamental Pastry-Making— of which Architecture is a Branch."

A final reflection upon the book, both as concerns matter and style, is that its author brought to its making the same principles of conduct which underlay the work of his Merrymount Press. The book could well have been an important but stiff and graceless presentation of facts but it is much, much more than that. In its preparation and composition as in his printing was the achieved desire "to make work better for its purpose than was commonly thought worth while"; or again in his words "to do common work well."

And so, good fortune to this third edition—the sixth printing in forty years—of *Printing Types*, itself a study in survival. What bliss it were to be reading it for the first time!

LAWRENCE C. WROTH

The John Carter Brown Library, Providence
February 12, 1962

PREFACE

THE Lectures on which this book is based were delivered as part of a course on the Technique of Printing in the Graduate School of Business Administration of Harvard University, during the years 1911–1916, and since then I have recast the material into a form suitable for publication. Each season that the talks were given I saw the necessity for amplification and abridgment of matter, and for modification of judgment, the results of which have been incorporated in these volumes; and now that my task is finished, I realize that further emendations could be continued with profit almost indefinitely. But while such a book can never, in any strict sense, be complete, it must be completed, though even the measure of perfection hoped for may not have been reached. It has been written in town and in country, amid the interruptions of business and in intervals of leisure — and "in time of war and tumults" that at moments made its subject, and all like subjects, seem trivial and valueless.

The chapters on Spanish printing are new — not having been part of the series of lectures. Outside Spain, little attention has been paid to its typography, and what has been written is devoted chiefly to the period of the incunabula. From 1500 to 1800 its typographical history is, to the general student, "terra incognita"; so these pages may give some information not heretofore available to the English reader. Other chapters dealing with this period — especially those upon French and English printing — have been amplified and virtually rewritten in the light of new material, or in an effort to improve the examples *of printing selected—a field that affords endless opportunity for revision.*

Mr. Rudolph Ruzicka of New York, Dr. Charles L. Nichols of Worcester, and Mr. John Bianchi have read my manuscript and given me the benefit of much helpful criticism. I am indebted for suggestions and corrections in certain chapters to Mr. William Addison Dwiggins, Miss Alice Bache Gould, Mr. S. Byington, Mr. Anselmo Bianchi, Miss Ruth S. Granniss, Librarian of the Grolier Club, New York, and Professor E. K. Rand of Harvard University. To Mr. J. W. Phinney, Mr. H. L. Bullen, and to many other friends and associates who have aided me in many ways, I am most grateful.

The chief part of the illustrative material has been taken from books in Harvard College Library, to the officials of which I am under particular obligation for the assistance and privileges they have so freely given me. Illustrations have also been reproduced from books and broadsides in the Boston Public Library and the Boston Athenæum; the John Carter Brown Library, Annmary Brown Memorial, and Public Library, Providence; the American Antiquarian Society, Worcester; the Library of Congress, Washington; and the Typographic Library of the American Type Founders Company, Jersey City. I have to thank the officials of all these libraries for their generous coöperation. To Mr. J. Pierpont Morgan I am indebted for permission to reproduce pages from his remarkable Caxtons and from other exceedingly rare books in his library; and to Mrs. J. Montgomery Sears, Dr. Charles L. Nichols, Mr. C. E. Lauriat, Jr., and Messrs. Houghton Mifflin Company, who have placed at my disposal books that could not readily be found elsewhere. More detailed acknowledgments are made in the list of illustrations. Where no credit is given, the illustrations are from books in my own collection.

The index is the work of Mr. George B. Ives. In some early researches, Mr. George L. Harding, now of Tacoma, helped me effectively; and a member of our staff, Mr. W. H. Smallfield, has been of the greatest assistance in the exacting task of seeing the work through the press. But perhaps the students who listened to the lectures, and who, by their interest and questions, encouraged — or obliged — me to better them, are those whom I should hold in most grateful remembrance; for they have most suffered for the truth's sake!

D. B. UPDIKE

The Merrymount Press, Boston
May-day, 1922

NOTE. *Mr. Updike's own collection, mentioned above, is now by legacy a part of the Updike Printing Collection of the Providence Public Library.* — L. C. W., 1962

PREFACE TO THE SECOND EDITION

I

THE first edition of *Printing Types* was published in 1922, and after its issue many letters brought new material to my notice or—what was less flattering but more salutary—called attention to mistakes. Most of these points were corrected in the second printing of 1923, which, since it contains important divergencies, should have been called a second edition. In 1927 a third printing was called for, in which a few corrections also were made. The present edition is, therefore, the third in fact, though the second in nomenclature, and accordingly supplies a basis for that kind of confusion so exciting to collectors, so puzzling to bibliographers, so annoying to publishers, and to the printer of no significance at all!

Since *Printing Types* was written many valuable investigations have been made, but to embody their results in my pages would mean re-writing the entire book. In the text of this edition I have made a number of minor changes—some of major importance—but rely on my notes to cover points needing full explanation. Even so I do not pretend to bring the volume up to date, or correct all my misstatements or errors. These I should like to excuse (to quote Dr. Johnson's Preface to the *Dictionary*) as the "wild blunders, and risible absurdities, from which no work of such multiplicity was ever free," if I did not remember that the Doctor when asked by a lady why he defined pastern as the knee of the horse, also replied, "Ignorance, Madam, pure ignorance."

The new material—apart from the Preface and those changes in the plates of the book already alluded to—is embodied in notes at the end of each volume, and consists in corrections and additions which cover later research by others, or change of opinion by me; references to the most important books bearing on my subject which have appeared since 1922; and additional facsimiles of the Garamond and Bell types. One value of *Printing Types* has been to provoke interest in a subject generally considered dull and to tie the typography of various times to the life about it; but its chief value is its use as a spring-board from which more adventurous souls have plunged into deeper waters than I have enough skill, patience, or knowledge to embark upon. *Vivat sequens.*

II

When I wrote *Printing Types* the Egenolff-Berner specimen-sheet of 1592 was not known to me, though discovered by Herr Mori in 1920. Its value historically lies in the fact that the names of the designers of its types are given, and thus it supplies us with authentic reproductions of fonts cut by Garamond and Granjon. A copy of the 1621 specimen-book of Jean Jannon of Sedan—though listed in Bigmore and Wyman's *Bibliography of Printing* in 1880—was, about 1927, found by Mrs. Beatrice Warde in the Bibliothèque Nationale. Her examination of it has quite upset the attribution to Garamond of the types called *caractères de l'Université* by the Imprimerie Nationale and has proved that they were cut by Jannon. Mr. Stanley Morison's papers in *The Fleuron* have thrown new light on the origin of an independent school of italic types not derived from Aldus. Mr. A. F. Johnson in his book, *Type Designs*, has gathered into a consistent whole much hitherto unrelated typographic history. He and Mr. Thomas and Mr. Lyell have prepared some useful books in the series "Periods of Typography," while Mr. Morison's book on John Bell, Mr. Keynes's volume on Pickering, and Mr.

Marrot's study of Bulmer and Bensley have added new knowledge about the types then used. Further discoveries concern the earliest date of Caxton's arrival in England, the German origin of Janson's so-called Dutch type, and the placing of Buell as the first American type-founder.

As their value as documents has been realized, founders' specimen-sheets and books have received more careful attention. An important work about them was Birrell & Garnett's *Catalogue of Typefounders' Specimens*, etc., covering over a hundred Italian, French, German, Dutch, and British items. This appeared in London in 1928. The *Catalogue of Specimens of Printing Types by English and Scottish Printers and Founders*, 1665–1830, by Berry and Johnson is a more ambitious effort and a valuable book; while Audin's *Livrets Typographiques des Fonderies Françaises créées avant 1800* does admirably for French, what the former book does for English, type-founding. In Germany much research has been made, among the most notable results being Herr Gustav Mori's hand-list of the exhibition of German specimens (1479 to 1840) held by the Society of Associated German Typefounders at Frankfort in 1926, and his papers on the Berner Specimen of 1592, on the Brothers Voskens, and the Egenolff-Luther Foundry. Appreciation of the value of such specimens is reflected in the reissue by Messrs. Tregaskis of the 1693 Oxford specimen of the Fell types; the facsimiles of Plantin's *Index Characterum* of 1567, Pierre Cot's specimen of 1707, and Fournier *le jeune's* specimen of Sedanoise and Nonpareille of 1757 all issued by Mr. D. C. McMurtrie; and the Connecticut Columbiad Club's excellent reprint of the 1809 and 1812 specimens of Binny & Ronaldson. It is evident that in recent publications, says an English critic, "Mr. Updike's historical approach has been transformed into a scientific one. There has been a conscious attempt during the last fifteen years to evolve sound canons of criticism, whether of type design or the disposition of types in book production or other work, and the beginnings of an exact terminology have been established." In this effort to classify early type-forms scientifically, the Germans have adopted a number of terms which indicate certain subdivisions of type-design better than the more general designations, *lettre de forme*, *lettre de somme*, and *lettre batarde;* and Mr. Morison and Mr. Johnson have also proposed a precise terminology applying chiefly to fifteenth and sixteenth century types. I have not considered it necessary or desirable, in a book of this general character, to adopt any more minute classification or discard the terms I have already used; for early type-forms do not much concern the reader of this book, which is intended to show what types have survived for modern use. And since doctors disagree on the exact terms to employ, I leave them to decide if *fere-humanistica* is preferable to *gotico-antiqua* or whether some yet uncoined word is better than either! The only objection —and that a minor one—to all this is, that one sometimes cannot see the wood for the trees. But far be it from me to discourage the arboriculturist—or even the botanist!

III

It is often asked if modern types still exhibit qualities significant of their time, and whither modern tendencies in typography lead? To the first question the answer is, that printing always reflects the tendencies of its period in forms of art and aims in life. But the question for the thoughtful printer is, how admirable is the life of to-day? Shall he be carried away by a phase which is transitory, or hold fast to certain principles that modern life ignores. It is urged that present-day printing should be dynamic rather than static—

expressive of motion rather than rest, and that the *tempo* of typography must be in keeping with the life about it. This is a confusion of ideas. Adequate craftsmanship—like great art—should convey a sense of order, security, and peace: not of restless excitement. One is automatically either a critic or an enthusiast of modern trends in literature, music, art, and daily living, so we unconsciously govern our printing by the kind of life we approve.

As to modernism in typography, apart from mere ignorance, forgetfulness, pose, and fashion, there are those who sincerely accept it as a new gospel; but in the remote past there were current gospels now styled apocryphal, and by the learned long since thought mere curiosities. Rousseau's revolutionary doctrine of a "return to Nature" influenced the landscape gardening of his day, but ended in a return to something much more natural. In printing, years ago, the *Art Nouveau* precariously flourished, but it never grew old. I should be disturbed by a few modern attempts "to blow up the whole of English typographical tradition," if not already familiar with the phenomenon of cast-off principles. What has become of those tenets so earnestly propounded some years since by designers and printers who assert with equal vehemence now the exact opposite of what they said then? Trajan's column was then much the mode. At present asymmetric tendencies seem to be the vogue; based, perhaps, on the leaning tower of Pisa which, to those who ascend it, produces that acute sensation of motion which we are told is desirable in modern typography. Not very long since it was a canon of book-making that illustrations should be on good terms with type — and that books should show illustrative and typographic team-play. We are now warned that type must not inhibit the freedom of an illustrator. The result is a divorce between the two, analogous to the reason for other divorces — that one must at no cost be prevented from self-expression! Slowly but unconsciously these aims lead back to the "table-book" of the 'sixties—which unwittingly displays the characteristics now thought modern, and which—*ad interim*—has been so thoroughly discredited.

The influx of foreign type-forms, markedly national in their character, have, both in England and the United States, been unfortunate for typography. For instance, some of the German types which since 1914 have been so constantly produced, while in many cases admirable in themselves, are in their national idiom Teutonic, and as many of those who affect them most have but little Anglo-Saxon tradition behind them, the result is unhappy. A New England philosopher once said, "What you are, speaks so loud I cannot hear what you say," and that is what many modern German, French, Italian, and other Continental types do. *Per contra* there are types which seem of international appeal and use—such as the modern Lutetia or the ancient Janson. Then, too, many types in present use, especially those employed for display—to one familiar with types of a hundred years ago—are mere revivals of an era of bad taste in typography. This search for foreign type-designs, the revival of discarded types, and efforts at their eccentric arrangement represent a revolt against tradition in the restless struggle for novelty in a changing world. But we must remember that reactions are often as violent and one-sided as that from which they re-act. As Mr. Morison says, "Typographic tradition is the embodiment of the common-sense of generations," and Royal Cortissoz writes, "Tradition is not a formula. It is the tribute which every true artist pays to the great men who have gone before him." Finally, to quote Santayana, "The merely modern man never knows what he is about. . . . Fidelity to tradition, I am confident, has and will have its reward. . . . New ideas in their violence and new needs in their urgency pass like a storm; and then the old earth, scarred and enriched by those trials, finds itself still under the same sky, unscarred and pure as before."

English and American printing — especially book-printing — will not, in the long run, be much affected by temporary fashions; and while for a time they seem to obscure the horizon, it is but for the moment. Fresh viewpoints are never useless, but the degree of utility that they possess cannot be evaluated until years have passed, and the pendulum swings back — for pendulums behave that way. Thus I believe that for those who use the English language the great stream of normal printing will continue in the Anglo-Saxon tradition.

I am grateful to the many who have valued a book written without thought that it would have even limited popularity. When first published its price placed it beyond the means of many of those who needed it most. In this edition, the difficulty has been remedied, though it has restricted the extent of my annotations. Perhaps its appeal now, as in the past, is because (to slightly paraphrase Lord Bacon), "I do not endeavour to convince either by triumphs of confutation, or pleadings of antiquity, or assumption of authority, . . . Nor do I seek to enforce men's judgements, but to lead them to things themselves and the concordances of things, that they may see for themselves what they have, what they can dispute, what they can add and contribute to the common stock."

D. B. U.

The Merrymount Press, Boston,
  May-Day, 1937

ACKNOWLEDGMENTS: 1937

I desire to acknowledge with many thanks the help given me by Messrs. Henry L. Bullen, W. H. Ivins, Jr., Douglas C. McMurtrie, Stanley Morison, and A. W. Pollard, who called my attention to errors in the first edition of 1922.

In preparing this edition I am under further obligations, for suggestions and corrections, to the late Mr. Leonard L. Mackall, and to Messrs. James F. Ballard of the Boston Medical Library, Ernst F. Detterer of the Newberry Library, Chicago, A. Ehrman, London, Karl Küp of the New York Public Library, Hellmut Lehmann-Haupt of Columbia University Library, New York, J. P. R. Lyell, London, Albert Matthews, Boston, William Davis Miller, Wakefield, R. I., Stewart Mitchell of the Massachusetts Historical Society, Edward M. Moore, Warrenville, Illinois, Gustav Mori, Frankfort, David T. Pottinger of the Harvard University Press, Carl Purington Rollins of the Yale University Press, Lawrence C. Wroth of the John Carter Brown Library, Providence, Rudolph Ruzicka, Dobbs Ferry, Professor E. K. Rand of Harvard University, Miss Alice Bache Gould, Boston, Miss Ruth S. Granniss of the Grolier Club, New York, and to Daniel B. Bianchi for valuable assistance in reading my proofs.

I am also most grateful to Mr. Milton E. Lord of the Boston Public Library, Mr. Walter B. Briggs of the Harvard College Library, and Miss Elinor Gregory of the Boston Athenæum—to the latter in particular for help in solving some puzzling questions.

D. B. U.

TABLE OF CONTENTS

VOLUME I

CONTENTS

LIST OF ILLUSTRATIONS

VOLUME I

*The plates, apart from a few placed in the text, either face the page
designated, or are grouped, with a few exceptions, immediately after it*

•.•

INTRODUCTION

THE purpose of this book is to supply a basis for the intelligent appreciation of the best printing types through the study of their history, forms, and use. As a preliminary we consider briefly the invention of printing, the cutting and casting of type, a font of type and its case, the measurement of type; supplementing this by a short account of the Latin alphabet and those manuscript book-hands which most influenced type-forms. This brings us to a study of the chief varieties of type in use in the fifteenth century, and from 1500 to 1800, in Germany, Italy, France, the Netherlands, Spain, and England. Coming to the nineteenth century, the types of Bodoni, Didot, and Wilson are discussed; the English and American revival of older type-forms, and the influence of this revival on printing at the present time. We now have a foundation for a reasoned judgment of type-design, and the practical application of this judgment is developed in suggestions as to the choice of types for a composing-room. Finally, some of the excuses made for not printing better to-day are — it is hoped — demolished in a paper on industrial conditions in the past.

It is a good thing to know about the ingredients of ancient and modern type-metal; about the old manner of making types, and to what degree their manufacture has been improved; about the names and relative proportions of early types and the development of the system of nomenclature and measurement in use to-day. But it is also needful to have a knowledge of the effect of types on the eye — of how their shapes originated, were elaborated or simplified, were improved or deformed, why these changes were made, and, in short, the reason for types being in the forms that they now are. By the time these pages have been read, and the books alluded to have been examined, one should be able to distinguish the various great type-families from one another, with the ease with which we recognize English, French, or Italian, when printed; and to choose intelligently the form of letter which, allowing for diversity in taste, is the most suitable to employ in any particular kind of printing; and should have, too, some knowledge of the skill and learning which, in successive centuries, men have devoted to this subject — a conception of how much there is to know, and an idea of how to know it.

The subject of type and type-forms follows a narrow path, a kind of "watershed" between biography and bibliography. I have not attempted to supply lives of printers or type-founders in any complete way, but merely to touch on those points in their careers which throw light on their types, and explain in part why they were what they were. This is equally true of books, which I do not try to describe bibliographically, but allude to only in so far as the types which were used to print them, or the manner of their use, illustrates my point. For, as Reed says of English types, "the *Catena on Job*, Walton's Polyglot, Boyle's Irish Testament, Bowyer's Selden, rank as type specimens quite as interesting as, and far more valuable than, the ordinary letter-founders' catalogues."

While access to all the books that I have mentioned will not be possible to all readers, most of them will be found in any great library. Only by having the books in one's hands and examining their types can a thorough training be acquired; for my illustrations, numerous as they are, merely show landmarks in the field under discussion. I have generally reproduced types in their actual size, composed in sentences, their exposition in alphabets and description of minute changes in letter-forms being intentionally avoided. Interesting as successive variations in the design of individual letters may be, it is the effect of these variations upon type in mass that is important for my purpose.

I have treated the technical side of my subject as briefly as is consistent with giving a clear idea of what is described. The historical, literary, and artistic aspect I have accented, in order to suggest to the student that immense mass of facts related to typography, without some knowledge of which it can only be imperfectly understood — and to serve as a counterweight to the vast amount of technical instruction and mechanical description given in most treatises on type and printing. "I prefer no claim to originality," said William Blades in one of his treatises, "but rather rest the utility of what I have to say, upon the advantage of bringing to one focus a number of facts hitherto scattered through a number of books, and by consequence but partially known." That is what I have tried to do in these pages.

In spite of the increasing interest in the history of printing, and the attention paid in many quarters to the work of famous typographers, a knowledge of standards among the rank and file of printers is still greatly lacking. To the average printer of to-day, type is type, printing is printing — it is all about alike; and he concerns himself only with alleged labour-saving contrivances, or new type-faces that ensure convenience at the expense of proper design. In a more advanced class is to be found the printer who, knowing something of the historical side of printing and realizing intellectually that there is a standard of excellence, yet has never considered the question as applying in any practical way to himself or his work. What he has heard or seen of people who profess to hold such standards seems to him, sometimes very rightly, faddish and impractical; and this helps him to dismiss the subject with a plausible generalization on the impossibility of doing successfully to-day what (for unexplained reasons) was somehow easy in the past. Lastly, there are printers who are seriously in earnest, but who permit themselves to be discouraged by the indifference of their fellows, or who with their idealism do not combine that uncommon thing — common-sense. It is precisely because all these groups of men are constantly told, and will no doubt constantly continue to be told, so much about the advantages of modern mechanical contrivances, that I lay stress upon the artistic and idealistic side of the subject in an endeavour to show that the best printing can be done only when a man is familiar with standards to which the best printers have always adhered.

Typography is closely allied to the fine arts, and types have always reflected the taste or feeling of their time. The charm of the early Italian types has perhaps never been equalled; and the like is true of the Renaissance manuscripts on which they were based — and of many other departments of art in that same wonderful time. Note, too, the relation of the French manuscripts and types of a slightly later date to the manuscripts and the types of the Italian Renaissance. It is very much the relation of French work in the fine arts of that period to Italian work of a little earlier date. There is about the French characters, as in design, a certain excess of elegance which makes them seem weak in comparison with the more sturdy and classical qualities of earlier Italian types. If this is at all true of French and Italian types, it is even truer of English types used in the middle of the eighteenth century and those used at the end of it. The mid-eighteenth century English types, of which Caslon was the designer, had precisely those honest, somewhat heavy, but workmanlike qualities exhibited in the early furniture of Chippendale and the architecture of Vanbrugh. The types of Baskerville (the influence of which subsequently found expression in the work of Bodoni and Didot) possess a fragile and affected elegance, which culminated in the light, clear, delicate characters used from 1780 to 1820 — types reflecting, in their elegance, thinness, and weakness, the distinguished but fragile decorations and furniture introduced into England at the end of the eighteenth century by Robert Adam. For the same reason that one fears to use Adam furniture, one is afraid to use late eighteenth century fonts; for both seem in danger of breaking to pieces! Within the recollection of some of us, heavier types were revived by Mr. William Morris, and they were nearly contemporaneous with furniture forms rendered in lumber — "Mission" furniture, so "sincere" in trying to escape the imputation of fragility that it made "spring housecleaning an affair of the derrick and the wrecking-crane!" The latest development in architecture seems to be a revival of Georgian or early American architecture and ornament, and a movement toward what is somewhat absurdly called, nowadays, "period" decoration. This is reflected in printing by a return to the Georgian or early nineteenth century types for the greater part of contemporary printing, and the appearance of "period" types — reproductions more or less accurate of styles of type famous at different epochs. Thus type, which one thinks of merely as the characters composing a printed word, does, when examined as design, reflect to some degree the tendencies current in other departments of contemporary art.

Just as the music of great masters like Palestrina makes some familiar compositions seem thin and trivial, so, by studying the monumental characters of early typography, do we learn to place in true perspective our types to-day. This means the study of types from a fresh point of view, and no study is ever a wholly amusing process if it is to be a serious training. Those who seek *will* find; but to the reader skeptical of results and critical of the value of any detailed consideration of type-forms, such a survey will seem either beside the mark or destructive. None the less, such study is the only way I know to establish a standard of taste in type-forms, or to contribute to the progress of printing as an art. For "the Arts have no real enemies except the ignorant."

PRINTING TYPES

THEIR HISTORY, FORMS, AND USE

PRINTING TYPES

CHAPTER I

THE INVENTION OF PRINTING: THE CUTTING AND CASTING OF TYPES IN RELATION TO THEIR DESIGN

THE invention of movable metal types in Europe, as we all know, has been generally attributed to Gutenberg — just as the invention of the steam-engine has popularly been considered that of Watt. But Watt did not invent the steam-engine; he perfected it, however, so highly as to make it almost a new invention. This is, I conceive, what Gutenberg did for printing; he was the first man to put typography on a practical and scientific basis. Before his day, printing from movable types was practised by the Dutch, and there is, perhaps, reason to believe that a man named Coster was the inventor of this process. Whether or no Coster was the first man to employ movable types, there certainly existed in Holland before Gutenberg's time, a series of books of primitive workmanship printed from type, and the roughness of the typography of some later printers — like Caxton — is considered one proof that a group of men were under the influence of this Dutch school of printing. It has always puzzled the casual student of *incunabula* to account for the perfection of the books printed by Gutenberg; but if it be true that Gutenberg did not originate printing from movable types, but simply greatly improved the whole practice of making them, then we can see that the early and crude typography of Holland was merely the sub-structure on which Gutenberg so splendidly built. As William Blades said of the Coster-Gutenberg controversy, "The evidence on each side may be enlarged in the course of years, but so far as it goes at present it is strongly in favour of a first rude invention of movable types in Holland by some one who may have been Coster. The claim of Gutenberg upon the respect of posterity rests on his great improvements — so great as to entitle him in a sense to be deemed the inventor.[1] . . . Just as astronomers have been unable to explain certain aberrations of the planets without surmising a missing link in the chain of their knowledge, so is it with early typography. That such finished works as the first editions of the Bible and Psalter *could be* the legitimate predecessors of the Costeriana, the Bruges, the Westminster press, and others, I cannot reconcile with the internal evidence of their workmanship. But admit the existence of an earlier and much ruder school of typography, and all is plain and harmonious. Side by side, the weakest gave place and the fittest survived, and soon, as in all survivals, the existence of the former became traditionary."[2] Endless discussions have arisen on this question, which has a whole literature to itself. Roughly speaking, the situation to-day stands much as it did in Blades's time. Later discoveries of early printing have been made, some new historical facts have come to light; but these have not much changed the theory that although there was an earlier Dutch school of unskilful printing, it was in Germany that printing as we know it to-day was first practised.[3] "We may take our stand," says Mr. Pollard, "on the distinction drawn by the Cologne Chronicle of 1499 between the Invention made at Mainz and the Prefigurement (Vürbyldung) which

[1] Blades's *Books in Chains*, London, 1892, p. 200.   [2] *Ibid.*, pp. 157, 158.
[3] The paper by Heinrich Wallau, *Gutenberg Techniker und Künstler*, published by the Gutenberg-Gesellschaft (*Vierter Jahres-Bericht*, Mainz, 1905), may be consulted for study of Gutenberg types. Seymour de Ricci's valuable *Catalogue Raisonné des Premières Impressions de Mayence* (1445-67), published by the same society in 1911, though primarily bibliographical, is useful to the student of types of this class.

he places elsewhere, or if it be preferred, on that subtler discrimination lurking in the word 'adinuentiones' applied to the achievements of Mainz, with its possible suggestion of earlier 'inuentiones' of another origin. Invention or Adinvention, whether that which was not first discovered at Mainz had been discovered at Strassburg or in Holland, it was in Germany and at Mainz that the Printed Book as the ambitious rival of the Manuscript first came into being."[1]

Gutenberg's invention consisted, apparently, in making brass moulds and matrices by which type could be *accurately cast in large quantities*. As Mr. De Vinne reminds us, relief printing, paper, wood-engraving, printed books, even the printing-press, and perhaps the idea of movable types were not attributable to Gutenberg. These had all been thought of already. Gutenberg availed himself of the different experiments of his predecessors and made something which, however it has been improved upon in detail to-day, has not been improved upon in theory.

The first type-cutters and type-founders were merely somewhat servile imitators of the manuscript letter-forms to which they were already accustomed. We can understand little about the design of our present printing types, if we are not familiar with the characters in the black-letter and Humanistic manuscripts which just preceded, or were contemporary with, the invention of printing.[2] There appears to have been no thought in the minds of early printers other than to reproduce manuscripts quickly and inexpensively; and although many early printed books were very beautiful, both in type and arrangement, because modelled on

---

[1] See Introduction to *Catalogue of Books printed in the XVth Century now in the British Museum*, London, 1913, Part III, p. ix.

[2] This is developed in the chapter on the Latin Alphabet.

fine manuscripts, I doubt if fifteenth century printers so consciously intended to make their books beautiful as is commonly supposed. What an early printer *was* intent upon
doing was to produce a printed book which resembled a
manuscript as closely as possible; and that such a man failed
to recognize any great divergence in theory between a book
in manuscript and a printed volume is shown by his obvious endeavour to follow in type the written letter of the
manuscript.[1] Because of this aim, the first printers made
certain errors in designing and cutting types, which have
profoundly influenced typography, and not always with
happy results. Intent upon imitating manuscripts, they felt
obliged to reproduce the kind of letters that a reader had
been accustomed to in volumes written by hand; and thus
they had neither time, opportunity, nor desire to consider
what types were, or to realize that they could never successfully reproduce in metal all the forms derived from the
pen. In other words, to the first type-cutters printing was
merely an evolution, and did not appear a new invention
in the sense that it obliged them to decide what forms of
letter were best adapted to the new medium they had to
employ. If these craftsmen had but thought of the whole
subject from a fresh standpoint, some of the calligraphic
black-letter types would never have existed, and italic and
Greek types, so far as imitative of handwriting, would have
been corrected. Instead of a long series of endeavours which
have not yet entirely adjusted type-forms to the medium

[1] "Almost invariably the style of the early printed book follows the contemporary MS. style of its place of production. In consequence we find strongly
marked national styles, though these were soon modified by the international
trade in books and especially by the influence of new classical texts distrib-
uted from Italy. In some places and in some other classes of books, local
conservatism was stronger." Syllabus of lecture on *Early Printed Books*, by
G. H. Palmer. London, 1913.

in which the type-cutter has to work, we should then have had characters designed with closer relation to the material from which they were fashioned.

Ever since the sixteenth century, elaborate diagrams have been published to show how letters should be drawn, as we shall learn from some accounts given of men who suggested new methods of designing them. Generally a diagram of minute squares was first made, and on this the design and dimension of each letter were determined. Jaugeon, who was appointed by the *Académie des Sciences* of Paris in the last years of the seventeenth century to supply a scheme or series of directions by which type should be cut, began by stating that "the eye is the sovereign ruler of taste." The rules which he set forth were extremely complicated — every Roman capital was to be designed on a framework of 2304 little squares. Grandjean, the first type-cutter who attempted to follow them, is said to have observed sarcastically, that he should certainly accept Jaugeon's dictum that "the eye is the sovereign ruler of taste," and accepting this, should throw the rest of his rules overboard!

In casting type the two schools of typography spoken of on an earlier page — one experimental and crude, the other sure and perfected — had probably different methods.[1] One cast letters in moulds of clay or sand; the other understood something of the punch, the matrix, and the adjustable mould, which they slowly perfected into much the kind of appliance we have now. The roughness of either form of type-casting no doubt accounts for the variation in appearance of the same letter in old books. The result of an accidental impression of a piece of type in a book printed in the last quarter of the fifteenth century is shown in the illus-

[1] Reed's *Old English Letter Foundries*, p. 29.

tration (*fig.* 1). This makes it clear that in appearance the earliest types much resembled those of to-day, though their heights were very irregular. While the quantity of type that was needed by any one printer was probably small, the different characters in a font were very many on account of the contractions, abbreviations, etc., then considered necessary.

All early types were cast by hand, and even down to the

1. *Impression of a piece of Fifteenth Century Type*
found on a page of Nider's Lepre Morale, printed at Cologne about 1476

first part of the last century hand type-moulds were in use. Into such a mould hot metal was poured, and the type-caster then gave it a quick shake, which forced the metal into all the crannies of the matrix. By practice it became apparent that some letters involved a different sort of motion, and were more difficult to make than others, so I suppose that the variations just spoken of between different impressions of the same letter in early fonts may also be attributable to the varying skill of the individual workman. In an account of an English foundry, where the use of ancient handmoulds survived well into the last century, mention is made of the uncouth movements and swaying figures of a group of gray-haired type-casters, who appeared as if demented to any one who did not know what they were about. Hand-casting was a slow and tiresome process, and according to Moxon[1] only about four thousand such letters could ordinarily be cast in one day.

In all probability lead, tin, and pewter were among the materials used for fifteenth century types. Where references are made in old books to the use of copper and bronze in type-casting, they may apply to the punches or matrices rather than to the types themselves. Steel, brass, copper, tin, lead, and iron wire were used as early as 1480 in Italy, as is distinctly stated in the "Cost Book" of the Ripoli Press[2] at

[1] Joseph Moxon, the first English writer on type-founding, was born in Yorkshire, in 1627. He was a maker of mathematical instruments and dabbled in all kinds of mechanics. He himself said that he had never been properly taught the art of type-founding, but had taken it up solely through his interest in the subject—as was the case with many celebrated type-cutters before and since. He issued a specimen sheet as early as 1669, showing characters which were not particularly good. In his book on the rules for the formation of letters ("useful for writing masters, painters, carvers, machinists, and for those who were lovers of curiosity," and dedicated to Sir Christopher Wren), he advises, as did Tory before him and Jaugeon after him, that letters should be first designed on a framework of minute squares. In 1667 he began a series of fourteen treatises in monthly numbers on the trades of the smith, joiner, carpenter, etc., and a second series, which comprised twenty-four numbers, was devoted entirely to printing, letter-cutting, and type-casting. This second volume appeared in 1683 and was inscribed to Dr. Fell (among others), benefactor of the Oxford University Press. Moxon's *Mechanick Exercises, or the Doctrine of Handy-Works* is the first English book on type-founding, and thus a classic in the literature of printing — though a very dull book.

[2] The Ripoli Press was in a Dominican monastery, originally founded at Piano di Ripoli and later moved into the neighbouring city of Florence. This press is interesting to the student of typography because it furnishes an early instance of the employment of women in composing-rooms; but specially because its treasurer kept very careful accounts of its expenses, which give valuable information about the materials employed in the work of the press, the cost of production, etc. The press had several faces of roman and black-letter type cut for it, as well as ornaments, initials, etc. It was most miscellaneous in its output. (See De Vinne's *Notable Printers of Italy in the Fifteenth Century*, p. 127, with facing plate.) Portions of the Ripoli "Cost Book" were edited in 1781 by P. V. Fineschi, under the title *Notizie Storiche sopra la Stamperia di Ripoli*, and a monograph by M. P. Bologna, entitled *La Stamperia Fiorentina del Monastero di S. Jacopo di Ripoli e le sue edizioni*, was published in the *Giornale storico della Letter. Ital.*, Vols. XX, XXI.

Florence—which throws a good deal of light on the conditions of fifteenth century printing-houses. Reed thinks that steel and brass were used for the mould, steel for the punches, copper for the matrices, lead and tin for the type, and iron wire for the mould or perhaps for stringing type together. An alloy was introduced later by adding tin and iron to the lead. In the fifteenth century the discovery of the properties of antimony gave the types their required hardness. The chief ingredients of type from the earliest times have been lead and tin, and these have been hardened either with iron and bismuth, or antimony.

In cutting type by hand to-day, the first thing a type-cutter does in following his design, or that supplied him, is to make a counter-punch. This consists in cutting out the spaces inside of certain letters, such as O, or the upper part of an A. This counter-punch is sunk into the end of a bar of steel, and when this is done the inside of the model letter is finished. The outlines of the model letter are then cut until it assumes its proper shape, numerous "smoke-proofs" meanwhile having been examined to see that the letter follows the form which the designer intends. After the punch is completed, the steel is hardened, and it is then punched into a bar of cold rolled copper, producing what is called a "strike." In this state it is really an unfinished matrix. It is then "fitted" so that it will cast in the proper position on its body. When this matrix is square on its sides, holds its letter in the same position as do the matrices of other letters of the new alphabet, and has the same depth throughout from the surface of the bar, it is finished. This is, roughly speaking, the process by which hand-cut punches and their matrices are produced.

But all type is not cut by hand to-day; in fact, quite the

contrary. The theory of the pantograph, understood as early as the seventeenth century, was adapted (in the second quarter of the nineteenth century) to producing wood type, which had hitherto been cut by hand. This invention required but one model alphabet, and from it an unskilled workman could cut on wood, on which nothing had been drawn, various sizes of letters. The principle was very naturally applied later to cutting metal punches. Benton of Milwaukee invented such a punch-cutting machine, thereby at once enormously simplifying the cutting of punches, as well as cheapening their production. At first sight it would appear that this was a wholly admirable invention; and it would be, if it did not tend to mechanize the design of types. But a design for a type alphabet that may be entirely successful *for the size for which it is drawn*, cannot be successfully applied to all other sizes of the same series. Each size is a law unto itself, and is often bettered by modifications in the original design made by the feeling and taste of the designer. To a trained eye, looking over impressions of a series of modern machine-cut types, it is often possible to tell which was the size originally designed because it stands out as the most harmonious and successful. In this particular size the designer's eye had most modified his rules, and in all others the necessary modifications proper to the varying sizes had not been so carefully made. An authority tells us that (ideally) a new model design should be made for every two sizes of type. It was because the punches for the older types were cut for each size by their designers with Jaugeon's maxim consciously or unconsciously in mind, that most old fonts were so pleasing in effect. Conversely, one reason why modern types are less mellow and agreeable to the eye is because, when cut from a model alphabet by machine, there is too much rule and too little taste. "Even with strict instructions and with best intentions," says Mr. Bruce Rogers,[1] "it is difficult for the habitual user of a very accurate machine *not* to insensibly smooth out what he has always been taught to consider 'imperfections' and to make as mechanically perfect a letter as is possible. . . . I have come to believe that perhaps only hand-cut punches, *cut by the designer of the type*, can preserve the real feeling of the design;" and he adds that the design should be drawn as nearly as possible to the exact size of the desired font.

In modern practice this is *exactly what is not done* by machine. Sizes from 6-point to 120-point, or as large as desired, are often cut from the same model letter; although contractions and expansions in either dimension of letter-design can be made when necessary to correct certain optical illusions.[2] I have sometimes questioned whether a machine can be so managed that it will ever produce those fine and almost imperceptible qualities of design given to it by the hand of a clever type-cutter — which mean so much to the appearance of type in the mass, and which vary in nature and degree in different sizes of the same series of characters. In point of fact, the first types produced by punch-cutting machines did seem to show a certain rigidity from the point of view of design. That there has been an improvement of late in type cut by machine is undeniable, and yet there has been practically no change in its mech-

---

[1] In a letter to the author.

[2] There are many optical illusions which must be guarded against in cutting an alphabet, the secrets of correcting which are still among the "mysteries and art of printing." If you have ever seen an inscription cut on stone in capital letters, where the v's or w's did not descend below the base of the other capitals, you will have experienced an illusion of this sort. In very large sizes of type it is necessary to make the o's descend below other letters as much as a sixteenth of an inch, to produce the effect of an even line. Round lower-case letters must extend above square lower-case letters as well as below, to appear to align.

anism. This improvement, I learn, has come to pass through a more sympathetic and subtle manipulation of the machine itself, and by modifications of rules by the eye of the workman who operates it. And so, after all, it seems to be the eye and the hand that determine the excellence of the product of a machine, and it is only when a machine is as flexible as the hand that it is as good as the hand. In the final analysis we come back to the eye as the great factor in the successful operation of a punch-cutting machine. For Jaugeon was right.

Nowadays all type is cast by machine. The difference, however, between early hand type-casting and modern mechanical type-casting is not so great as one would suppose, and is nothing more than the substitution of the movement of a machine for manual dexterity. The modern type-casting machine has the advantage of infinitely greater production; and as much more care is taken in examining the types produced and discarding those with imperfections, its product is more uniform and perfect than in earlier fonts cast by hand.

The use of hand-moulds survived for a time for casting small and special sorts, kerned letters and script types. The modern type-casting machine is now, however, employed in the United States for everything.

The ingredients of modern printing types are, roughly speaking, lead, tin, antimony, and sometimes a little copper; these vary in proportion, according to the size of the type being cast. The end aimed at in type-metal is to obtain a material which shall be dense, ductile, and fusible at a low temperature. Lead is too soft to be used alone; antimony is therefore introduced to give it hardness; as are copper and tin to give toughness, the last having the property of cementing metals which fuse at different temperatures. This amalgam of metal does not rust, has the advantage of shrinking less than any other alloy, and fills the mould and matrix very perfectly.

As to the wearing qualities of type, small faces of type, with lines more delicate and closer together, wear less well than large faces, and the counters in small faces, being shallow, fill more easily. Types also wear out because of careless handling, and by constant setting, distributing, correcting, and planing down; and therefore much depends upon good workmen who handle their types carefully and, above all, keep them clean. Certain printing papers cause types to wear much more than others. Such are many of the interesting hand-made papers; especially rough-surfaced papers when printed dry. So it is not alone important that types should be made of proper ingredients and should be made well, but they should be carefully handled and thoughtfully employed.[1]

---

[1] For detailed accounts of the processes of ancient type-cutting and type-casting, see Reed's *History of Old English Letter Foundries*, Introductory Chapter, and Moxon's *Mechanick Exercises*. For modern type-cutting and type-casting, see De Vinne's *Plain Printing Types*, and Legros and Grant's *Typographical Printing-Surfaces*. The last is especially valuable for its diagrams.

CHAPTER II

A FONT OF TYPE AND ITS CASE: THE TYPOGRAPHICAL
POINT: POINT–SET AND LINING TYPES

TYPE is defined as a right-angled, prism-shaped piece of metal, having for its face a letter or character, usually in high relief, adapted for use in letter-press printing; and type in the aggregate is described as an assemblage of the characters used for printing. In a single type the chief points to be described are the face, counter, stem, hair-line, serif, beard or neck, shoulder, body or shank, pin-mark, nick, feet, and groove.

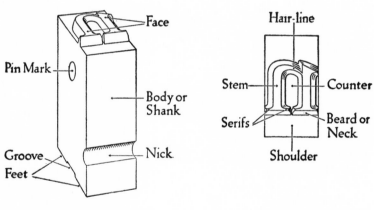

2. *Diagram of Type*   3. *Plan of its Face*

The accompanying diagram of a piece of type (*fig.* 2) shows its face, body, nick, groove, feet, and pin-mark; and the plan of the face (*fig.* 3) shows the stem, hair-line, serif, counter, beard, and shoulder.

The *body* (or *shank*) of a piece of type is the metal between the shoulder and the feet (described later), and the term "body" is also used to denote the size or thickness of types, leads, etc. The *pin-mark* is an indentation on the upper part of the body, made by the pin in casting. The *nick* is the groove across the lower part of the body of the type, and is a guide to the position in which it is to be set up.[1] The *feet* are the projections on each side of the groove on which the type stands, the *groove* being the hollow left between the feet where formerly was the jet.

The *face* of a type is the letter on its upper end which carries the ink to be impressed upon the paper; the *counter* is the cavity left by the surrounding lines of the face. The *stem* is the thick stroke or line of the letter; the *hair-line* is the thin stroke of the letter. The *serif* is a short cross-line which occurs at the ends of the unconnected lines in the type-face.[2] The *beard*, sometimes called the *neck*, is the slope between the outside edge of the face and the shoulder, the *shoulder* being the flat top of the body which supports the neck or face.

A standard font or fount of letters consists of all the char-

[1] In American, English, and German types, the body carries the nick on the front, but in French and Belgian type on the back. Besides showing the position for setting, this aids both founder and printer in distinguishing the different faces of the same type-body — by the number, kind, or situation of the nick on the bodies of the various faces. An extra nick is sometimes cut on small capitals — o, s, v, w, x, and z — to distinguish them from lower-case letters. Small capital ı is so marked in old style faces to distinguish it from the arabic figure.

[2] The serif is an important feature in type-design and usually varies by the style of its attachment to the body strokes, according to the face of the type. In old style lower-case letters it is a sort of blunt spur; in many modern French and Italian types it is a delicate hair-line; in modern "Scotch-face" it is curved or bracketed on the inside where it meets the main line. But the design of types is not absolutely determined by the shape of the serif. The stems of letters in the great type-families, and particularly the swellings and depressions in the forms of their lower-case letters, are also important to the design of a type-face and yet independent of the shape of the serif. Serifs, taken by themselves, may resemble each other in quite different type-faces.

acters usually needed in composition, and is made up of the following sorts:

ROMAN

Capitals: A, B, C, D, E, F, G, H, I, J, K, L, M, N, O, P, Q, R, S, T, U, V, W, X, Y, Z, &, Æ, Œ.

Small capitals:[1] A, B, C, D, E, F, G, H, I, J, K, L, M, N, O, P, Q, R, S, T, U, V, W, X, Y, Z, &, Æ, Œ.

Lower case: a, b, c, d, e, f, g, h, i, j, k, l, m, n, o, p, q, r, s, t, u, v, w, x, y, z, æ, œ, ff, fi, fl, ffi, ffl.[2]

Accented letters: á, à, â, ä, é, è, ê, ë, í, ì, î, ï, ó, ò, ô, ö, ú, ù, û, ü.

Figures: 1, 2, 3, 4, 5, 6, 7, 8, 9, 0.

Marks of punctuation: - , ; : . ? ! — ' [ ] ( ).

Marks of reference: *, †, ‡, §, ||, ¶, ☞.[3]

ITALIC

Capitals: *A, B, C, D, E, F, G, H, I, J, K, L, M, N, O, P, Q, R, S, T, U, V, W, X, Y, Z, &, Æ, Œ.*

Lower case: *a, b, c, d, e, f, g, h, i, j, k, l, m, n, o, p, q, r, s, t, u, v, w, x, y, z, æ, œ, ff, fi, fl, ffi, ffl.*

Accented letters: *á, à, â, ä, é, è, ê, ë, í, ì, î, ï, ó, ò, ô, ö, ú, ù, û, ü.*

Figures: *1, 2, 3, 4, 5, 6, 7, 8, 9, 0.*

Marks of punctuation: *- , ; : . ? ! ( ).*

Spaces: en quadrat, and 3 to em, 4 to em, 5 to em, 6 to em, and hair spaces, used to separate words.

[1] There are seldom any italic small capitals.

[2] A greater number of ligatured letters occur in Caslon's fonts, *viz.:* ﬅ, long ſ in its combinations ſb, ſh, ſi, ſk, ſl, ſſ, ſt, ſſi, ſſl, both in roman and italic. **Some** other old faces or their reproductions — *i.e.,* the Garamond italic — **show** *as, is, us, ﬅ, fr, ll, ſp, ﬅ, tt.*

[3] Note references, except in rare instances, are the same for roman and italic.

Quadrats: em quadrats, and three sizes of large quadrats, viz., 2 em, 3 em, and 4 em, used chiefly to fill out lines.

Miscellaneous: braces in different lengths, dashes, leaders, fractions, mathematical signs,[1] degree marks, commercial signs (such as $, @, ℔), and so forth.

Occasional Characters: liturgical signs, ℣, ℟, and ✠ (for the sign of blessing), characters denoting contractions (such as p̄, q̄, o̊, đ, ꝣ, p̓), unusual fractions, etc.

The characters which make up a complete font of type fall into six classes, which Mr. De Vinne tabulates as: "(1) Full-bodied letters, like Q and j, that occupy the entire body of the type; (2) Ascending letters, like A, b, d, h, that occupy the upper three-fourths of the body; (3) Descending letters, like p, y, g, q, that occupy the lower three-fourths of the body; (4) Short letters like a, o, that occupy about one-half of the body in the middle part; (5) Small capitals, that are sometimes in height more than one-half of the body, but not as high as the ascending letters; (6) Irregular characters, like the *, that have no arbitrary height, but do have a definite position." In a type of "modern" face, the figures all belong to the second class, but in "old style"[2] fonts they are variously short, ascending, and descending.

[1] As far as is known, the mathematical signs + and − were first used by Widmann in a book published at Leipsic in 1489, though he does not speak of them as if they were a novelty. Robert Recorde first employed them in an English book. In *The Whetstone of Witte* (1557) Recorde employed = as the sign of equality (chosen because "noe two thynges can be moar equalle" than two parallel straight lines), though this sign had long before appeared in mediaeval manuscripts to represent the word *est.* William Oughtred showed the × or sign of multiplication in his *Clavis Mathematica*, issued in 1631. See Franz Steffens's *Paléographie Latine. 125 Fac-similés en phototypie acompagnés de transcriptions et d'explications, avec un exposé systématique de l'histoire de l'écriture latine.* Trèves and Paris, 1910. Edited by Remi Coulon and translated into French from the *second* German edition of *Lateinische Paleographie*, p. xl.

[2] To understand the terms "old style," "modern face," and "modelled" letter, it must be remembered that the earliest roman and italic types were

A "sort," understood in connection with printing, is one of the pieces in a font of type considered in reference to supply or lack. To be "out of sorts" is to lack some of the necessary types in a case. To "order sorts" is to order more of the kind in which the font is deficient. The term "out of sorts," therefore, means destitute or without equipment.

The word "ampersand" is a corruption of "& per se = and," meaning the character & by itself.[1] In some italic ampersands the letters e and t are easily distinguished, as in the examples shown, $\mathcal{E}$, &, &, &.

The Arabic numerals have an interesting history. The best forms to employ are mentioned on a later page. Arabic figures are not cast in italic except in very modern fonts.

Types have much better appearance when composed in certain languages than in others. Latin is an ideal tongue for type composition, no other language having anything like the same dignity and monumental appearance when well composed in fine type — probably one reason why Latin quotations have so long survived in specimen books. This is due to the many u's, m's, and n's, the lack of y's, and the paucity of other descending letters. A page composed in Latin and a page composed in English, placed so that the lines of type are perpendicular to the eye, will at once show the difference in effect between them.

It was an early custom to display black-letter types in

of much more uniform line throughout than now. In time they began to show increasing differentiations of weight between the stem and connecting lines. The earlier form of letter, with slighter differences in contrasting weight of stroke, we now call "old style;" the much later form, exhibiting greater contrasts of thick and thin lines, constitutes a "modern face" letter. And the greater the variation of weight of line in the design of a letter, the more it may be called "modelled."

[1] The *per se* was used with A, O, and I, to indicate that the letter, standing by itself, made a word. This led to the term *a per se*, to denote what we should call now, A No. 1. For instance, "London, thowe arte of townes A per se."

the words of the *Pater Noster* or sometimes (as in Ratdolt's fifteenth century specimen sheet) of the *Ave Maria*. Classical quotations were used to show off roman type. No doubt the familiar opening of Cicero's oration, "*Quousque tandem abutere, Catilina,*" has had (since Caslon's time[1]) considerable influence on the shape of the capital letter Q; for this sentence became so consecrated to type-specimens that most eighteenth century type-founders felt it necessary to employ it, and in order to outdo each other, they elongated the tails of their Q's more and more. I do not say that Q's have long tails because Cicero delivered an oration against Catiline; but that the tails of some Q's would not be as long as they are if the oration had begun with some other word! Ultimately the tail became so long that many capital Q's with their companion u were cut as logotypes, *i.e.*, Qu.

In casting a font of type, the proportion of its letters varies according to the language for which the type is to be used. Latin and French require more of the c, i, l, m, p, q, s, and v than English. This variation of proportion applies to almost all modern languages in different degrees. It is easy to see that in English many more letters of one sort are needed than of another. Indeed, the arrangement of type-cases is a hint as to the proportion used. This leads us to the consideration of the printer's case, which has some points of interest.

A case is a wooden tray divided into various compartments or "boxes" of different areas but of a uniform depth of about an inch, and a printer's font of type ordinarily requires two of these trays, one placed above the other on frames or sloping desks. The higher tray is called the upper case; the lower tray is called the lower case; and it is from these trays and their position that the characters are described as upper-case and lower-case letters, a term which

[1] Caslon appears to have been the first letter-founder to employ this quotation.

is merely descriptive of the relation of the cases to each other
and to the compositor (*fig.* 4).

The ordinary upper case has 98 equal-sized boxes and
contains capital letters in order from A to Z, except for the
omission of J and U, which follow the Z. The remaining

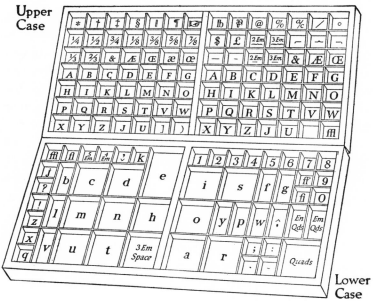

4. *A Pair of Printer's Cases*

boxes on the right hand are occupied by commercial signs,
dashes, braces, diphthongs, the ampersand, and the lower-
case ffl. The left-hand side of the upper case contains small
capitals, arranged like the capitals on the right-hand side,
and the other boxes are filled with fractions (sometimes
replaced by accented letters), reference marks, such as the
asterisk, dagger, section mark, etc., diphthongs for small
capitals and lower case, the small capital ampersand,
brackets, and parentheses.

The lower case, which has 54 boxes or compartments, is laid (for that is the term used in speaking of placing type in a case) on the principle of placing the letters most needed nearest the hand of the compositor. Of these, e comes first, having the largest compartment allotted to it of any character; and the next commonest letters are: c, d, i, s, m, n, h, o, u, t, a, and r, together with 3 em spaces and quadrats. The third class of letters, of which about half as many are required, comprise the remaining letters of the alphabet (except j, k, q, x, and z), to which add the comma and em and en quadrats.

Lower-case j, k, q, x, and z, the ligatured letters, figures, and the rest of the marks of punctuation, and 4 em, 5 em, 6 em, and hair spaces, occupy small boxes along the edge of the case. They are, in a sense, suburban letters, and live in a small way in outlying districts; whereas the more popular letters live in the middle of the town; like a city in which — unlike most cities — the busiest inhabitants live in the best and largest houses![1]

In early times the capital letters U and J did not exist, V being used for U, and I for J. From the eleventh to the sixteenth century the letter I represented both the vowel sound of I and the consonant sound of J.[2] Its likelihood of being

[1] The cases described are intended for book work. For job work — that is, for circulars, advertisements, etc. — a different case is required. This "job case" is a single case somewhat varied in its arrangement from that used for book composition.

[2] The lower-case i and j were first differentiated in Spain, where (when printing was introduced) j was used for the consonant and i for the vowel. At first the capital I stood for both I and J, as it now does in German type, and should in all black-letter — although some very strange J's have been made by modern type-founders to supply a black-letter variant. The capital J appeared in Spanish before 1600. Louis Elzevir, who worked at Leyden between 1595 and 1616, is supposed to be the first printer who made the distinction of u and v, i and j, lower case.

The capital letters U and V began to be differentiated by printers in

confounded with one of the strokes of some letter near it led
to various efforts in writing to keep the two sounds distinct
by a differentiation in the character, and from this effort came
the curve of the j, though the dot of the i survived in the
lower-case letter when the tail was elongated.

When these two new capital letters were first rendered
in type, it is obvious that printers had become accustomed to an upper case arranged without them. To introduce them in their proper places, *i.e.*, the J after I and the
U after T, proved an inconvenience to the printer who had
been trained to cases in which there were no such letters.
At any given moment, it would have caused too much
trouble and confusion in a printing-house to make this reform, and by this *vis inertiae* the J and U still follow the Z in
the upper cases, as they always have, and probably always
will.

Efforts at improved arrangement of cases have been
many. Lord Stanhope invented a case which varied from
that described, by discarding some of the double letters,
which he considered logotypes, and by introducing some
new combinations. He also modified the height of the front
partition of each box, in order to facilitate the compositor's
work. But while his invention may have induced improvements in the arrangement of cases, it was considered rather

---

Italy as early as 1524. In England, although various attempts were made in
the sixteenth century to introduce u and j, their use was by no means general
until 1630. At first V continued its double function as a capital, but subsequently U was adopted, — derived from an uncial form of V dating from the
third or fourth century. This kind of capital U was employed up to the end
of the seventeenth century, when it gave way to the present form. The modern English use of U u for the vowel and V v for the consonant dates from
about 1700; but their interchangeable use survived until well into the nineteenth century. Words beginning with U are still entered under V in the
catalogue of the British Museum. In Chambers' *Encyclopedia* of 1786, words
beginning with U and W are placed under V.

too radical.[1] Lefèvre, author of the classical *Guide du Compositeur*, who was "prote" (or foreman) to Didot, also arranged a case which, by an elaborate series of calculations, he shows would save twenty-three days' time in a period of three hundred working days.[2] In some of his proposals he foreshadowed the present idea of simplification of effort and movement as an important factor in economical production.[3]

There must be a variation in cases used for foreign languages. In general, European languages employing the Roman letter have cases differing slightly from one another, while cases for Greek and languages employing non-Roman characters have a great divergence. Greek cases vary in different establishments; and a model of a Greek case, with the simplifications proposed by Lefèvre, may be consulted with profit.[4]

The names given to the various sizes of types in current use in England in the seventeenth century were as follows: French canon, two-line English, double pica, great primer, English, pica, long primer, brevier, nonpareil, and pearl; and small pica was also occasionally used. Half a century later, two-line letters of double pica, great primer, and pica were added; and paragon, small pica, bourgeois, and minion were to be found in most printing-houses. Pica, equivalent

[1] For illustrations of Lord Stanhope's proposed cases, logotypes, etc., see Savage's *Dictionary of the Art of Printing*, London, 1841, p. 102.

[2] Lefèvre's *Guide Pratique du Compositeur*, Paris, 1883, p. 556, and facing plate.

[3] Of late years much has been said in regard to "scientific management," and much unused or wasted energy has been liberated or saved by it. But the effects of scientific management, pushed to an extreme, on the trades in which elements of fine art or personal taste are factors, would often lead to artistic inefficiency.

[4] Lefèvre, p. 242; for plans of cases for various languages, see plates in the same work.

to 12-point, was the standard English and American body and common unit of measurement for types, leads, etc., until the adoption of the point system.

The irregular bodies like small pica and bourgeois originated through the widespread use of Dutch fonts by English printers. This predilection for Dutch material forced English founders to supply types cast to the Dutch standard. Some of the Dutch body-sizes were almost the same as English regular sizes, and were consequently called by the usual English name, which would thus come to stand for two or more slightly different bodies. But when a new font was imported, or cut by an unskilful English workman, which would not fit any regular English body, it was cast on an irregular body and given a new name.[1]

The names of the old type-bodies varied in different countries. Although they are practically abandoned to-day, it is useful to know what their original names were — a part of the literary history of type which explains many allusions in early books on printing that would be otherwise unintelligible. At first the name was descriptive of both body and face. Later it was applied to the body only. For instance: English was the name used to describe one size and all faces of *black-letter* type; and thus some specimen books display black-letter of 14-point size under the heading "English English." Indeed, until about the end of the eighteenth century an "English" face was *understood* to be black-letter. The old names of the chief English,

---

[1] " To confess the truth," says Rowe Mores, " the irregular bodies owe their origin to the unskilfulness of workmen, who when they had cut a fount which happened to vary from the intended standard gave it the name of a *beauty*, and palmed it upon the printers as a purposed novelty — such are *Paragon, Nonpareil, Pearl, Minion, Robyn* and *Diamond*." *Dissertation upon English Typographical Founders and Founderies*, London, 1788, p. 20.

French, German, Dutch, Italian, and Spanish types with their approximate equivalent in points are shown in the accompanying lists.[1]

That the sizes of ancient type-bodies were arbitrary was deplored by writers as early as Moxon. In his *Mechanick Exercises* he gives tables showing the number of squares of a certain body which should make up an English foot. For instance, 184 squares or ems of a pearl body, or $17\frac{1}{2}$ of the great-canon body, were comprised in one English foot. The relation, however, of these types to one another was extremely irregular. Dominique Fertel, of St. Omer, in his *Science Pratique de l'Imprimerie*, written in 1723, alludes to the lack of precision and uniformity in sizes of type current in his time. It was to remedy this that Pierre Simon Fournier[2] formulated his "point system" in the tractate issued at Paris in 1737, entitled *Tables des Proportions qu'il faut observer entre les caractères;* describing and developing it further in the preface to his *Modèles des Caractères de l'Imprimerie* of 1742; and finally giving an elaborate description of his perfected scheme of the "typographic point" in his *Manuel Typographique* of 1764. I do not know how the scheme of proportion of type-bodies proposed in the original formulation of 1737 compares with that proposed in 1742, but the latter is neither as complete nor as practical as is the plan finally developed in 1764. In the *Modèles* Fournier took for his unit of measurement a line

---

[1] For names of types in French, English, German, Spanish, Dutch, Italian, and Magyar, see lists in *Vocabulaire Technique de l'Éditeur en Sept Langues*, Berne, 1913, p. 303. The derivations of these names are of considerable interest, and are treated at length in Reed's *Old English Letter Foundries*, pp. 35–40; also in De Vinne's *Plain Printing Types*, pp. 62–68.

[2] Commonly called Fournier *le jeune*. He sometimes styled himself S. P. Fournier, as in the *Table des Proportions* reproduced on a later page.

No. Points	English	French	German	Dutch	Italian	Spanish
48-point	Canon	Double Canon	Kleine Missal	Parys Kanon	Reale	
44-point	2-line Double Pica	Gros Canon	Grobe Canon	Groote Kanon	Corale	Canon Grande
36-point	2-line Great Primer	Trismegiste	Kleine Canon	Kanon	Canone	Canon
28-point	2-line English	Petit Canon	Doppel Mittel	Dubbelde Augustyn	Sopracanoncino	Peticano
24-point	2-line Pica	Palestine	Roman	Dubbelde Mediaan	Canoncino	
22-point	Double Pica	Gros Parangon	Text or Secunda	Dubbelde Descendiaan (or Ascendonica)	Ascendonica	Misal
20-point	Paragon	Petit Parangon	Parangon	Parangon	Parangone	Parangona
18-point	Great Primer	Gros Romain	Tertia	Text	Testo	Texto
14-point	{ (Large English) / English	Gros Texte / Saint-Augustin	Grobe Mittel / Kleine Mittel	Augustyn	Soprasilvio / Silvio	Atanasia
12-point	Pica	Cicéro	Cicero	Mediaan	Lettura	Lectura
11-point	Small Pica	Philosophie	Brevier	Descendiaan	(Filosofia)	
10-point	Long Primer	Petit Romain	Corpus or Garmond	Garmond	Garamone	Entredos
9-point	Bourgeois	Gaillarde	(Borgis)	Burgeois or Galjart	Garamoncino	
8-point	Brevier	Petit Texte	Petit or Jungfer	Brevier	Testino	Breviario
7-point	Minion	Mignone	Colonel	Colonel	Mignona	Glosilla
6-point	Nonpareil	Nonpareille	Nonpareille	Nonparel	Nompariglia	Nonpareli
5-point	Pearl	{ Parisienne or Sedan / Perle }	Perl	{ Joly / Peerl }	{ Parmigianina }	
4½-point	Diamond	Diamant	Diamant	{ Robijn / Diamand }		

Names of Sizes of Type in Various Countries

of six points, and a 10-point type would therefore be measured as one line and four points—a plan somewhat cumbrous and inconvenient (*fig.* 5). But in the *Manuel* of 1764 he did away with the line and took the point as his unit— a much simpler plan, and one which by its practicality commended itself to printers then, as it has done ever since. His description of the first successful endeavour to place the measurements of types on a rational basis is quoted on a later page.

Before Fournier began experiments with the typographic point, there had been already some regulation of the height of French types; and a standard measurement of type-bodies had been proposed as early as 1733. But the standard to which types were to conform was set arbitrarily by some characters which happened to be found in one particular office, and the regulations which were issued at the time, not having any fixed principle of universal application, were useless. The idea was that one type should be equal to the body of two other types, but what the form of those two other bodies was to be was not decided. Of course, so ill-defined a plan ended in nothing.

Fournier describes his invention as something "new and unknown." "I give it a place here," he says in his *Manuel*,[1] "in order to explain the new proportions which I have applied to type bodies by the fixed measures which I call typographic points, . . . introducing in this department of typography an orderliness which it has never before had. Through the invention of typographic points, I think I have been fortunate enough to succeed with an exactness and precision which leave nothing to be desired. The typo-

[1] *Manuel Typographique, Utile aux Gens de Lettres, & à ceux qui exercent les différentes parties de l'Art de l'Imprimerie.* Par Fournier le jeune. Paris, 1764. Tome I, pp. 125 *et seq.*

TABLE
DES PROPORTIONS
DES DIFFERENS CARACTERES DE L'IMPRIMERIE.

Par S. P. FOURNIER, Graveur & Fondeur de Caractéres d'Imprimerie.

Nombre	CORPS.	ECHELLE DE ⟨scale⟩ DEUX POUCES.	Lignes.	Points.
1	PARISIENNE.	. . . .		5
2	NOMPAREILLE.	. . . .		
3	MIGNONE.	. . . .	1	1
4	PETIT-TEXTE.	. . . .	1	2
5	GAILLARDE.	. . . .	1	3
6	PETIT-ROMAIN.	—— 2. PARISIENNES.	1	4
7	PHILOSOPHIE.	—— 1. Parisienne , 1. Nompareille.	1	5
8	CICERO.	—— 2. NOMPAREILLES. ‖ 1. Parisienne, 1. Mignone.	2	
9	SAINT-AUGUSTIN.	—— 2. MIGNONES. ‖ 1. Nompareille, 1. Petit-Texte.	2	2
10	GROS-TEXTE.	—— 1. PETITS-TEXTES. ‖ 1. Parif. 1. Philofophie. ‖ 1. Nompareil. 1. Petit Romain. ‖ 1. Mignone, 1. Gaillarde. ‖ 2. Parif. 1. Nomp.	2	4
11	GROS-ROMAIN.	—— 2. GAILLARDES. ‖ 3. Nompareilles. ‖ 1. Nomp. 1. Cicéro. ‖ 1. Mign. 1. Philofoph. ‖ 1. Pet. Text. 1. Philofoph. ‖ 2. Parif. 1. Pet. Text. ‖ 1. Parif. 1. Nomp. 1. Mignone.	3	
12	PETIT-PARANGON.	—— 2. PETITS-ROMAINS. ‖ 4. Parifiennes. ‖ 1. Nomp. 1. Saint-Auguftin. ‖ 1. Pet. Text. 1. Cic. ‖ 1. Gaill. 1. Philofoph. ‖ 2. Parif. 1. Pet. Rom. ‖ 2. Nomp. 1. Pet. Text. ‖ 2. Mign. 1. Nomp. ‖ 1. Parif. 1. Nomp. 1. Gaill. ‖ 1. Parif. 1. Mignon. 1. Pet. Text.	3	2
13	GROS-PARANGON.	—— 2. PHILOSOPHIES. ‖ 1. Nomp. 1. Gros-Texte. ‖ 1. Pet. Text. Saint-Aug. ‖ 1. Pet. Rom. 1. Cic. ‖ 2. Parif. 1. Cic. ‖ 1. Parif. Pet. Rom. ‖ 2. Mign. 1. Pet. Text. ‖ 2. Pet. Text. 1. Nomp. ‖ 1. Parif. 1. Nomp. 1. Philofoph. ‖ 1. Nomp. 1. Mign. 1. Gaill. ‖ 2. Parif. 2. Nomp. ‖ 3. Parif. 1. Mignon.	3	4
14	PALESTINE.	—— 2. CICEROS. ‖ 3. Petits-Textes. ‖ 4. Nompareilles. ‖ 1. Nomp. 1 Gros-Romain. ‖ 1. Pet. Text. 1. Gr. Text. ‖ 1. Pet. Rom. 1. Saint-Aug. ‖ 2. Parif. 1. S. Aug. ‖ 2. Nomp. 1. Cic. ‖ 2. Mignon. 1. Pet. Rom. ‖ 1. Gaill. 1. Nomp. ‖ 1. Parif. 1. Mign. 1. Cic. ‖ 1. Parif. 1. Gaill. 1. Pet. Rom. ‖ 1. Nomp. 1. Mign. 1. Philofoph. ‖ 1. Nomp. 1. Pet. Text. 1. Pet. Rom. ‖ 1. Mign. 1. Pet. Text. 1. Gaill. ‖ 2. Parif. 1. Mign. ‖ 3. Parif. 1. Gaill.	4	
15	PETIT-CANON.	—— 2. SAINTS-AUGUSTINS. ‖ 4. Mignones. ‖ 1. Nomp. 1. Gros-Parangon. ‖ 1. Pet. Text. 1. Petit-Parangon. ‖ 1. Pet. Rom. 1. Gr. Rom. ‖ 1. Cic. 1. Gr. Text. ‖ 2. Parif. 1. Gr. Rom. ‖ 1. Nomp. 1. Gr. Text. ‖ 2. Mign. 1. S. Aug. ‖ 2. Pet. Text. 1. Cic. ‖ 2. Gaill. 1. Pet. Rom. ‖ 2. Pet. Rom. 1. Pet. Text. ‖ 1. Philofoph. 1. Nomp. ‖ 2. Parif. 2. Gaill. ‖ 2. Nomp. 2. Pet. Text. ‖ 2. Parif. 3. Nomp. ‖ 3. Nomp. 1. Pet. Rom. ‖ 4. Parif. 1. Pet. Text. ‖ 1. Mign. 1. Gr. Text. ‖ 1. Nomp. 1. Pet. Text. 1. S. Aug. ‖ 1. Parif. 1. Gaill. 1. S. Aug. ‖ 1. Parif. 1. Philofoph. 1. Cic. ‖ 1. Nomp. 1. Pet. Rom. 1. Cic. ‖ 1. Mign. 1. Gaill. 1. Cic. ‖ 2. Nomp. 1. Mign. 1. Gaill. ‖ 2. Mign. 1. Nomp. 1. Pet. Text.	4	4
16	TRISMEGISTE.	—— 2. GROS-ROMAINS. ‖ 3. Cicéros. ‖ 4. Gaillardes. ‖ 6. Nompareilles. ‖ 1. Pet. Text. 1. Petit-Canon. ‖ 1. Cic. 1. Paleftine. ‖ 1. S. Aug. 1. Gr. Parang. ‖ 1. Gr. Text. 1. Pet. Parang. *(On peut encore augmenter de beaucoup l'affemblage de ce Corps & des fuivans.)*	6	
17	GROS-CANON.	—— 2. GROS-PARANGONS. ‖ 4. Philofophies. ‖ 1. Pet. Text. 1. Trifmégifte. ‖ 1. Gr. Text. 1. Pet. Canon. ‖ 1. Pet. Parang. 1. Paleftine.	7	2
18	DOUBLE-CANON.	—— 2. PETITS-CANONS. ‖ 4. Saint-Auguftins. ‖ 8. Mignones. ‖ 1. Cic. 1. Gr. Canon. ‖ 1. Pet. Parang. 1. Trifmég.	9	2
19	TRIPLE-CANON.	—— 2. TRISMEGISTES. ‖ 4. Gros-Romains. ‖ 6. Cicéros. ‖ 8. Gaillardes. ‖ 12. Nompareilles. ‖ 1. Gr. Text. 1. Doubl-Canon. ‖ 1. Pet. Can. 1. Gr. Can.	12	
20	GROSSE-NOMPA-REILLE.	—— 4. PALESTINES. ‖ 8. Cicéros. ‖ 12. Petits-Textes. ‖ 16. Nompareilles. ‖ 1. Paleft. 1. Triple-Canon.	16	
	Tous les Caractéres doivent avoir dix lignes & demie géométriques de hauteur en papier , fuivant les Réglemens ; ou onze lignes trois points , mefure de l'Echelle.	*Les Caractéres de l'Imprimerie n'ayant point eu jufqu'à préfent d'ordre parfait, (les Corps étant plus forts ou plus foibles , fuivant les Imprimeries) je leur donne ici un corps fixe & une correfpondance générale ; en confervant , autant que j'ai pû, les forces de corps ordinaires : ce qui a été approuvé des perfonnes les plus expérimentées dans l'Art. Et pour l'éxécution , j'ai fait une Echelle que je divife en deux pouces , le pouce en douze lignes , & la ligne en fix points ; où il faudra prendre exactement le nombre de lignes & de points que je marque pour chaque Corps.*		

5. *Fournier's Table of Proportions of Bodies of Different Types*
From Modèles des Caractères de l'Imprimerie. Paris, 1742 (reduced)

graphic point is nothing but the division of the type body into equal and definite degrees which are called *Points*. By this means any one can know exactly the degree of difference and the relation of type bodies to one another. One may combine them as numerals are combined; two and two make four; add two and you will have six; double this and you get twelve, etc. So a Nonpareille, which is six points, with another Nonpareille would make a Cicéro, which is twelve points. Add still a Nonpareille and you would have eighteen points, or a Gros-Romain. Double this total, which would make thirty-six points, and you have the Trismegiste, and so on with the others, as you will see by the table of proportions. . . .

"To combine the bodies it is sufficient merely to know the number of typographical points in each. To do this, these points or given units should be invariable, so that they will serve as standards in printing-offices, like the *pied du roi*, the inch, and the line in geometry. To this end I have fixed the exact size which the points should have, in a scale which is at the head of my Table of Proportions, and to insure invariable exactitude in casting types, I have devised an instrument which I have called a prototype. . . .

"The invention of these points is the first tribute which I rendered to typography in 1737. Obliged since then to start on a long, difficult and laborious career by engraving all the punches necessary to the establishment of my foundry, I found no rule to guide me in fixing the body of the characters which I was obliged to make. I was therefore forced to formulate my own principles, which I have done, and which I have rendered comprehensible by the following table (*portions shown by figs. 6 and 7*).

" At the head of the table is a fixed and standard scale which I have divided into two inches, the inch into 12 lines, the line into 6 of these typographic points, making 144 points in all. The first little divisions are of two points, which is exactly the distance between the body of the Petit-

TABLE GÉNÉRALE
DE LA PROPORTION
des différens Corps de Caractères.

ÉCHELLE FIXE
de 144 points Typographiques.

Nomb.	CORPS.	Points
1	PARISIENNE.	5
2	NOMPAREILLE.	6
3	MIGNONE.	7
4	PETIT-TEXTE.	8
5	GAILLARDE. . . . , ...	9
6	PETIT-ROMAIN. — 2 Parifiennes.	10
7	PHILOSOPHIE. = 1 Parif. 1 Nompareille.	11
8	CICÉRO. — 2 Nomp. = 1 Parifienne, 1 Mignone.	12
9	SAINT-AUGUSTIN. — 2 Mignones. = 1 Nompareille, 1 Petit-texte.	14

6. *Fournier's perfected Table of Proportions for his Point System
From Manuel Typographique. Paris,* 1764

texte and the body of the Petit-romain, or from this last size to the body of the Cicéro, etc. The number of points which I have assigned to each of the bodies must be measured by this scale. If these measures are carefully taken for each body and verified by the prototype, this will establish the

Nomb.	Corps.	Points
	TABLE	
10	GROS - TEXTE. — 2 Petit-textes. = 1 Parif. 1 Philofophie. = 1 Nomp. 1 Petit-rom. = 1 Mignone, 1 Gail. + 2 Parifiennes, 1 Nompareille.	16
11	GROS-ROMAIN. — 2 Gaillardes. — 3 Nompareilles. = 1 Nompareille, 1 Cicéro. = 1 Mign. 1 Philofophie. = 1 Petit - texte, 1 Petit-romain. + 2 Parif. 1 Petit-texte, + 1 Parif. 1 Nompareille, 1 Mignone.	18
12	PETIT-PARANGON. — 2 Petit-rom. — 4 Parifiennes, = 1 Nompareille, 1 Saint-Auguftin. = 1 Petit-texte, 1 Cicéro. = 1 Gaillarde, 1 Philofoph. + 2 Parif. 1 Petit-rom. + 2 Nomp. 1 Petit-texte, + 2 Mign. 1 Nomp. + 1 Parifienne, 1 Nomp. 1 Gaill. + 1 Parifienne, 1 Mign. 1 Petit-texte.	20
13	GROS-PARANGON. — 2 Philofoph. = 1 Nomp. 1 Gros-tex. = 1 Petit-tex. 1 Saint-auguftin. = 1 Petit-romain, 1 Cicéro. + 2 Parifiennes, 1 Cicéro. + 2 Nomp. 1 Petit-rom. + 2. Mign. 1 Saint-auguftin. + 2 Petit-textes, 1 Petit-texte, + 2 Petit-tex. 1 Nomp.	

Nomb.	Corps.	Points
	+ 1 Parif. 1 Nomp. 1 Philofophie. + 1 Nomp. 1 Mignone, 1 Gaill. + 2 Parif. 2 Nomp. + 3 Parifiennes, 1 Mignone.	
14	PALESTINE. — 2 Cic. — 3 Petit-tex. — 4 Nomp. = 1 Nomp. 1 Gros-rom. = 1 Petit-tex. 1 Gros-tex. = 1 Petit-rom. 1 Saint-auguft. + 2 Parifiennes, 1 Saint-auguftin, + 2 Nomp. 1 Cic. + 2 Mign. 1 Petit-rom. + 2 Gaill. 1 Nomp. + 1 Parif. 1 Mign. 1 Cic. + 1 Parif. 1 Gaill. 1 Petit-romain. + 1 Nomp. 1 Mign. 1 Philofophie. + 1 Nomp. 1 Petit-tex. 1 Petit-rom. + 1 Mignone, 1 Petit-texte, 1 Gaill. + 2 Parif. 2 Mign. + 3 Parif, 1 Gaill.	24
15	PETIT-CANON. — 2 Saint-auguftin. — 4 Mign. + 1 Nomp. 1 Gros-par. + 1 Petit-texte, 1 Petit-parangon. + 1 Petit-rom. 1 Gros-rom. + 1 Cic. 1 Gros-texte. + 2 Parif. 1 Gros-rom. + 2 Nomp. 1 Gros-texte. + 2 Mign. 1 Saint-auguftin. + 2 Petit-textes, 1 Cic. + 2 Gaill. 1 Petit-romain.	28

7. *Fournier's perfected Table of Proportions for his Point System (continued)*
From Manuel Typographique

general relation between all bodies of types, as will be shown by the following combinations.

"This scale contains in its totality twelve bodies of Cicéro. After printing this same table, which I published in 1737, I perceived that the paper in drying had shrunk the proper dimensions of the scale a little, and in the present table I have forestalled this fault by adding what should be allowed for the shrinkage of the paper."

Fournier's general table of proportions of the different bodies of characters is interesting. His idea of correcting the lack of system in casting types was excellent, but in the exact plan which he was proposing it was risky to make merely a rough and ready allowance for shrinkage of the paper on which his table was printed, if he intended to arrive at any exact result. Books at that period were printed on wet paper, and its shrinkage was very variable. It is perfectly possible, therefore, that the elaborately introduced scale, with its 144 points, varied by at least a point in different copies of Fournier's *Manuel*. His prototype was of metal, a large measure of 240 points, something like a composing-stick, and was intended to correct this fault; but the prototype itself was probably subject to slight variations in manufacture, and was in no sense an instrument of precision.

In the succeeding steps by which the present point system was arrived at, the next advance was made by François Ambroise Didot, of the celebrated French family of typographers. Realizing the weakness of Fournier's basis of measurement, he adopted as his standard the authoritative *pied du roi*, containing 12 French or 12.7892 American inches. He preserved Fournier's subdivisions, making 72 points to the French inch. Nor did he find it difficult to adjust the smaller sizes of type to his new system. With large bodies, Didot was less fortunate. Cicéro, which was, like our 12-point or pica, the standard for determining sizes, he changed from twelve to eleven points, which proved rather disastrous in its working out. The traditional names of types he threw over, substituting for them (with French lucidity) the number of points which the type-body covered, as we do to-day; and this was perhaps the valuable feature of Didot's performance. At the loss of a certain historical and picturesque nomenclature, it placed type sizes upon a basis comprehensible to the meanest intelligence. The introduction of the Didot system of points was not made without confusion, however; for many printers, especially in the French provinces, persisted in using the system of Fournier — a persistence continued until late in the last century. The Didot point is used in most of the foundries of Austria, Asia Minor, Belgium, Brazil, Denmark, Germany, Hungary, Rumania, Serbia, Sweden, Switzerland, and Turkey. Fournier's point is scarcely used nowadays, except in Belgium.

At the time that the Didot system was introduced the French metric system had not been adopted, and it is only fair to say that until a type system is formulated which is in full and regular accordance with the metric system, perfection will not be attained. But the advance made has been very great and has infinitely simplified type-setting, the facility with which the numerical nomenclature indicates the sizes of types as compared with one another, being a by-product of a still greater mechanical advantage.

In this country, George Bruce of New York formulated, in the first quarter of the nineteenth century, a plan based on the theory that bodies of types should increase by arithmetical progression — that small pica should be made as much larger than long primer as bourgeois was larger than brevier. This system, which De Vinne calls ingenious and scientific, was not adopted except in Bruce's own foundry.

Further advances were made, in which western type-founders took the lead. Marder, Luse & Co. of the Chicago Type Foundry began to produce types on point bodies about 1878. Influenced by this, in 1886 the United States Type Founders' Association named a committee to consider the point system. It was found that the pica body selected as a standard could be made to accord (irregularly) with the metric system, 83 picas being equal to 35 centimetres. The unit was gained by dividing the pica into 12 equal parts, each part being called a point. As in France, the old names were discarded, great primer becoming 18-point, pica becoming 12-point, long primer, 10-point. This was very much the system of Fournier and of Didot; the only difference being that the pica selected was of a slightly different body from their standard body. It is known as the American point system, and many American printers proudly suppose that it is called so from having been wholly invented here!

The common measure for all bodies of type was decided by the Type Founders' Association to be 35 centimetres or 83 picas in length. To gain a standard for determining the height of type it was proposed that this same standard of 35 centimetres should be chosen, and 15 type-heights were to build up to the 35 centimetres. There is a slight difference here between the old standard of $\frac{11}{12}$ of an inch and the new standard. The difference amounts to only about $\frac{1}{500}$ part of an inch, but this is sufficient to make it impossible to use types of the old heights in combination with those of the new.

The Type Founders' Association also considered the advisability of adopting the Didot point; but this, which had a great advantage in permitting the interchange of types between France and America, would have involved too much of a departure by American founders, and was thought impracticable.

It is not fair to expect from the adoption of the American point system that all difficulties will be overcome. Trouble in types may still be caused by defective moulds, by the overheating of the metal, or by careless dressing; and types of the same bodies from different foundries cannot *always* be used together with safety. There is still the great obstacle of a lack of uniformity in the height of the types themselves.[1] But in spite of all this, typographical practice has been enormously simplified by the "point" system. It was adopted in England in 1898, though it had been in use by her nearest continental neighbour for well over a hundred and fifty years!

The adjustment to units of the width or set of types, as well as their height-to-paper and their body, has also been considered. In 1883 Mr. Linn B. Benton took out a patent for types made to units both in body and width — called "self-spacing" type. In 1894 a western firm introduced this system of self-spacing types, every type in their entire output being placed on a body the width of which was equal to an even division of the standard "pica em." Later the more logical unit of a point was adopted — hence the term "point-set." This was to result theoretically, as indeed it did practically, in each line ending evenly, and for the workman trouble in spacing was avoided; but the shapes of letters and the space around them were arbitrarily rearranged by

---

[1] The dimension of a type as to height is measured from the face to the foot, and is termed "height-to-paper." The standard height-to-paper is 0.918 inch. Types exceeding or falling short of this measurement are termed respectively "high-to-paper" and "low-to-paper."

such a method. Types have definite shapes already determined. The bodies on which they are cast cannot be wid-
ened or narrowed merely to aid mechanical convenience,
with successful typographical results. In comparing fonts
cast according to the old system of irregular sets and those
cast on the point-set system, we find that the older font had
more than ninety different sets, while the latter has but from
thirteen to twenty. Something suffers when ninety different
adjustments are reduced to from thirteen to twenty, and the
"something" that suffers *is the effect of the type.*

Point-line — another so-called improvement — was introduced by the same western house in 1894; and has been
so generally adopted by American and English foundries
that it is now known as the Standard Lining System. There
are mechanical advantages inherent in this scheme, but
they are attained at the expense of the correct proportion
of certain letters. The convenience of being able to align
different sizes of type by the use of 1-point leads or their
multiples is no doubt appreciated by the compositor; but
to make this possible, types below 18-point are arranged,
so far as "line" is concerned, in but three groups: in the
first are 5 and 6-point types; in the second, 7 to 10-point
types; and in the third, 11 to 16-point. Taking the second
group for illustration, the "descenders" of g, j, p, q, and y
can be no longer in a 10-point than in a 7-point face; and
as they are none too long in 7-point they become much too
short in 10-point. This disregard for proportionate length of
descenders of types of different sizes pervades the whole
scheme; and consequently no size of type (excepting possibly 7-point and 11-point) which is cast on Standard Line
can have descenders of adequate length; while in some sizes
they are so "chopped off" as to produce real deformity. It is
fair to say, however, that a few series of roman and italic

types have been arranged on Standard *Script* Line, which permits descenders of proper length in all except small sizes.

The shortened descender is objectionable from two points of view. In the first place, if the type in mass (especially in larger sizes, and when leaded) is not to present a squat and rolling appearance, the ascenders and descenders must be of adequate length to counteract this tendency. And in English, especially, the slanting and vertical lines of descenders are particularly required to offset the preponderance of round, short letters. With the descenders shortened the page loses that texture or "woven" look which is an integral part of elegance in typography. It is objectionable, secondly, because the legibility of a letter has a direct connection with its form; and to disregard this, for mechanical or any other reasons, makes type less "friendly to the eye."

One convenience of the lining system is that all faces of a given size, whatever their character, line with one another. This enables the compositor to give emphasis to a certain word in the body of a page by using heavy-faced type, without the necessity of "justification." A good typographer seldom, if ever, *wishes* to give emphasis to a word in the middle of a sentence by setting it in heavy type; nevertheless there are cases, especially in catalogue work, where it is necessary to use some heavy-faced type to pick out a title or some salient feature akin to it. But a so-called advantage which offers facilities for wretched typography is that any italic will line with any roman—which has hitherto been difficult and "would to God were impossible!"

In these point-set and lining types (offered to the printer on the ground of labour-saving and economic advantages) care about distortion of the shape of letters, ill-fit to bodies or mixture of faces, or the effect which all this results in, was cast to the winds. Instead of being combated by larger foun-

dries, both point-set and lining schemes were at once followed for business reasons. But the lining system was not
adopted without some objection from printers, which is now
making itself distinctly felt, and type-founders are again
offering fonts with long descenders — a movement that has
extended to the makers of type-setting machines.

Shortened descenders are nothing new. Italian printers
used such deformed types in the fifteenth century, but they
had no lasting vogue. The Elzevirs used them in the seventeenth century, — one reason why Elzevir books as reading
editions now are failures, — but they did not survive. In the
eighteenth century Caslon showed them as variants to his
famous fonts, and Fournier possessed such types; but they
went the way of all flesh. The shortened descender tried
in our day is again going out of use; for no type-founder
or machine-maker can permanently "buck" the proper proportions of letters.

A lining system which mutilates descenders, and self-
spacing or point-set schemes which involve either lateral
distortion of letters or too much space between them, may
for the moment seem clever, convenient, lasting, and money-
saving "improvements," but they are merely unintelligent,
temporary, and inartistic expedients. The reason that such
schemes met at first with instant success is attributable to
that lack of standard on the printers' part to which I have
alluded before. Their waning vogue has come from a little
study and education. Men must show their faith by their
works; and it is of little use to admire early typography
when one is willing for money-making reasons to destroy, or
permit the destruction of, the elements which made it admirable. But apart from all this, the fundamental trouble
with these schemes is, that they make types hard to read.

CHAPTER III

IN the preceding chapter we considered how type was
made, the sizes of types, and the systems which have
been devised for their measurement. We must now
learn something about the history and design of type itself.

Whence are derived the shapes of the characters in
which you read the sentence before you; and whence comes
the type in which this sentence is printed? The type of this
book is a font *transitional* between the "old style" types
of the school of Caslon and the English equivalent of the
pseudo-classic types made at the beginning of the nineteenth
century under the influence of Didot of Paris, Bodoni of
Parma, and Unger of Berlin. These pseudo-classic types
were modifications of that old style type (as we should
now call it) which was in use in England and throughout
Europe in the middle of the eighteenth century. The English
old style types of the seventeenth and eighteenth centuries
were chiefly derived from Dutch models of the middle of
the seventeenth century; and these seventeenth century
types in turn were modelled on earlier roman[1] types common in Europe which were introduced into Italy at the time
of the Renaissance. Any one familiar with the earliest printing will note that many of the early types were black-letter
characters derived from manuscripts, and at first sight it is
a little perplexing to know where Roman characters come
from. But the Roman characters of the Italian Renaissance
were a revival, along with the revival of antique learning,
of the lettering in which antique learning had been pre-

[1] In this book the words Roman and Gothic, when describing handwriting,
manuscript, style, form, etc., are capitalized. But when denominating printing types, they are not.

served at the period of Charlemagne; and this antique lettering, preserved in the calligraphic revival of the ninth century, was in part a return to the early Roman characters which go back to a period coeval with the Christian era. Thus the type of this page is tied historically to the written characters of the Romans.

In tracing the ancestry of any modern type-form, it is by no means sufficient to limit our research to the earliest types, for it cannot be too clearly understood that the *first* printed books (as has before been said) were nothing more than imitations of *late* manuscripts. " The discovery of typographic printing did not all at once produce, it is to be understood, a radical change in the general aspect of the book. The first works which left the hands of the printers were astonishingly like the manuscripts of the same period, especially up to about 1475; so exactly indeed that at first sight one cannot always say, whether one has before him a piece of early printing, or a manuscript. . . . The letters of the printed text present the same characters as those which were written by the calligraphers. . . . The same abbreviations, the same ligatures, and the same punctuations are found as in the manuscript. The disposition of the printer's text is the same as that of the manuscript text."[1]

So it is clear that we can have no knowledge of the types of to-day and their history without knowing the history of types back to the invention of printing, and that we can have no knowledge of the first types or their relative place in the scheme of things unless we know how earlier calligraphers formed the letters of their manuscript book-hands. Nor can we tell how the letter-forms themselves came to be unless

---

[1] See Leo S. Olschki's *Incunables illustrés imitant les Manuscrits. Le passage du manuscrit au livre imprimé*, Florence, 1914, p. 5. See also the illustrations of illuminated incunabula.

we know the history of the alphabet, of the various forms of Latin writing, and its vicissitudes in different countries up to the invention of printing.

Alphabetic writing had generally five successive stages. It began with ideograms, which were pictures, representing to those who made them either :

(1) objects;

(2) thoughts.[1]

Then came phonograms, which were merely ideograms by which sounds had come to be signified instead of things, and of these there were three sorts:

(3) signs which stood for words;[2]

(4) signs which stood for syllables;

(5) alphabetic signs which stood for the elementary sounds which constitute the syllable.

This last is what our alphabet is now; its letters being "phonograms which by the process of long continued detrition have reached an extreme stage of simplicity both as regards form and value. If the history of any one of our

---

[1] The Roman numerals are supposed by some to be ideograms—I, II, III representing the fingers of the human hand, and V representing the hand open, and signifying 5. Again IV = 1 less finger than a hand, represents 4. VI = 1 more finger than a hand, gives us 6. X was a picture or ideogram of two hands = 10. In fact, we call these figures digits = fingers.

The zodiacal and planetary signs used by astronomers are also ideograms. The symbol ☿ is the caduceus of Mercury entwined by two serpents; ♀ is the mirror of Venus, with its handle; and ♂ is the shield and spear of Mars. The symbol ♃, which denotes Jupiter, resolves itself into an arm grasping a thunderbolt; while ♄ , which stands for Saturn, is a mower's scythe. " Among other ideograms which we employ may be enumerated the crown and the broad arrow, sundry trademarks and armorial bearings, together with several printer's signs, such as ☞ ; ! , and =." Taylor's *The Alphabet*, London, 1883, Vol. I, pp. 7, 8.

[2] Such symbols as £, s, d, though alphabetic in their origin, are now used simply as convenient phonograms, standing for the words "pounds," "shillings," and " pence." *Ibid.* Also such signs as $, ℔, cwt. (c = 100, wt. = weight), etc.

alphabetic symbols be traced backwards, it will be found to resolve itself ultimately into the conventionalized picture of some object." [1]

The next question is, Where does our alphabet come from? We derive our Latin alphabet from the Greeks and the Greeks received theirs from the Phœnicians, but from whom the Phœnicians derived their alphabet we do not know. Sixty or seventy years ago it was supposed that it could be historically connected with the Egyptian hieratic writing, but this theory is either erroneous, or at the present moment out of fashion.

The Greek alphabet had a close relation to the Phœnician, or (as perhaps it is more properly called) the Semitic alphabet. In the first place, the forms were in many cases very much alike. The word "alphabet," which gives a clue to the connection, is derived from *alpha* and *beta*, the names of the first and second letters of the Greek alphabet. "The names of the Semitic letters," Sir Edward Maunde Thompson tells us, "are Semitic words, each describing the letter from its resemblance to some particular object, as, *aleph*, an ox, *beth*, a house. When the Greeks took over their Semitic letters, they also took over their Semitic names." [2] Both the names of the letters and their order in the two alphabets are the same. This alphabet was employed by the Phœnicians, by the Jews, and by the Moabites, and from early inscriptions, the primitive Phœnician alphabet, consisting of twenty-two letters, can be made up.

---

[1] Taylor's *The Alphabet*, Vol. I, p. 8.
[2] See Sir E. Maunde Thompson's *Introduction to Greek and Latin Palaeography*, Oxford, Clarendon Press, 1912, p. 1: referred to henceforth as Thompson. It is not to be confused with the same author's *Handbook of Greek and Latin Palaeography*, published by Kegan Paul, Trench, Trübner & Co. in their *International Scientific Series*, first issued in 1893 and since republished.

The Greeks learned the art of writing in the ninth century B.C.—perhaps earlier. The primitive Greek alphabet
was generally known as the Cadmean alphabet, and it had
many varieties. The alphabets first in use were written from
right to left; then the *boustrophedon* method of writing came
into vogue, in which the lines ran alternately from right to
left and from left to right, like the furrows of a plough; and
finally writing all ran from left to right as it does to-day.

The Latin alphabet had twenty letters of the Greek
western alphabet and three letters in addition, G, Y, and Z.
Our English alphabet has twenty-six letters, the additions
being (as we know) J, an alternate form of I; U, which is
a similar form of V; and W, which is simply two ligatured
V's equivalent to a double U.

Manuscripts in the Latin alphabet go back to the first century of our era, and the history of Latin writing is divided
into five periods, each distinguished by its characteristic
group of handwritings. These, according to Steffens's[1] convenient divisions, are as follows:

   i writing of the Roman period;

   ii national handwritings;

   iii the Carolingian minuscule;

   iv the Gothic minuscule;

   v Humanistic writing and modern Gothic hands.

Under each epoch there were many subdivisions. For
instance, the writing of the Roman period was of several
kinds, namely:

   (*a*) a capital letter hand (further subdivided);

   (*b*) ancient Roman cursive handwriting;

[1] Steffens's (Franz), *Paléographie Latine. 125 Fac-similés en phototypie acompagnés de transcriptions et d'explications, avec un exposé systématique de
l'histoire de l'écriture latine.* Trèves and Paris, 1910. (Edited by Remi Coulon and translated into French from the *second* German edition of *Lateinische
Paléographie.*)

(*c*) uncial letters;

(*d*) later Roman cursive handwriting;

(*e*) a half-uncial letter.

These belonged to the Roman period of writing alone. It is not necessary to describe all these variations here, except to say that there were at a very early period different kinds of handwriting intended for special purposes; just as later certain types were employed to print special classes of books. For instance, in the writing of the Roman period we find there were two forms of capital letters, which are called the square capital (or *capitalis quadrata*, *elegans*, or *scriptura monumentalis*),[1] and the rustic capital, which is called *capitalis rustica* or *scriptura actuaria*.[2] The former is a square, rigid, formal letter used for inscriptions and more stately kinds of manuscripts; the latter—the rustic—is somewhat freer, though employed for fine manuscripts as well. The works of the great poets were written in these styles — for the *edition de luxe* of books by celebrated authors is a very ancient institution.[3] What the difference is between these two forms is plain. Rustic letters were easier to make and could be written more rapidly than the formal, square hands, but both forms of capitals were intended for manuscripts of books.

Now it is not to be supposed that letters, accounts, receipts, and scribblings were written in these hands. The Romans had, as we have, a current running handwriting which they used for commercial and ordinary purposes, and which they called *scriptura cursiva*, or *littera epistolaris*, to distinguish it from the straighter book-hand, which was

[1] *Paléographie Latine*, pl. 12; or Thompson, fac. 82.

[2] *Paléographie Latine*, pls. 10, 19; also Thompson, facs. 84, 85, 86.

[3] This difference appeared also in inscriptions in stone. See Votive Inscription on marble, in square and rustic capitals, reproduced in Steffens's *Paléographie Latine*, pl. 7.

called *scriptura erecta*, or *libraria*.[1] This old Roman cursive, while it was cursive, *was a cursive of capital letters*, and in course of time these letters began to show certain ligatures as well as inequalities in their height.[2] In the history of any art or craft there is constant development; and it was so in the history of writing. Letters were all the time evolving special characteristics. The capital book-hands, for instance, fell under the influence (especially in rustic forms) of cursive capital handwriting coexistent with them; and inversely the cursive capital hands, as they progressed, became modified by the influence of literary book-hands of capital letters familiar to the same scribes. So the next step in the writing of capital hands showed itself in a development of what was called the uncial letter, which we shall hear a good deal about.

The uncial was distinguished from the capital of the book-hands by the round character of certain letters; the chief characteristic "test-letters" being A, D, E, H, and M.[3] In other words, the old informal, cursive capital hand had broken into the square capital, formal hand, and produced these uncial capitals, which, because they were much easier to write, followed cursive rather than square capitals in shape. This uncial hand began to show itself as early as the third century, but was in its heyday in the fifth and sixth centuries. By the eighth century it greatly degenerated, although there was an attempt to revive it for certain ornamental purposes.[4]

---

[1] *Paléographie Latine*, pl. 9.

[2] *Ibid.*, pl. 13; also *Tables of Latin Cursive Alphabets*, in Thompson, pp. 335–337.

[3] Strange's *Alphabets*, London, 1898, pl. 2.

[4] See *Paléographie Latine*, pls. 15 (showing both early and later uncials), 17, 18; or Thompson, facs. 87, 88.

The later or new Roman cursive hand which succeeded the older cursive, like it was characterized by flowing ligatures between letters and by characters of unequal height; but these became much more frequent and striking. The style of the letters showed that their forms had changed through the effect of rapidity and freedom of execution. Ligatured letters became more common and more varied, and from this kind of writing the black-letter ff ultimately is derived. But a chief distinction was the marked difference between tall and short letters; and from this hand, thus developed, the first minuscule alphabet— the beginnings of a printer's "lower-case" alphabet — is derived. The first square capitals were drawn as if they were between *two* parallel lines. The more cursive capitals and uncial capitals showed some tendency to break through these lines, and a certain number of characters actually did so. The later Roman cursive appears as if arranged between *four* parallel lines. The short letters are compressed between the two middle lines, the bodies of other letters still coming between these two lines, but ascending and descending letters touch almost the first and fourth line of the four imaginary lines alluded to just as they do in type to-day.[1]

Finally, there was also a half-uncial letter which differed from uncial writing in this way — that while uncial writing was composed of capitals with a few intrusions of minuscule (or as a printer would say "lower-case") letters, the half-uncial was generally based on minuscule (or "lower-case") forms, with occasional intrusions of capital letters. This style of handwriting was revived as a part of that calligraphic reform in which the abbey of St. Martin at Tours played so important a part in the ninth century.[2]

[1] *Paléographie Latine*, pl. 22; Thompson, facs. 110, 111.
[2] Thompson. facs. 98, 99, 100; or *Paléographie Latine*, pl. 20.

Here we have a fuller development yet of our present "lower-case" alphabet.

It has been said that Latin writing was divided into five classes, viz:

    i writing of the Roman period;

    ii national handwritings;

    iii the Carolingian minuscule;

    iv the Gothic minuscule;

    v Humanistic writing and modern Gothic hands.

We have so far touched solely on the handwriting of the Roman period and the five classes into which that was subdivided; *i.e.* (*a*) the capital letter-hand, (*b*) the old Roman cursive handwriting, (*c*) the uncial letters, (*d*) a later Roman cursive, and (*e*) a half-uncial letter. What is learned thus far? Merely from this we see whence we derive capital letters, whence we derive certain uncial forms of capital letters with which we are familiar in black-letter types, and whence we derive our lower-case alphabet. Furthermore, we learn that there were three forms of writing — a formal, less formal, and informal; and perhaps it may be said that in type, capitals answer to the formal square capital hands, lower-case letters to the less formal half-uncial letter, and italic to the informal later Roman cursive hands. The square capital, the old Roman cursive, the uncial, and especially the later Roman cursive and half-uncial hands, are the sources from which we derive our present type alphabet.

From what has been said only of the Roman period, the importance of all the different epochs of the history of Latin writing, in their effect upon letter-forms, may be guessed. But we are not considering the history of all stages and variations of Latin writing except as they have to do more directly with printing types, explain the shapes which these have taken on, and the uses to which they have been put. We need, therefore, only touch on the remaining four great groups of manuscript hands:

ii the national hands;

iii the Carolingian minuscule;

iv the Gothic minuscule;

v Humanistic writing and modern Gothic hands;

—hands which had either an enormous influence on the letters of our present alphabet, or else actually survive in types in daily use.

During the existence of the Roman Empire different western countries continued to employ Roman cursive writing. But on its fall, while at first the handwriting of the professional scribes preserved more or less the old traditional forms of uncial, half-uncial, etc., the cursive characters employed for literary scripts slowly took on, in various countries, changes analogous to those which the Latin tongue underwent in the Romance languages. In Italy there was an old Italian cursive, a Curiale, an old Italian manuscript hand, and the better-known Beneventan writing. These were all Italian hands, but were all derived from later Roman cursive writing. They were also all minuscule hands. In France their equivalents took on a different development into what was called the Merovingian letter, a French national hand originally derived from Roman cursive characters but with marked, though slowly developed, French peculiarities. The Visigothic writing was nothing more than the Roman hand isolated and changed by the national genius of Spain into its characteristic Spanish form. What were called the Insular hands—i.e., Anglo-Saxon and Irish—had, too, whatever their origin, a characteristic development within themselves and formed a particular style of writing entirely distinguishable from French, Italian, or Spanish. The student may see what these hands were by consulting facsimiles of Visigothic, Merovingian, Franco-Lombardic, and Pre-Carolingian writing.[1] "In the Visigothic hand," says Thompson,—and the same is true of other national book-hands,—"there is the national character inherent in the script, which, quite independently of any peculiar forms of letters, reveals the nationality of a handwriting as clearly as personal handwriting reveals the individual." It will be seen later that this is true of the national printing types which succeeded these national manuscript-hands. Roughly speaking, all these forms of letter were what in type we call "lower-case," though in them some capital forms were included. These national hands profoundly influenced the earliest type-forms in their respective countries; as, for instance, in certain sorts of well-known black-letter types in use to-day, which are directly derived from English and French manuscripts.

In all books on early writing, Carolingian minuscules are mentioned: a term that is readily comprehensible if it be remembered that "minuscule" may be taken for our purposes as meaning merely a lower-case letter, and that "Carolingian" indicates the epoch of Charles the Great, otherwise Charlemagne. This ruler, in the revival of learning that marked his reign, not alone collected manuscripts preserving works of antiquity, but in copying them desired that the form of letter adhered to as a model by scribes should be the most beautiful that could be found. This was effected by a partial return to the letter-forms of Roman manuscripts.[2] As has been happily said of the revival of classical forms in ornament of Louis XVI's time: "We can see its

[1] Thompson, facs. 115–131.

[2] It should be said, however, that the revival of classical literature under Charlemagne was preceded by classical studies in Ireland, where the priesthood showed an instinct for the preservation of classical literature. Their spread as missionaries all over Europe played a large part in the preserva-

inspiration taken from the classic which it wished to re-produce, together with its fortunate inability to do so, and its consequently successful creation of something entirely original but yet filled with classic spirit."

"The reign of Charlemagne," says Thompson, "is an epoch in the history of hand-writings of Western Europe. With the revival of learning naturally came a reform of the writing in which the works of literature were to be made known. A decree of the year 789 called for the revision of church-books; and this work naturally brought with it a great activity in the writing schools of the chief monastic centres of France. And in none was there greater activity than at Tours, where, under the rule of Alcuin of York, who was abbot of St. Martin's from 796 to 804, was specially developed the exact hand which has received the name of the Carolingian Minuscule. . . . The general practice followed in the production of fine MSS. in this school, and no doubt in other contemporary schools also, which set the fashion for the future, was to employ majuscule letters, either capitals or uncials, for titles and other ornamental parts of the volume; for the general text, minuscule script; but for special passages which it was desired to bring into prominence, such as tables of chapters, prefaces, and intro-ductory sentences or paragraphs of sections of the work, a handsome style of writing was reserved which was adapted from the old half-uncial script of the fifth and sixth centuries."[1] This last served the purpose of what a printer would to-day call "display type."[2]

"The immense services rendered by the Carolingians to the Latin classics consist, therefore," says Hall, "not in their

tion of ancient manuscripts. The monasteries of Bobbio, near Pavia, and St. Gall, near Lake Constance, were both founded by Irish priests. Manuscripts executed at these monasteries are important in the history of paleography.

[1] Thompson, p. 367.　　　[2] *Paléographie Latine*, pl. 47.

attempts at recension which could never be systematic, but in the accuracy with which they copied the good manuscripts which were still accessible, and in the legibility of the script in which they copied them. The last service is equally important with the first. At Tours, Fleury, Micy, and elsewhere in France, there was evolved from the ugly Merovingian script, with its numberless ligatures and contractions, and from other sources, the handwriting known as the 'Caroline minuscule.' This clear and beautiful alphabet, in which every letter is distinctly formed, spread rapidly over the whole of Europe, and is the parent of the modern script and print which is still used by the majority of the Western nations. The difficulty of the earlier hands such as the uncial and half-uncial had often been severely felt. . . . If a difficult handwriting such as the Irish had been widely adopted in early times the havoc wrought in Latin texts by slovenly monkish scribes during the later period would have been much greater. Even the painstaking scholars of the Renaissance were completely at a loss when they were confronted with the Irish hand or the Lombardic (*e.g.* in Tacitus). The soundest texts — with the exception of the few fragments of greater antiquity that are preserved — are those which are attested by manuscripts of the ninth and tenth centuries. The succeeding centuries witness only an increase in corruption."[1]

The "Carolingian Reform" is important *to us* because the letter then adopted furnished a model for the types which we use in printing; for this Carolingian minuscule spread throughout France, had a profound influence in Italy, Spain, and England, became the dominant handwriting of western Europe, and superseded all these national handwritings except that of Ireland. It was introduced into Eng-

[1] F. W. Hall's *Companion to Classical Texts*, Oxford, 1913, pp. 89, 90.

land in the tenth century, but at first, apparently, only for Latin texts.[1] It was generally adopted in England after the Norman Conquest, and became common in Spain in the eleventh and twelfth centuries. Its characteristic was also — for Tours — to banish cursive forms, to make letters independent of each other, to avoid ligatures (or if ligatured, the ligature made slight changes in form), and to *spread the letters.* It is obvious that these tendencies adapted themselves to movable types when the time came to make them.[2]

But the time had not yet come. "Even with this widespread use of the reformed hand, uniformity of character could not be ensured. National idiosyncrasies show themselves as manifestly in the different scripts of different people as they do in their mental and moral qualities ; and although the Carolingian minuscule hand formed the basis of all modern writing of Western Europe, which thus started with more chance of uniformity than the old national hands . . . yet the national character of each country soon stamped itself upon the adopted script. Thus in the later Middle Ages we have again a second series of national hands developed from the Carolingian minuscule and clearly distinguishable from each other."[3]

This second national development began in the twelfth century. "It is the period of large volumes, with writing on a large scale, and adorned with initials and borders of bold design. With the increasing diffusion of literature, MSS. rapidly multiplied, and now the book-hands of the several countries of Western Europe, all now derived, as we have seen, from

[1] Differentiations were made between the kind of books for which these various hands were used. Analogously, in the beginnings of typography certain types were used for one kind of book and others for another — not merely as a matter of taste *but as a matter of tradition.*

[2] *Paléographie Latine*, pls. 47, 51, 52, 60, and Thompson, facs. 132, 133.

[3] Thompson, p. 403.

the Carolingian minuscule, exhibit their individual characteristics; each one developing its own national style and, in
course of time, diverging more and more from the rest. The
MSS. of the northern countries of Western Europe are now
to be distinguished from those of the south; the book-hands
of England, France, and the Low Countries being modelled
on one pattern, and, especially at first, bearing a family resemblance to each other; and those of Italy, Southern France,
and the Peninsula being of a type which was the creation of
the Italian scribes. The German script, which belongs to the
northern group, rather holds a place by itself, being generally of less graceful character than the others."[1]

The Gothic minuscule of the Middle Ages was nothing
more than an angular form of lower-case black-letter, the
intermediate result of this second national development. It
is distinguished by its pointed shape, by letters which are
taller than they are wide, and by their closeness to each
other. "This form of writing," says Steffens, in a passage
which is full of interest, "developed little by little, and insensibly, at the precise period at which, in architecture, the
round arch gave place to the ogee." He adds that "just as
Gothic architecture had in each country certain special
characteristics, so did Gothic writing receive everywhere
a national impress. In the fifteenth century the humanists
returned to the Carolingian writing, and it was they who
gave to pointed writing (as they did to the Ogival style of
architecture) the name of Gothic; that is to say, barbarous."[2] In these various forms of writing are the precursors
of black-letter types which we shall meet later on.[3] It cannot

[1] Thompson, p. 436.

[2] This supports what has been already suggested — that typography and calligraphy are closely related to the decorative and architectural feeling of
their time.

[3] *Paléographie Latine*, pls. 101, 104, 106, 109 (Cicero), 111.

be made too clear that there was no gap between the earliest
types and the Gothic minuscule characters of manuscripts of
the time immediately preceding them; and that the reason
the earliest German printing types were what they were, was
because German manuscripts were what *they* were, and that
the same thing is true of the early types of other countries.[1]

Finally, we come to Humanistic writing and modern
Gothic hands; for from the fourteenth century there were
in western Europe these two schools of writing. The Humanistic writing was round, and was a revival of the old
Carolingian minuscule hand *as then understood*. The Gothic
or black-letter hand was pointed and was a survival of the
Gothic minuscule of the Middle Ages.

The Humanistic hand was a logical result of the revival
of learning at the Renaissance. In their demand for the works
of antiquity the Humanists began to revive the Carolingian
minuscule in which these works had earlier been copied, and
their versions of it furnished the basis of our roman type
to-day.[2] It was a clear, readable hand, which grew more and

[1] To trace more fully the stages by which the mediaeval minuscule book-
hand, derived from the Carolingian minuscule, evolved into a black-letter
hand, the student is advised to consult Thompson's *Greek and Latin Palaeography*, facs. 157–201, noting *specially* facsimiles 186, 187, 188, 191, 192,
193, 194, 199, for their resemblance to early black-letter printing types.

[2] There were *two revivals*: first, that of Charlemagne in the ninth century;
second, that of the Italian Humanists at the Renaissance, "which period,"
says Hall, "may conveniently be taken to extend from the age of Petrarch and
Boccaccio to the sack of Rome by the troops of Charles V in 1527. It is not
to be supposed that the classical literatures would have perished but for that
revival. Both, however, were at a critical period of their history. Latin might
have suffered irreparable losses from the continuance of mediaeval neglect,
while Greek literature, which, as far as can be seen, was but little affected
by the fall of Constantinople in 1453, might have been gravely impaired by
that disaster, had not the study of Greek been transplanted from Byzantium
to Italy at least a century before the final victory of the Turks." (Hall's *Companion to Classical Texts*, p. 97.) For an interesting account of the vicissitudes of Latin and Greek manuscripts from the Age of Charlemagne up to
and during the Italian Renaissance, see Chapters IV and V.

more in favour, though for a long time used only for secular literature; black-letter alone being considered proper for sacred literature. It had various names, being called in Italian "Antiqua" (the name adopted by printers), although paleographers preferred to call it "handwriting of the Renaissance" or the "Humanistic hand." Its roundness seemed to be an Italian tendency.[1] In the first half of the fifteenth century, the earliest examples of this Italian hand are found; and by 1465, Sweynheym and Pannartz, at the first printing-house set up in Italy, showed the influence of this Humanistic writing in their semi-gothic types, which they soon abandoned for a distinctly roman letter. In this they were followed by many other printers, and thus the roman types spread all over Europe. It must be remembered, however, that in Sweden, Norway, and Denmark these roman types (like Italian handwriting) have been employed only in the course of the last century. In Germany to-day the roman letter is used only for certain classes of literature — that being the only important country where a debased mediaeval book-hand, translated into type, still persists.

Humanistic writing was, of course, subdivided into groups, as were all such schools of writing. There was a Humanistic writing for books which was at its best in the fifteenth century, but which, by the sixteenth century, printing type had driven out.[2] It is interesting to compare examples of the Carolingian minuscule with the Humanistic hand based upon it.[3] Then there was a Humanistic cursive — a flowing form of the straighter Humanistic Roman, inclined as in writing,[4] and for which there seems

---

[1] Even in Italian Gothic hands of the period a much greater roundness was preserved than in most other national Gothic texts (Thompson, fac. 194).

[2] *Paléographie Latine*, pl. 115.

[3] *Ibid*. Compare pls. 60 and 115.   [4] *Ibid*., pl. 116.

to have been no model in the Carolingian minuscule. Spreading through Italy as a cursive letter, this later became the common handwriting of all countries which had adopted for books the Humanistic form of Roman letter. Aldus based his italic printing types on this Humanistic cursive letter, and all italic types are based on it. The handwriting which we employ to-day and the tasteless, typographical script equivalent thereto, is simply the cursive of our own time and country.

Nothing more need be considered, except so-called modern Gothic writing. This modern Gothic writing was a cursive form of black-letter. After the invention of printing, the old formal pointed Gothic book-hands were given up by scribes and transmuted into type-forms. Such books as *were* written, were in a cursive Gothic hand, which, like the national book-hands, developed characteristic national traits. The French *lettre batarde*,[1] perhaps the most characteristic of these Gothic cursives, was, however, soon rendered into type; and in England the same letter in coarser form and equivalents of the most popular current English hands were likewise adapted to typography. The close connection between English Gothic vernacular book-hands[2] and the earliest English types is obvious if we compare Thompson's reproduction of the page of a Wycliffite Bible, written before 1397,[3] and the *lettre de forme* used by Caxton in his Boethius.[4] Thompson also shows a page of a manuscript Chaucer of about 1400,[5] which in writing is very like the types Caxton used in his *Ars Moriendi.*[6] An early fifteenth

[1] Thompson, fac. 196. [2] *Ibid.*, pp. 472–490. [3] *Ibid.*, fac. 209.
[4] Duff (E. Gordon), *Early English Printing. A Series of Facsimiles of all the Types used in England during the XVth Century*, etc. London, 1896, pl. II.
[5] Thompson, fac. 210.
[6] Gordon Duff, pl. VII, second type in lower facsimile.

century manuscript of Occleve[1] also suggests early English typography. The Netherland printers' uncouth fonts closely followed the equally uncouth writing of their locality and time. And as for Germany (as has been said), its present type is simply a survival of the early German cursive Gothic, in a debased form;[2] for in other European countries this cursive Gothic letter was, fortunately, superseded by Humanistic writing. "If Humanistic writing had not been adopted," says Steffens, "to-day, according to all probability we should have a great number of different national writings, difficult to read, just as in the early mediaeval days before the Carolingian minuscule had come to supplant the national hands."[3]

To recapitulate : there were in use among the Romans divers forms of writing, which continued, with various developments, until the fall of the Roman Empire. Then these forms developed still further in character, in different countries, according to the national genius. Some of these forms, through their fitness, survived; others perished. The roman character that we employ to-day is the offspring of a form of letter partly revived from antique days by Charlemagne and partly the creation of its period. The splendid hand of this revival after a time again yielded to the play of national influences. A second time revived at the Renaissance—a second time revived through this same devotion to classical learning—on the invention of printing, this

[1] Thompson, fac. 212.

[2] *Paléographie Latine*, pl. 121.

[3] In addition to the hands employed for books, there were a certain number of Gothic hands employed for documents—such as the French *Civilité*, etc. (*Paléographie Latine*, pl. 119)—which were occasionally rendered into fonts of printing type; but they were uncommon and held much the same position in reference to type then, that modern script types hold to other types now.

letter was transmuted into type and became the roman letter of our modern printing.[1] In ancient times, in the Middle Ages, and in the period immediately before the invention of printing, we can seem, too, to trace three forms of writing: the formal, to which in type our capital letter answers; the less formal, to which our lower-case type is equivalent; and the epistolary or cursive, which is now rendered into type called "italic." Broadly speaking, all types, like all hand-writings, fall into these classes. What we have now to know, therefore, is about these three great classes of types, at various periods, and in their different forms, down to our own day.

[1] The reader should examine *throughout* Steffens's *Paléographie Latine*, in the French edition cited, and the less conveniently arranged, but more available volume, Thompson's *Introduction to Greek and Latin Palaeography*. On these two works most of this chapter is based.

CHAPTER IV

THE next step in the study of type is to learn to recognize the various forms or "tribes" of type and the subtle differentiations between varieties of the same general form of type-face. These differences are very slight; often to the casual observer no differences appear. There is no way to learn to recognize them except by training the eye. There is no better way to train the eye than to familiarize it with the type-forms common to the fifteenth century in the countries where printing was then practised, and to follow this by an examination of the type-forms of these same countries from the sixteenth to the eighteenth century. By the time the end of the eighteenth century is arrived at, one will be fitted to consider intelligently the nineteenth and twentieth century types in use to-day. For unless we know the history of early type-forms, we cannot choose, nor have adequate reasons for choosing, the good types which should equip a modern composing-room. This is true, because much type to-day which seems desirable to the novice, to a trained eye is merely a corrupt version of older and better types; and also because unless we know something of the historical and literary associations connected with certain type-forms, we shall not have a sense of the fitness of things in their use—that sense which prevents a man from printing the *Marseillaise* in German fraktur, or the *Ode to a Grecian Urn* in French black-letter. Then, too, we must learn to know where modern type-forms stand in reference to earlier type-forms, if we are not to give undue importance to various modern types; just as we must know where the earliest types stand in relation to the manuscripts

which preceded them.[1] It was Benjamin Franklin who said:
"A Calf is a Big Beast, until you see a Cow!"

This detailed historical study of type-forms is of such practical value, that I do not hesitate to inflict it upon the reader, although, before he has finished, he will no doubt wonder where he is "coming out;" and wonder, too, if there be no shorter way of arriving at this knowledge.

Less than thirty-five years — from 1454 to 1487 — covered the spread of printing, as we now know the process, throughout Europe. The dates at which it was introduced into the various countries were as follows: not later than 1454 in Germany; in 1465 in Italy; in 1468 in Switzerland; in 1470 in France; in 1473 in Holland — if we except the *Speculum* and "Costeriana," which were executed before that time; in Belgium in 1473; Austria-Hungary, 1473; Spain, 1474; England, 1476; Denmark, 1482; Sweden, 1483; and Portugal, 1487.

The type-forms used in the fifteenth century fall into two classes: Gothic (a corrupt national following of the Carolingian minuscule),which was used earliest, and Roman (a fairly faithful return to the Carolingian minuscule), which

---

[1] As a study in "comparative typography," it is useful to see how the same book was printed at different periods, and any student who will select an early and famous book, like the *Inferno* or *Decameron*, in a first edition, and compare successive editions with it, will find that the different editions furnish almost a history of typography. The more characteristically national the book, the better it is for purposes of comparison of styles in the national typography which it represents. But in comparing the printing of various countries, it is better for the student to choose a classic which belongs to the literature of them all — like the texts of Horace, Virgil, or Cicero. In this way one may study typography both "perpendicularly" and "horizontally" — perpendicularly, where we take a given book of an early date and trace its progress chronologically; and horizontally, where we look at its editions in various countries at the same epoch. The special collections of the works of a particular author, found in most large libraries, are very illuminating when used in this way.

came in later. *By Gothic, the mediaeval text or black-letter is always meant.*[1]

Fifteenth century Gothic type-forms may be roughly subdivided into Pointed, sometimes called *lettre de forme;* Round, sometimes called *lettre de somme,* and a vernacular Cursive black-letter, like the French *lettre batarde.* Although our examples are the English *lettre de forme* (*fig.* 8), and the French *lettre de somme* (*fig.* 9) and *lettre batarde* (*fig.* 10), they show the characteristics of these types sufficiently for our purpose. These three type-forms were the black-letter equivalents of the formal, less formal, and cursive manuscript-hands of the Roman period. Between the members of the Gothic type-families of the fifteenth century there is the same likeness that appears in the manuscripts of the period immediately before the invention of printing; and, too, much the same divergencies.

Roman forms of type of this period may be divided into Transitional (from Gothic to Roman) and pure Roman, the precursor of the types we now commonly use.

The first type employed in Germany was a gothic or black-letter character. The earliest *dated* piece of printing from German gothic type known is the Letters of Indulgence, issued at Mainz in 1454. This indulgence was granted by Pope Nicholas V to all Christians who, during three years preceding, had given money to help on the war against the Turks. The agents who sold manuscript copies, which were brought out in the early months of the same year (1454), apparently had heard, meanwhile, of printing, and recognized its utility for producing leaflets of this sort in quantity.

[1] What is called "gothic" by type-founders has no relation to any Gothic style; and is purely an arbitrary name—unless it hints at the artistic abilities of its inventors. It is nothing but a diagram of a letter—all qualities of design having been left out.

Domine omnipotens, Deus patrum nostrorum Abraham, et Isaac et Jacob, et seminis eorum justi, qui fecisti coelum et terram cum omni ornatu eorum; qui ligasti mare verbo praecepti tui; qui conclusisti abyssum, et signasti eam terribili et laudabili no= mine tuo; quem omnia pavent et tremunt a vultu virtutis tuae, quia importabilis est magnificentia gloriae tuae, et insustentabilis ira comminationis tuae super peccatores; immensa vero et investiga=

8. *Lettre de Forme*

Domine omnipotens, Deus patrum nostrorum Abraham, et Isaac et Jacob, et seminis eorum justi, qui fecisti cœlum et terram cum omni ornatu eorum; qui ligasti mare verbo præcepti tui; qui conclusisti abyssum, et signasti eam ter// ribili et laudabili nomine tuo; quem omnia pavent et tremunt a vultu virtutis tuæ, quia importabilis est magnificentia gloriæ tuæ, et insustentabilis ira com// minationis tuæ super peccatores; immensa vero et investigabilis misericordia promissionis tuæ: quoniam tu es Dominus, altissimus, benignus, longaminis, et multum misericors, et pœnitens super malitias hominum. Tu, Domine, secundum multitudinem bonitatis tuæ promisisti pœnitentiam et remissionem iis, qui peccaverunt tibi, et multitudine miserationum tuarum decrevisti pœni// tentiam peccatoribus in salutem. Tu igitur, Domine Deus justorum, non posu// isti pœnitentiam justis, Abraham, et Isaac et Jacob, iis, qui tibi non peccave// runt; sed posuisti pœnitentiam propter me peccatorem, quoniam peccavi, super

9. *Lettre de Somme*

Domine omnipotens, Deus patrum nostrorum Abraham, et Isaac et Jacob, et seminis eorum justi, qui fecisti cœlum et terram cum omni ornatu eorum; qui ligasti mare verbo præcepti tui; qui conclusisti abyssum, et signasti eam terribili et laudabili nomine tuo; quem omnia pavent et tre/ munt a vultu virtutis tuæ, quia importabilis est magnifi/ centia gloriæ tuæ, et insustentabilis ira comminationis tuæ super peccatores; immensa vero et investigabilis misericordia promissionis tuæ: quoniam tu es Dominus, altissimus, benignus, longaminis, et multum misericors,

10. *Lettre Batarde*

de facultatibus suis pre erogauerunt merito huiusmodi indulgentie gaudere debet · In veritatis et
pntibus litis testimonialibus est appensum Datum m Opido Myntie Anno dni Occcdquito die vero pi

Forma plenissime absolutionis et remissionis in vita

Isereatur tui zc̄ Dns noster ihesus xp̄s p sua sanctissima et piissima mia̱z te absoluat Et
apostoli eius ac auc̄te aplica michi omissa z tibi c̄cessa Ego te absoluo ab omnibus penis tuis c̄tritis c
excessibus criminibus atq̄ delictis quatucuq̄z grauibus sedi aplice refuatis Necnō a quibusc̄uq̄z ex
Atinisq̄z sentencie censuris z penis ecclesiasticis a iure vel ab hoīe p̄mulgatis si quas incurristi dan̄
indulgentia̱ z remissionē Inquatū clauis sancte matris ecclie in hac parte se extendūt · In noie p

Forma plenarie remissionis in mortis articulo

Isereatur tui zc̄ Dns noster zc̄ Dns noster ut supra Ego te absoluo ab omnibus penis tuis c̄tritis c̄fessi
fideliū z sacramentis ecclesie Remittendo tibi penas purgatorij quas propter culpas z offensas
pc̄cōz tuoz remissionē· Inquantū clauis sancte matris ecclie in hac parte se extendūt· In noie pa

11. Portion of 30-line Letters of Indulgence, Mainz, 1455

Iuxta dicti indultum de facultatibus suis pie eroga   .merito huiusmodi indulgentiis gaud
nium Sigillum ad hoc ordinatum presentibus litteris testimonialibus est appensum Datum
die vero   Mensis

Forma plenissime absolutionis et remissionis

Misereatur tui &c. Dominus noster ihesus xps per sua sctissima et piissima mia; te absoluat Et auct
Aplorum eius ac auctoritate aplica michi cōmissa et tibi cōcessa Ego te absoluo ab omnibz petis tuis cōtritis cōf
bz excessibz criminibz atqz delictis quātucūqz grauibz Sedi aplice reseruatis Necnon a quibuscūqz excōicacōm
aliisqz sntīis cēsuris z penis ecclesiasticis a iure vel ab hōīe promulgatis si quas incurristi dando tibi plē
gentiā z remissionē Inquātū claues sancte matris ecclesie in hac pte se extendūt. In nomine patris z f

Forma plenarie remissionis in mortis articulo

Misereatur tui &c. Dominus noster &c. Ego te absoluo ab omnibz petis tuis cōtritis cōfessis z
ti fideliū z sacramentis ecclesie Remittendo tibi penas purgatorii quas propter culpas et offensas in
oīm veatorū tuorū remissionē. Inquātū claues sce matris ecclesie in hac parte se extendūt. In nōie pris z

12. *Portion of 31-line Letters of Indulgence, Mainz, 1455*

tr ut applicarēt ad castra iudeo=
rum:et pcuterēt eos subito.Et
filij qui erant ex arce erant illis
duces.Et audiuit iudas:1 sur=
rexit ipe 1 potētes pcutere virtu=
tem exercituū regis : que erant
in ammaū.Adhuc eūi disper=
sus erat exercitus a castris.Et
uenit gorgias ī castra iude noc=
tu:et neminē inuenit.Et quere=
bat eos in montib;: qm dixit:
fugiūt hij a nobis.Et cum di=
es factus esset apparuit iudas
in campo cū trib; milib; viror
tantū:qui tegumēta 1 gladios
non habebāt.Et viderūt castra
gentiū valida:et loricatus 1 e=
quitatus incircuitu eorū:et hij
docti ad preliū.Et ait iudas vi=
ris qui secū erāt.Ne timueritis

13. *Type of* 36-*line Bible, Mainz, not later than* 1461

So they ordered copies of the Indulgence in two styles: one set in 30-line form, of which there were three issues — one in 1454 and two in 1455 (*fig.* 11), the other in 31 lines, of which four issues are known — three dated 1454 and one 1455 (*fig.* 12). The gothic type was of two sizes: the larger and more pointed being used for head-lines and important words, and a smaller, rounder type for the text. Blanks were left to be filled in with names, etc. In the 30-line Letter of Indulgence[1] this larger character appears to be much like that used in the 42-line Bible commonly ascribed to Gutenberg, but printed, perhaps, by Fust and Schoeffer at Mainz about 1455[2] (*fig.* 14). This book, which it took several years to complete, was in process, it is supposed, at the time the Indulgences were printed. The larger type in the 31-line Indulgence is the same as that used in the 36-line Bible, printed not later than 1461, at Mainz (*fig.* 13). Nothing can be more pointed or Gothic than these large black-letter Bible types copied from the German manuscripts of the period. It is the characteristic form of the earliest gothic type-letter of Germany.[3] The Germans called this kind of *lettre de forme*

[1] *Facsimiles from Early Printed Books in the British Museum*, London, 1897, facs. 3, 4, which show Indulgences in complete form.

[2] Burger's *Monumenta Germaniæ et Italiæ Typographica*, Berlin, 1913, pl. 137, for facsimile of entire page with rubrication.

Facsimiles of the types used in *incunabula* are contained in the *Catalogue of Books printed in the XVth Century now in the British Museum*. The Library of the British Museum contains about nine thousand books printed before 1500. The work is to be completed in six parts, and four parts are now published: I, Xylographica and books printed with types at Mainz, Strassburg, Bamberg, and Cologne (with 29 plates showing 240 types). II, Germany: Eltvil to Trier (30 plates showing 254 types). III, Germany: Leipzig-Pforzheim, German-speaking Switzerland and Austria-Hungary (18 plates showing 175 types). IV, Italy: Subiaco and Rome (13 plates showing 110 types). The facsimiles in most cases give only a few lines of type; so, as its introduction admits, "those who would know the glories of early printing must consult Burger's *Monumenta*." But it can be used where Burger is deficient or not available.

[3] *Paléographie Latine*, 1910, pls. 104, 111.

"textur" — because the effect of a page set in it was like a tissue or weave. It afterward was simplified into the type called "fraktur." The smaller type of the Indulgences, which is a rounder black-letter, has certain peculiarities later found in "schwabacher" fonts (*figs.* 11 *and* 12).

A book which shows clearly the form of the early gothic types of Germany is the famous Latin Psalter printed by Fust and Schoeffer at Mainz, August 14, 1457 — the first book to which the printers put their names and date of publication. This monumental volume shows a larger letter than the 42-line Bible, but of much the same pointed Gothic form[1] (*fig.* 15). The famous *decorated* initials were probably stamped in after the pages were printed, one stamping being used for the blue and the other for the red impression.

The same sort of letter is shown in a Missal printed at Bamberg by Sensenschmid in 1488, in type a size between that of the Mainz Psalter and the 42-line Bible.[2] There are other examples much like it, such as the *Missale Salisburgense* printed at Nuremberg by Stuchs in 1492,[3] and the Mainz printer Neumeister's edition of Turrecremata's *Meditationes* of 1479.[4] These all show the pointed, angular black-letter of Germany, the earliest form of type used there. The larger types of this kind were generally intended for folio volumes used in the offices of the Church ; some of the characters which appear in the Bamberg Missal of 1481[5] being almost three-quarters of an inch high. Such volumes are rough in execution compared with manuscripts, yet nevertheless magnificent in effect.

[1] *Druckschriften des XV bis XVIII Jahrhunderts,* Berlin, Reichsdruckerei, 1884–87, pls. 61, 62, 63.

[2] *Ibid.*, pl. 25.   [3] Burger, pl. 117.   [4] *Ibid.*, pl. 76.

[5] *Ibid.*, pl. 105. The right-hand plate shows a reproduction of part of the Canon of the Mass. Its ordinary pages are printed in a type much more Italian or Spanish than German in character, and of different design.

Quod cũ audiſſet dauid:deſcendit in
preſidiũ.Philiſtijm autem venientes
diffuſſi ſunt in valle raphaim.Et cõ=
ſuluit dauid dũm dicens.Si aſcendã
ad philiſtijm·et ſi dabis eos ĩ manu
mea? Et dixit dñs ad dauid.Aſcende:
q̃a tradens dabo philiſtijm in manu
tua.Venit ergo dauid ad baalphara=
ſim:et percuſſit eos ibi et dixit.Diuiſit
dñs inimicos meos corã me:ſicut di=
uidunt aque.Propterea vocatũ ē no=
men loci illi⁹ baalpharaſim.Et reliq̃=
runt ibi ſculptilia ſua:q̃ tulit dauid et
viri ei⁹.Et addiderunt adhuc philiſti=
im ut aſcenderent:et diffuſſi ſũt ĩ valle
raphaim.Cõſuluit autē dauid dũm.
Si aſcendã cõtra philiſteos:⁊ tradas
eos in manus meas? Qui rñdit.Nõ
aſcendas cõtra eos ſed gira poſt tergũ
corũ:⁊ venies ad eos exaduſo pirorũ.
Et cũ audieris ſonitũ clamoris gra=
dietis ĩ cacumie piror̃ tũc inibis pliũ:
q̃a tũc egrediet̃ dñs ãte faciē tuã:ut p=

14. *Type of 42-line Bible, Mainz, c.* 1455

Sctē Justine, ora

Sācte Egidi, ora

Scē leonarde, ora

Sācte Goar, ora

Sācte libon, ora

Omnes sancti cōfes=

sores, orate p nob

Omnes sci Mona=

chi z heremite, orate

Scā maia magd.

Scā katherina o.

15. *Type used in Latin Psalter: Fust and Schoeffer*
Mainz, 1457

Cupiẽtes emere libros infra notatos veniẽt ad hospi
ciuz subnotatum.Venditorem habituri largissimum.

Cum plurimoꝝ pꝪoꝝ ſnīa ſit.oībus in actōnibꝯ maiorē curā abbibēdā eſſe.vt viœ
ppetuitate ꝓſtare poſſim̄?: ad hāc quidẽ ꝓſꝗndā.ꝗlibet mortalis tenef totis viri
bus inſudare.Qꝺ et aſſeꝗ poſſe.a nr̄is maioribꝯ creditū ē:ſi ſingl̃is meditatōnibꝯ
opibuſꝗ honeſti forā accuratiſſime ꝓponat.Sed in hmōi plimaꝝ affectōnū genē
a nōnullis illuſtribꝯ viris.huiuſcemōi glīa diuerſo calle ꝗſita eſt.Naz ab alijs phīa
nat̃alis.vt platōe et areſtotele:alijs moral.vt ſeneca:nōnullis poemata.vt fama
ē de homero ꝗ virgilio:pleriſꝗ etiā eloꝗntia.vt demoſtene ꝗ cicerone.Alijs tū ebē
bis.tū ꝗuerſābis admiſtrābiſꝗ legibꝯ.vt legit de ligurto.ſolone.et traꝑano impa
tore:necnō de iuſtiniano.ꝗ ꝓſuſuz iuris corꝑ? in lucē reduꝝit.ꝗ reductōe ꝗplures
iuriſcōſulti.viœ ppetuitatē ꝓſeꝗ arbitrati ſūt:veluti Quit̃?muti?. paul? vlpian?.
mltiꝗꝗ pꝫterea ꝗs lōgū eēt receſere.Aeꝗ qꝫ theologia ſacra oīm ſciaꝝ corona ē:ma
rime circa materiā ꝗ exigit canōibꝯ legibuſꝗ fulcīta.Quibꝯ eīm ꝓficit hō ſi natu
rali.poeſi.eloꝗntia ſuꝑ aſtra volitās:ſi apicibꝯ vēuſꝗ iuris diuitias.ꝓgreget:etiā
ſi vniuerſū mōm lucref:aīa vo ſui detrimētū patiaf?Si xꝑm ſcis(ait melliſluus
boctor)ſatis ē.et ſi cetera neſcis.Quo pmot? vir ꝓſilioꝝ clariſſim?: dns Antonin?
olim cauſaꝝ romãe ſedis pitiſſim?: demū archieꝑs florẽtin?.Sūmā egregiā ī ꝗtu
or ꝑtes biſtinctā ꝓgeſſit:ꝗ vt vere viœ ppetuitatē ꝓſeꝗ facile poſſem?.Parte pri
ma creatoris imenſitatē.creaſeꝗꝫ hūane nobilitatē.atꝗ ne ab ea laborē diuīa le
ge fulcitā pduꝝit.Secūda pte crimioſas enormitates ꝗbꝯ hō a ſua nobilitate etiaz
hobie labif:ſubiūꝝit.Tercia pte ſtatibꝯ vniuerſoꝝ ſacmētalia remedia ꝗbꝯ ꝗlibet
reſtitueref:ꝓſcripſit.Et ꝗrta pte ne recidiuū pateref ꝓbuatiua ſtutū.graꝑ ꝗ bo
noꝝ ſpuſſcēi:coabiūꝝit.Et qꝫ ſapiẽtiſſimo teſte ꝗ abbit ſciam:abbit ꝗ laborē.pꝫtes
beterriti magno ſūptu ꝗ ī ꝓpābis volumībꝯ impẽbēb?erat.otio aut ignauie bebi
ti.vel ab alia ſe poti?opa trāſtulef̃t.Quoꝝ tāte nccitati: ſiue hūano artificio:ſi
ue biuīa ope ſubuef̃tū ē:vt iuenta nr̄a etate hac īprimēbi lf̃aꝝ facilitate.pleriꝗꝫ ſe
ſtubijs bedicarūt:ꝗ ꝗuo ſūptu plīma libroꝝ volumīa:breui tpe ꝓnītes.ī viros cla
ros euabē nitunf̃.Et ꝗuis iā be magno volumīnū nūero ꝑ haꝝ lf̃aꝝ impſſores ꝑ
fice volẽtiū nccitati puīſū ſit:neo tñ eoꝝ ib nouiſſimū(qꝺ qꝫ modernū ꝗ vtilimū)
op̃ex ītegro aggreſſ?ē:beterriti(vt opinor)magna cobicū ꝗ lf̃aꝝ mltitubie.Re
uolẽtes igif̃ hoc ī aīo.theologie ſacre quibē alumni.rez ſatiſdignā.ꝗ tãꝗ nouis
morbis.nouis ātibotis neceſſariā.hac lf̃aꝝ effigie characterizata op?pſectū ꝗ cor
rectū biligẽter explicarūt.Quare volẽtes ī ſuiꝑi?agnitōe ꝑficere.ꝗ ſaluti primoꝝ
ſalubriter ꝓſulere:omī conamīe curare bebẽt hmōi ſūmā Antonīnā ſe penes bf̃e.
Cupiẽteſꝗ ſibi ꝓpare ab hoſpitiū ſeſe recipiãt ſubſcriptū vēbitore bituri benignu;

In theologia

Sūmaz Antonini egregiā in ꝗtuor
ꝑtes biſtinctā.vt ſupra claret.
Pantheologiā id ē totā theologiā.
Biblias ameniſſime impſſas.
Gloſam ordinariaz Petri Lombar
bi ſuper pſalterio.
Specula vincencij quatuor.
Item Vitaſpatrum
Sūmā piſani al's piſanella
Rationale biuinoꝝ officioꝝ.
Queſtiōes ō potẽtia bei.b.Thome.
Secūbā ſecunœ beati Thome.
Concordantias maiores Biblie.
Item vitam xp̃i.

Sermones

Diſcipulum be tempe ꝗ ſanctis per
totum annum.
Hugonez be Brato per totū annū.
Leonhardū be Vtino be ſanctis.
Quabrageſimale leōbardi ō vtino.
Quabrageſimale gritſch benuo cor
rectū fibelif̃ꝗꝫ ipſſuz boctoris eximij
Vocabulariū Salomonis
Boeciū be conſolatōne phīe

In medicinis

Auicennam.
Aggregatorem.
Pandecta;

16. *Advertisement issued by Koberger, Nuremberg, c. 1480*
(reduced)

cipiebat.cui tamen idem ꝓpheta dicit.Nonne cor
meū in p̄senti erat qn̄ reu̇sus est homo curro suo
in occursum tibi. ¶Postq̄ de ꝓphecie tēpibus trac
tauimus.restat ut de modis eius et qualitatibus
aliqua disseramus.Spiritus q̄ppe ꝓphecie nec sem
per nec eodem modo ꝓphete animū tangit.aliqn̄
enim spiritus ꝓphecie ex p̄senti tangit animuȝ ꝓ
phetantis et ex futuro nequaq̄ tangit aliqn̄ uero
ꝓphecie spiritus animū ꝓphetantis ex futuro tan
git.et ex p̄senti non tangit.aliqn̄ ꝓphetantis ani
mū ex p̄senti pariter et ex futuro tangit.aliquan
do autem ex p̄terito et ex p̄senti atq; ex futuro.
ꝑiter animus tangit̄ ꝓphetantis.aliqn̄ uero pro
phecie spiritus ex p̄terito tangit animuȝ nec tan
git ex futuro.Aliqn̄ uero ꝓphecie spiritus tangit
ex futuro nec tangit ex p̄terito.Aliqn̄ uero in p̄
senti ex ꝑte tangit et ex ꝑte non tangit.Aliquan
do uero spiritus ꝓphecie in futuro ex ꝑte tangit
et ex ꝑte non tangit.Iteȝ scias q̄ ꝓphete quidaȝ
ex ꝓximo tanguntur atq; e longinq̄ minime tan
guntur.quidam uero tangunt̄ elonginquo et nō
tanguntur ex ꝓximo.quidam uero et e longinq̄
tangunt̄ et ex ꝓximo.¶Aliqn̄ auteȝ prophecie
spiritus ꝓphetis deest nec semꝑ eoꝝ mentibȝ pres
to est.q̄tinus cū hunc non hn̄t se.hūc cognoscant
ex dono habere cū habent.vnde helizeus cū flentē
sunamitē mulierem a suis pedibus ꝑ giezi puꝝ a
uelli ꝓhiberet dixit dimitte illā.anima eniȝ eius
in amaritudine est et dominus celauit me et non
indicauit michi.Item amos.q̄ eadem hora qua
requisitus est ꝓphecie sibi spiritum deesse sensit de
se ueraciter dixit.Non sum ꝓpheta.ut dixi in ar
mentum.Sic quoq; cū iosephat de futuris requi
reret.et ꝓphecie ei spiritus deesset psaltē fecit ap
plicari ut prophecie ad hunc spiritus per laudem
psalmodie descenderet atq; eius animum de uentu
ris repleret.vox etenim psalmodie cū ꝑ intencō
nem cordis agit̄.ꝑ hanc omnipotenti ad cor iter

17. *Round Gothic Type of Catholicon: Gutenberg Mainz*, 1460

Koberger of Nuremberg used, about 1480, a type less pointed than the first gothic types, reminding one a little of the early black-letter types of Italy and Spain. The reproduction here shown (*fig.* 16) is interesting not only for its type but because it is an example of one of the earliest advertising circulars. In the fifteenth century, printers and booksellers who did business in a large way put agents "on the road" with a stock of their books, and circulars for distribution. This particular sheet advertised a theological work by Antoninus, Archbishop of Florence, and its writer, after praising literature in general, says that, theology being the crown of all sciences, the author wrote this monumental *Summa Theologica;* that until then, readers could not afford to buy the expensive manuscripts of the work, and printers, owing to its enormous length, had been afraid to publish it. But at last its printing had been accomplished by Koberger and the "long-felt want" (sacred to advertisements) had been filled! Quite in the modern manner, it is stated that the advertisement is printed in the same type as the book, and that if any one wishes to buy the volume, he can do so at a certain inn, where the agent has lodgings. So it would appear that travelling salesmen and book canvassers are no new thing![1]

Besides the pointed gothic type, or *lettre de forme*, used in Germany, there was a rounder gothic type known as *lettre de somme.*[2] Examples are to be seen in the Mainz *Catholicon,* printed probably by Gutenberg, in 1460 (*fig.* 17), and in the *Rationale Divinorum Officiorum* by Durandus, printed

[1] For reproductions of similar early advertisements, see Burger's *Buchhändleranzeigen des* 15. *Jahrhunderts.* Leipsic, 1907. The earliest printed book advertisement known is that of Heinrich Eggestein of Strassburg, issued in 1466.

[2] The *lettre de somme* is said (without much authority) to derive its name from the *Summa* of St. Thomas Aquinas, for which, as well as for other scholastic works, it was early employed.

by Fust and Schoeffer in 1459.[1] The *lettre de somme* was copied from less studied and formal book-hands, and was less massive in effect than the pointed *lettre de forme*. For convenience it may be called a "round gothic type." In a sense this letter-form was transitional, for by extending its design a little further toward modern ideas of clearness, a resemblance exists between this round gothic type of the *Catholicon* and the gothicized roman invented by those German printers who became influenced by Italian models.

In addition to pointed and round black-letter types, German printers had a vernacular type — intended primarily for printing books in German — later commonly known as "schwabacher." Some *elements* of this type may be seen in Koberger's German Bible printed at Nuremberg in 1483, in which we find the looped b, d, h, l, the tailed f and s, etc., characteristic of schwabacher fonts.[2] We may see it employed in a form which is clearly different from the pointed fraktur, in Peter Schoeffer's *Hortus Sanitatis* (*fig.* 18), printed at Mainz in 1485. It flowered into the type now recognizable as schwabacher in the last decade of the fifteenth century. Although intended for books in German, it was used for many Latin books as well.

Thus in the fifteenth century there was a tendency in German gothic types toward the forms of letter which we associate with German text of to-day — a tendency showing itself in German manuscripts very early and persistently. Andreae's *Baum der Gesippschaft*, issued at Augsburg by Johann Baemler in 1474, was printed in a pointed letter which shows a form distinctly German as we now understand the term (*fig.* 19). This is markedly shown, too, in the rounder type-forms employed in Koberger's German

[1] *Druckschriften*, pl. 41; or Burger, pl. 73.
[2] Burger, pl. 20.

Alcamia eyn baum also genãt   Cap·xlvij.

Lcamia latine·grece Ciprus·arabice kenne·   Der meiſter
Galienus in dem·vij·büch genant ſimpliciũ farmacarũ· in
dē capitel Ciprus·id eſt alcamia ſpricht daz diß ſy ein baũm
der wechſet hynder dem mere vñ in Cicilia·vnd diß bletter vñ blomen nutzet man in der artzney   In dem büch circa inſtans beſchri-
ben vns die meiſter vñ ſprechen daz des baũmes faſt viel ſtat in cici-
lia·Die ſelbigen pulueriſeren die bletter vñ blomen vñ ſchicken das
puluer durch die lande·   Diß puluer iſt ſwartzlicht von farben vñ
das mag man viel iare behalten vnnerſeret an ſyner natuer   Der
meiſter Paulus pandecta vñ Platearius in dem capitel Alcamia
ſprechen daz diß ſy kalt an dem erſten grat vñ drucken an dē anfang
des andern grats·   Serapio ſpricht daz diß puluer güt ſy den dye
do haben alcolam das ſynt wyß bletterlyn in dem müde·   Itē diß
puluer geſotten mit gerſten waſſer vnd geſtrichen wo ſich eyner ge-
brant hait zuket viel hitz vß·Die verharten glied der oder verlemten
do mit geſtrichen oder geſalbet machet ſie weich vnd glietlich· Vnd
diſſe ſalbe ſal alſo bereyt werden· Nym baũm öley als viel du wilt
vñ miſche dar vnder des puluers alcamie   Platearius ſpricht daz
alcamia habe alle dogent in ym die dan hait ſanguis draconis· vñ
wan man nit haben mag alcamiam ſo mag man an ſyn ſtat nemen

18. *Type prefiguring Schwabacher: Peter Schoeffer, Mainz,* 1485

Den der on leiberben abgeſtorben iſt/erbend ſein vatter vnd
müter. vñ ander vorfaren ob die allayn verleÿbend auß nã
hin der grad/der vatter vor dem anherrn ob ſÿ baid jn leben
weren. Vnd die jn gleichem grad ſeind erbend geleich/die vã
terlichen halb vnd die müterlichen halb/wie wol ir zal vnge-
leich iſt. Ob aber mit den vorgemelten vorfaren vor hannden
weren des abgeſtorben eelich leiplich brieder/von vatter vñ
müter /die erbten mitſampt vatter vnd müter/jr ÿeglichs als
vil als das anndez /on vnderſchaid des geſchlechts vnd vãt-
terlicher gewaltſamin.

Ceſſante

Wañ weder aufffteigend vorfaren/noch abſteigend leibs er -
ben vor hannden ſeind. So erbend zü erſt/der brüder vnd des
abgeſtorben brüd kind/an jrs vatters ſtat. Der brüd/ſag ich/
vnd brüders kind/die von vatter vnd müter-des brieder ge-
weſen ſeind/des erbſchafft vor hannden iſt. wellich perſon er-

19. *Pointed Gothic Type: Baemler, Augsburg,* 1474

Bible just mentioned, or in his *Nuremberg Chronicle* of 1493,[1] which are easily recognized as German in feeling (*fig.* 20). By the end of the fifteenth century and through the sixteenth century, two thoroughly German forms of text letter had developed from the earlier and purer German blackletter characters.

But all the type used in Germany was not of Gothic form. Fonts of roman character were employed there by a few printers. Mentelin, the first Strassburg printer, used a gothic type which pointed towards roman in his *Biblia Latina*, finished in 1460 (*fig.* 21). But the font of the "R Bizarre," as it is often called, was the first roman letter used in Germany (*fig.* 22). This ungainly roman type was used by Adolph Rusch of Ingweiden ("the R Printer"), who printed in it an edition of the *Rationale* of Durandus, at Strassburg, as early as 1464. Rusch married a daughter of John Mentelin, and to his business he later succeeded. Other roman types of early date were used in a *Speculum Historiale* printed about 1473 by Mentelin,[2] and at Augsburg in 1471 by Zainer, in his *Lateinischer Einblattkalendar* for 1472,[3] who is said to have brought this font from Italy. The Zainer type was a fairly pure roman character, as we now understand the term, although the fitting of the type on its body is rather uncertain in effect. Pollard says that but ten fonts of roman were known to him as employed in Germany before 1480. Its use was revived in the last years of the century, when the accumulation of standard ancient literature (chiefly by foreign authors and formerly available only through manuscripts) had been pretty well ex-

[1] Also Burger, pl. 258. For further examples see *Druckschriften des XV bis XVIII Jahrhunderts*, pls. 72, 53, 35, and 26, of books dated respectively 1474, 1485, 1492, and 1494.

[2] *Druckschriften*, pl. 93; or Burger, pl. 91.

[3] Burger, pl. 1.

hausted by printers. Then the contemporary author began to appear, and roman type began to be used for these modern books as well as for editions of the classics. In Germany roman type is still called "Antiqua" in allusion to its classical origin.

There were also semi-gothic types like that used by Mentelin, and puzzling transitional roman-gothic fonts, of which an interesting example is that used by Holle at Ulm in 1482 in his first dated book — the *Cosmographia* of Ptolemy (*fig.* 23).

The German fifteenth century press was conspicuous for its fine editions of law books and its liturgical printing, in both of which departments Fust and Schoeffer stood first. Pictorial and decorative capital letters were used by many of the best printers, and some of the page-borders used in books were fine, though they were not very commonly employed. Large sizes of type were cut, no doubt, mainly to save the expense of printing in two colours in lines needing to be "displayed" — as in the Indulgences. Printers who used roman fonts got over this difficulty by picking out "features" of their books in lines or masses of roman capital letters; but massed capitals of black-letter — the type chiefly employed in Germany — were almost unreadable. This was possibly a second reason for large sizes of types, which for purposes of convenience were ordinarily made double the size of the text types with which they were used. One reason that the books of the earliest Mainz printers had such an immediate success was that they were such good imitations of the manuscripts with which they had to compete. If German scribes and illuminators had been as clever as those of France or Italy, the divergence between books and manuscripts would have offered an obstacle to their sale. But this was not so; and by a happy accident the German manu-

euus abſ𝔮𝔷 miſericordia.Q̈uia non addã vltra
miſereri domui iſrl': ſed obliuione obliuiſcar
eo𝔲. Et domui inda miſereboꝛ: et ſaluabo eos ĩ
dño deo ſuo: et nõ ſaluabo eos m arcu et gladío
et ĩ bello et ĩ equis et ĩ equitibꝫ. Et ablactauit eã
que erat abſ𝔮𝔷 miſericordia. Et cõcepit: et pepit
filiũ. Et dixit ei. Voca nomen euus non ꝓplus
meus. Q̈uia vos nõ ꝓplus meus: et ego non
ero veſter deus. Et erit numerus filiorũ iſrl' q̈ſi
arena maris q̈ ſine mẽſura ẽ: et nõ nnmerabiꞇ.
Et erit m loco vbi diceꞇ eis nõ ꝓplus meus vos:
diceꞇ eis filij dei viuẽtis. Et cõgregabunꞇ filij iu꞉
da et filij iſrahel pariter·et ponẽt ſibimet caput
vnũ: et aſcẽdẽt de terra: q̈a magnus dies ihezra꞉
icite fratribꝫ veſtris ꝓplus ⅡⅭ hel.
meus: et ſoꝛoꝛi veſtre miſericoꝛdiã cõſe꞉
cuta. Iudicate matrẽ veſtrã iudicate: qm̃ ipſa
nõ vxoꝛ mea: et ego nõ vir eius. Auferat for꞉
nicacões ſuas a facie ſua·et adulteria ſua de me
dio vbeꝝ ſuoꝝ: ne foꝛte exſpoliẽ eã nudã et ſtatuã
eã ſcdm̃ diẽ natiuitatis ſue : et ponã eã q̈ſi ſoli꞉
tudmẽ·et ſtatuã eã velut terrã inuiã et interfi꞉
ciã eã ſiti: et filioꝝ illius·non miſereboꝛ·qm̃ filij
foꝛnicationũ ſũt: quia foꝛnicata eſt mater eoꝝ.
Cõfuſa ẽ que cõcepit eos: q̈a dixit. Vadã poſt
amatoꝛes meos qui dant panes michi: et aquas
meas lanã meã et linũ meũ oleũ meũ 𝒶 potũ
meũ. Propꞇ hoc ecce ego ſepiã viã tuã ſpinis:

21. *Semi-Gothic Type: Mentelin, Strassburg*, 1460

fequebant dimiffis nõ ad Seleucũ ut fibi antea perfuafũ fuerat: fed in cheroneffũ
Syrie virũ perduxit ibiq3 firmis cuftodns prefidiifq3 adhibitis eũ reliquit . Hoc
igitũ in loco relegato Demetrio & anguftis finibus circũfepto :omnia que ad uitã
fplendidã & cultũ regiũ pertinebãt iuffu Seleuci parabãt . Nam & regales edes
& iocunda pomeria & orti uariis arboribus confiti ei abunde erant :amicis & fa-
miliaribus fuo arbitratu utebatur :qui cum crebro ad eum ufendum accederent
femper modeftos fermones a Seleuco afferebant quibus virum hortabantur bono
ut animo effet omniaq3 de falute fua & Seleuci liberalitate fperaret fe cõpertum
habere dicentes Antiochi & Stratonicis aduentum a Seleuco expectari quorum
gracia liberam ei abeundi quocumq3 uelit:q3 primum poteftatem fore :In hac mi
fera fortuna conftitutus Demetrius defperatis iam omnibus rebus ad Antigonũ
filium & eos qui Corinthum Athenafq3 regebant nuntios mifit : qui fuo nomine
eos monerent : ne deinceps figno & litteris fuis fidem preftarent : fe ueluti de-
functum arbitrarentur . Deniq3 Antigono filio quoad per eos fieri poffet : pro
antiqua benuolentia regnum ftatumq3 feruarent Antigonus ea tempeftate cum
Patras ueniffet:hoc acerbiffimo nuntio accepto uehemẽter grauiterq3 ingemuit:
atq3 lugubri uefte affumpta confeftim in omnes partes litteras mifit:quibus Reges & principes obfecrabat ut pro falute patris Demetri apud Seleucũ interce-
derent .Ipfum autem Seleucum inutis precibus rogatum mifit :ut quicquid fibi

22. *First Roman Type used in Germany: Rusch, Strassburg, c. 1464*

SCYTHIE INTRA IMAVM MON
TEM SITVS

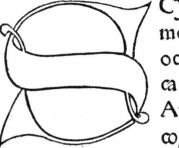 CYTHIA intra Imaū montem terminatur ab occaſu Sarmaria Aſiatica ſcđm lineā expoſitā A ſeptentrione terra incognita. Ab oriēte Imao monte ad arctos vergente ſcđm meridianā ferme lineā q̄ a p̄dicto oppido vſq̄ ad terrā incognitam extenditur. A meridie ac etiam oriente Satis quidē & Sugdianis & Margiana iuxta ipſorū expoſitas lineas vſq̄ oſtia oxe amnis in byrcanū mare exeūtiſ ac etiā parte q̄ hinc eſt vſq̄ ad Rba amnis oſtia q̄ gradus habet 87 ż 48 ż ʒ̄. Ad occaſum aūt vergitur in gradib₂ 84 44 ꜣ̄

Rhymmi ff oſtia	91	48 ꜣ̄
Daicis ff oſtia	94	48 ꜣ̄
Iaxarti ff oſtia	97	48
Iſtai ff oſtia	100	47 ʒ̄
Polytimeti ff oſtia	103	44 ż
Aſpabotis ciuitas	102	44

23. *Transitional Roman-Gothic: Holle, Ulm*, 1482

scripts of that day lent themselves very well to typographic rendering.

The sack of Mainz in 1462 influenced the spread of typography, for it wiped out commerce there, and the consequent lack of money led printers, who were established in a kind of industrial group, to scatter widely. This accounts for the German names we find among the earliest printers in other countries throughout Europe. Where these men continued to work in Germany, their difficulties were slight, and this was true where they were invited to set up their presses in some foreign place, and financial support was assured them. But in many cases the wandering printer had to take his chances as to where he might find employment, and to travel into a far country whose language was unfamiliar to him, before he reached an apparently favourable spot for his enterprise. As books were printed, at first, page by page,[1] and galley proofs were unknown, if he desired to produce a large book with any speed, a number of presses would be required, and there was the cost of other materials to be counted. So a good deal of courage, ingenuity, and financial ability to see the undertaking through was needed, if he was to succeed. Even then it was very easy to make mistakes in the choice of books, or in the way they were printed, and either error might lead to disaster. For these men were obliged to be not merely printers, but publishers; they had not alone to make their books, but to sell them.

Such printers found their chief customers in churches, monastic libraries, the clergy, teachers and their students, lawyers, doctors, and professors of philosophy; and there were, too, general readers and educated lovers of literature.

[1] It was not until between 1470 and 1480 that two pages were printed at the same moment.

For monastic libraries printers often supplied books which may be classed among those volumes "which no gentleman's library should be without," and which so few gentlemen ever read! Both in France and Germany, many printed service books were required, although in Italy manuscripts for some time held their own as the more orthodox form of liturgical book. "Helps for the clergy," skeletons of sermons, etc., appealed to parish priests, and law-books, school-books, and medical treatises also had their market. Then, too, there were editions of the classics which were, however, mostly produced in Italy for the rest of Europe.

As we have to do chiefly with type, the kind of types which these printers made most interests us. Mr. Pollard, in the illuminating paper on Early Printers with which he prefaces the catalogue of the Annmary Brown Memorial library,[1] tells us that "At first there were special church types for service-books and Bibles, but these were soon reserved for the large service-books for use in choir, in which the type was necessarily massive and clear, both to avoid mistakes in reading and sometimes also to enable the book to be shared by several singers. Save for a few experiments, roman types in Italy and gothic in Germany were at first used for books of all kinds, but the tendency was to regard roman as specially appropriate to editions of the classics, to use upright and rather plain gothic for other Latin books, and a more sloping gothic for books in the vernaculars. . . . Besides these subject-divisions of types the local schools of

[1] *Catalogue of Books mostly from the Presses of the First Printers showing the Progress of Printing with Movable Metal Types through the second half of the Fifteenth Century. Collected by Rush C. Hawkins, catalogued by Alfred W. Pollard, and deposited in Annmary Brown Memorial at Providence, Rhode Island.* Oxford, 1910. The Printers, pages xix *et seq.* The early printer has been treated with great charm by Mr. Pollard, and I commend his paper in its entirety as indispensable to a clear idea of the subject we are considering.

handwriting had great influence on the forms of letters, more especially in the early days of printing, and this accounts for the great variety in the founts used before 1480. After about that date, types of the same general character and often indistinguishable in nearly every detail were in use in places long distances apart, in some cases because the later printers found it easier to imitate an already existing type than to adapt written characters to their needs, in others, in all probability, owing to the sale of punches or matrices.

"While great care had to be taken in choosing a good design for a type, a single fount often served an early printer for several years. There were no title-pages in these first days, and the printer's business was only to print the text of his book, leaving headings and headlines, as well as ornamental capitals, to be supplied by hand to suit purchasers' tastes. As the cry for cheapness grew louder printers found it necessary to leave less and less to be done by the scribes, whose bill for rubricating a book must have added very materially to its cost to the buyer. Special types were then cast for use in headings and headlines and on title-pages, and many printers provided themselves with fine sets of woodcut capitals."

Thus we see that the printer's choice of types was almost entirely governed by the kind of manuscript popular in the particular locality of the country in which he found himself. The design of his type was also dependent on the kind of book to be printed; as various classes of books—I speak of black-letter books—employed particular forms of black-letter.

In closing, it may be noted that most Mainz printers went to Italy; none of them, apparently, to Holland. Perhaps this was because they knew that the art of printing, in rudimentary form, was already practised there.

CHAPTER V

THE popularity of the Roman character in Italian manuscripts was due to the Renaissance revival of classical learning, and it has already been briefly shown to what sources this letter was traceable. Italy being the seat of the Renaissance, printing in roman types very naturally became general there earlier than in any other European country. The best roman types are to be found in Italian books printed before 1500. These, as has also been said, were modelled on Humanistic characters, which were in their turn revivals of the Carolingian book-hands. To see how closely these two forms of writing agreed in general effect, it is only necessary to compare Carolingian manuscripts of the ninth with Italian manuscripts of the fifteenth century.

"At the period of the early Renaissance," says Walter Crane, "two streams met, as it were, and mingled, with very beautiful results: the freedom, the romance, the naturalism of the later Gothic, with the newly awakened Classical feeling, with its grace of line and mythological lore. The rich and delicate arabesques in which Italian designers delighted, and which so frequently decorated, as we have seen, the borders of the early printer, owe also something to Oriental influence, as indeed their name indicates. The decorative beauty of these early Renaissance books was really, therefore, the outcome of a very remarkable fusion of ideas and styles. Printing, as an art, and book decoration attained a perfection it has not since reached. The genius of the greatest designers of the time was associated with the new invention, and expressed itself with unparalleled vigour in the woodcut; while the type-founder, being still under the influence of a fine traditional style in handwriting, was in perfect harmony with the book decorator or illustrator."[1]

The first press in Italy was set up at the Benedictine Monastery of Subiaco, near Rome. Some Germans were members of this community, and perhaps that was one reason why the German printers, Conrad Sweynheym and Arnold Pannartz, were welcomed by its abbot, Cardinal Turrecremata. Sweynheym, a clerk of the diocese of Mainz, was possibly one of Fust and Schoeffer's workmen. Pannartz belonged to the diocese of Cologne. The theory that both men were refugees from Mainz in 1462, that Nicolas Jenson accompanied them in their flight, and that he cut the font used by them at Subiaco, as well as that subsequently employed at Rome, has been advanced by reputable authorities.[2] Be that as it may, a very beautiful type was produced at Subiaco, which appears to us gothic, but which they probably considered roman; for these printers, accustomed to gothic types, found themselves in a country where manuscripts in the Humanistic character were the fashion. So, while their type has many details of Gothic design in it, it has roman capitals, and lower-case letters very roman in structure — though their thickness of line gives, in mass, the effect of gothic type. There is, too, a certain amount of white between the lines of type, which results in a clearness usually characteristic of books printed in roman fonts.[3] While not a roman type as we should now understand the term, it is, in spite of its general effect, a font well on the

[1] Crane's *Decorative Illustration of Books*, p. 125.
[2] For Claudin's account of this episode, see his *Histoire de l'Imprimerie en France au XVe et au XVIe siècle*, Vol. I, pp. 10 *et seq.*
[3] Burger, pl. 45.

way thereto. Three books were printed at Subiaco—Cicero's *De Oratore* (which, though undated, is generally considered the first one), appearing either at the end of 1464 or the beginning of 1465; the *Opera* of Lactantius, printed in 1465; and the *De Civitate Dei* of St. Augustine, finished in 1467 (*fig.* 24). Possibly earlier than all of these was a Donatus, of which no copy exists, but of which there is a record.

The end of the year 1467 finds Sweynheym and Pannartz in Rome, where they set up a press in the palace of the De' Massimi family. Their first book printed in Rome was Cicero's *Epistulæ ad Familiares* of 1467, followed by the Lactantius of 1468. These were set in a new font which, though far less attractive than the Subiaco letter, was a much more roman type (*fig.* 25). Besides the books at Subiaco (four, if we count the Donatus) they printed about fifty at Rome, where they worked together until 1473. A roman type was also produced at Rome in 1468 by Ulrich Han for editions of Cicero's *De Oratore* and *Tusculanæ Quæstiones*, but whether it was a roman letter under Gothic influence, or a gothic letter under Roman influence, it is hard to say. In general effect it was certainly greatly inferior to the Sweynheym and Pannartz types.[1] In all three fonts, whatever the form of lower-case letter, the capitals were distinctly roman. Many roman types of varying degrees of purity and attractiveness were used by Italian printers of this period. It was reserved for John and Wendelin de Spire to show a roman type which to-day appears roman to us. In the font used in the Venice editions of Cicero's *Epistulæ ad Familiares* and Pliny's *Historia Naturalis* of John de Spire, printed in 1469, and the *De Civitate Dei* printed in the next year by John and Wendelin de Spire (*fig.* 26), this very modern quality can be clearly recognized.

[1] Burger, pl. 83.

agit. ut humana diuinis tribuat auctoritatē: cū potius humanis diuina de‑
buerint. Quę nūc sane omittamus. ne nihil apud istos agamus. et ī infinitū
materia ꝓcedat. Ea igī̄ quęramus testimonia. qbus illi possint aut credere:
aut certe non repugnare. Sibillas plurimi et maximi auctores tradiderūt
gręcoꝗ: Aristoricus: et Appollodorus: Erithreus: nostroꝗ Varro et Fe‑
nestella. Hi omēs ꝓcipuam et nobilem pręter cęteras. Erithream fuisse cō‑
memorāt. Appollodorus qdē ut de ciuī ac populari sua gloriāt. Fenestella
uero etiā legatos Erithreos a senatu eē missos refert. ut huius Sibillę car‑
mina Romā deportarēt. et ea consules Curio et Octauianus ī capitolio
quod tūc erat curante Quīto Catulo restituendū: ponēda curarēt. Apud hāc
de summo & conditore rerū deo huiusmōi uersus reperiūtur. Αφθαρτος
κτιστης αιωνιος αιθερα ναιων τοις ακακοις ακακον προ‑
φερων πολυ μειʒονα μισθον τοις δε κακοις τε αδικοις τε
χολον και θυμον ετειρων. id est ī corruptibilis et conditor ęternus
in aere habitans. bonis bonū ꝓferens. tustis multo maiorē mercedem. in‑
tustis aūt & malis iram et furorem excitans. Rursus alio loco enumerans.

24. *First Type used in Italy: Sweynheym and Pannartz, Subiaco, 1465*

credendum eſt. quia neceſſe fuit populū aliquãdo ad
ludum conuenire.& uoluerunt ut ſquit philoſopbuſ
determíata eē loca ludendi:ne in diuerſorriſ p̄uatiſq̃
lociſconuenticula fatienteſ: p̄broſa & contumelioſa
aliqua perpetrarent ☙Huiuſmodi itaq̃ mechanice
arteſ & uiuendi genera b̄oeſtiſſime a quolibet b̄oeſto
uiro ualent exerceri. Nam & ſacra ſcp̄tura buiuſmōt
neceſſariaſ arteſ cō mendat inquiēſin eccleſiaſtico. In
manu artificiſomiſopera laudabit́.unuſ ex ppbetiſ
ait.í porta regiſartificeſnegotiátur. Aut ſi forte cete/
raſarteſingenio preditaſperoptaſ:elige tibi liberaleſ
arteſ.preſertim quatuor ultimaſ quaſ mathematicaſ
uocant. que plerunq̃ magno ſplendore bomineſ eaſ
ſectanteſ illuſtrant. Legiſti Sulpitiū Gallū aſtro/
nimū plurimū bonoriſ& utilitatiſactuliſſe romaniſ.
Qui cum bello p̄ximi eſſent contra parſaſ:ea nocte
luna eclipſata eſt. quo ſigno ſtupefacti romani deli/

25. *Second Type of Sweynheym and Pannartz, Rome,* 1467
From the Speculum Humanæ Vitæ of 1468

feliciter uiuant: quod deos suos posse afferunt in corporibus igneis: Iouéq̃ ipsum eorum regem in omnibus corporeis elementis: Nam si animę ut bta fit corpus est omne fugiendum: fugiant dii eoꝝ de globis syderum: fugiat Iuppiter de cęlo & terra: aut si non possunt miseri iudicentur. Sed neutrum isti uoluut:qui neque a corporibus separatioñe audent dare diis suis: ne illis mortales colere uideantur: nec beatitudinis priuationem:ne infelices eos eē fateantur. Non ergo ad beatitudinem cōsequendam omia fugienda sunt corpora: sed corruptibilia: grauia:moribunda:non qualia fecit primis homibus bonitas dei:sed qualia esse compulit peccati **poena.**

Sed necesse est inquiunt: ut terrena corpora naturale pondus uel i terra teneat:uel cogat ad terram: & ideo in caelo esse non possunt. Primi quidem illi homiēs in terra erant nemorosa atque fructuosa: quae paradisi nomen obtinuit.Sed quia & ad hoc respondendū est:uel propter cbristi corpus cum quo ascendit in caelum:uel propter sanctorum 'qualia in resurrectione futura sunt: intueantur paulo attentius pondera ipā terrena. Si enim ars humana efficit: ut ex metallis quę in aquis posita continuo submergunt:quibusdam

26. *John and Wendelin de Spire's Roman Type, Venice,* 1469

From De Civitate Dei of 1470

Nicolas Jenson, whose celebrated roman types are now to be considered, was a Frenchman, a native of Somme-voire, Haute-Marne, and for some time was mint-master at Tours. The legend is, that Charles VII of France sent Jenson, in 1458, to Mainz, to inform himself on the subject of the new art of printing and to acquire sufficient knowledge to work in it on his return. But if Jenson ever went to Mainz, he never returned to France, and we find him in 1468 at Venice. The first roman characters, which were used by John de Spire, and for which De Spire obtained an exclusive privilege for five years, have been sometimes attributed to Jenson. In any case, De Spire's death in 1470 lifted the restrictions on roman types from other Venetian printing-houses, and Jenson produced in that year his famous roman letter (*fig.* 27). The tractate *De Præparatione Evangelica* of Eusebius is generally considered his first book. If we look at the best Humanistic manuscripts of the period, it is readily seen whence he derived his inspiration.

The characteristics of Jenson's font were its readability, its mellowness of form, and the evenness of colour in mass. Analyzed closely, his letter-forms were not very perfect; had they been so, their effect would not have been so good; for, as an authority has said, "a type too ideal in its perfection is not an ideal type." The eye becomes tired when each character is absolutely perfect. Thus the good effect of the type in mass depends somewhat upon the variations in, and consequent "movement" of, its integral parts. Jenson's roman types have been the accepted models for roman letters ever since he made them, and, repeatedly copied in our own day, have never been equalled. There were other printers in Italy whose types rivalled his, but no other man produced quite so fine a font, or had better taste in the composition of a page and its imposition upon

paper.[1] The presswork of his volumes is perhaps their weakest point. Apparently a lighter ink was used for his roman
than for his gothic types—for Jenson also used a gothic letter.[2] He printed about a hundred and fifty books in some ten
years, and as he prospered in the enterprise we may draw
from his history the unexpected moral that if only a man
does a thing *well enough*, it will reward him—in reputation,
or in money—perhaps in both. For Jenson in his own day
had a great reputation, both as a publisher and printer. He
died at Rome, in 1480, whither he went at the invitation
of Pope Sixtus IV. Jenson's material passed into the hands
of Torresano of Venice, father-in-law of Aldus, who, after
the latter's death, carried on the Aldine printing-house.

At the head of a broadside advertisement of various
classes of books,[3] printed (in bold gothic type) by Jenson
and his associate and successor, Herbort, and brought out
by the latter not many months, it is believed, after Jenson's
death, there are some prefatory remarks which were perhaps written by a theologian of a Humanistic turn of mind.
We quote them as a testimony to the esteem that Jenson's
work enjoyed in its own day : even allowing for the exagger-
ation incident to advertising. After an invocation to Christ
the Illuminator of the World, it reads :

"It has appeared to me to be an undertaking which
would redound to the common advantage of all men, that
I should in this little discourse of mine set forth to every
people the extreme usefulness of the works printed in the
famous city of Venice, especially of those which are from

---

[1] *Druckschriften*, pl. 67.   [2] *Ibid.*, pl. 34.

[3] Discovered in the library of the Capuchin Cloister at Burghausen, Upper
Bavaria, pasted inside three books printed by Jenson in 1478. It is now in the
State Library at Munich. For facsimile, etc., see *Wiegendrucke und Hand-
schriften. Festgabe Konrad Haebler zum* 60. *Geburtstage.* Leipsic, 1919,
p. 22.

qui omnibus in aquarum submersis cum filiis suis simul ac nuribus
mirabili quodã modo quasi semen huãni generis conseruatus est:quẽ
utinã quasi uiuam quandam imaginem imitari nobis contingat:& hi
quidem ante diluuium fuerunt:post diluuium autem alii quorũ unus
altissimi dei sacerdos iustitiæ ac pietatis miraculo rex iustus lingua he-
bræorũ appellatus est:apud quos nec circuncisionis nec mosaicæ legis
ulla mentio erat. Quare nec iudæos(posteris eni hoc nomen fuit)neqʒ
gentiles:quoniam non ut gentes pluralitatem deorum inducebant sed
hebræos proprie noiamus aut ab Hebere ut dictũ est:aut qa id nomen
transitiuos significat.Soli qppe a creaturis naturali rõne & lege inata
nõ scripta ad cognitioné uen dei trasiere:& uoluptate corporis cõtẽpta
ad rectam uitam puenisse scribunt:cum quibus omibus præclarus ille
totius generis origo Habraam numerãdus est:cui scriptura mirabilem
iustitiã quã non a mosaica lege(septima eím post Habraã generatione
Moyses nascitur)sed naturali fuit ratione consecutus fũma cum laude
attestatur.Credidit enim Habraam deo & reputatũ est ei in iustitiam.
Quare multarum quoqʒ gentium patrem diuina oracula futurũ:ac in
ipso benedicẽdas oẽs gentes hoc udelic& ipsum quod iam nos udeũs
aperte prædictum est:cuius ille iustitiæ perfectioẽm non mosaica lege
sed fide cõsecutus est:qui post multas dei usiones legitimum genuit
filium.quem primum omnium diuino pfusus oraculo circũcidit:&

enim id ſcrutādum nobis modo eſt. Poſt Habraam filius eius Iſaac in pietate ſucceſſit: fœlice hac hæreditate a parētibus accæpta: q̄ uni uxori coniunctus quum geminos genuiſſet caſtitatis amore ab uxore poſtea dicitur abſtinuiſſe. Ab iſto natus ē Iacob qui ꝓpter cumulatū uirtutis prouētum Iſrael etiam appellatus eſt duobus noibus ꝓpter duplicem uirtutis uſū. Iacob eīm athletā & exercétem ſe latine dicere poſſumus: quam appellationé primū habuit: quī practicis operatioibus multos pro pietate labores ferebat. Quum autē iam uictor luctando euaſit: & ſpeculationis fruebaťbonis: tūc Iſraelem ipſe deus appellauit æterna premia beatitudinéq ultimam quæ in uiſione dei conſiſtit et largiens: hominem enim qui deum uideat Iſrael nomen ſignificat. Ab hoc. xii. iudæorum tribus ꝓfectæ fūt. Innumerabilia de uita iſtorum uirorum fortitudine prudentia pietateq dici poſſunt: quorum alia ſecundum ſcripturæ uerba hiſtorice conſiderantur: alia tropologice ac allegorice interpretať: de q̄bus multi cōſcripſerūt: & nos in libro q̄ inſcripſius

27. *Jenson's Roman Type used in Eusebius, De Præparatione Evangelica, Venice, 1470*

the excellent workshop of Master Nicolas Jenson the
Frenchman. And in order that what is maimed and imper-
fect be not bought and prized as the equal of the best, and
that bad printing be not so praised as to cause men to
neglect and not purchase what has been printed with the
utmost care and painstaking, I made up my mind to com-
municate this letter to the public. For the excellent Master
Nicolas Jenson employs proofreaders who are skilled in
both languages, and he seeks out the most famous men of
learning and greater numbers of them, with the result that
works published by him have the power of illuminating
the entire world, and contain neither too much nor too little,
as you will well understand if you will read through his
books with the most heedful attention. Furthermore, they
contain discussions, on this side and that, by the most competent men, in order that the truth may through the variety of arguments be revealed. For, as Cicero says in the
Paradoxes, 'there is nothing so rough and unkempt that it
cannot be glorified by the proper treatment.' But the quality
and value of the types that he uses is another marvel to
relate, for it ought to be ascribed rather to divine inspiration than to human wit, so that all may say and truly, that
Master Nicolas easily surpasses all his rivals; so that men
might justly venture to repeat the saying of Virgil in the
Bucolics—'but she bears her head as high among all other
cities as any cypress will do among trailing hedgerow
shoots.' For his books are no hindrance to a man, nor do
they produce weariness, but rather give delight by their
exactness and precision; they do not harm one's eyes, but
rather help them and do them good. Moreover the characters themselves are so methodically and carefully finished
by that famous man that the letters are not smaller or
larger or thicker than reason demands or than may afford

pleasure: which he could not have done unless filled by some divine inspiration. Hence our debt to that excellent man Master Nicolas Jenson is great indeed: for through his diligence and toil all peoples, barbarous as well as Latin, have in their hands works which before could scarcely be procured: now they have these works printed with correct texts in most excellent, beautiful and agreeable books, so that they deserve praise and reverence in the highest degree. I for my part determined to narrate briefly their good qualities, not because of any spite or jealousy toward others, but as I have already said, for the common advantage of all men: on which we ought to insist much more than upon our own advantage: lest men, when they buy, should buy and possess the false instead of the true, the ugly instead of the beautiful, the incorrect instead of the most accurate."

Five or six roman fonts were cut for the great Venetian printer-publisher, Aldus Manutius. His first roman letter, in which Bembo's *Ætna* appeared, was not particularly successful, but the third roman font, designed by the celebrated Francesco da Bologna (Griffi), who afterward cut the Aldine italic character, was excellent. This roman type was used in that famous book, Colonna's *Hypnerotomachia Poliphili*, or "The Strife of Love in a Dream," printed by Aldus in the last year of the century. It is remarkable for its delightful illustrations, drawn in a line which harmonizes with the tone of the pages of roman letter. From one of these decorations the famous Aldine printer's mark of dolphin and anchor was derived; although the original of this design is to be found on a coin which Erasmus says was sent to Aldus by the Renaissance scholar, Bembo. A specimen of this Aldine roman font is shown in the facsimile from a page of the *Hypnerotomachia* (*fig.* 28). It is distinctly inferior to Jenson's roman characters, and perhaps

POLIPHILO INCOMINCIA IL SECONDO LIBRO DI
LA SVA HYPNEROTOMACHIA. NEL QVALE PO-
LIA ET LVI DISERTABONDI, IN QVALE MODO ET
VARIO CASO NARRANO INTERCALARIAMEN-
TE IL SVO INAMORAMENTO.

NARRA QVIVI LA DIVA POLIA LA NOBILE ET
ANTIQVA ORIGINE SVA. ET COMO PER LI PREDE
CESSORI SVI TRIVISIO FVE EDIFICATO. ET DI QVEL
LA GENTE LELIA ORIVNDA. ET PER QVALE MO-
DO DISAVEDVTA ET INSCIA DISCONCIAMENTE
SE INAMOROE DI LEI IL SVO DILECTO POLIPHILO.

E MIE DEBILE VOCE TALE O GR A
tiofe & diue Nymphe abfone perueneráno &
inconcíne alla uoftra benigna audiétia, quale
laterrifica raucitate del urinante Efacho al fua-
ue canto dela piangeuole Philomela. Nondi
meno uolendo io cum tuti gli mei exili conati del intellecto, & cum la mia paucula fufficié
tia di fatiffare alle uoftre piaceuole petitione,
non riftaro al potere. Lequale femota qualúque hefitatione epfe piu che
fi congruerebbe altronde, dignamente meritano piu uberrimo fluuio di
eloquentia, cum troppo piu rotunda elegantia & cum piu exornata poli
tura di pronútiato, che in me per alcuno pacto non fi troua, di cófeguire
il fuo gratiofo affecto. Ma a uui Celibe Nymphe & ad me alquáto, quan
túche & confufa & incomptaméte fringultiéte haro in qualche portiun-
cula gratificato affai. Quando uoluntarofa & diuota a gli defii uoftri &
poftulato me preftaro piu prefto cum lanimo nó mediocre prompto hu-
mile parendo, che cum enucleata terfa, & uenufta eloquentia placédo. La
prifca dunque & ueterrima geneologia, & profapia, & il fatale mio amore
garrulando ordire. Onde gia effendo nel uoftro uenerando conuentuale
confpecto, & uederme fterile & ieiuna di eloquio & ad tanto preftáte & di
uo ceto di uui O Nymphe fedule famularie dil accefo cupidine. Et ítan-
to bénigno & delecteuole & facro fito, di fincere aure & florigeri fpirami-
ni afflato. Io acconciamente compulfo di affumere uno uenerabile aufo,
& tranquillo timore de dire. Dunque auante il tuto uenia date, o belliffi-
me & beatiffime Nymphe a quefto mio blacterare & agli femelli & terri-
geni, & pufilluli Conati, fi aduene che in alchuna parte io incautamente

A

nia bona. lauſ:honoꝛ:virtuſ
potētia: ꝛ gratiaꝛ actio tibi
chꝛiſte.Amen.

Viue deū ſic ꝛ vines per ſecula cūcta. Pꝛouidet ꝛ tribuit deus omnia
nobis. Pꝛoficit abſque deo nullꝰin
oꝛbe laboꝛ. Illa placet tellꝰ in qua
res parua beatū. Me facit ꝛ tenues
luxuriantur opes.

Si foꝛtuna volet fies de rhetoꝛe conſul.
Si volet hec eadem fies de cōſule rhetoꝛ.
Quicquid amoꝛ iuſſit nō eſt cōtēdere tutū
Regnat et in dominos ius habet ille ſuos
Vita data é vtēda data é ſine fenere nobis.
Mutua:nec certa perſoluenda die.

Vſus ꝛ ars docuit quod ſapit omnis homo
Ars animos frangit ꝛ firmas dirimit vꝛbes
Arte cadunt turres arte leuatur onus
Artibus ingenijs queſita eſt gloꝛia multis
Pꝛincipijs obſta ſero medicina paratur
Cum mala per longas conualuere moꝛas
Sed pꝛopera nec te venturas differ in hoꝛas
Qui non eſt hodie cras minus aptus erit.

29. *Ratdolt's Gothic Type, from his Specimen of* 1486

to those of the Venetian printer, Ratdolt. Besides roman types, Aldus possessed fonts of his celebrated italic character in two sizes, and several fonts of Greek type. Aldus died in 1515, and when he lay in state his books were grouped about him. He directed in his will that punches begun by a certain cutter should on no account be completed by an inferior hand.

One other Venetian printer (and type-cutter) should not be forgotten — Erhard Ratdolt, who came from Augsburg, and began to print at Venice in 1476. His books are the first with decorative title-pages, and he also employed extremely fine borders and initial letters.[1] He issued his beautiful type specimen-sheet in 1486.[2] It is dated Augsburg, April 1, 1486, but was probably printed at Venice, just before Ratdolt left for Augsburg, and was to be used there. In this, the earliest specimen-sheet known, the *Ave Maria*, in its older form (which begins it with a charming initial A), is printed in a large gothic letter, derived from fourteenth century Italian manuscripts.[3] The sheet exhibits ten sizes of excellent gothic letter, four of which are here reproduced (*fig.* 29). There are three sizes of roman — all good — and a specimen of Greek letter of excellent early form (*fig.* 30). Ratdolt's books were among the most distinguished of the Venetian press. Indeed, by the sixteenth century, Venice was a centre for printing, and had some hundred and fifty printing-houses; and over four thousand books, of remarkable excellence in workmanship, came from

---

[1] De Vinne thinks that Ratdolt's initials were probably cut in high relief on metal, as it was expensive and not particularly practical to cast these ornamental letters in a mould. In books of the period much that is considered engraving on wood, especially when of a delicate kind, is really engraving on metal. De Vinne's *Plain Printing Types*, New York, 1900, p. 84.

[2] Burger, pl. 5, for entire sheet.

[3] Thompson, fac. 194.

its presses. The work of Venetian printers and type-founders was considered a model for the rest of Europe. Publishers wishing to commend their books announced that they were printed in the *carattere Veneto*.

The attempts of the first Italian printers, Sweynheym and Pannartz, to print in semi-roman types, have led us naturally to consider first the development of these types into pure roman letter; but gothic types were also used in Italy by Jenson, as has been said, and by many other printers. A fine specimen of Jenson's work in gothic fonts is the *Codex Decretorum* of Gratian, printed in 1474.[1] The forms of Italian gothic types, while pointed, in the larger sizes were rounder and less compact than the like kinds of German black-letter. In the smaller sizes this attenuated quality is very striking, and makes the character almost a condensed type. A similarly condensed letter was employed in manuscripts of a little earlier date.

For head-lines, a large, round gothic letter similar to some Spanish gothic characters was often used; and sometimes roman capitals. Not merely the types, but their arrangement in general, were modelled on manuscripts of the fourteenth and fifteenth centuries. The famous manuscript Virgil, with notes, which belonged to Petrarch (now in the Ambrosian Library at Milan), shows a character of letter and an arrangement of text which were closely followed in many subsequent printed editions of Virgil. The manuscript commentary on the Decretals of Gregory IX (1353) in the Vatican Library is also very much like some books printed from Italian gothic fonts.[2]

The important series of plates of Italian types issued by the Type Facsimile Society (alluded to more fully later) are

[1] *Druckschriften*, pl. 34.
[2] *Paléographie Latine*, pls. 101 and 106.

Eſt homini uirtus fuluo precioſior auro: ænæas
Ingenium quondam fuerat precioſius auro.
Miramurq; magis quos munera mentis adornãt:
Quam qui corporeis emicuere bonis.
Si qua uirtute nites ne deſpice quenquam
Ex alia quadam forſitan ipſe nitet

Nemo ſuę laudis nimium lętetur honore
Ne uilis factus poſt ſua fata gemat.
Nemo nimis cupide ſibi res deſiderat ullas
Ne dum plus cupiat perdat & id quod habet.
Ne uę cito uerbis cuiuſquam credito blandis
Sed ſi ſint fidei reſpice quid moneant
Qui bene proloquitur coram ſed poſtea praue
Hic erit inuiſus bina q̃ ora gerat

Pax plenam uirtutis opus pax ſumma laborum
pax belli exacti præcium eſt præciumque pericli
Sidera pace uigent conſiſtunt terrea pace
Nil placitum ſine pace deo non munus ad aram
Fortuna arbitriis tempus diſpenſat ubi
Illa rapit iuuenes illa ferit ſenes

κλιω Τευτερπη τε θαλεια τε μελπομενη τε
Γερψιχορη τερατω τε πολυμνεια τουρανιη
τε καλλιοπη θεᾱη προφερεςατη ἐςιναπα
σαωψ ιεσυς χριςους μαρια τελος.

30. *Ratdolt's Roman and Greek Type, from his Specimen of* 1486

qui ingenio subferuiunt crassiores hēt:ppeaqȝ minus pspicaces sunt.AT Neqȝ dedeco
rant.Dedecorauit alexandri defe iudiciū cherilus:qui nō correspondit iudicio suo.Ergo
nō recte iudicauit Alexander.Tu uero auguste cōtra de Virgilio et Vario poetis recte iu
dicasti:Nā prepositi a te respōderunt iudicio tuo.Laus ergo ista et octauianū et hos poe
tas simul pingit.CVM Multa laude dantis.Magna.n.laus datoris ē munera et beneficia
bene collocare.AE Nea signa.Diuisa ē syllaba metri cā;ut aenea quatuor sit syllabarum.

Ad libros & ad hæc musarū dona uocares
Boeti in crasso iurares aere natum.
At neqȝ dedecorant tua defe iudicia:atqȝ
Munera quæ multa dantis cū laude tulerūt
Dilecti tibi uirgilius uariusqȝ poetæ.
Nec magis expressi uultus p aenea signa:
Quā p uatis opus mores animiqȝ uiuorū
Clarorū apparēt nec sermones ego mallem
Repēres p humū quā res cōponere gestas
Terrarūqȝ situs & flumia dicere & arces
Mōribus impositas:& barbara regna:tuisqȝ
Auspiciis rotū cōfecta duella p orbē:
Clausstraqȝ custodē pacis cohibentia ianū.

Snia est:qȝ carmie boni poete
melius exprimūt uirtutes ma
gnorū uirorū:q̄ exprimaT eo
rundem corpora p sculpturā:
NEC Sermones ego.Ego ̃et
libentius heroica scribere:et
illis res ꝑgregias clarorum du
cū exprimere:q̄ sermōes.i.hu
iuscemodi carmia infimo stilo
descripta:fed nō possum quod
cupio.REPentes.quod est pe
dibus carentiū.Ergo repēres
p humū.i.infimos.C Lausfra
cohibētia ianū.Hanc romano
rū cōsuetudinē qȝ in pace iani
templū clausū essetin supiori
bus abunde profecuri fumus.
PARThis. Quoniam ab eo
per Ventidium ducem supera
ti fūt.TVA MAIestas.i ma

31. *Part of a page of Horace: Miscomini, Florence, 1482*

material to be consulted for the general effect of books printed in gothic letter in the last half of the fifteenth century.[1]

Italian transitional fonts merged almost imperceptibly from a distinctly gothic into a fairly clear roman type. Starting from the pure gothic types, the first differentiation appears in a wider leading of lines and wider spacing of the type itself.[2] The next advance shows gothic fonts with somewhat roman capital letters. This was followed by books in which head-lines and dates were set in pure roman capitals. An increasing clearness in cut and further separation of letters and a constant use of roman capitals finally developed into tentative roman fonts. These changes can be interestingly traced by looking at the earliest type of Sweynheym and Pannartz (*fig.* 24), and the improvement in the type used by them only a little later at Rome (*fig.* 25); or, better still, the four types used by Ulrich Han in the same city.[3] These transitional types form the "bridge" between Italian gothic and roman types. Italian printers were not always very particular about the unities, and sometimes mixed gothic head-lines with roman text, while some books (although but few) were set in a roman lower-case letter with gothic capitals.

The fonts of Italian roman vary greatly. The finest all have that rich, mellow character which no types before or since have ever had in such degree. While Jenson's type was undoubtedly the best, it was pushed hard by some other roman fonts, such as those employed at Venice by John and Wendelin de Spire and Ratdolt, by Miscomini at Venice and Florence, by Servius at Rome, and others.

[1] Type Facsimile Society. Publications of the Society for the years 1901–09, inclusive.

[2] *Ibid.*, pl. 1903 m.

[3] Burger, pls. 23, 84, 83 [1], 83 [2], in this order.

A page like Miscomini's Florentine Horace of 1482, where notes surround the text, is an admirably practical piece of work. The notes are perhaps a little closely set, but the page is fine and straightforward, and of a pleasant solidity which gives the reader confidence (*fig.* 31). Almost all Italian roman fonts in the last half of the fifteenth century had an air of "security" and generous ease extremely agreeable to the eye. Indeed, there is nothing better than fine Italian roman type in the whole history of typography.

It is not fair, however, to take the finest of these and think of it as representative of Italian fifteenth century type. Only by seeing many examples can one get a general idea of *that*. And for this purpose, the publications of the Type Facsimile Society, issued in England through the influence of Robert Proctor between 1901 and 1909, are admirable. If the reader can divide a set of the loose plates into groups of roman and gothic types, and then sort them into groups under each country, in chronological arrangement, he will obtain a conspectus of national type-forms which is invaluable. He has, in fact, but to glance through the gothic and roman Italian types shown in facsimiles thus arranged, to comprehend the general tendency of type-forms in either class of character; and will realize how high an average of excellence, especially in the roman letters, the fifteenth century Italian printers attained. This publication is rare, and this use of it diverts it from the bibliographical purposes for which libraries cherish it—though it does not divert the librarian! But for the student I do not know a more valuable work, nor a more valuable way to use it.

When we compare even the best early printed books with the Italian manuscripts which they copied, we see how far they fell short of their model. "As compared with other national scripts," says Maunde Thompson. "the high level of general excellence maintained by the Italian scribes is very striking. And it was this general excellence that placed them in the position to take the lead at the crucial moment of the adoption of printing in Europe. . . . And when the art of printing was established, and after the early type-cutters had selected their first models in the contemporary MS. book-hands of their several countries, it is no wonder that, in the end, the type copied from the Italian script prevailed over all others."[1] For the characters employed in the best Humanistic manuscripts are, in their way, among the masterpieces of human endeavour.

[1] Thompson, p. 464.

CHAPTER VI

TYPE AND TYPE-FORMS OF THE FIFTEENTH CENTURY
IN FRANCE

PARIS was the first place in France in which printing, as we know it to-day, was practised. But before
any press was set up there, essays in typography
had already been made at Avignon, as early as 1444, by
Waldfoghel, a Bohemian goldsmith of Prague. He had some
secret process which he called the art of writing artificially.
He declared under oath upon the Gospels and before wit-
nesses, that the said method of writing artificially was real,
easy, possible, and useful to those who wished to work in it.
In association with a watchmaker, or locksmith, who came
from Treves, and with the help of others who supplied money
for the project, he set up some sort of a printing establishment, the material of which consisted of two steel alphabets, two iron forms, a steel instrument called a vise, and
other accessories. He also made an alphabet of twenty-seven
Hebrew letters, with a so-called engine and accompanying
instruments of wood, tin, and iron. It is possible that Waldfoghel had earlier been associated with men who were, in
turn, connected with Gutenberg, at Strassburg or Mainz. At
the latter place there were men who were experimenting in
the art of printing besides Gutenberg. Waldfoghel, though
lacking means fully to develop his ideas, seems to have arrived at something much like Gutenberg's process. However that may be, his experiments did not continue after
1446. Eleven years later, Fust and Schoeffer's Latin Psalter
of 1457 appeared at Mainz — the first *dated* book printed
from movable types.

In Paris, printing was begun in 1470 under the auspices
of two men whose origin casts some light on the *personnel*

of the printing-house (really "a private press for the benefit of public studies") which they established. One was Johann Heynlin, called *de la Pierre*, from his birthplace, Stein, in the Duchy of Baden. He had been prior and rector of the Sorbonne. He was a booklover, and, coming from the banks of the Rhine, was in relation with Mainz printers. Worried by the carelessness of copyists, he succeeded in interesting Fichet, professor of *belles-lettres* and rhetoric at the Sorbonne, in a scheme to import printers to Paris, so that learned works could be more correctly printed — a plan which aroused considerable opposition among the powerful associations of writers and copyists. The printers for whom he sent were three — Freiburger, a man of education, an old friend of Heynlin, and a former fellow student at the University of Basle; and two others, Ulrich Gering and Martin Kranz, both workmen of the higher class. These men reached Paris in the early months of 1470. Before printing anything, they were obliged to manufacture the tools of their trade, to set up a press, and to fit up their workroom. Last, but not least, they were obliged to cut their type — a roman font for which Heynlin furnished a model from the types of an edition of Caesar's *Commentaries*, which was printed at Rome in 1469 by Sweynheym and Pannartz. As the prior (who was to correct the proofs of the books to be printed) was nearsighted, a large roman character, which did not tire the eye, was preferred to the Gothic manuscript-letter, at that time generally used in France. The type was awkward in cut, but readable (*fig.* 32).

The first book printed in this font was *Gasparini Epistolæ,*[1]

[1] Claudin's *Histoire de l' Imprimerie en France au XVe et au XVIe siècle*, Paris, 1900-14, 4 vols., Vol. I, p. 23.

See also the same author's *First Paris Press. An Account of the Books printed for G. Fichet and J. Heynlin in the Sarbonne*, 1470-1472. (Bibliographical Society's Monographs, No. VI, 1898.) Consult facs., pp. 91-100.

a collection of letters by Gasparino Barzizi of Bergamo, which was considered an example of an excellent Latin style. A second book, *Gasparini Orthographia,*—a treatise by the same author on the orthography of Latin words,—was printed in the same type. With a copy of it which Fichet sent as a present to a former pupil, Robert Gaguin, he despatched a letter in which is this paragraph:

"The printers say here to whoever is willing to listen to them, that it is a man named John, called Gutenberg, who first invented in the neighborhood of Mainz the art of printing, by the means of which books can now be made, not with the aid of the reed, as in old times, nor by the pen as in our days, but with letters of metal, quickly, correctly, and well. ... Bacchus and Ceres were made divinities for having taught humanity the use of wine and bread, but Gutenberg's invention is of a higher and diviner order, for it furnishes characters by the aid of which all that is said or thought can be written, transmitted, and preserved to the memory of posterity."

A Sallust and other books followed, always printed in this same font. This press, as primarily founded, ended its work in 1472. In the next year, Fichet having left for Italy, and Heynlin no longer taking an active oversight of its production, the printers decided, or were obliged, to leave the Sorbonne and set up their workroom outside it. It has been said that, as an institution, the Sorbonne was active in procuring the services of these printers, but this is untrue; it was merely by the initiative of two men connected with that institution that the printers came to Paris. The press itself, however, was undoubtedly under the roof of the Sorbonne, for such a printing-office, with but one kind of type and a small daily production, took up very little space.

The printers then installed themselves at the Sign of the

coacticɋ affentiremur habere· Qʒ fi uidemur
belli fortuna fecum participare·́cófultius effe
fato,opponere fe illis q humilioribus dnãtͨ́
ɋ uirum focium a finibus erigere , ac fe ultro
romanis hoftes oftendere ;

      ❡Brutus trallianis ;

Nͨunciatũ mihi eft ɋ menedotius uefter,
dolobellę inimico meo hofpes & amicuf
exiftens,effecit·́ut intra loca nͣ̄a caftra metanf
inde abire nõ urgerͤtͨ· & nͧ̄c quærit ut intra
urbem cũ exercitu recipiaͭͨ·Qʒ dolobellæ pʒo
deffe ipfe uel quis alius operatus fit·́id mihi
moleftũ nõ eft·nec anïaduertͤdos cuiufpïã er
rores hactenus exiftimo·́confiderata amicicia
& hofpitalitate eorum·Sed ne in antea aliqd
anïaduerfioïs dignũ ppetretis·́ipfũ menedoꝛ
e ciuitate in exilium eiciatis·́nͣ̄o commodo &
utilitati profpicientes·ex quo ipfe patrïã de
uendendo·́ fuũ dumtaxat commodũ quæritat·
Necɋ dolobellam quocɋ pacto recipiatif·́fed a
finibus ueftris expellatis·Qʒ fi refifteret·́ui
& armis cogatis·Quippe fi nõ parebitis·́non
menedori opera uos dolobellam recepiffe·́fed

32. *First Roman Type used in France: Freiburger, Gering
and Kranz, Paris*, 1470

ferens! ꝗ michi peccatori aliquā-
tulā scintillulam intelligētie im-
partiri dignatus est. Illa autem
que minus benedicta fiunt! mee
ignorātie, aut inaduertētie ascri-
bens, caritatiue corrigat. et ꝓ me
peccatore ꝑcef ad dñm fundat;

¶Doctissimi viri domini guidonis
de monte rocherij liber, manipu
lus curatozum vulgariter dictus
finit feliciter. Qui completus ē
parisius ꝑ industriosos impꝛesso-
rie artis libzarios atꝗ magistros
Michaelē de columbaria, Ujdal-
ricū gering, et Martinū cꝛantz
Anno dominice natiuitatis Mil-
lesimoquadringentesimoseptua-
gesimotertio, Menfis marij die ve
ro vicesimoprimo;

scz ita firmiter tenebimus deum!
ꝗ nullo mo timebimus eum amittē
Et de ista tentioe dicit in canticis·
Tenui eum·nec dimittā·Et ista fir
ma tentio succedit virtuti spei·Ter
tia dos anime beate erit ꝑfecta frui
tio·scz quia anima beata ꝑfecte fru
etur deo·et adherebit ei·et satiabi
tur·et delectabit in eo·Uñ psalmi-
sta·satiaboz cum apparuerit gloria
tua·Et ista ꝑfecta fruitio succedit
amoꝛi caritatis·Et de istis tribus
dicit augustinus·videbimus,amabi
mus,et laudabimus·Et istud offici-
um habebimus in paradiso·scz vi-
dere,amare,⁊ deum laudare·
¶Post resurrectionē autē habebi
mus quattuoꝛ dotes ex parte coꝛpo
ris·quia coꝛpoꝛa nostra erunt agilia
id est mouebunt ꝑ quātumcunꝗ
spacium sine aliqua fatigatioē et la
boꝛe·Erunt etiā impassibilia·quia

33. *First Gothic Type used in France: Freiburger, Gering, and Kranz, Paris, 1473*

A B C D E F G H I L M N O P Q R S

T V Y Z : ꝯ - a b c d ꝺ e f g ɓ i k l m n o p q r ꝛ ſ s ʒ

t u v x y z . ꞑ ꞇ ꞇ ꞇ ꞇ ꞇ ff fl ꞇ ꞇ ꝥ ꝥ ꝥ ꝗ ſſ ꞇ ſt

ā ꝉ ꝏ ꝺ̄ ē ḡ ꝉ ō p ꝓ ꝑ ꝓ ꝓ ꝗ́ ꝗ̀ ꝗ̃ ꝗ̃ ꝗ̃ ꝷ ꞃ é ꝉ ꞇ ū v̇ ꝫ

34. *Type used for first Bible printed in France: Freiburger, Gering and Kranz, Paris,* 1476

Publii Virgilii maronis mantuani uatis clariſſimi
Carmen Bucolicum fœliciter incipit.

Hic deflet melibœus profugiat quod iniquē.
Tityrus aſt letus quis contulit ocia dicit.

        Melibœus   Tityrus
¶   Ityre tu patulę recubās ſub tegmine fagi:
       Silueſtrē tenui muſā meditaris auena.
       Nos patrię fines et dulcia linqmus arua.
       Nos patriā fugim⁹:tu tityre lētus ī ūbra
Formoſā reſonare doces amaryllida ſiluas;
O melibœe deus nobis hæc ocia fecit.   Tityrus.
Namcɜ erit ille mihi ſemper deus:iſtius aram:
Sepe tener noſtris ab ouilibus imbuet agnus.
Ille meas errare boues(ut cernis)et ipſum:
Ludere(quę uellem)calamo permiſit agreſti.
Nō equidē inuideo.miror magis.undicɜ totis, Me.
Vſcɜ adeo turbatur agris.en ipſe capellas
Protinus eger ago.hanc etiam uix tityre duco.
Hic inter denſas corylos modo namcɜ gemellos,
Spem gregis(ah ſilice iu nuda)connixa reliquit:
Sepe malum hoc nobis(ſi mens non leua fuiſſet)
De cælo tactas memini predicere quercus:
Sæpe liniſtra caua prædixit ab ilice cornix.
Sed tamen iſte deus qui ſit:da tityre nobis.
Vrbem quā dicunt romā:melibœe putaui   Ti.
Stultus ego huic noſtrę ſimilem:quo ſæpe ſolemus
                                    .a.ii.

35. Roman Type used in Virgil by Gering, Paris, 1478

Golden Sun in the Rue St. Jacques, a street consecrated for centuries to the commerce of the book — as indeed it still is. Their next type (employed for a manual for the clergy, called *Manipulus Curatorum*, issued in 1473) was a gothic font of transitional character, more roman, however, than the like types of Schoeffer. This was the first gothic type used in France. In this book it was set in double-column, with the initial letters and paragraph marks put in by hand (*fig.* 33).[1]

A new font, of letters larger in size than any of these previous types, was cut for the imposing Bible which they issued in 1476 — the first Bible printed in France. The type is a heavy, rounded gothic, but capitals are roman, a feature not so inharmonious in effect as would be expected (*fig.* 34). The small type used in this Bible was the same as that employed in the first book printed after they left the Sorbonne.[2]

In 1477 Kranz and Freiburger returned to Germany, leaving Gering alone. Laying gothic fonts aside, Gering cut for himself two new types, both pure roman, though heavy in effect. In comparing these with the Bible type, they appear to be only an evolution of some elements clearly discernible in the earlier gothic character. The throwing back of the dot on the i is a feature to be noticed. In the smaller font Gering printed two theological books; in the larger, editions of Virgil (*fig.* 35) and of Sallust. After 1484 there seems to have been a cessation in his activities, but meanwhile other printers had taken up work in Paris, and had procured new fonts of gothic and roman letter. Later, in association with Berthold Rembolt, a native of Strassburg, he employed in the *Bréviaire de Paris* of 1492 a delicate gothic type. It was cut by Wolf, a printer, who during an

[1] Claudin, I, p. 63, for full page, rubricated.
[2] *Ibid.*, p. 77, for full page, rubricated.

interim in Gering's management took charge of the press.[1]
They used also two other gothic fonts.[2] In the Paris Missal,
which was printed by Gering and Rembolt for Simon Vostre
in 1497, some fine woodcuts were introduced;[3] and the initials used by them are also of considerable decorative value.[4]
In the last year of the century this office was still effective
and prosperous. Ulrich Gering has always been popularly
considered the patriarch of Parisian typography.

Now that the history of the first Paris press has been
traced, I shall keep more closely to the types themselves.
The first French types were, as we know, roman. These
were transitional roman letters, but after a few years they
gave way to gothic, for the popular taste was entirely for
gothic forms such as were used in the *Missale Parisiense*
printed by Jean du Pré in 1479.[5] A few fonts of roman
letters, modelled on the Italian letter, appeared in French
publications at the very end of the fifteenth century. For the
more stately liturgical books gothic type was of a pointed
character — the real *lettre de forme*.[6] For other books the
rounder *lettre de somme* was employed. But the characteristic form of French gothic letter used by French printers
up to 1500 was the *lettre batarde*,[7] first brought out by Pas-

[1] Claudin, I, p. 98.   [2] *Ibid.*, pp. 99–102.   [3] *Ibid.*, pp. 105–107.
[4] *Ibid.*, pp. 112–117.   [5] *Ibid.*, p. 211.

[6] In writing *de forme* each letter was formed separately and complete. This
was the writing to be taken as a model or form; or, according to the sixteenth century expression used by Geofroy Tory, as "canon." Mores says,
"The curious Mons. Torin (Tory) . . . divides typographical letter into *la
lettre de forme* and *la lettre bastarde;* the former of which he tells us was
called Canon. The inference is that the former were cut *secundum normam,*
the latter by no rule at all." Mores's *Dissertation*, etc., p. 21.

[7] *Batarde* — called *bastardella* or *bastarda* in Spain, and anciently called in
France *escritura italienne bastarda à la française* — was named so because
it was composed of elements of various sorts of writing. It is really derived
from the Italian chancery-hand, and the writing-books of Palatino and others
show its various forms.

ne honte que les grecz lui auoïet faitte.
les greiois qui moult furent couroucïez
de ceste chose sesmeurent et bindrent
assieger trope. a ce siege qui .r.ans du
ra furent occiz tous les filz au roy pri
ant. mais que bng appellé elenus il et
la royne ecuba sa femme. la cite fut ar
se et desruicte le peuple et les barons
occis.mais aucuns eschapperent de ceste
pestilence et plusieurs des princes sespã
sirent en plusieurs et diuerses parteis
du mõde pour querre nouuelles habita
cions cõme elenus encas anthenoret

Ce premier chappitre parle cõ
ment les francois descendirẽt
des troyens.

Batre cens et qua
tre ans auant que
Romme fust fõdee
regna priant en
trope la grant. il
enuoia paris laisne
de ses filz en grece
pour rauoir la royne helaine la femme
au roy Menelaus pour soy bengier du

36. Lettre Bâtarde used in first book printed in French: Bonhomme, Paris, c. 1477

La pfeffion de frere oliuier maillard.

OÛte psõne qui deƒire eƒtre ƒauluee de neceƒſite pʒient quelle ƒoit en la grace de dieu, car ſans elle nul ne puet eƒtre ſaulue. Ceƒte grace eƒt cõme vne cite qui ſaulue tous ceulx qui ſõt en peril de leurs ennemis qui voulent ſe reduire a elle ꝗ Lon y entre p̃ deux poztes. La pʒemiere eƒt le bapteſme, et eƒt bien ayſe a entrer en my la dicte cite, car ſans faire mille peine exterio relon puet eƒtre baptiſe et auoir la grace de dieu en faiſant trois fermenes et pʒomeſſes. Ceƒt que lon renõcie au diable ꞇ a tout peche moztel, et que lon croye les articles de la foy et que lon vueille garder les cõmandemẽs de la loy. Mais que lon garde ces trois pʒomeſſes et que lon ſoit baptiſe : ſans nulle doubte lon demoura en la grace de dieu. Mais pource ꝙ bien peu en y a qui gardent les pʒomeſſes fai ctes en bapteſme, par quoy ilz ſont deʒectes de la cite de grace. et ſont en danger deƒtre prins de ennemis iſernaulx. Jl a pleu a la

ce a coulpe du pechie moztel elle peche moʒ tellemẽt cõ il eƒt eſcript en la huittieme ꞇ tier ce diſtiõ au chapitre. Qui p̃deƒt, et au cha pitre error cui nõ reſiſtif approbat' ſelon Jn nocent cõme par exẽple ſe le pere ou la mere veoiẽt a leur enſant faire aucũ pechie moztel et ilz ne le corrigẽt quãt ilz le peuuẽt biẽ faire ilz pechẽt moztellemẽt et auſſi doit entẽdre de tous ceulx ꞇ celles qui ont auctorite ꞇ puiſ ſance de coʒriger les manuaiſtics de leurs ſub gets; ꞇ ne le ſont la ou ilz le peuẽt biẽ faire ilz pechent moztellement. Et cecy eƒt quant aux oeuuʒes faictes pʒe ſon pʒochain.
Ainſi ſont acõplies neuf reigles, par leſquel le lon peut facillemẽt cognoiſtre tout peche moztel. Jmpʒimees a pʒis on colliege de nar boune. En lan mil quatrecens quatre vingtz vñg Le vigtieſme iour de Nouẽbʒe.

a.i

37. Condensed Gothic Type used by Bötticher, Paris, 1481

quier Bonhomme. This was entirely different from the gothic types used up to that time, and imitated French cursive Gothic manuscripts of that day. It is a charming type, characteristically French—nervous and spirited. At first introduced in rather a crude form, it developed into a beautiful letter, principally, if not always, used for the printing of French. It was in type of this family that the first book in French printed at Paris, viz., *Croniques de France*, was produced by Bonhomme about 1477 (*fig.* 36). Like other early types it was derived from a literary hand, founded on a cursive legal script which was used in the north of France and in some parts of the Netherlands contiguous thereto.[1]

Besides these characteristically French types, fonts of which to-day form part of the equipment of some French printing-offices, condensed gothic types were employed in certain books in small *format* printed at Paris. The first of these appeared in 1481 — *La Confession de frère Olivier Maillard* (*fig.* 37). Gothic type was used with roman capitals,[2] and other fonts appear that are reminiscent of Italian and Flemish models. There was also a difference in the kind of gothic type employed for Latin and French books, the former being printed in the pointed gothic character, and the latter in various forms of *batarde*— following in this use the manuscripts which preceded printing. Some fonts, the provenance of which is puzzling, we find were imported from Basle, from Nuremberg, or elsewhere.

Placed on the first page of French books of this period were inscriptions, cut on wood, in very large letters (usually imitative of calligraphy), of a round or pointed Gothic form. These and calligraphic initials, adorned with masks

[1] Thompson, fac. 196.
[2] Claudin, I, pl. facing p. 200.

or grotesque heads—such as that used in the well-known
Mer des Hystoires of 1487[1]—were characteristic of popular
French book-making. A particular feature of the French
press of the fifteenth century was the exquisite manner in
which type and decorations were harmonized and combined.
The work produced by Le Rouge, Pigouchet, Vérard, Du
Pré, Vostre, and Tory shows a delicacy of execution and
refinement of taste not hitherto apparent. It was in the
Books of Hours produced by this group of men, says Pollard, "that the genius of French printers first strikingly
evinced itself. For more than a century the decoration of
manuscript *Horæ* had invited all the skill of the finest illuminators of Europe, and it was in France alone that the
attempt was successfully made to rival the glories of the
scribe and painter by those of the printer and engraver.
The names of Antoine Vérard, Philippe Pigouchet, and
Simon Vostre, as printers and publishers, are inseparably
connected with these Books of Hours, which for some
quarter of a century from 1488 onward constitute the
chief glories of the French press. More than 300 editions
were issued altogether, in which some forty different printers had a share, Jean du Pré at the beginning of the series,
and Geoffroy Tory, as late as 1525, being the most important after the three already named" (*fig.* 38).

The use of roman type in the French printing-houses of
the fifteenth century was slight, after the first essay in it by
the Sorbonne press. It is only toward the very end of the
century that the roman letter is again employed, generally in
editions of the classics, though Kerver and Tory later used
it for Books of Hours. With roman lower-case types, roman
capital letters, floriated and ornamented, were combined—
as in the work of the second Paris press of César and Stoll.

[1] Claudin, I, p. 459.

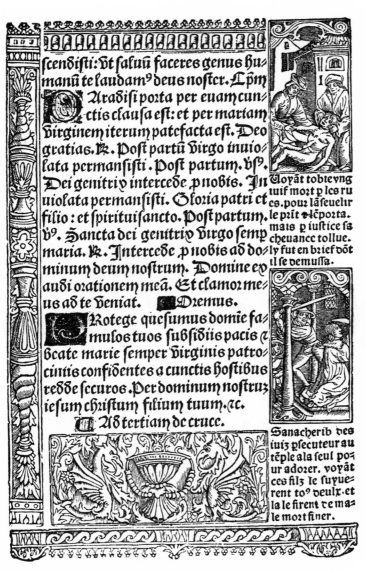

scendisti:vt salvũ faceres genus hu-
manũ te laudam⁹ deus noster. Cpm
Aradisi porta per euam cunctis clausa est: et per mariam
virginem iterum patefacta est. Deo
gratias.℟. Post partũ virgo inuio-
lata permansisti. Post partum. vs⁹.
Dei genitrix intercede p nobis. Jn
uiolata permansisti. Gloria patri et
filio : et spiritui sancto. Post partum.
vs⁹. Sancta dei genitrix virgo semp
maria. ℟. Jntercede p nobis ad dominum deum nostrum. Domine ex
audi orationem meã. Et clamor meus ad te veniat.   Dremus.
Rotege quesumus domie fa-
mulos tuos subsidiis pacis z
beate marie semper virginis patro-
ciniis confidentes a cunctis hostibus
redde securos.Per dominum nostrũ
iesum christum filium tuum.zc.
Ad tertiam de cruce.

Voyãt tobie vng
tuif mort p les ru
es.pour lã seuelir
le prit z lẽporta.
mais p iustice sa
cheuance tollue.
ly fut en brief dõt
il se demussa.

Sanacherib des
iuiz psecuteur au
tẽple ala seul po-
ur adorer. voyãt
ces filz le suyue-
rent to⁹ deulx.et
la le firent re ma-
le mort finer.

38. *Page from Book of Hours in Transitional style*

Longo ſufflamie:id eſt longo ambitu litis. ¶ Coranum:hunc ponit pro eo qui captatur æmulatione Horatii. Horatius: Captatorꝗ dabit riſus naſica corano. Corani alterius meminit Martialis:ſed hic pro eo tantum qui captatur. ¶ Mere tem æra caſtrorum:id eſt qui locupletatur ſtipendiis:laudat legem ꝗ ſcilicet bo- na caſtrenſia ſint tantum filioruꝫ. ¶ Torquibus:torques militares erant ſumpto

Aſt illis quos arma tegunt:& balteus ambit.

Quod placitum eſt illis præſtatur tpũs agẽdi:

Nec res atteritur longo ſufflamine litis.

Solis præterea teſtandi militibus ius

Viuo patre datur:nam quæ ſunt parta labore

Militiæ:placuit non eſſe in corpore cenſus:

Omne tenet cuius regimen pater:ergo coranũ

Signorum comitem:caſtrorũꝗ æra merentem

Quãuis iã treul?captat pater:hũc labor æquꝰ

Prouehit:& pulchro reddit ſua dona labori

Ipſius certe ducis hæc referre uidentur:

Vt qui fortis erit:ſit fœliciſſimus idem:

Vt læti phaleris omnes:& torquibus omnes.

more a gallis: unde tor- quati. Strabo in decimo ita ſcribit: ſimilia ſunt & quæ apud Thraces cele- brãtur: Quæ cocytia & mendidia dicũtur: apud quos & orphica initium habuerũt. ipam ſane Co cyn : quæ apud edonios colitur:& eius inſtrumẽ ta memorat Aeſchylus. Hic manibus bombicã tornatam tenens digitis tactilẽ modulos implet. Quo ex loco planũ eſt Aeſchilũ appellaſſe Ce- rerem Cocyn:quam Iu- uenalis Cocyto dixit.nã ut teſtimõio Ouidii do cuimus coniuncta erant Cereris cum Baccho ſa- cra.cocytia ſacra comme morat etiam Porphyrio.

Iunii Iuuenalis Aquinatis Satyrarũ libri impreſſi Lugduni diligentiſſime arte & in- genio Iohãnis de Prato. Anno chriſti.M. cccc.lxxxx.ſecunda die Decembris:

39. *First Roman Type used at Lyons: Du Pré*, 1490

The effect of their quaint forms is less disagreeable than one would suppose.[1]

Lyons was scarcely inferior to Paris in the number of its printing-houses. By its situation it was one of the centres of fifteenth century commerce, and fairs were held there frequented by purchasers from all parts of Europe. The Lyons printing trade was more prosperous, because less restricted, than in Paris, where the theological censorship in particular became extremely active. The products of the Lyons press, which produced popular literature — poetry, histories of chivalry, etc. — show some interesting variations in French typography. In general the same types are used as at Paris, but the type-setting seems rougher and perhaps freer in execution. Many Lyons books were executed in a *lettre de forme* which recalls the products of early Netherlands printers.

Guillaume Le Roy was the first Lyons printer. His patron was Barthélemy Buyer, to whom he held somewhat the same relation that the first Paris printers did to Fichet and Heynlin. Le Roy's first book, the *Compendium Breve* of the Cardinal-Deacon Lothaire, issued in 1473, was executed in a heavy, roughly cast gothic type, just mentioned as recalling that of the Netherlands. He also employed a round gothic font, identical with that used by Wendelin de Spire at Venice in 1473, for his *Miroir de Vie Humaine* of 1477. Lyons had the credit of producing the first illustrated book printed in France, *Le Mirouer de la Rédemption*, printed there in 1478 by Martin Husz or Huss.[2] The woodcuts for this book came from Basle, and so, in point of fact, did the types. If Lyons printing seems puzzling because of the fre-

[1] Claudin, I, pp. 124, 131.
[2] *Ibid.*, III, pp. 159–164.

quent resemblance of its types to those of other countries, the reason is, that types of other countries were so often employed! Some Lyons fonts can be traced to Nuremberg, others to Basle,[1] to Vienna, and to Venice,[2] for Venetian types had begun to have wide vogue. Besides these fonts, the foreign origin of which is known, there are others evidently of Italian origin or design.[3]

One of the finest Lyons books produced in *lettres de forme* was the *Missale secundum usum Lugduni* of Neumeister, of 1487.[4] Neumeister employed magnificent pointed gothic types, and his Lyons Missal recalls in many ways Gutenberg's work; quite apart from the fact that he actually came from Mainz to France by the invitation of Cardinal Amboise, and was traditionally Gutenberg's pupil and companion. This Missal was almost equalled by that printed by Hongre in 1500, in a most Italian and also most imposing character, though not especially typical of the French press.[5]

Besides pointed gothic or *lettre de forme*, there were in use at Lyons, as we have just seen, some round gothic fonts. When Lyons printers wished to employ such type, they seem to have turned to the Italian form of gothic letter for their models, or else they actually procured it from Italy. Proctor believes that there existed in the fifteenth century, independent of Venetian printers, some Venetian typefoundries, where types not only could be bought, but also could be hired. This transfer of the types of one country to the workshops of another, by purchase or otherwise, is

[1] Claudin, III, pp. 166, 167.
[2] *Ibid.*, facing p. 194, and pp. 195, 196, 215.   [3] *Ibid.*, p. 219.
[4] *Ibid.*, p. 360 and facing plate, p. 361, plates between pp. 366 and 367, and plate facing p. 368.
[5] *Ibid.*, pp. 344, 345.

a puzzling feature in any attempt to identify types geographically.

The *lettre batarde*, the characteristic French gothic letter used in Paris, was also common in Lyons, but, as a rule, in a rougher and less attractive form. Examples of the use of this heavier form of it may be seen in the work of Mathieu Husz and of Du Pré. The latter's Lyons edition of *La Mer des Hystoires* shows pages in this massive character which are splendid in effect,[1] especially when used in connection with such sumptuous woodcuts as those of the Baptism of Clovis and the Battle of Tolbiac.[2] A very decorative pillar which appears in the centre of this plate forms an ingenious division between its two subjects.[3]

Many of these Lyons books were arranged with a line of large, round, Italian gothic type at the head of the page; types several sizes smaller forming the text. Large calligraphic initials were also features of the Lyons press; and square initials engraved on wood, with black backgrounds (such as were used by Le Masson and his associates), added brilliancy to somewhat heavy typography.[4] As the end of the century approached, the popularity of Venetian types increased more and more — a fact which foreshadowed some of the tribulations of Aldus, who, in the next century, found no more unscrupulous imitators of his italic type than Lyons printers. Roman characters were not used in Lyons until 1490, Jean du Pré employing them in his annotated Latin text of the *Satires* of Juvenal, issued in the last month of that year. Proctor thinks these types have a

---

[1] Claudin, III, pp. 495, 496.

[2] *Ibid.*, p. 498.

[3] For a comparison of Le Rouge's Paris edition of this same book, see Claudin, I, pp. 459–463.

[4] Claudin, III, pp. 232, 233.

Gothic look. They appear to be a very fine form of a transitional roman character (*fig.* 39).

French fifteenth century types may be roughly classed as:
  i transitional roman;
  ii pure roman on Italian models;
  iii pointed gothic or *lettre de forme;*
  iv round gothic or *lettre de somme;*
  v contemporary manuscript gothic letter or *lettre batarde;*
  vi gothic fonts showing foreign influence, sometimes of foreign source.

Of all these French gothic types, the characteristically national or vernacular letter was the *lettre batarde,* derived from contemporary French manuscripts. Other gothic types employed are sometimes akin to those of other countries, but the *lettre batarde* is distinctly French. In fineness of cut and spirited delicacy of design — when at its best — it produces a beautiful effect, especially when used with the decorations so cleverly designed to accompany it.

As a whole, French printing was more delicate and distinguished, but less virile, than that of Germany or Italy. The Gallic feeling shows itself in the best fifteenth century French books, in a certain brilliance and elegance which is purely French. Less archaic than the German, less monumental than the Italian, the work of the best early French printers, like so much else that is French, is charming.[1]

---

[1] For a survey of early French types, I recommend the student to the facsimiles in Thierry-Poux's *Premiers Monuments de l' Imprimerie en France au XVe Siècle.* Paris, 1890.

CHAPTER VII

TYPE AND TYPE-FORMS OF THE FIFTEENTH CENTURY IN THE NETHERLANDS — HOLLAND AND BELGIUM

THE year from which Dutch printing is usually officially dated is 1473, but some sort of printing was done in Holland before that time. The name of the printer of the *Speculum Salvationis*, which is probably the work of the earliest Dutch press, is not known. The first Dutch books of which we have any knowledge, which may be called "Costeriana" (*i.e.*, the editions of Coster and his successors), or which may be attributed to the printer of the *Speculum*, were executed from rough gothic types of the kind known as *lettres de forme*. There is in Holtrop's *Monuments Typographiques* a series of plates[1] of type-pages which throw a great deal of light, not alone on printing in the Low Countries, but on the whole subject of its beginnings. These show that the first books were roughly executed in a heavy, black, and awkward *lettre de forme*. On glancing through these plates — for it is impossible, owing to their rarity, to look at the originals — one realizes what Blades meant in his allusions to the crude school of printing which preceded that of Gutenberg. If we examine the facsimile of a Donatus printed with the types of the *Abecedarium*,[2] is it conceivable that the printer of this book could have known anything about the exact methods of making type, or of printing with it, which Mainz printers so well understood? The *Abecedarium* formerly in the possession

[1] Holtrop's *Monuments Typographiques des Pays-Bas au Quinzième Siècle*. La Haye, 1868. Twelve plates beginning 11 [3]; *i.e.*, plate 11 in sequence in the bound book, but plate 3 in sequence of original issue. The references are confusing unless this is remembered, for the plates *as bound* have no consecutive folios.

[2] Holtrop, pl. 11 [3].

of the Enschedés at Haarlem (*fig.* 40)—what a wretched little book it is! how primary in every sense! While the fragments of other Donatuses are considerably better, the uneven ending of lines, which indicates that no composing-rule was used at the time, is obvious in the facsimiles of the Donatus of 28 lines,[1] and in the *Voyage de Jean de Manda-ville.*[2] As to the four editions of the *Speculum*,[3] these books, rather ambitious from a decorative point of view, call for better typography than that which accompanies their illustrations.[4] Although some impressions are better than others, these plates show printing as an art in its infancy, and hold out very little prospect of its ever growing up! The *Speculum* may have been executed at Utrecht some time between 1471 and 1473. The other fragments of which Holtrop shows facsimiles are those of books or editions brought out before the latter year, perhaps all from one printing-office, perhaps from different printers.[5] In these early fragments and a few complete books, about eight different fonts of type are found; and with these types perhaps eighty different editions were printed. The gothic types used in these books were the first models of the style of black-letter which we recognize as characteristic of the country (*fig.* 41).

But the *Speculum* and its mysterious companions are not the books from which Dutch printing is scientifically dated. Ketelaer and Leempt, who printed two books in Utrecht in 1473, were the first printers in Holland who dated their

---

[1] Holtrop, pl. 13 [49].   [2] *Ibid.*, pl. 121 [4].

[3] *Ibid.*, pls. 17 [19]–22 [1].

[4] The pictures were printed in brown ink, in one impression, and the type, which was of uneven height and indented the paper badly, at another printing. Two of the four copies are in Dutch prose, two in Latin verse. Some turned letters in the text show that it is printed from movable types, and is not a block-book.

[5] Holtrop, pls. 24 [37]–33 [97].

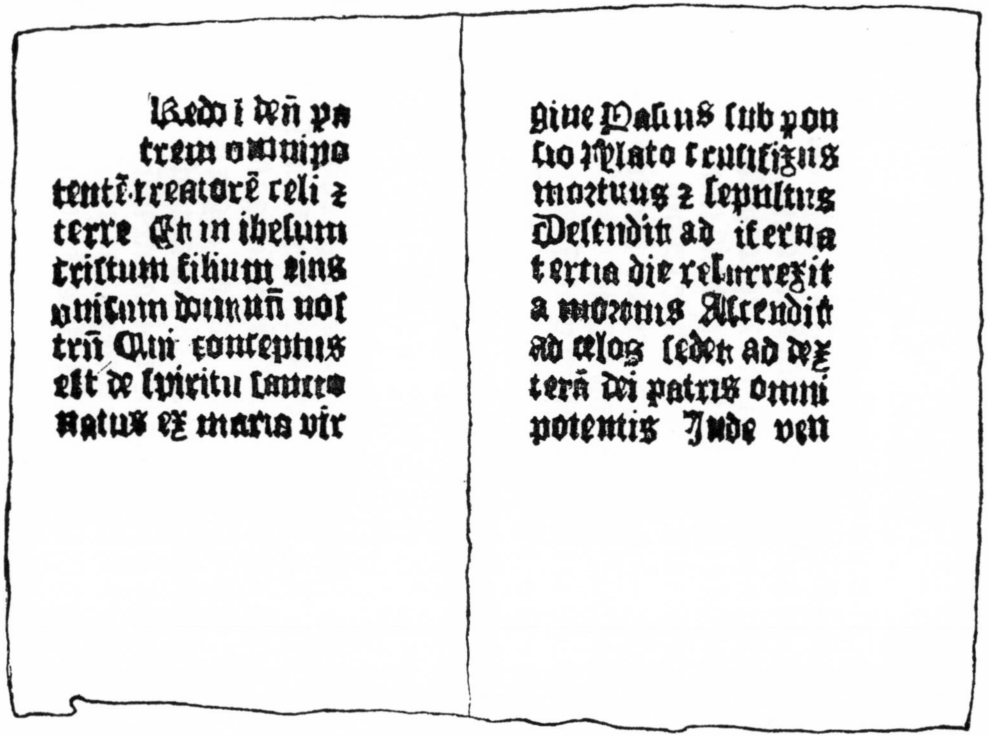

40. *Two pages of an Abecedarium*

Hec preter p vi deo pteris exdpe pradi
P canlus fu iGgr neutro paffma fecund
D as deo di l fu gcmiṇas ve fupia dat i fu
S it fewo feffum reddit tamē ff gcminatu
G audeo gauifu pbet wlt regula gaufum
P cetriês i vi dat iwi nullu ve fupiũ
S i fadt l ut r ante geo ri littera longa
V el dypṛōg? hab3 p vi geo cetera format
P rebet vi nullu fi p fu:ricp fadt dum
D ic tamē indultu f3 prcenê vegeo nullu
-A ddita muta leo fadt eui vicp fadt tum
S ic leo fic oleo de fe fadt omne creatũ
E ĝ quandocp tamē olui reperitur itumcp
E x oleo p vi venifcia die z i eui
E tum z itum dicns adolere p vltu
D uplex pter itu reddit duplexcp fepinu
H inc et adultus erit
I unctacp muta leo patcs hic oleocp leocp
C etera verba leo p vi fadt abfcp fupino
S ed oleo dat itum foleo valeocp fupinu
S i queo fumcp fadt tu in tu placp reddit
D at deo vi p tum pi format vbicp fupinu
E x vi nil remoues facis tu nil fupadfs
E xdpe pas ca fa fe la fol vol ag cog z a fe
D at cauueo cautu faueo fautu fed amiau
E x amicie fadt foluo ul uoluo dat utu
D e fewo fume fatu lauo lotu paftoz paftu
A g ul cognfco dat itum fepelice fepultu .
érifeo vi dat fiue bui conniueo vi ri
D i tum dante preis vocalis nō breuiata
Q ui fi d fa li I demeutur z ide creata
De deo dcp geo leo ul queo l neo dictu

41. *Gothic Type used by Printer of the Speculum, c.* 1471
From Doctrinale of Alexander Gallus

books. Pollard, in his series of valuable introductory notes to the national divisions of his Catalogue of the Hawkins Collection, says: "From 1473 onwards, the history of printing in Holland is normal and straightforward, native and German printers being found working simultaneously in the usual way. Presses were set up in thirteen places after 1473,—in Deventer, Delft, and Gouda in 1477, in S. Martijnsdijk in Zeeland in 1478, in Nijmegen and Zwolle in 1479, in Hasselt in Overijssel in 1480, in Leiden, Kuilenburg, and Haarlem in 1488, in 's Hertogenbosch (Bois-leduc) in 1484, in Schoonhoven in 1485, and in Schiedam in 1498. Seven of these towns were only visited by a single printer. At Utrecht, Delft, Gouda, and Zwolle there was a moderate output. The only really prolific printers were Richard Paffraet and Jacobus de Breda at Deventer, who must have produced between them over five hundred incunabula, though most of these were small educational books. The total Dutch output at present registered may be roughly estimated at between eleven and twelve hundred, its characteristics being akin to those of Germany, but with a much greater proportion of schoolbooks, and strikingly few large folios."

"Printing was introduced into seven towns within the limits of modern Belgium in the fifteenth century," says Mr. Pollard in the same volume, "into Alost in 1473; the next year into Louvain, where much excellent work was done by Johann of Paderborn; into Bruges, by Caxton and Colard Mansion, probably in 1475; into Brussels, by the Brothers of the Common Life, in March of the same year. After a long interval printing began at Audenarde in 1480, and at Antwerp a year later still, the rear being brought up by Ghent in April, 1483. Gerard Leeu's work gave distinction to Antwerp as that of Johann of Paderborn did to Louvain, and these two cities between them account for over two-thirds of the registered output of 'Belgian' incunabula, the total of which is probably somewhat under a thousand. Belgium in the fifteenth century had, of course, no separate existence, nor were the boundaries of Holland those of the modern kingdom. It may be noted, however, that in the 'Belgian' books there is a much greater preponderance of Latin than in the Dutch, though a few printers were tri-lingual, printing in Flemish, French, and Latin."

The Netherlands fifteenth century types were chiefly, as has been said, crude *lettres de forme*,[1] but later they became more refined. A few types showed the influence of the ro-man letter, but pure roman letter was as yet rare. The *lettre batarde* of France appears in Holland, uncouth, irregular, badly aligned, badly fitted on its body, awkward in cut,[2] al-though employed in 1480 by Veldener, who was one of the most distinguished printers of the Netherlands. Thierry Martens of Alost and Antwerp, the first Belgian printer, em-ployed that fine familiar type, the round Italian gothic.[3]

Three black-letter types used in the Netherlands are interesting. The first is the bold, coarse *batarde* character used by Colard Mansion at Bruges (*fig.* 42). Mansion employed two kinds of type, a *batarde*, and a sort of very rough transitional *lettre de forme* (though sometimes called *lettre de somme*), which he used in 1477.[4] His *batarde* was merely an imitation of the Burgundian writing of the period. It was to Dutch printing just what a *lettre batarde* was to French printing — a sort of vernacular type, dependent for its form upon the locality in which it was found, and found there simply because based on the writing which preceded it in that neighbourhood. The earliest of Mansion's impres-

[1] Holtrop, pl. 125 [30].   [2] *Ibid.*, pl. 40 [24].
[3] *Ibid.*, pl. 46 [6].   [4] *Ibid.*, pl. 60, *c* [131].

¶ Du dieu esaulapius et de
sa figure

Esaulapius le dieu de
medecine doit estre fi
gure et paint en guise de vn
homme aiant longue barbe
laquele il atouchoit de sa des
tre main . Et en sa senestre
tenoit vn baston entour du
quel estoit entorteillie vn
serpent: sicomme il sera cy a
pres declairie ou il cherra a
point . Ces choses ainsi
premises il est temps de co̅
mencier ou premier liure de
nostre acteur ouide . Et pre
mierement aux tables de
chascun liure

42. *Mansion's Ancienne Batarde, Bruges,* 1484

Este Brieue doctrine est ordonnee
pour quatre manieres de pson
nes. Premierement pour les
simples curez prestres qui se
meslent de oyr confessions.
Item pour les simples personnes autres.
soyent seculiers, ou religieus qui noyent

Explicit feliciter.

Aspice presentis scripture gracia que sit
Confer opus opere. spectetur codice codex
Respice q mun de. q terse. q q decore
Imprimit hec ciuis Brugesis Brito Johannes
Inuenies artem nullo monstrate miradam
Instrumeta quoqz non minus laude stupeda

43. *Lettre Batarde used by Brito, Bruges*

is gemeyn in allen drogē malaetſcappē
meer dā in die vuchte ēñ vlieten roo-
len der meeſter vingherē en traechlic
voorſi groot met als ſi coemt ſo maect
ſi cloeuinge en kenninge en dat witghe
togen bloet is vā donckere veruen en
voorſchier ghecoaguleert en hoe dat-
ment meer wrijft hoe dattet ſwarter en
harder woor en midzen ſijn daer oft wit
te zeenken waren of telgeren vā zenen
en dat is ghemeyn in alle malaetſcheit
Jtem die malaetſcap coemt van meni-
gerhande ſaken behaluē den voorſcre-
uen ſaken als vā medewoningen ende
mede etinge der malaetſcher en datter
een mēdighe dicwile mede ſpreect en vā
dert want het is een leuende ſuuct en
de venijnt die gene die daer bi ſijn ende

ſubſtācie der leden corrūpeerde van de-
ſen en vā menigen anderē ſakē wert eē
menſch wel malaetſch mē mach te qua
liken geneſen dan mitter godliker hant
na dien dat ſi volcomelic ge confirmeert
is nochtans mach menſe lappē en boe
ten dz ſi traechliker coemt Item die ſie
ke ſal hem wachten van ſpiſen die hem
deerlic ſijn en te voorſten vā ſpiſen dye
ſwarte colera maken en van ſpiſen dye
heet bloet maken Ēn men ſal hē goede
en bequaem dpete ordineren en dz hat
telic gecorrumpeert of diſeert en wort
Is daer bloet mē ſaken als allopicia ſo
ſal men eerſt bloet laten daer na medecijn nemen die ſuuerende is Jnden an-
deren ſal farmacia dat is coppenſetten
medecijn voer gaen daer na iſt noot ſal

44. *Black-letter used by Bellaert, Haarlem, 1485*

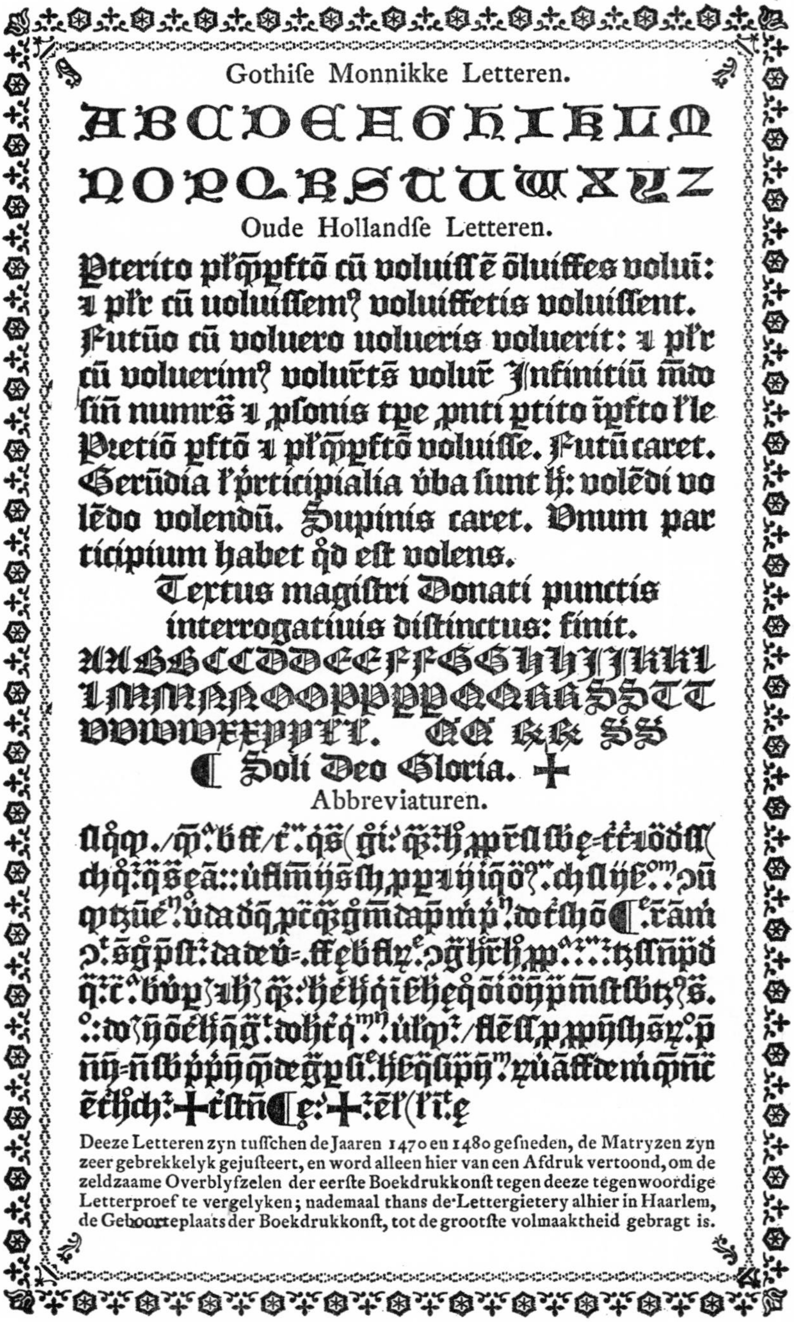
Gothiſe Monnikke Letteren.

ABCDEFGHIKLM
NOPQRSTUVWXYZ

Oude Hollandſe Letteren.

Pterito plq̄ppfcō cū voluiſſē ōluiſſes volui: ⁊ plr cū uoluiſſem⁊ voluiſſetis voluiſſent. Futūo cū voluero uolueris voluerit: ⁊ plr cū voluerim⁊ volurtš volur Infinitiū mō ſiñ numrš ⁊ pſonis tpe pnti ptito ipfto l'le Pretiō pftō ⁊ plq̄ppftō voluiſſe. Futū caret. Gerūdia l'prticipialia vba ſunt h̄: volēdi vo lēdo volendū. Supinis caret. Unum par ticipium habet q̄d eſt volens.

Textus magiſtri Donati punctis
interrogatiuis diſtinctus: finit.

AABBCCDDEEFFGGHHIJKKL
LMMNNOOPPPPQQRRSSTT
VVWWXXYYZZ. ÆÆ KK SS

Soli Deo Gloria. ✝

Abbreviaturen.

Deeze Letteren zyn tuſſchen de Jaaren 1470 en 1480 geſneden, de Matryzen zyn zeer gebrekkelyk gejuſteert, en word alleen hier van een Afdruk vertoond, om de zeldzaame Overblyfzelen der eerſte Boekdrukkonſt tegen deeze tegenwoordige Letterproef te vergelyken; nademaal thans de Lettergietery alhier in Haarlem, de Geboorteplaats der Boekdrukkonſt, tot de grootſte volmaaktheid gebragt is.

45. *Fifteenth Century Saint Augustin Flamand: Enschedé's Proef van Letteren, Haarlem*, 1768

sions show lines which were not spaced out to the full width of the page. This is one argument for the independence of the Netherlands and Bruges school of typography from that of Mainz; for it cannot be believed that if a man like Mansion knew how to use a composing rule (as he must have known, had he ever been in touch with Mainz printers), he would have abandoned it. He began to print before 1476, and it was only in 1478 that properly spaced lines appear.

The second type to which attention should be paid is that used by Brito at Bruges, and perhaps cast by him, and later by William de Machlinia at London. This type-form somewhat resembles the types used by Caxton. It is another rough form of the *batarde* letter, but without the charm of the French *lettre batarde* (*fig.* 43).

A third type to be remembered is the font used by Bellaert, to which the English black-letter types, which later became the national English face and size of letter, bear a close resemblance (*fig.* 44).

There is a very interesting Dutch gothic type shown in the specimen-book of 1768 issued by Enschedé, the celebrated Dutch founder, which it is believed was engraved about the end of the fifteenth century—between 1470 and 1480—a *St. Augustin flamand* (*fig.* 45). It was probably cut by a Dutch printer and type-cutter, Henric of Delft, who called himself, in the colophons to his works, *letter-snider*, or graver of characters, and who furnished types to several printers. We have records of this font being employed in Paris printing-offices. A letter much the same in cut, of *gros-romain* size, may also be seen on the last page of Enschedé's specimen of 1768 (*fig.* 46).

As for fifteenth century roman fonts in the Low Countries, John of Westphalia, at Louvain, employed a very dis-

tinguished roman letter, Italian in effect, and evidently derived from an Italian source (*fig.* 47). Another roman font
which is of interest, with a charming quality of pen-work
about it, is the *St. Augustin romain*, considered by Enschedé
as older even than the Flemish character cut by Henric the
letter-snider. The man from whom Enschedé bought it in
1768, Jacques Scheffers (a printer at Bois-le-Duc, where
his ancestors had practised their trade for a long time), was,
according to tradition, a descendant of Peter Schoeffer of
Gernsheim. Enschedé, when he bought some sixty matrices
from Scheffers, purchased a copy of a book printed by
Schoeffer himself; and believed that these punches actually
came from Peter Schoeffer. This point cannot be decided;
but the types have great charm. In recent years the Messrs.
Enschedé completed the defective font, some missing letters
being obtained by adding to or subtracting from existing
characters, and when this was not feasible, a few new letters
being cut in the style of the old ones.[1] Our plate shows this
reconstitution of the font (*fig.* 48).

The output of the fifteenth century Netherlands press is
historically interesting, but artistically monotonous. It is difficult to be enthusiastic over these fonts, which contrast
unfavourably with better types of similar style in other
countries. But their historical interest is indubitable. They
form a link between the Continent and England, and are
the starting-point of English typography.

[1] See Ch. Enschedé's *Fonderies de Caractères et leur Matériel dans les Pays-
Bas du XVe au XIXe siècle*, Haarlem, 1908, pp. 30, 31, and 32. For a survey of fifteenth century Dutch types this work will be found of great value.

𝔄 𝔄 𝔄 𝔄 𝔅 𝔅 ℭ ℭ 𝔇 𝔇 𝔈 𝔈
𝔉 𝔉 𝔊 𝔊 𝔥 𝔥 𝔍 𝔍 𝔎 𝔎 𝔏 𝔏
𝔐 𝔐 𝔑 𝔑 𝔒 𝔒 𝔓 𝔓 𝔔 𝔔 𝔯 𝔯
𝔖 𝔖 𝔗 𝔗 𝔘 𝔘 𝔚 𝔚 𝔛 𝔛 𝔜 𝔜

Oude Hollandfe Letteren, van 1470 à 1480.

℧ Dit is die ploghe vand fpeghel
onfer behoudeniffe· ✠

Ꞩ wie ter rechtuaerdichet ve
Ꞩ le mēfchē leren felle blenckē
alfe fterrē in die ewighe ewic
heden· Hier om ift dat ic totter leri
ghe vele mēfchē dit boeck heb aēge
dacht te vgaderē Indē welkē die ghe
ne diet lefen leringhe gheuē en ötfan
ghē fellen· Jc vmoede dat gheen dinc
dē mēfche nutter is in defē teghēwo
erdighe leuē·dan te bekeñē fŷn fce
pr fŷ condicie eñ epghe wefen·✠

𝔄 𝔅 ℭ 𝔇 𝔈 𝔉 𝔊 𝔥 𝔍 𝔎 𝔏 𝔐 𝔑 𝔒
𝔓 𝔔 𝔯 𝔖 𝔗 𝔘 𝔚 𝔜 𝔯 ✠

Abbreviatuuren.

℧ pp ā̃p̃ p̃c̃h̃ dꝛ ll̃ tꝛ ꝛ a fiñh̃ ll̃ r̃q̃ ll̃ h̃g̃ dēm
ph / ēh̃ūm̃ tōp̃ d̃ŵ ēꝓ̃ñ ? ꝓd̃ꝼ : ōꝓ̃ ꞓ̃uñ̃ꝓ
q̃ ā āñq̃ / ꝙ̃ h̃ ꝓ̃ h̃ꝓ̃ ꝗ̃ : · ꝓꝓ ꝛ h̃ñ̃ꝗq̃ ~ : ꞵ̃ ✠

Deeze Letteren, en voornaamenlyk de Matryzen,
zyn ongemeen raar en zeldzaam.

46. *Fifteenth Century Gros-Romain Flamand: Enschedé's*
Proef van Letteren, Haarlem, 1768

Regraciatoria.& aliquid de studiis hūanitatis.

Eneas siluius.Salutem plurimam dicit.Magnifico& gene-
roso comiti.galeazio de archo.Aggressus est me nudiust-
ertius uir suauis.& tui amātissimus,iacobus ledroneus mi
les.tuasqg & magnifici germani tui comitis francisci litteras aperu
itque magno mihi testimonio fuerunt amoris:erga me uestri: cū
in utrisqg.multa salute iussus me esset iacobus impertiri.Quod &si
perfuasum ante mihi esset:quia noui animi uestri constancia.Iuuit
me tamen cernere.quod meditabar.Sed ne pluribus immorer.scr̃
uos uolo.non truncum a uobis coli:qui non sentit: neqg asinum q
non intelligit-sed hominem quātus pusillum: beneficioqg tamē me
morem& qui nunq animo est ingrato.Non est quod nunc scribam

47. *John of Westphalia's Roman Type, used at Louvain*

BERNARDVS NERLIVS PETRO MEDICAE LAVRENTII
FILIO .S.

Vm doctiffimorum hominum & horum grauiffimorum fen-
tentia: grecas litteras non folum latinis plurimum ornamenti
afferre: Sed etiam perneceffarias effe animaduerterem: omni
ftudio ac labore ad hec ftudia percipienda me conuerti. Sed cu
uiderem non nullos litterarum grecarum ftudiofos ob inopiaz
librorum magno affici icomodo: qd & ipfe una cum illis expiebar: operepre-
tium me facturum exiftimaui: fi eadem ratione tum horum tum mee incomo
ditati occurrerem: qua latinas litteras difcentibus iam pridem confultum effe
uidebam. Itaqz ut & de grecis litteris bene mererer: & earum ftudiofis aliquo
modo prodeffem: utqz alii copia librorum allecti: ad hec ftudia magis incitare
tur: decreui grecum aliquem auctorem: qui et apud eos nobiliffimus effet: &
nobis difcentibus perutilis foret: imprimendum fufcipere. Quod et fi arduuz
& perdifficile uidebatur: tamen cum ea que ad hoc opus conficiudu neceffaria
erant: in hac noftra ciuitate concurrerent: eiufmodi occafionem minime pre
termittendam putaui. Nam ut omittam Nerii fratris liberalitatez: & Ioannis
Accaioli auxilium: Demetriiqz Cretenfis dexteritatem: id inprimis mihi opor
tunum fuit: maximeqz optatum: quod ad hanc rem Demetrium Chalcondyle
Athenienfem nactus eram: Virum profecto tempeftate noftra doctiffimum:
preceptoremqz meum: a quo huiusmodi opus accuratiffime recognofci poffet.
Perdifficile enim mihi uidebatur fine eruditiffimo uiro id operis caftigatiffi-

48. *Fifteenth Century Roman Type attributed to Schoeffer*
(*as reconstituted by Enschedé*)

CHAPTER VIII

TYPE AND TYPE-FORMS OF THE FIFTEENTH CENTURY
IN SPAIN

ALTHOUGH Spanish typography has not had much influence on printing in other parts of Europe, it is both interesting and extremely individual. For the most part, the first printers both in Spain and Portugal were wandering Germans, who brought to the Iberian Peninsula, as they did to so many other parts of Europe, their knowledge of the new art. The introduction of printing was, however, rather late,—not until the year 1474,—and for that reason we do not find in either country, as Haebler[1] says, "those precursors of the typographic art—woodcuts accompanied by text more or less 'padded,' nor xylographic books, of which we find so many examples in Germany and the Netherlands." He adds that if Spanish books were sometimes rather archaic in appearance, this was due to unskilled workmen rather than to the state of the art when introduced in Spain; for typography, when brought there, was no longer in its experimental stage, but a developed industry. The Spaniards very early occupied themselves with this new trade, and established workshops quite independently of the German printers; but the first printer who came to Spain was of German or Flemish origin, and the printing-houses most distinguished for the excellence of their work were either actually directed by Germans or else inaugurated under a German master.

The chief output of the Spanish press was, as one might guess, theological, and the clergy played an important part in the propagation of typography. Besides missals and breviaries, of which no copies are extant, and which are known

[1] *Typographie Ibérique*, p. 1.

only from existing records, there were a very large number of liturgical books printed in Spain up to 1500, and an enormous production of forms for indulgences. Even so, in addition to these, similar books and documents were constantly procured from abroad — and for a long time continued to be — because there were not enough printing-houses in the Peninsula to produce them in sufficient quantities. As in other parts of the world, monasteries established printing-offices in their precincts, and some of the secular clergy were themselves printers; while among higher ecclesiastics there were many who bore the expense of printing their own works, or who paid the cost of printing the works of others. Haebler believes that more books were published by the aid of the clergy in Spain than in any other country where printing existed prior to the Reformation.

It has just been said that printing was introduced in Spain as a developed art; and it is for that reason that almost all Spanish books have "signatures"—a feature which appeared rather late in English typography. Initials engraved on wood are to be found in Spain almost as early as anywhere else. And, too, as did the Venetians, Spanish printers enjoyed "privileges" which protected their work. Indeed, Spanish printing-houses profited from almost all the advances made in typography in other lands. In the commerce of legal forms, multiplied by the help of printing, Spain was ahead of other nations.

"In spite of the fact that the masters [in printing] were all Germans . . . ," says Haebler, "it cannot be said that the style of their production showed their national origin. On the contrary, the productions of Spanish presses, from a very remote period, have something special about them. At a very early date a Spanish style was developed which is readily recognizable even in the production of men who were newcomers to Spain. For this reason, as we have said, the influence of a particular school of printing cannot be recognized in books printed in Spain. One finds types imitated from those employed by the printers of Venice, Basle, and Lyons, and other types which seem to have been used elsewhere. But it is very rare to find a Spanish book which one would suppose to have been printed anywhere else. I know of but one printer who worked in Spain with an outfit which was decidedly French, namely, Jean de Francour at Valladolid. But even he appears soon to have changed his fonts of type, and to have adopted others of a kind more in accord with Spanish taste.

"The Spanish had a marked predilection for gothic characters. The first books printed in Spain, it is true, are in roman characters, but the very master who executed them procured gothic fonts some years later, and employed them to the end of his career. If we were to count up the books printed in gothic characters and compare them with those in roman types, we should find that the majority printed in gothic is enormous. Nevertheless, it should be remembered that the number of roman fonts which, one by one, have been discovered in books printed in Spain, is quite considerable. It is of course true that only one of all the printing-houses of Spain produced books in quantity printed in roman types. This was the anonymous printer of Salamanca, and it is easy to explain this peculiarity: for that establishment was under the influence, perhaps actually under the direction, of Aelius Antonius Nebrissensis, who printed classical texts and his own commentaries on the writers of antiquity, following the lead of the Humanists of Italy. The books of the latter were commonly printed in roman characters (which were, on that account, called Italian), which accounts for the isolated fact that so many books in roman characters were printed in this particular city. In the rest of Spain books in Italian characters were uncommon. Almost all printing-houses of importance had one or two fonts of roman. But the number of books printed in those types was exceedingly small; and such fonts were rarely renewed; while gothic fonts (from the very beginning stocked in greater quantities) were renewed and revamped very frequently."[1]

This statement brings up an interesting point, *i.e.*, that in spite of the German origin of printers who came to work in Spain, their style soon became something characteristically Spanish. In looking through Spanish incunabula, one feels that it *is* a very special school of typography; rugged yet effective, and reminiscent, to one who knows Spain, of its rough, careless splendour, its grave, sad magnificence. The finest productions of the Spanish press before 1500 are scarcely second to the best contemporary work done in Germany and Italy, and this Spanish quality existed particularly, perhaps, in these incunabula. But it is also extremely apparent at the end of the eighteenth century in the production of the first modern Spanish type-cutters, who somehow, even when copying the ornaments of Baskerville and Caslon, and the types and decorations of Fournier, put into them a Spanish flavour which makes it quite clear that they are Spanish and can be nothing else.

[1] *Typographie Ibérique du Quinzième Siècle*, 1902, p. 2. Haebler's books on Spanish printing are the works most available to the European and English student. His *Typographie Ibérique du Quinzième Siècle* (in Spanish and French) —a work specially valuable for its facsimiles of almost all the types at present known to have been used in Spain and Portugal up to the year 1500— has a delightfully clear and complete, though brief, prefatory notice of the introduction of typography in the Peninsula. The same author's *Early Printers of Spain and Portugal* (Bibliographical Society's Monographs, No. IV, London, 1897) was written in English five years earlier. It is excellent, though not so comprehensive.

Proctor, in his *Early Printed Books in the British Museum*, takes up the cities in Spain in which printing was established from the date of its introduction at Valencia in 1474, to the last year of the fifteenth century; and in the notes describing the types of Spanish printers, he constantly alludes to the material of presses in other countries which these Spanish types recall. It is plain that many of the types *were* from foreign sources; and yet there are some which do not resemble any foreign types and seem to be of Spanish workmanship. These, it is to be supposed, were cut by the early printers, who were, as elsewhere at this period, type-cutters too. But even this does not wholly account for that particularly Spanish quality which crept into so much of the work of men from other nations, often using types derived from other countries. One can explain it only by the influence of Spanish manuscripts and the national school of writing in which they were executed, which were—as was printing—governed by the subtle influences emanating from the soil and skies of Spain itself—the ethos of a country to the last degree individual, which therefore showed itself very markedly even in work which would not appear capable of such impregnation. Many of these early German printers married Spanish women, and in a generation became completely merged in the land of their adoption. This was not an isolated instance of such Spanish assimilation. In the third quarter of the eighteenth century large agricultural colonies of Bavarians—six thousand of them, grouped in thirteen villages (the chief of which was called *La Carolina*) in the Sierra Morena—were brought to Spain by ministers of Carlos III. In a comparatively short period these absolutely disappeared from a "national" point of view, and became merged in the Spanish population. Later in the same reign, a great many English, Scotch, and Irish were established in Seville and Madrid to direct or take part in the new manufactories or industries which the Government was establishing. In Madrid these families practically died out, or else were assimilated by the Spanish: for the spirit of the country seems always to have become too strong for the foreigner.

The decorative features of Spanish incunabula, too, show, like their types, certain marked Spanish peculiarities. The fifteenth century title-pages are often very magnificent; and this magnificence of effect is usually arrived at by large and splendid decorations placed above very meagre titles. On the title-page of Vagad's *Cronica de Aragon,* printed by Pablo Hurus, at Saragossa (1499), an enormous decorative woodcut appears above a title in black-letter, consisting of but three words! This was entirely in consonance with the huge decorations and heraldic bearings commonly used in all departments of Spanish art—churches with their entire fronts covered by a coat of arms, the door of the church being as subsidiary to the decoration above it as was a title to the decoration on a title-page. These heraldic emblems were characteristic—*cosas de España*—for, as Ford says, "few countries can vie with Spanish heraldic pride and heraldic literature." What Spaniards did in books was only what they did in architecture—they printed as they built—another instance of the interlocking of the artistic side of printing with the art of a given period. Then, too, in some of the borders to printed pages, we see ornament which is reminiscent of Saracenic or Arabesque design; and this again seems to reflect

—sad stories of the death of kings.

In other words, the characteristic of Spanish printing was that it was so essentially Spanish — more obviously "Spanish," it seems to me, than Italian printing was "Italian," or French printing was "French," perhaps because the nationality of Spain is more intense than that of any other country (or Latin country) of Europe. A friend who read these lines said to me, "What is meant by 'essentially Spanish'?" But like the flavour of olives, "Spanish" cannot be described!

During the latter part of the fifteenth century, Valencia was a great seat of foreign commerce, and, like Lyons, a meeting-place for foreigners; it was therefore natural that, printing having been brought to Spain by foreigners, the first Spanish press should be set up in Valencia. It was established by Lambert Palmart, who was probably of Flemish origin, and who produced at this press some fifteen books. What is generally thought to be the first book printed in Spain—Fenollar's *Obres e trobes*—a collection of poems in honour of the Blessed Virgin, though undated, was probably issued in 1474. It was printed in a rough roman type. Five books were printed in this roman font by Palmart, of which the earliest with a date was the *Comprehensorium*, issued in 1475 (*fig.* 49). He then procured gothic types, in which he continued to print until the end of his career. One characteristic of his work is the extreme leading of the type in some of his books, which gives them an effect not at all consonant with ordinary ideas of fifteenth century printing. When printing his *Biblia Valenciana* in 1477–78, a Spanish printer was in association with him, Alonso Fernandez de Cordoba, who also printed on his own account. Fernandez de Cordoba was a silversmith by trade, and probably cut the punches of the gothic types employed in the Bible. Palmart died in 1490.

The second press in Spain was set up at Saragossa in the autumn of 1475, by a certain Matthaeus of Flanders, who printed the first book in Spain in which its printer's name is given — an edition of *Manipulus Curatorum* — Palmart's books before 1477 being without an imprint. Very little is known of Matthæus, who thenceforth vanishes from view.

The other chief cities out of the twenty-four in which printing was introduced between 1474 (the probable date of its introduction) and the end of the century, were Seville, Barcelona, Salamanca, Burgos, Toledo, Valladolid, and Granada — Madrid having no printing-press until the Court had its permanent seat there in 1565. The most famous of these Spanish printing-houses were the Burgos press of Fadrique de Basilea (Friedrich Biel of Basle); the Saragossa press of Juan and Pablo Hurus of Constance; that at Seville belonging to Ungut and Stanislaus, and the establishment of the Unknown Printer of Salamanca. Arnald Guillen de Brocar of Pamplona should be mentioned, although his fame came to him in the next century as printer of the Complutensian Polyglot; for which he was called to Alcalá. Of these presses, those at Seville and Valencia were among the most productive. That of Salamanca is interesting for its classical books issued in roman type. Some of the best work was done in the office of Pablo Hurus at Saragossa, where illustrated volumes were brought out; the *Officia Quotidiana* issued in the year 1500 by his successor, Coci, Haebler calls one of the finest specimens of work executed at any time and at any place in the world.

The first book printed in Spain was from a font of coarse roman letter, but the rank and file of Spanish work was executed in a round, massive black-letter. This was something like the Italian black-letter of the same period, but had a peculiar Spanish twist to it. It was based on a round Spanish book-hand. The larger sizes of this type were ex-

Amarchilentus·a·u·plenus amarore
Amarus·a·u·qui non eſt dulce amarus
et inſuauis qui queq̃ non ncuit ad ſuum
ꝗfortiũ aliꝗ mutare dulcedine/et cõpaꞇ
amarior·ſſim9·unð amare·ri9·me·adů·
Amaſa·e·m·proprium nomen viri
Amaſco·cis·incho·incipio amare
Amaſia amica ſed amaſia luxurie amica
caſtitatis·eſt femeninum.
Amaſias ꝓpum inꝑretã ꝑſm tollés
Amaſio idem ꝗ amaſius
Amaſiola di·parua amaſia
Amaſiolus paruus amaſius.
Amaſiunculus·di·amaſioli
Amaſius·ii·pronus ad amorem luxurie

Ambidexter·tri·qui v̇traꝗ manu v̇tiꞇ
pro dextera
Ambiglom9 triangulus qui ebctem an /
gulum babeꞇ
Ambagna ouis que cũ duobus agnis im
molabaꞇ·q·ex utraꝗ ꝑte agnum habens
Ambifaria aduerbiuz diſcretinum·i·ex
ambabus partibus
Ambigo·gis·egi·ctũ·n·i·dubitare
Ambiguitas·i·dubictas
Ambiguoſ9·a·u·dubitabilis uel plenus
ambagibus
Ambigu9·a·u·dubi9 et comparaꞇ ambi
gu9 magis·ambigu9·ſſim9·et ambigue
aduerbium

49. First Roman Type used in Spain: Palmart, Valencia, 1475
From Johannes, Comprehensorium

Bernardi Villanoua nauarro in artib⁹ magiſtri. et in ſacra theolo gia bachallary rudimenta artis grammatice perutilia incipiunt.

Rāmatica eſt ars recte lo quendi recte ſcribendi recte que ſcriptā ſūt pnūciandi:eſtǫ initium &fundamen tū omnium diſciplinarum: poetaᵹ & au torum lectionib⁹ obſeruata ¶ Partes gramaticæ ſunt Quatuor. Littera.Syllaba.Dictio.& Oro ¶ Littera eſt minima pars vocis conpōitæ vt a b. ¶ Dicta eſt autē littera quaſi legittera ǫ legendi iter prebeat:vel a litturis vt quibuſdam placet ǫ plerūnǫ antiqui ince ratis tabulis ſcribere ſolebant:& poſtea delere ¶ Alii dicunt a lino dicta ē littera: ǫ inſcribendo illinitur: hoc eſt leuiter inducitur atramētum ¶ Litteras etiam elementorum nomine aliqui nuncupauerunt ad ſimi litudinem mundi elementorum:quia ſicut elementa coeuntia oīe corpus perficiunt:ſic etiam litteræ con iunctæ litteraᵹ vocem quaſi corp⁹ aliquod conponūt ¶ Inter litteras & elemēta hoc inter eſt ¶ ǫ elemēta pprie dicuntur iſæ pronuntiationes· ¶ Literæ vero ſunt notæ:& ſigna elementornm.1.pronuntiationum ¶ Abuſiue tamen & elementa plitteris: & literæ pro elementis vocātur ¶ Litteræ accidunt tria nomen figura & poteſtas. ¶ Nomen litteræ eſt quo littera nominatur vt a b. ¶ Figura litteræ eſt qua littera depingitur· ¶ poteſtas litteræ eſt iſa pnuntiatio qua valet. ¶ Litterarum aliæ ſunt vocales aliæ ſunt cōſo nantes. ¶ Vocalis eſt littera que p ſe vocem pſicit &

a iii.

50. *Spindeler's Roman Type, Valencia*, 1500

ceedingly fine, especially in Hurus's work; and on title-pages and for head-lines of chapters, large sizes were used with very imposing effect. There were also many somewhat condensed pointed gothic fonts of great richness of colour, almost like the handwriting of a manuscript as contrasted with rounder and more typically Spanish forms. Except for a few quartos, most of the books were set in double column. By referring to the plates in Haebler's *Typographie Ibérique* one can get a very clear idea of what fifteenth century Spanish types and composition were. Many of the volumes to be referred to came from the well-known presses just mentioned.

As roman characters were the first used in Spain, though less interesting than gothic types, we will consider them first. The roman type used by the prototypographer Palmart at Valencia, in 1475, in the *Comprehensorium* was, as our plate shows, of a very rough sort; and another roman font used in the *Commentum Ethicorum* of Saint Thomas Aquinas, printed by Spindeler and Brun at Barcelona in 1478, also is of an extremely primitive style.[1] In Villanova's *Rudimenta Grammaticæ*, printed by Spindeler at Valencia in 1500, we have a more regular type, better fitted, but of a heavy cut—this heaviness being a mark of many Spanish roman fonts (*fig.* 50). The Unknown Printer of Salamanca employed a roman font with a certain condensed quality, which points to derivation from Gothic characters. This he used in the *Grammatica* of Fliscus about 1485.[2] The very virile roman font employed at Burgos about 1497 by Fadrique de Basilea in the *De Hispaniæ Laudibus* of Marineus Siculus shows a distinct advance in its type-cutting and fitting; but in effect it is almost as heavy as black-letter.[3] This is true of a font used in the

[1] *Typographie Ibérique*, No. 12.   [2] *Ibid.*, No. 34.   [3] *Ibid.*, No. 51.

same printer's Latin edition of Brant's *Stultiferæ Naves*, though the massive appearance of such close-set type certainly accords well with the woodcut above it (*fig.* 51). These very heavy roman fonts are evidently Spanish renderings of Italian type of that epoch, but renderings "with a difference." In the Ungut and Stanislaus edition of Alfonso de Palencia's *Epistula de Bello Granatensi* (Seville, no date), we have a fine roman font which is even more Italian in effect (*fig.* 52). In many of these pages, gothic types, for head-lines, etc., are mixed with roman; the excessive colour of the roman fonts making this less discordant than would be expected.

The gothic types used by Palmart were a somewhat round yet slightly condensed black-letter — but by no means *as round* as some other Spanish gothic fonts. A page from the *Cosmographia* of Pomponius Mela, printed by Palmart in 1482, is composed in two sizes of this type (*fig.* 53). By comparing this with such type as was used in the *Espejo de la Cruz* by Cavalca, printed by Martinez at Seville in 1486, we see what this gothic type so much used in Spain was in *rounder* form.[1] A splendid example of it appears in the *Manuale Burgense*,[2] printed at Saragossa in 1497 by Hurus, whose books are among the most workmanlike and interesting of the early Spanish press. An even finer font of round gothic was that employed by Brocar at Pamplona in the *Libros Menores* of 1499, shown in our illustration (*fig.* 54). Small sizes of this character were used in the *Carcel de Amor* of San Pedro, printed at Burgos by Fadrique de Basilea in 1496.[3]

More condensed kinds of black-letter (like the French *lettre de forme*) were also employed by the same printer in 1493, in the *Introductionum Latinarum, Secunda Editio*, of

[1] *Typographie Ibérique*, No. 9.   [2] *Ibid.*, No. 75.   [3] *Ibid.*, No. 50.

tentes caſte uixerūt: nõ ſolũ uiſionē ſingularē habebūt : uerũetiã
cãtabūt quaſi cãticũ nouũ qd dicere aliorũ nemo poterit. neqʒ mi
nus de auditu eiuſqʒ obiecto q̃ de uiſu addubitauerūt philoſophi
Vnde Aulus gelius dicto li.v.cap.xv. Vetus atqʒ ppetua quæſtio
inter nobiliſſimos philoſophorũ agitata eſt. corpus ne ſit uox an
aſomatũ.i.incorporeũ. Corp⁹ aũt eſt aut efficiẽs aut patiẽs. Quã
definitionē ſignificare uolẽs Lucretius ita ſcripſit. Tãgere eni aut
tangi niſi corpus nulla poteſt res. Alio quoqʒ modo corp⁹ eē græ
ci dicũt:triplici dimēſione diſtans. Sed uocē ſtoici corpus eſſe cõ-
tendũt: eaqʒ eſſe dicunt ictũ aera. Plato aũtẽ non eſſe uocē corpus
putat. Non enim penſſus inquit aer : ſed plaga ipſa atqʒ percuſſio
uox eſt: nõ tñ ſimpliciter plaga aeris uox eſt. Nã digitus quoqʒ ae-
rem percutit: non ita tamẽ uocẽ facit. Sed quanta plaga? & uehe-
mens & tanta ut audibilis fiat. Democritus ac deinde epicurus ex
indiuiduis corporibus uocē conſtare dicunt. Eamqʒ ut ipſis eorũ

51. *Fadrique de Basilea's Roman Type, Burgos,* 1499

procul ab ipfa urbe fita. Quid non diruiffet illa in
numerabilis multitudo:ut plurimũ in difcriminibus
bellicis exercita ? Mirabitur fortaffe lector: q̃uis. a
ueritate cãlamus nihilo abfcedat.Ducẽta armatorũ
milia capiebat intra fe ciuitas Granatenfis. Horum
uix mille trecentũ equites erant.partim ex induftria
ut equis alimẽta nõ deeffent.partim qm̃ paruus iam
equorũ nũerus in circũuicinis urbibus fuperat.quũ
in cõgreffionibus diuturnis equi nõ pauci cecidiffẽt.
& ex Mauritania nullus iam effet acceffus ad trãfue
hendos in hifpaniã equos.Rex igitur Fernãdus pro
culdubio fœliciffimus:rem difficillimã aggreffus eft
ubi apte cognouit ueteres pactiões effluxiffe:uelut ĩ
caffum:& fub diuturna diffimulatione infideles que
fiuiffe fibi aliquã faltẽ cõfidentiã priftinæ libertatis.
Quã Alphaquifii: ac fi deũ coluiffent profitebant̃
deliris hoĩbus cito affuturã. Nam populus ad fuper
ftitionẽ præceps repente fidẽ adhibuit.& tam fupbe
atcp petulanter extulit fe:ut rex Boadelis iunior p̃ter
mentẽ fuerit coactus uulgi fententiã illico cõprobare
cp fi forte uel morofius:ul'languidius acceptaffet:far
racenico infultu dilaceratus fuiffet. Itacp aliud nihil
fe facturũ cum iureiurãdo promifit:q̃ queritare aftu
tius oportunitatẽ:qua ualeret chrifticolas longa fœ
licitate elatos penitus cõterere:quũ poffet unius diei
iactura exterminare noftros:iam ad populationem
agri Granatenfis intentos:tali clade.ut quecuncp in
multis expeditionibus obtinuiffent:confeftim amit
terent. Quibus infideliũ cognitis nouitatibus.Illu

52. *Roman Type used by Ungut and Stanislaus, Seville, n.d.*

Pōponii melle cofmographi
de fitu orbis. Liber primus.
Probemium.

Rbis fitū dicere
aggredior ipeditū꜕ opus
꜕ facūdie minime capax.
·Conftat enim fe re genti
um locorūq꜕ nominibus
꜕ eorum perplexo fatis
ordine: quem perfequi longa eft magis q̄ be
nigna materia: Uerum afpici tamē cognof/
ciq꜕ digniffimum: ꜕ quod fi non ope ingenij
orantis: at ipfa fui contēplatione pretiū ope
attendentiū abfoluat. Dicā autē alias plura
꜕ exactius: Hūc aut vt queq꜕ erunt clariffi/
ma et ftrictim. ac primo quidē que fit forma
totius: que maxime partes. quo fingule mo
do fint: vtq꜕ habitētur expediā. Deinde rur/
fus oras omnium et littora vt intra extraq꜕
funt. atq꜕ vt ea fubit ac circūluit pelagus: ad
ditis que in natura regionum incolarumq꜕
memorandos funt: Id quo facilius fciri pof/
nt atq꜕ accipi: paulo altius fumma repetef.

Mundi in quatuor
partes diuifio.

53. *First Gothic Type used in Spain: Palmart, Valencia,* 1482

Los libros que en este volumē
se cōtienen son los siguientes.
El caton conel libro llamado cō-
této cuya obra es de sāt bernardo
El floreto el qual cōtiene seys prī
cipales partes.
La primera cōtiene los articulos
de nuestra sancta fe.
La segūda los diez mādamiētos
La.iiſi.los siete pecados mortalef
La quarta los siete sacramentos
La quínta las virtudes morales
τ theologicas.
La.vi.morte y las cosaſ dla muerte
Contiene mas las quinqz claues
dela sabiduría cōlas cinco propri
edades que a de tener el maestro.
Contiene las fablas del esopo
Cōtiene mas los hymnos con o-
tros muchos que faltauan.
Cōtiene mas las lectiones d̄ iob
conel credo.salue regina. el pater
noster.conel aue maria.

Antonio de Nebrija — very elegant in the smaller size.[1] Fine pages set in a still more pointed character were produced by Pablo Hurus at Saragossa in 1496. The latter has that peculiar quality of penwork which keeps cropping up in Spanish printing fonts (*fig. 55*).

Condensation, and this pointed quality in type, varied in degree. An idea of the rich, massive quality of Spanish black-letter is given by the illustration just referred to and by pages of the *Suma de Confesion* printed by Hurus in 1499;[2] in Hagenbach's Toledan Missal of 1500;[3] or in the *Leyes por la Brevedad de los Pleitos*, printed at Toledo by Hagenbach about 1499.[4]

A peculiarity of composition in some Spanish books, namely, the excessive leading of gothic types, may be seen in the Valencia edition of the *Epistolæ* of Phalaris, printed in 1496;[5] or the *Ecloga* of Teodulus, printed at Zamora in 1492.[6] This was sometimes done to allow annotations or "glosses" to be interlined; hence a small size of Spanish type used for notes is called *glosilla*.

In early Spanish illustrated books, Pollard says that "pictorial title-cuts are not so common as in those of other countries, because of the Spanish fondness for filling the title-page with an elaborate coat of arms;" adding, however, that "nearly all their early bookwork is strong and effective, and the printer who placed a cut on a title-page nearly always secured a good one."[7] Spanish title-pages are interesting, and show certain peculiarities in ornament and arrangement. For instance, white letters on a black background was a very Spanish style of decorative writing — a style splendidly employed later by the calligrapher Juan

---

[1] *Typographie Ibérique*, Nos. 48 and 49.   [2] *Ibid.*, No. 77.
[3] *Ibid.*, No. 132.   [4] *Ibid.*, No. 130.   [5] *Ibid.*, No. 19.
[6] *Ibid.*, No. 37.   [7] Pollard's *Fine Books*, pp. 163, 164.

de Iciar.[1] Ungut and Stanislaus, at Seville, in 1494, cleverly took advantage of it, in a wood-block for the title-page of Columna's *Regimento de los Principes*.[2] There is a similar instance of white lettering on a black background in the well-known title-page of *Obra Allaors de S. Cristofol*, printed at Valencia by Pedro Trincher in 1498.[3] Another book printed by Ungut at Seville in 1495 — *Lilio de Medicina* — has a magnificent title-page which is distinctly Spanish in effect — a very important decoration bearing the words of the title, with a block of massive round black-letter beneath it (*fig.* 56). The Salamanca edition of *Leyes del Quaderno nuevo delas rentas delas alcavalas ı fraquezas*, etc., printed about 1496, with its four lines of gothic text beneath an immense and brilliant heraldic shield, is reminiscent of the huge armorial bearings used in decoration in other branches of Spanish art (*fig.* 57). Another title-page in the same style is that of Vagad's *Cronica de Aragon*, printed by Pablo Hurus at Saragossa in 1499.[4] Then there was a good deal of work in small *format* treated in the same way, such as the extraordinary xylographic title-page of Lucena's *Repeticion de Amores, e arte de axedres* (Salamanca, 1496), by Hutz and Sanz.[5]

[1] Juan de Iciar, Spanish calligrapher, and the designer of one of the finest writing-books ever printed. It is entitled *Recopilacion subtilissima : intitulada Orthographia pratica*. The first edition was published in 1548, at Saragossa. Some of the plates are copies of those in Italian books, but many of them are original with Iciar. Mr. Strange believes that the running hands in the book show certain Moorish influences. The original volume is rare, but plates from it are reproduced in most books on calligraphy. There is a short account of Iciar in Sir William Sterling Maxwell's *Annals of the Artists of Spain*, and Mr. Strange's paper, *Writing-Books of the Sixteenth Century* (Transactions of the Bibliographical Society, Vol. III, p. 41), may also be referred to.

[2] *Early Printers of Spain and Portugal*, pl. xxiii.

[3] *Typographie Ibérique*, No. 155.

[4] *Early Printers of Spain*, pl. xviii.   [5] *Ibid.*, pl. x.

℣ Finiūt oēs fori aragonū tā antiqui ꝗ nouissimi: vſꝗ ad Ferdinandū
Secundū regē aragonū ⁊ castelle:nunc feliciter regnātem:vna cū obser
uantijs ⁊ duab⁹ epistolis:vna quidē ſup diuiſione bonoꝝ:ſoluto matri
monio:altera vero de ordine magistrat⁹ iuſticie aragonū.qui fuere cor
recti:p̄ egregiū doctorē dūm Gondiſſaluū garſiā de ſancta maria: alte
rum ex vicarijs iuſticie aragonū:vna cū ordine tituloꝝ:⁊ quaſi repto-
rio:ab eodem dūo Gondiſſaluo:edito. Et ex iuſſu impenſiſꝗz Pauli
hurus:Cōſtancienſ. Germanice nacionis:apud vꝛbē Ceſaraugustā:
impreſſi. Aūo a natiuitate dūi. M.ccccxcvj.die vero.v.mēſ Augusti.

55. *Gothic Type used by Pablo Hurus, Saragossa*, 1496
(*reduced*)

Lilio de
mediana.

Lo contenido eneste presente volumen de Bernar
do Gordonio es lo seguiente. Primera mente los sie
te libros que se intitulan Lilio de medicina. Lo segū
do: Las tablas delos ingenios. Lo tercero: el Regi
mięto delas agudas. Lo quarto: el Tractado delos
niños conel Regimiento del ama. Lo quinto y po
strimero: Las pronosticas.

56. *Title-page of Gordonio's Lilio de Medicina: Ungut and Stanislaus
Seville, 1495 (reduced)*

Leyes del Quaderno nueuo delas rentas delas alcaualas
e frãquezas. Fecho enla vega de Granada. Por el qual el Rey
e la Reyna nuestros Señores reuocan todas las otras leyes ó
los otros quadernos fechos de antes.

57. Title-page of Leyes del Quaderno, etc., Salamanca, c. 1496
(reduced)

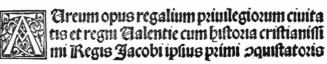

Areum opus regalium priuilegiorum ciuita
tis et regni Ualentie cum historia cristianiffi
mi Regis Jacobi ipsius primi aquistatoris

58. *Title-page of Aureum Opus: Diego de Gumiel, Valencia*, 1515
(*reduced*)

In the Burgos edition of *Oliveros de Castilla*, printed by Fadrique de Basilea, the page of text with its mass of rich black-letter and decorative picture of an archbishop wedding the hero to the daughter of the king of England, is an example of an illustrated edition of a popular romance — the kind over which Don Quixote lost his wits.[1] The calligraphic initial, and title in large, round gothic letters, are reminiscent of early French printing. These title-pages, cut on wood, are common in Spanish books of the time. The opening page of another famous story of chivalry, *Tirant lo Blanch*, printed at Valencia by Spindeler in 1490, shows a rich border with something Oriental about its decorations.[2] How the illustrations appeared when placed in the text may be seen in San Pedro's *Carcel de Amor* (Rosenbach, Barcelona, 1493) and G. G. de Novarra's *Contemplaciones sobre el Rosario*, etc. (Ungut, Seville, 1495).[3] The initials used in Spanish incunabula were very brilliant in effect. Those employed by the Unknown Printer of Salamanca in 1498, 1499, and 1500[4] are fine and characteristic examples.

Although of later date than 1500, there is one example of Spanish decoration so remarkable in design that I include it here. It is the title-page of a small folio book entitled *Aureum opus regalium privilegiorum civitatis et regni Valentie* — being the second part of the Chronicle of Jayme el Conquistador. This fine black-letter book was issued at Valencia "by the art and humble industry of Diego de Gumiel" in 1515 (*fig.* 58). It exhibits three very Spanish features: (1) an heraldic design (2) in white on black (3) above very little text; and shows what is meant by "Span-

[1] *Typographie Ibérique*, Nos. 52 and 53.   [2] *Ibid.*, No. 17.

[3] *Early Printers of Spain*, pls. II and XXIV.   [4] *Ibid.*, pls. XI and XII.

ish" better than any words can do. It is a very romantic, courageous, and effective style of decoration.[1]

Facsimiles, however well reproduced, give very little idea of the splendour of Spanish incunabula. The books themselves must be seen. Then only a true idea of their effect is gained. The typography of these books was comparatively simple, the sizes of type were few, the decorations were strong and masculine, and the composition, as a rule, so compact that a page of it looks like some dark weave laid upon a sheet of paper. I am not saying that these books are the finest that were ever printed, but they were in one way among the finest. For if entire unity with the life about it makes great printing, these books were great.

[1] All the facsimiles in Haebler's two books — *Early Printers of Spain and Portugal*, and *Typographie Ibérique du Quinzième Siècle* — should be looked through. For a guide to the rarest and most important productions of the Spanish press, the reader may consult the Salvá catalogue, *Catálogo de la Biblioteca de Salvá, escrito por D. Pedro Salvá y Mallen*. Valencia, 1872. 2 vols. It is illustrated and also contains many typographical reproductions (not very well done) of title-pages of the more famous works. For facsimiles without bibliographical descriptions the student may consult *Bibliografía Grafica, Reproducción en facsímil de portadas, retratos, colofones y otras curiosidades*, etc. Pedro Vindel, Madrid, 1910. 2 vols. The work contains upwards of 1200 facsimiles of Spanish printing and engraving from the introduction of printing to the early years of the nineteenth century. It is rich in reproductions of the early work touched on in the foregoing chapter. A guide to some titles of fifteenth century Spanish books is supplied by Henry Thomas's *Short-title Catalogue of Books printed in Spain and of Spanish Books printed elsewhere in Europe before* 1601 *now in the British Museum*. London, 1921. The *Catalogue of the Spanish Library and of the Portuguese Books bequeathed by George Ticknor to the Boston Public Library, together with the Collection of Spanish and Portuguese Literature in the General Library* may also be consulted for titles of books to be examined. This was published in 1879, and since that date many volumes have been added to the collection. It contains a number of books interesting to the student of Spanish printing. The library of the Hispano-American Society, New York, is the *best* collection of Spanish typography which exists in this country. It numbers over 100,000 volumes, and the incunabula (splendidly displayed) include many rare and beautiful books. No printed catalogue has been published. The Society has issued a number of the rarest Spanish books in facsimile.

CHAPTER IX

TYPE AND TYPE-FORMS OF THE FIFTEENTH CENTURY IN ENGLAND

PRINTING was introduced in England in 1476 by William Caxton, who owes his fame, however, to more than the fact that he was England's proto-typographer. For he was not only the first of English printers — he was also "the first in a long line of English publishers who have been men of letters . . . and was like-wise one of the earliest in the succession of English mer-chants and men of affairs who have found recreation and fame in the production of literature."[1] His services to liter-ature in general, and particularly to English literature, as a translator and publisher, would have made him a com-manding figure if he had never printed a single page. In the history of English printing he would be a commanding figure if he had never translated or published a single book. But with him printing was not the sole aim; and this ex-plains in part why his printing was not so remarkable as his reputation might lead us to expect. He was a great Eng-lishman, and among his many activities, was a printer. But he was not, from a technical point of view, a great printer.

For our purpose, a summary of his life which throws into relief his typographical activities is enough. Born about 1421, and apprenticed to a London merchant who after-wards became Lord Mayor, Caxton some time after 1441 went to Burgundy; being abroad, as he tells us in 1469, "for thirty years, for the most part in the countries of Brabant, Flanders, Holland, and Zealand," and being for some time "Governor to the English Nation" (*i.e.*, English merchants) at Bruges — the seat of the Burgundian court. After hold-

[1] Winship's *William Caxton*, Doves Press, Hammersmith, 1909.

ing this post with success, and negotiating some important commercial arrangements in behalf of the English Crown, he retired from active work, and it was then that he began, as a pastime, his translation of the *Recuyell of the Histo-ryes of Troye*—a French book popular at court, written by Raoul Le Fèvre, chaplain to Philip, Duke of Burgundy. Of this he completed but little and laid it aside. In 1469, when attached as secretary to the household of the new Duchess of Burgundy, sister to Edward IV, he happened to mention his English translation, and as the Duchess became interested, he promised her to go on with it. Taking the work with him on a visit to Germany, he finished his task at Cologne in 1471.

The new art of printing was then practised at Cologne, and it is supposed that Caxton visited one of its printing-houses and had a hand in the production of an edition of Bartholomew's *De Proprietatibus Rerum*. To support this theory, there is the testimony of Wynkyn de Worde, foreman of Caxton's printing-house and his successor, who says, in his prologue to an English translation of *De Proprietatibus*, which he issued about 1495:

> And also of your charyte call to remembraunce
> The soule of William Caxton first prynter of this boke
> In laten tonge at Coleyn hymself to avaunce[1]
> That every well disposyd man may thereon loke.

On his return to Bruges, Caxton gave his completed translation to the Duchess, and somewhat later set up a press to supply the demand for copies of his *Recuyell*. In an epilogue to the third part, Caxton says: "Thus ende I this book whyche I have translated after myn Auctor as nyghe as God hath gyuen me connying, to whom be gyuen the laude and preysing. And for as moche as in the wrytyng of

[1] *i.e.*, in learning the art.

the same my penne is worn, myn hande wery & not sted-
fast, myn eyen dīmed with ouermoche lokyng on the whit
paper, and my corage not so prone and redy to laboure as
hit hath ben, and that age crepeth on me dayly and febleth
all the bodye, and also because I have promysid to dyuerce
gentilmen and to my frendes to addresse to hem as hastely
as I myght this sayd book, Therfore I have practysed &
lerned at my grete charge and dispense to ordeyne this said
book in prynte after the maner & forme as ye may here see,
and is not wreton with penne and ynke as other bokes ben,
to thende that euery man may have them attones, ffor all the
bookes of this storye named the Recule of the Historyes of
Troyes thus empryntid as ye here see were begonne in oon
day, and also fynysshid in oon day."

In this production Caxton had associated with himself
Colard Mansion, who had previously been a clever calligrapher. Authorities differ as to whether Caxton persuaded
Mansion to exchange his old industry for that of printing,
or whether Mansion, as seems more likely, had, shortly before his connection with Caxton, set up a press of his own.
About 1475, Caxton and Mansion also printed at Bruges
The Game and Playe of the Chesse. The type of these books
differs from all other fonts used by Caxton. It is of rough,
angular, awkward design, which shows clearly its relation
to current Flemish handwriting, which was rough, angular, and awkward too (*fig.* 59). Some authorities have supposed its design based on Mansion's handwriting, and that
the type was cast by him; others have thought it came from
Veldener of Louvain. Its provenance is not clear. "Its general
appearance," says Blades, " is more free and manuscript-
like than would be thought the case from the square-set
figure of each individual letter. This is, to a considerable
extent, caused by the great variety of letters, there being

only five for which there were not more than one matrix, either as single letters or in combination : for, although the differences between the various matrices of the same letter may be but very slight, we have here the fundamental principle of freedom, namely, a recurrence of modified sameness. The execution of the type is good, sharp, and decided, with sufficient differences between the repetitions of the same letter to indicate independence of tracing or mechanical contrivance; hence probably the work of one accustomed to cut letters." This type was never brought into England, but was employed by Mansion after Caxton's departure.

Caxton returned to England in 1476, and set up a press in the Abbey precincts at Westminster—at the Sign of the Red Pale—and also brought with him some type and equipment.

The remaining seven fonts of type that Caxton used fall into two classes : *batarde* types of the Burgundian school; and *lettres de forme* more on the model of pointed gothic types of the Mainz school.

Caxton's Type 2 and its variant 2*, his Type 4 and its variant 4*, and his Type 6, are all versions of the Flemish *batarde* character. In his Type 2 he printed at Westminster in 1477 *The Dictes or Sayengis of the Philosophres* (*fig.* 60) — the first book printed in England with a date and place of printing. "This type," says Blades, "has a more dashing, picturesque, and elaborate character than type No. 1. It is an imitation of the 'gros-batarde' type of Colard Mansion, with some variation in the capital letters, which are extremely irregular, not only in size but also in design, some being of the simplest possible construction, whilst others have spurs, lines, and flourishes."

Caxton's Type 3 is particularly interesting to students

ther Are whiche redounded in to the ayer and reysing
as they that felde not of heuen ne of erthe vpon ther
enemyes began to fighte / certes whan the troians sawe
the centaures mountyd on horsbacke reynyng as the
hors they were so aferd and affrayed that they fledo
and were neuer to haue seen fyght day / how wel they
toke corage and aboo them / and the centaures foughte
so myghtily among them that celse oon of them Bare to
the erthe a troian wyth the poynt of his spere and
among other gamincdes was born doun to the erthe
among them / and som were hurte a parte and some
refeurs of hurtyng / and som were wyth oute hurte / whan
gamincdes felte hym self among the ...
in this fierce batayle and saw the grete ...
he woke ... grete dispyte and ... arose ...
... and sayd / and Answerd angrily ...
... that he sette ... and ...
swerd and ... the centaures ...

59. Caxton's Type 1. From *The Recuyell of the Historyes of Troye* (*first book printed in English*)
Caxton and Mansion, Bruges, c. 1475

Werkis/take compaynie With Wyse men and studie in their
bookis/fle lesinges/ for the lyers speth not but for Vnkno-
Wing of reason and of her saules/the lest harme that can fall
to alyer / is that no man bileueth him of nothing that he
saith/neuirthelesse man may bettir be Ware of a theffe than
of alyer (And sayd the hertis of good people accordeth
togiders /like as renning Watre With the Watre of the see,&
the hertis of euill people can not lightly accorde/all be it that
they be togidres/as the Vnreasonable bestes that playe & lepe
togidre & sodaynly falle to fighting (And said/ordeigne
that your offices and auctoritees ben yeuen to theym that
loueth & foloweth trouth & rightwysnes and cause them to
haue rigorous peynes þ ben harmedoers & loueth falshode &
deception (And said/ If ye haue doute in eny thing counseile
you to Wysemen & if they dispraise you therof be ye neu Wroth

60. *Caxton's Type 2. From* The Dictes or Sayengis of the Philosophres, *Westminster*, 1477
First book printed in England with date and place of printing

If it plese ony man spirituel or temporel to bye ony
pyes of two and thre comemoracios of salisburi vse
enprynted after the forme of this present lettre whiche
ben wel and truly correct, late hym come to westmo-
nester in to the almonesrye at the reed pale and he shal
haue them good chepe ⸪

Supplico stet cedula

61. *Caxton's Type* 3. *Used in his Handbill, Westminster, c.* 1477

Here begynneth the boke Jntituled Eracles, and also of God
frey of Boloyne, the Whiche speketh of the Conquest of the hol
londe of Jherusalem, conteynyng diuerse warres and noble faytes
of Armes made in the same Royāme, and in the contrees adiacent
And also many meruayllous Werkes happed and fallen as W
on this syde, as in tho partyes this tyme duryng, And how th
valyant duc Godefrey of Boloyne conquerd With the Werd t
sayd Royamme, And was kynge there,

The ffirst chapitre treateth how Eracles conquerd Perse an
slewe Cosdroe, and brought in to Jherusalem the very crosse, a
pitulo   prime

He Auncyent hystoryes saye that Eracle
was a good crysten man and gouernour
thempyre of Rome, But in his tyme Mach
met had ben Whiche was messager of the deu
And made the peple to vnderstonde, that
was a prophete sente from our lorde, In th
tyme of Eracles was the fals lawe of m
chomet sowen and sprad abrode in many partyes of thoryent, a

62. *Caxton's Type* 4. *From Godfrey of Boloyne, Westminster,* 1481

of English printing, for it is the type that we have come to know, both in face and size, as English. It is a *lettre de forme*, much finer than his *batarde* types, and not unlike the ancient Flamand type in the Enschedé collection (*fig.* 46), though not so massive. It was used by Caxton for three books: an *Ordinale seu Pica Sarum*, in 1477, and a Psalter and *Horæ ad usum Sarum*, both printed in 1480. This type is shown in our illustration (*fig.* 61), which is interesting because it reproduces a copy of Caxton's handbill advertising Pyes of Salisbury Use—probably the earliest advertising leaflet printed in England. The "Pye" was a collection of rules to show how to deal with the concurrence and occurrence of festivals; pyes of two and three Commemorations possibly being separate portions of the *Ordinale seu Pica Sarum* of 1477. The type of the advertisement was that used in the Pyes. After Caxton's death, Type 3 passed into the hands of Wynkyn de Worde, who employed it frequently. The variant of Caxton's second type, called Type 2*, appears to have been cast from matrices made from trimmed-up letters of Type 2. Caxton's *Mirrour of the World*, printed about 1481, shows the use of this type.[1] It has some changes and additions, but is scarcely more attractive than its original.

In the *Godfrey of Boloyne* of 1481 Caxton employed his Type 4, a disagreeable, rough, and more compact letter, resembling some used by Machlinia in his *Speculum Christiani* about 1486, and that used at St. Albans in 1481. Ugly as it is, it was apparently a favourite of Caxton's (*fig.* 62). Its variant—Type 4*—is a recasting on a little larger body,[2] and Type 4 and Type 4* may be distinguished by the different form of the lower-case w.

Caxton's Type 5 is a relief to the eye—a church type of the Flamand school, but not so fine as the large "church"

[1] *Early English Printing*, pl. III.   [2] *Ibid.*, pl. v.

letter called Type 3, which is considered above. "The large Lombardic capitals used with this font," says Blades, "have a bold and striking appearance. Unlike any former font of Caxton's, they are all cast with the largest face the body will bear, and without the least beard. They are used, more or less, in every book printed with this type. . . . They do not look at all well when used as initials to a word, on account of their size preventing them ranging with the sequent letters." Caxton printed *The Doctrinal of Sapience* in Type 5, about 1489. It is a good type as Caxton's types go—and very English and ecclesiastical in effect, as we understand English "church type" to-day (*fig.* 63).

Type 6, a variant of Type 2, first used in the *Ars Moriendi* of 1490, calls for no remark, for it is another of Caxton's series of *gros batarde* letters (*fig.* 64).

Caxton's Type 7 was a small size of rough, compact English black-letter, and was discovered by Henry Bradshaw, the learned Cambridge bibliographer. In its delicacy it is somewhat French. It was used in an Indulgence brought out in 1489. Blades does not mention this type in his account of Caxton's books, for he was never convinced that it was—as it certainly seems to have been—used by Caxton (*fig.* 65).

Type 8, of French origin, is a *lettre de forme* of the conventional type. It appears in the first four lines of the opening page of the *Ars Moriendi* mentioned above, and in the fourth, fifth, sixth, twelfth, and thirteenth lines of the left-hand column in our illustration (*fig.* 64).

Caxton's press turned out about a hundred books. Gordon Duff tells us that "from the time Caxton first started printing it is interesting to notice how he gradually introduced various improvements. His earliest books have no head-lines, no numbers to the pages, no catchwords and no signatures;

in this fair bode/that ye wyl remembre how the poure soules be
leyed in the fyre of purgatorie. And therwyth he departed: wha
the clerke was leyd down in his fair bede he myght nother sle
ne reste whan he remembred the wordes that the prechour
had said to hym   On the morn whan he was rysen he gaf all
that he had for the loue of god & entred in to relygyon: after
was an holy man ¶ Now seest thou how it is good to take the
word of god/Jt is flouthe whan thou goost not gladly now we
ought to do whan thou art rysen out of thy bedde for to
comande the to god/& in good trouthe thou art all thy werkes &
besynes shall fare the better yf thou so do . Example ¶ we
rede of thyr crafte ¶ That
sar whyche was patryarke of alexandrie recounteth of two
auncers which were goossho & lyuen by thyr crafte That
one was right a good werkman and had not grete mynde
in his hous. and was alle poure: alleway he allewary he
to werke/That other was no good werkman but he toucled god
hushold and grte mainep. but he toucled worke our lord god.

63. *Caxton's Type 5. From The Doctrinal of Sapience, Westminster, c. 1489*

man And that I shuld do neuer
so moche penaūce and pdee my self;
do to the fyre to be brente and gyf
alle my good to fede poore folkes
If I haue not loue this loue in
god and to alle folkes for god all
thys shuld no thynge profyte/for
as seyth the holi abbot moyses All
the penaūce that we suffer and o-
ther good werkes that we do or
cause to be don/ne be but Instru-
mentis for to awey the herte that
loue maymore sone growe ther in
thys holy anocon/ and thys mai
as see be ensample If a man sol/

fynce nexe. And ther & alle other
wcddes of their charge to pray for
the soule of the sayde translatour
¶ Canticū beate marie & volo
re suo in passione filii sui pleni
two legis est dilectio:

The apostel seinte pou
le seyth the fulfyl-
lyng of the lawe ys
Loue & Septe gre;
goxy seyth

¶ Quicquid precipitur in sola
caritate solidatur/
All thys that ys comaunded in ꝓ
oke lawe and in the newe is/or

64. Caxton's Types 6 and 8. From Tretyse of Love, Westminster, c. 1493

the ends of the lines are not always even,[1] and we see in the paper the holes made by the points which kept the paper straight. . . . In some of these books printing in red is found, not worked off by a separate impression, but pulled at the same time with the black, a peculiar method of printing used also by Colard Mansion in the books which he printed alone."

Caxton introduced signatures in 1480, and began to use woodcut illustrations in about the same year, and very rough they were. Few ornamental initials are found in his books. "Such improvements as Caxton adopted," says Gordon Duff, "were only made from necessity, to keep himself abreast of his rivals."

It was unfortunate for early English typography that Caxton lived so long in the Low Countries, and modelled his printing on the work about him, rather than upon that of France or Italy. But unlike his rivals, he was, says Gordon Duff, "the editor or translator of most of his publications, and, unlearned as he calls himself, his labours have made a lasting mark in the history of the English language." Thus

[1] This was because Caxton, following the practice of the Dutch school of printing, at first used no composing-rule. As Blades says in his essay on Caxton's printing-office, "Placing rough types *upon* rough types admits of very little shifting or adjustment, and to this fact, I imagine, we must attribute the practice of leaving the lines in early books of an uneven length. An attempt to push along the words of a line in order to introduce more space between them, without some plan of easing the friction, would be certain to break up the line altogether, and so the lines were left just as they happened to fall, whether full length or short. Sometimes, when a word would come into the line with a little reduction of the space between the last two words, the space was reduced accordingly; but more often a syllable at the end of the line was contracted, such as 'men' into 'mē,' or 'vertuous' into 'vertuo⁹.' Most often the compositor, knowing the practice to be understood by his readers, would finish his line with just so many letters as his measure would take, and accordingly it is common to find words divided thus:—why-||che th||at w||ymen w||iche m||an. But when once the 'setting rule' was brought into use all that was altered, and the various words of a line could be pushed about, and the spaces between them augmented or reduced with ease."

the historical significance of Caxton's types, and the interest that attaches to him as a man, must make up for the lack of beauty in his books.[1]

Caxton's material at his death, in 1491, passed to Wynkyn de Worde, a native of Wörth in Alsace, who had been his assistant. He at first used only Caxton's types; the fonts he owned being 3, 4*, 6, 7, and 8. These he employed in five books published from 1491 to 1493; among them the *Golden Legend*, printed in the latter year.[2] The first type of his own that he used, in a *Liber Festivalis* in 1493,[3] has somewhat the appearance of the French *lettre de forme* of the period. "It was," says Gordon Duff, "probably formed on a French model, though it retains several characteristics and even a few identical letters of Caxton's founts." Of the variant capital I's, one much resembled that in Caxton's Type 4*. The black-letter in *The Boke of St. Alban's*, printed by De Worde in 1496, was derived from Gotfried van Os of Gouda, from whom, on his departure from Gouda to Copenhagen, Caxton bought types and a supply of the rather awkwardly designed initials to be found in De Worde's books. This type

---

[1] In De Ricci's *A Census of Caxtons* (Bibliographical Society's Monographs, No. XV, 1909), Caxton's eight types are reproduced in facsimile, printed on rough paper, and showing full pages of the types. There are also lists of the books printed at Bruges and Westminster, giving the number of existing copies, untraced copies, and fragments. A list of the books printed at Paris for Caxton and the books printed by Wynkyn de Worde after Caxton's death, but with Caxton's types, is followed by a list of Caxton's books classified by *types;* finally, a list of Caxton's books in chronological order, showing the types used in each year, is appended. There is also an index of libraries which contain or have contained Caxtons.

This book is supplementary to Blades's *Life and Typography of William Caxton*, London, 1863, 2 vols., which is now made more or less incomplete by later knowledge; but Blades's volumes, Gordon Duff's *Early English Printing* and *Life of Caxton* (Caxton Club of Chicago), and De Ricci's *Census* furnish a fairly complete equipment to the student. Mr. Winship's delightful paper, *William Caxton*, should also be consulted.

[2] *Early English Printing*, pl. viii.   [3] *Ibid.*, pl. xi (of later editions).

Iohannes De Giglis aliae de filiis Aplicus Subdiacon̄q Et in Inclito Regno Anglie fructuū e prouentuū canunr apl̄ice debl̄/
tor̄ Collector / Et Dor̄t9 de Maluinis decanus Eccl̄e Sancti michael̄ de Ippoleto Bar̄omē Sanctissimi domini nr̄i papc
Cubicularius Sedis apostolice Nuntii et commissarii per eundem sanctissimum dominum nostrum papam admitta scripta deputati
In spiritu anglie regno/ Uniuersis presente littere Inspectoris Salutem e Sinceram in domino caritatem/Noueritis q̄ sanctissi/
mus in cr̄ito patr̄ e dn̄e nr̄ piatus Nobis Iohānis e Petro cōmissariis pnominatis cōcedendi bn̄uersis cr̄isti fidelib3 In regnis
Anglie / e dominio bptente Lorisq3 ac teris quibuscūq3 iuristi regni dicioni subiectis qui per se vel aliū Intra temp9/ad sr̄issimi dn̄i nr̄i
e sedis apl̄ice br̄iplaciti duratur3 e bisquequo eiusdem br̄iplaciti reuocato aut ob̄entoq3 in suis literis suspensio facta fueret sc̄om tenorē
ipsar3 literaq3 aplicaq3 /Qui ad ipugnandū infideles e resistendū eoq3 conatib3/Tantū Quatuor Tres vel Duos vel br̄ui florenos auri
Uel tm̄ qntum per nos Cōmissarios prefatos desuper deputatos/seu cū Collectorib3 ; a nobis super hc ostituendis vel facultatē habitibus
conuenerint /e cū effectu persoluerint/Ut Cōfessor pdons9 presbiter secularis vel cuiusuis ordinis etiam mendicantiū Regularis curat9
bel nō curat9/quē quiskt eoq3 dugerit eligendū/eligeris e eligentium cōfessione audita seu cōfessionib3 respectiue auditis pro cōmissis
per cū vel eos peccatis criminib3 e excessib3 quibuscūq3 qntūcūq3 grauib3/crū si talia foret propter que sedes aplica ett
quouismodo cōsulenda/Cr̄picacōe In romanū Pontificē e in predictam sedem apl̄icam/e iniectionis manuū biolētas In Epos ett
Inferiores prelatos e crimibue dū tapat excepto Secnō a censure e pena ecclr̄alium quibuslibet quomōcūq3 influctis a Jure vel ab
spie semel in vita e in alio dicte sedi nō reseruatis casib3 e peccatis quocies id petiurint eis auctoritate Apl̄ica de absoluturonis br̄ficio
prouidere e bam semel m bita q̄ in mortis articulo plenariam oim suoq3 petōq3 remissionem e absoluciōe; cū ea plenaria Indulgentia quā
etiā assequerentur In bisitatione liminū Beatoq3 apl̄oq3 Petri e Pauli/e Basilicaq3 sancti Iohānis lateranen Et br̄ade Mar̄remaioris
de urbe ac recuperatione terre sancte eorūdem infidelium expugnatiō3/ac Anno Iubileo que etiā ad preī obiecta e deuocione sr̄issimi dn̄i nostri e successor lurq3
bus cōcessi foret cōcedendi Ipsis in sinceritate fidei e bnitate sc̄e Romane ecclr̄e ac obediērtia e deuocione sr̄issimi dn̄i nostri articulo
Romanoq3 Pontificū Canonice intrācium persistentib9 impendere e salutare penitenciā iniungere Ita br̄t si ipsis in br̄moī mortis articulo
sepius cōstitutis absolucio ipsa impendat/Nichilomin9 iterato in vero mortis articulo possit impendi e impensa suffragetur eisdem auctō
ritate apl̄ica de apl̄ice potestatis plenitudine cōcessit facultatem prout in Ipsis litteris apl̄icis super hoc emanatis plenius continetur
Cū aut; Magr̄lr̄ fr̄ānnus Aboft
dicti beneplaciti de facultatib3;suie Competentem quātitatem ad opus fidei br̄ici ac ad expugnationem Infidelium Contulerit /Ideirco
deinoe presentium br̄moī Confessoris eligendi et Auctoritate apostolica qua In hac parte fungimur satisfacto tamen his quibus fueret
satisfacio impendenda plenam ac liberam tribuim9 facultatem/Datum Sub Sigillo Sancte Cruciate Anno Incarnacionis Dn̄ice
Mill̄imo Quadringētesimo Octuagesimo Nono Die brrtima quarto Mensis Iplis

Justa presenti sepus

65. Caxton's Type 7. Used in Indulgence, Westminster, 1489

Pzefatio in nominü generä

Finem operis quicücp bides:ꝗ noſtra pzobaſtl.
Scripta:pzccoz faciles in tua bota deos
Et tu liuoz edax:qui non hic carpere iure.
Quid'potes/ꝗ rodis lurida fella crepa.
Grammata ſulpitii toto relegentur in ozbe
Atꝗ erit in pzecio noſtra nunerua ſuo.

Sulpitii berulani in opuſculum
de generibus nominü pzefatio

Ogitanti mihi ꝗ tentanti ſepe/ꝗ curioſi/
qua via poſſent:ꝗ facilius ꝗ melius pficere pueri in arte grä-
tica:compertum eſt doctrine clara ꝗ breuia pzecepta vberi⁹ illis
ꝗ obſcura conferre. Itacp cü de nominum declinatione ꝗ verboz ceterarücp
ozationiſpartium conſtructioe duos libzos compendioſos nup ediderim. In
ceſſit mihi de nominü generib⁹:ꝗ de verboz pteritis ꝗ ſupinis (duobus alijs
exiguiſcp voluminib⁹) ſcribendi libido. Omnis eni pueroz difficultas in decli
natione genere:pteritis ꝗ ſupiuis ꝗ conſtructioe conſiſtit.Qua qui dem ſi ego
illos bzeuitate claritateꝗ efficaciü pceptoz leuauerim:videboz pietati mee
feciſſe ſatis:atꝗ mei labozis pmium glozia habiturus.Admiroz aüt ſup ieus
etatis homines aut veteranos ludimagiſtros hanc ſibi puinciä nö aſſump-
ſiſſe:maluiſſeꝗ Alexandri obſcuritatib⁹ ꝗ erroribus imbuere adoleſcentes.
Puto ſane labozis'fuiſſe preſum:aliquos inuidiſſe minozib⁹:vt ea dipi didice
rint difficulter:alios nö minoze docerent laboze diſcentü :nec poſteris aptioz
eſſet ad emergendü via.aliquos (tancp religionem) ventos eſſe rudimeuta
mutare:ꝗ ne apud gentem pſuaſam neuellum opus meritä fozet auctozitate
conſecutuz.Continere em omnes iäpude ſupuacaneü in Alexädzo tempus
ꝗ conterunt:illü ſolü ex grämaticis nozüt.Illü pzecipue habēt :illü euoluunt:
nec alios attingunt:illum pueris explanant:in illo totos cöterüt dies ſp diſci-
pulos infelices:p quä regulä ꝗ rogitando dicerē litteraz exptes:niſi etiam ex
doctis aliquot hec ipa tractare velut valde peculiaria ſcirem. Sed quanta
ib faciunt (vt pace eoz dixerim) impzudentia:nam pueros quī lacte cibiſcp
delicatiſſimis:faciliſcp ſolutionis alendi ſunt:multo abſintheo:cibiſcp ruſticis
ꝗ duriſſimis nutriunt male:reddunt aut inualidos ꝗ deformes:aut pzo ping-
uibus turgidos.Rñdebunt illos facilius Alexandri carmen qð quidē contin
git in multis.Multi quocp melius pzoſam ꝗ carmē ediſcüt.Sed eſto ita quð
de arte grämatica copioſe ꝗ clare ſcribe carminibus pöt. Sciant memoriter
Alexandrü.Quid demü pzoficere cü non intelligant ꝗ Intelligent (inquunt).
paulatim quouſcp tñ nü ad terciü:nü ad quartü:nü'ad quintü:ſextüve annum

66. *Gothic Types used by Wynkyn de Worde, Westminster*, 1499

is the square, Netherlands *lettre de forme* of the period.[1] The lower-case w's of this type are peculiar in shape, and should be examined.

De Worde's *Speculum* of 1494[2] was printed from Caxton's Type 8, which was a *lettre de forme*. De Worde had also two other types, both of which he used before the end of the fifteenth century in his *Opus Grammaticum* of Sulpitius (*fig.* 66). The larger of the two was a text type, the smaller being employed for notes. The first seems to be French; the smaller has a round quality which is a little like the Italian gothic types of the time. Gordon Duff says that these characters were imported, and that some French printers possessed almost identical fonts. The small type is a charming character and was the work of a very clever founder. De Worde printed about one hundred books before 1500, and nearly eight hundred in all—if new editions and broadsides are included.

One of the methods of placing De Worde books chronologically is curious, *i.e.*, from the condition of the woodcuts. An engraving on wood of the Crucifixion, which was first used in Caxton's *Fifteen Oes*, was employed so much by De Worde, that in 1498 it began to crack. And in 1499, while an edition of the *Mirror of Consolation* was in process, the block split in two. The progress of time was thus marked by the fissure in the plate.

The types of the printer Julian Notary, who worked in connection with Barbier and another unknown printer, and produced several books for De Worde, are also of the *lettre de forme* family. His Sarum Missal shows these fine characters admirably composed; for the French elegance in typesetting exhibits itself very clearly in this book, which was printed about 1498 (*fig.* 67); and also in the Sarum *Horæ*

[1] *Early English Printing*, pl. x.   [2] *Ibid.*, pl. ix.

of 1497. Barbier was of French origin, and probably came to England at De Worde's invitation.

In the work of John Lettou we see this same mastery of composition; but there is a distinct foreign quality in the letter shown in his *Quæstiones Antonii Andreæ*. This type, in effect, resembles a form employed at Rome (possibly by the same printer) in 1478–79. It looks like the transitional gothic types which showed the influence of Roman letter-forms (*fig.* 68). This book was the first volume printed in England in which double columns were employed. After its appearance Lettou went into partnership with William de Machlinia, and it was by them jointly that the two types employed in Littleton's *Tenores Novelli* were used. One was a Burgundian (or "Caxton") sort of *batarde* letter, the other a pure *lettre de forme*.[1] After printing some five books in association with Lettou, Machlinia carried on the business by himself. A square *lettre de forme* was used by Machlinia in the *Revelation of St. Nicholas*, and a picturesque condensed gothic type in the *De Secretis Naturæ* of Albertus Magnus of 1484.[2] Machlinia's two remaining fonts were a heavy, square *lettre de forme*, rather like Caxton's Type 3, and a coarse *lettre batarde flamande*, identical with types used by Veldener at Utrecht and Brito at Bruges — another proof of the close connection between Netherlands printers and the English fifteenth century press. These were employed in a *Speculum Christiani* brought out about 1486.[3]

The printer Richard Pynson was a Norman by birth. He had two rough forms of transitional *lettre de forme* (in which he printed Chaucer's *Canterbury Tales* and *Dives and Pauper*)[4] and a more delicate *batarde;* his remaining types being *lettres de forme*. The *lettre batarde* in which *The Fall of*

---

[1] *Early English Printing*, pl. xvi.   [2] *Ibid.*, pl. xvii.
[3] *Ibid.*, pl. xviii.   [4] *Ibid.*, pls. xx and xxi.

Tu credis in filium dei? Respondit ille et dixit. Quis est domine ut cre-
dam in eum? Et dixit ei Iesus. Et
vidisti eum: et qui loquitur tecum
ipse est. At ille ait. Credo domine: et pro-
cidens adorauit eum. Off[erto]. Be-
nedicite gentes dominum deum nostrum
et obaudite vocem laudis eius qui po-
suit animam meam ad vitam: et non de-
dit commoueri pedes meos: benedictus?
dominus qui non amouit deprecatione[m]
meam et misericordiam suam a me. A[lleluia].
Jubilate deo omnis terra psalmum di-
cite nomini eius: date gloriam laudi eius.

S Upplices te rogam[us] D[omi]ne
omnipotens deus: ut his sa-
crificiis peccata nostra munden-
tur:quia tunc veram nobis tribu-
is et mentis et corporis sanitate[m].

tes eius:quia timebant iudeos. Ia[m]
enim conspirauerant iudei: ut si
quis eum cofiteretur christum: et
extra synagogam fieret. Propterea
parentes eius dixerunt: quia etate[m] habet: ipsum interrogate. Vocaue-
runt ergo rursum hominem qui fuerat cecus:et dixerunt ei. Da glo[ri]-
am deo. Nos scimus:quia hic homo peccator est. Dixit ergo ille. Si
peccator est nescio:vnum scio.quia
cecus cum essem.modo video. Dixerunt ergo illi. Quid fecit tibi:
aut quomodo aperuit tibi oculos
Respondit eis. Dixi vobis iam: et
audistis. Quid iterum vultis au-
dire? Numquid et vos vultis disci-
puli eius fieri? Maledixerunt ergo
ei dixerunt. Tu discipulus illi[us] sis

67. *Lettres de Forme used by Notary and Barbier, Westminster, 1498*

gnat et qd concipitur sub mo .cu̅ g̅o p̅batur o̅n̅a qd i̅de significa̅t plurale τ singulare τ i̅de includit · dico qd no̅ e̅ simile . qt singulare i̅ cludit conceptu̅ . τ mo̅du̅ concipie̅di su̅t re pugnantia . τ i̅deo singulare includit·q̅i in se ro̅em uera̅ p̅ ut includit conceptu̅ τ mo̅dum concipie̅di, plurale aut̅ p̅ ut i̅cludit illa duo includit q̅i in se ro̅em fa̅la .cuius p̅tes repug na̅t .τ io̅ no̅ sequitur q̅ plurale sit ueru̅ d̅ plurali sicut singulare de singulari . q̅o d̅ sub iecto cuius ro̅ de se est falsa nihil uere pot̅ p̅ dicari . ita ee̅ falsa bo̅ irronalis insensibilis currit τ sic de aliis similibus ¶ Ad sco̅m dice̅du̅ cu̅ dicit̅ q̅ illa p̅po maior n̅ e̅ p̅ma, f3 reducit̅ ad i̅sta ·oc̅ ens i̅perfectu̅ reducit̅ ad p̅ fcm f3 qd oc̅ ens p̅ p̅ticipato̅es i̅ps̅m τ tm illud ens est p̅scm qd est ens p̅ essentia̅. ideo sequitur illa maior q̅ oc̅ ens p̅ p̅ticipato̅em τc .illa aut̅ p̅po oc̅ i̅p̅fectu̅ reducitur ad p̅ fectu̅ sic intelligentes est .na̅ aliquid est i̅p̅rfe que .s̅. no̅ nco̅b3 i̅p̅rfecto̅em a̅ne̅p̅a q̅ non

R̅o̅. ctu̅ dupliciter ·uno s̅co̅3 p̅rfectio̅em sidpliciter

res deos est inco̅possibile τ i̅ncludat repugna̅ tia̅ ut o̅n̅fum est multiplex̅ . τ io̅ non est meli us esse plures deos .qd e̅ non est melius nisi ep̅o̅e i̅co̅possibiliu̅ non est melius,i̅mo nec to nu̅ siipliciter .sicut illud qd non n̅isi ep̅o̅e in possibili τ repugnantia̅ include̅te non e̅ o̅ino seu i̅possibile est ip̅m esse uel poni i̅nesse te̅e. 5̅o concludit philus q̅ non est bonum in uni uerso pluralitas principatuu̅ .unus g̅o est p̅n ceps totius uniuersi qui est deus benedictus uiue̅s τ regna̅s sup̅er uniuersa̅m creaturam̅ a seculo usq3 in seculum.

A M E N .

¶ Excellentissimi sacre theologie p̅fessoris ? Anthonii Andree ordinis fratru̅ minou̅ su per duodecim libros Methaphisice questioni bus per uenerabilem uiru̅ magistru̅ Thoma̅ penketh ordinis fratru̅ Augustinensiu̅ emen datis finis impositus est . per me Johannem lettou ad exp̅ensas Wilhelmi Wilcock impres sis. Anno dn̅i. M.CCCC.lxxx.

68. *Transitional Gothic Type used by Lettou, London, 1480*

In his moost rich royall apparayle
Cast in hir chaunges to yeue him a sharpe shoure
By assaundre of grece entierpoure

Unto purpos I wyll my penne dresse
for to declare and make mencion
Howe proude darye in his moost noblesse
was by fortune from his sete cast doun
for anone after the coronacion
Of assaundre in macedoyne kinge
This was the procesfe anone of his wedkinge

He nat delayed nor made no longe date
In purpos fully of pre to procede
Of perce and mede the scepters to translate
All their trichesses to conquere and possede
Perpetually for to abyde in dede
Under Grekys mighty obeisaunce
In macedoyne to haue gouernaunce

Howe Darie kinge of Perce and mede was out-
rayed by assaundre kinge of macedoyne

N Assaundre called Epitoffes
Helpff as nowe no lenger for to tarye
Slayne at mischeef for he was rechelees
Double of corage for he caude chaunge and barye
for turne I wyll my penne to binge darye
Which that whilom who so lift take hede
Moost mighty regnyd in perce and mede

And amonge other notable wetzours
Lyke as I deme by heuynly influence
Duly by title of his predecessours
And through his prudent royall excellence

69. Lettre Batarde used by Pynson, London, c. 1494

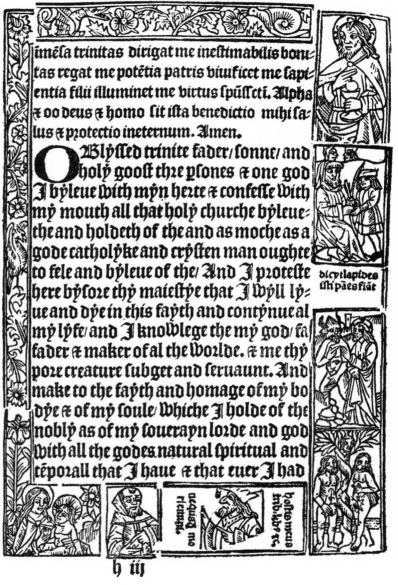

imēſa trinitas dirigat me ineſtimabilis bonu:
tas regat me potētia patris biuificet me ſapi:
entia filii illuminet me birtus ſpūſſcti. Alpha
⁊ oo deus ⁊ homo ſit iſta benedictio mihi ſa:
lus ⁊ pzotectio ineternum. Amen.

O Blyſſed trinite fader/ ſonne/ and
holy gooſt thze pſones ⁊ one god
J byleue with myn herte ⁊ confeſſe with
my mouth all that holy churche byleue:
the and holdeth of the and as moche as a
gode catholyke and cryſten man oughte
to fele and byleue of the/ And J pzoteſte
here byfoze thy maieſtye that J wyll ly:
ue and dye in this fayth and contynue al
my lyfe/ and J knowlege the my god/ fa:
fader ⁊ maker of al the wozlde. ⁊ me thy
poze creature ſubget and ſeruaunt. And
make to the fayth and homage of my bo
dye ⁊ of my ſoule/ whiche J holde of the
nobly as of my ſouerayn lozde and god
with all the godes natural ſpiritual and
tēpozall that J haue ⁊ that euer J had

h iij

70. *Lettre de Forme used by Pynson, London, c.* 1495

Princes was printed, about 1494 (*fig.* 69), is somewhat like the fonts common in France. Pynson's *lettres de forme* are shown in the larger type of his Sulpitius of 1494—a square Netherlandish letter—and in the very handsome *lettre de forme* which he used with beautiful effect in an *Horæ ad Usum Sarum* of 1495 (*fig.* 70), and in a Sarum Missal of 1500.[1] His small black-letter types for notes are rather Italian in feeling. The Sarum Missal of Pynson is a really fine piece of work, which shows taste and ability, though the borders are very rough in execution. Pynson was the most tasteful of the fifteenth century English printers.

In addition to the London presses, there were printing establishments at Oxford and St. Albans. Of the seven types employed at Oxford, some narrow, upright gothic types produced striking pieces of typography.[2] The other fonts call for little comment here. In the St. Albans press(the third place where printing was done in England) we have three different types, and this press also used Caxton's Type 3. Of these three fonts, the type used in the Augustinus Dactus is the most interesting.[3] Besides the books that were printed in England, a great many volumes were printed abroad for the English market—some at Antwerp, Paris, and Rouen,[4] others at Basle, Louvain, and Cologne. These do not concern us in our study of English type-forms, though in passing it may be said that they were more finished than the books printed in England.[5]

In a final survey of the types used in England in the fifteenth century, they group themselves into three classes

---

[1] *Early English Printing*, pl. xxvi.   [2] *Ibid.*, pl. xxix, Cicero.
[3] *Ibid.*, pl. xxxii.   [4] *Ibid.*, pls. xxxv–xxxviii.
[5] Excellent facsimiles of the types of Caxton and *other early English printers* are appended to Gordon Duff's *Fifteenth Century English Books* (Bibliographical Society's Monographs, No. XVIII, 1917).

of black-letter fonts, for the roman character was not introduced into England until well into the sixteenth century.

The first was a pointed *lettre de forme* much resembling
the French. In this the most attractive books were issued;
and certain of them are particularly interesting as giving in
type the English national letter-form, based on earlier manuscripts, of which I have spoken more than once. This still
survives.

The second group is the *lettre batarde*, based on the Burgundian *batarde*. Fonts of this appear in all sizes and varieties, from the rough and ugly characters used by Caxton
down to the refined imitation of French *batarde* types employed by Pynson.

The third group of types is miscellaneous, made up of
characters which were imported, and others which may
have been copies of importations. None of them are characteristic of purely English typography, though they are
sometimes better than the native English types.

CHAPTER X

FROM our survey of fifteenth century types it would appear that every country had its formal pointed black-letter; every country, save England, its classical roman type; and every country — except, perhaps, Spain — its cursive vernacular black-letter type, copied from the handwriting of the locality and time. Before 1500 Italy had no vernacular type simply because the current handwriting of Italy (which was not of the black-letter school) was only translated into type-forms at the beginning of the sixteenth century. Italic was the Italian cursive vernacular type, and it ultimately drove out all other vernacular types wherever roman letters came into general use. It was produced by Aldus in 1501; but it was modelled so clearly on fifteenth century cursive hands, that it comes within the range of fifteenth century fonts. So to complete our review of the earliest type-forms, we must consider this famous italic.

We cannot understand the work of Aldus Manutius and the Aldine printing-office, or the innovation made by books in small *format* printed in italic type, unless we know something of the intellectual condition of Europe at the time of Aldus, and about an experiment which he made in type-cutting some years earlier. "In 1500, men were thinking of new things," says Pollard. "New editions of many of the old religious and didactic treatises, the old poems and romances, continued to be printed, though mostly in a form which suggests that they were intended for a lower class of readers; but the new publishers would have little to do with them. Scholarship, which till now had been almost confined to Italy, spread rapidly to all the chief countries of Europe, and, amid the devastation which constant war soon brought upon Italy, was lucky in being able to find new homes. With the new literary ideals came new forms for books, and new methods of housing them. . . . The men for whom Aldus catered wanted books which they could put in their pockets and their saddlebags, and it was not long before the publishers of Paris and Lyons outdid Aldus in the smallness and neatness of their editions."

The *reasons* for the invention of a new condensed type were (like most reasons for things) so simple that they are in danger of being overlooked. Small books had come into vogue—the kind of volume that inspired Dr. Johnson when he said, "Books that you may carry to the fire and hold readily in your hand, are the most useful after all." It probably occurred to Aldus that simple, compact volumes might be popular, and thus commercially successful; so for these small books a condensed type was designed, which permitted a good deal of matter to be printed on a page. That he meant these 16mo editions of the classics to be in the nature of a "handy-volume" collection is shown by the dedication of the Juvenal, issued in 1501—the first year of his use of italic—which runs as follows:

"*Aldus, to his friend Scipio Carteromachus, Greeting.*

"We have printed, and are now publishing, the Satires of Juvenal and Persius in a very small *format*, so that they may more conveniently be held in the hand and learned by heart (not to speak of being read) by everyone; this we do at a time when every vice has reached a point still higher than had been reached when these Satires were composed —for I do not doubt that Life will here read, and recognize, its own Manners and Morals. We send these Satires to you, my dear Scipio, that they may through their brevity become once more your intimate friends, as they were formerly during your stay at Rome as a young man, when you possessed them as thoroughly in your memory as your own fingers and finger-nails."

The Aldine 16mo books were in reality a sort of Venetian Everyman's Library, and held the same position with regard to other books that the various series of books in handy *format* do now ; and they bore somewhat the same relation to other books in their price. In these popular editions Aldus was merely returning to classical usage.[1]

So much for the reasons that appear to have suggested these books in small *format* for which the Aldine italic was designed.

The adoption of an imitation of a cursive hand by Aldus for his new fonts is not wholly explicable by the wish for a compact type. His italic types were only a development of an idea already put into effect in his Greek fonts. The older Greek manuscripts employed formal, simple characters, separate from each other and with comparatively few ligatures or contractions, which adapted them very well to translation into type;[2] but Aldus preferred to imitate the cursive Greek handwriting of his time, which was filled with an immense number of ligatures, contractions, and unneces-

---

[1] "We think of the cheap book and the public library as blessings coming direct from the invention of the printing-press, and at first thought we may be inclined to suppose that in Rome, when copies had to be written by hand, books must have been as dear as they were during the Middle Ages. . . . This was not the case. Copyists had been trained to attain such a speed in writing, and slave labor was so cheap, that in the first century of our era, as Martial tells us, the first book of his poems, which contains about seven hundred lines, could be had at a sum amounting to thirty or forty cents, while his *Xenia* could be sold for twenty cents. At these rates, books did not cost more than twice what they do to-day." Abbott's *Society and Politics in Ancient Rome*. New York, 1909.

[2] Like the Greek font used in the Complutensian Polyglot (*fig.* 228).

sary complications.[1] Despite their faults, these cursive Greek fonts hit the popular taste (*fig.* 71). So when a small, compact type was wanted for editions of Latin classics, etc., I suppose it may have seemed to Aldus natural and clever, to do for Latin letter-forms what he had done for old Greek letter-forms. It may be, too, that Aldus adopted a cursive letter for his new font because it suggested the popular and informal character of his projected series. Whatever his reasons, the result was the Aldine italic.

The punches for these types were cut by Francesco da Bologna (whose name was Griffi, and is not to be confused with Il Francia), who had already designed roman types for Aldus. Tradition says that he intended to imitate the handwriting of Petrarch[2] — too picturesque a fib to give up, though comparison with specimens of Petrarch's handwriting upsets the theory. The high-flung names of Aldus Manutius, Francesco da Bologna, and Petrarch have dazzled us into forgetting that the production of these little books printed in italic was a simple business affair. If Aldus had been named "Brown," Da Bologna "Smith," and Petrarch "Jones," the venture would appear to us more what it appeared to the Venetians of that day. The first books printed in the new font were the Virgil and Juvenal of 1501 (*fig.* 72).

The Aldine italic was founded upon a Humanistic cursive Italian handwriting of a somewhat earlier period, of

[1] For some of the contractions supplied by ligatured Greek letters, see Savage's *Dictionary of the Art of Printing*, pp. 300–302. While simplifications of Greek type took place in France under the Estiennes, and still more changes have been made since, the original misunderstanding has never been corrected.

[2] Probably based on a misconception of the phrase, *tolto con sommissima diligenza dallo scritto di mano medesima del Poeta*, occurring in the colophon of the 1501 Aldine edition of Petrarch's *Cose Volgari*. This means merely that the text of the edition has been carefully transcribed from a manuscript in Petrarch's autograph. The statement is twice repeated, in varying phrase but with identical meaning, in the address entitled *Aldo a gli Lettori*.

ΦΙΛΟΣΤΡΑΤΟΥ ΕΙΣ ΤΟΝ ΑΠΟΛΛΩΝΙΟΥ ΤΟΥ ΤΥΑΝΕΩΣ ΒΙΟΝ

ΒΙΒΛΙΟΝ ΤΕΤΑΡΤΟΝ·

Ἤδη δὲ εἶδον τὸν ἄνδρα ἐν Ἰωνίᾳ παρελθόντα ἐς τὴν Ἔφεσον, οὐδὲ οἱ βάναυσοι ἔτι πρὸς ταῖς ἑαυτῶν τέχναις ἦσαν, ἀλλ' ἠκολούθουν, ὁ μὲν σοφίας, ὁ δὲ εἴδους, ὁ δὲ διαίτης, ὁ δὲ σχήματος, οἱ δὲ πάντων ὁμοῦ θαυμαστοὶ ὄντες. λόγοι τε περὶ αὐτοῦ ἐφοίτων, ὁ μὲν ἐκ τοῦ Κολοφῶνι μαντείου, κοινωνὸν τῆς ἑαυτοῦ θρίας, καὶ ἀτεχνῶς σοφὸν, καὶ τὰ τοιαῦτα τὸν ἄνδρα ᾄδοντες· οἱ δὲ, ἐκ Διδύμων· οἱ δὲ, ἐκ τοῦ περὶ τὸ Πέργαμον ἱεροῦ· πολλοὺς γὰρ τῶν ὑγείας δεομένων, ὁ θεὸς ἐκέλευε προσφοιτᾶν τῷ Ἀπολλωνίῳ· τουτὶ γὰρ αὑτῷ τε βούλεσθαι, καὶ δοκεῖν ταῖς μοίραις. ἐφοίτων καὶ πρεσβεῖαι πρὸς αὐτὸν ἐκ τῶν πόλεων, ξένον τε αὐτὸν ἡγούμενοι, καὶ βίου ξύμβουλον, βωμῶν τε ἱδρύσεως, καὶ ἀγαλμάτων· ὁ δὲ ἕκαστα φύτων, τὰ μὲν ἐπιστέλλων, τὰ δὲ ἀφίξεσθαι φάσκων, διωρθοῦτο. πρεσβυσαμένης δὲ καὶ τῆς Σμύρνης, καὶ ὅ,τι μὲν δέοιτο οὐκ εἰπούσης, ἐλιπαρούσης δὲ ἀφικέσθαι, ἤρετο τὸν πρεσβευτὴν ὅ,τι αὖ τοῦ δέοιντο· ὁ δέ, Ἰδεῖν ἔφη, καὶ ὀφθῆναι. ὁ δὲ Ἀπολλώνιος, Ἀφίξομαι εἶπε, καὶ δοίητε ὦ Μοῦσαι καὶ ἐρασθῆναι ἀλλήλων· τὴν μὲν δὴ διάλεξιν τὴν πρώτην, ἀπὸ τῆς κρηπῖδος τοῦ νεὼ πρὸς τοὺς Ἐφεσίους διελέχθη, οὐχ ὥσπερ οἱ σωκρατικοὶ, ἀλλὰ τῶν μὲν ἄλλων ἀπάγων τε, καὶ ἀποσπουδάζων. Φιλοσοφίᾳ δὲ μόνῃ ξυμβουλεύων, καὶ προσημπελάσαι τὴν Ἔφεσον μᾶλλον, ἢ ῥαθυμίας τε, καὶ ἀγερωχίας, ὁπόσην εὗρεν· ὄρχη τῶν γὰρ ἥττημένοι, καὶ πρὸς πυρρίχαις αὐτοὶ ὄντες, αὐλῶν μὲν πάντα μεστὰ ἦν, μεστὰ δὲ ἀνδρογύνων, μεστὰ δὲ κτύπων· ὁ δέ, καίτοι μεταθεμένων τῶν Ἐφεσίων πρὸς αὐτὸν, οὐκ ἠξίου περιορᾶν ταῦτα, ἀλλ' ἐξῄρει αὐτὰ, καὶ διέβαλλε τοῖς πολλοῖς. τὰ δ' αὖ ἄλλας διαλέξεις, περὶ ἄλση τὰ ἐν τοῖς ξυστοῖς δρόμοις ἐποιεῖτο. διαλεγομένου δέ ποτε περὶ κοινωνίας, ἢ

71. *Greek Type used in Philostratus: Aldus, Venice,* 1501

IVNII IVVENALIS AQVINA
TIS SATYRA PRIMA.

EMPER EGO AVDITOR
tantum?nunquám ne reponam
V exatus toties raucí theſeide
Codri?
I mpune ergo mihi recitauerit ille
togatus?

H ic elegos?impune diem conſumpſerit ingens
T elephus?aut ſummi plena iam margine libri
S criptus, et in tergo nec dum finitus, Oreſtes?
N ota magis nulli domus eſt ſua, quàm mihi lucus
M artis, et æoliis uicinum rupibus antrum
V ulcani . Quid agant uenti, quas torqueat umbras
A eacus, unde alius furtuæ deuehat aurum
P elliculæ, quantas iaculetur Monychus ornos,
F rontonis platani, conuulſáq; marmora clamant
S emper, et aſſiduo ruptæ lectore columnæ .
E xpectes eadem a ſummo, minimóq; poeta .
E t nos ergo manum ferulæ ſubduximus, et nos
C onſilium dedimus Syllæ, priuatus ut altum
D ormiret. ſtulta eſt clementia, cum tot ubique
V atibus occurras, perituræ parcere chartæ .
C ur tamen hoc libeat potius decurrere campo,
P er quem magnus equos Auruncæ flexit alumnus,
S i uacat, et placidi rationem admittitis, edam.
C um tener uxorem ducat ſpado, Meuia thuſcum
F igat aprum, et nuda teneat uenabula mamma,
P atricios omnes opibus cum prouocat unus,

A ii

72. *Aldine Italic as used in Juvenal and Persius*
Aldus, Venice, 1501

which there are endless examples.[1] As a type it had several particularly distinguishing features: first, originality of character; second, a large number of tied letters, of which there are about *sixty-five* in the Aldine Dante and Virgil; and third, the use of roman capitals shorter than the ascending lower-case italic letters—indeed, the dot of the lower-case i stands above a roman capital I. In pages of Dante's *Purgatorio*, the capital belonging to the first word of the first line of each three-line stanza is set off from the rest of the word, following in this Italian manuscripts of the period. Tied letters were used to produce a cursive appearance. For these tied letters an elaborate case was necessary, and thus composition became much more difficult; but in the later Aldine editions fewer tied letters were used, without great loss of effect. Aldus employed his italic as a text type for an entire book. It was a character entirely independent of roman. Placing italic fonts on bodies corresponding to roman fonts was the outcome of its later use in connection with roman for purposes of differentiation, emphasis, and for "liminary and preliminary" matter.

This Aldine character became the model for most subsequent italic types. In its own day it had a great success, and, like most typographic successes to-day, was widely and inaccurately imitated; but although the Venetian Senate gave Aldus an exclusive right to use the character, a patent confirmed by three successive Popes, counterfeiting went on. The Italians called the character *Aldino*. By others it was called *Italic*, either because they did not care to give Aldus so obviously the credit for inventing it, or did not wish to appear to have stolen it from anybody in particular!

A rival printer, for whom Griffi made another set of

[1] *Paléographie Latine*, pl. 116 a—Brief of Sixtus IV, 1472.

punches, published Aldus's own edition of Virgil in this type, so that his literary text as well as his type was pirated. This same edition of Virgil was reproduced at Lyons, with a counterfeit Aldine device upon it. Aldus issued a printed protest, and pointed out mistakes made by the Lyons printer in his reprint. This document was at once used in producing a new and more correct Lyons edition. Several series of these Aldine counterfeits appeared in Lyons, of all degrees of imperfection; the worst, perhaps, being produced by a sort of Jack-of-all-trades named Bartholomew Trott, who in these volumes described himself (as no one else was likely to do) as "the honest book-seller." The Giunti of Florence also copied the Aldine editions.

To the Lyons printers we owe the *slanting italic capital* letters now adopted for all italic fonts. Artistically this was not wholly an improvement, as roman capital letters gave a page of italic lower-case type an agreeable perpendicular movement which italic capitals do not supply. So what was generally considered a fault in the Aldine italic was, typographically, one of the best things about it. The Aldine printing-house, however, itself adopted italic capitals about 1560, some fifty years after the death of Aldus. Six different sizes of its italic type had meanwhile appeared.

The Aldine italic is often spoken of as an admirable invention, and from certain literary points of view, it may have been. But italic became a workable type for the printer only when precisely that characteristic was discarded which made it most Aldine, *i.e.*, imitation of a cursive hand. Though the character on which Aldus based his italic was more quickly written than the older book-hands, it was far slower to set up as he rendered it in type: and it certainly was foolish to try to imitate written characters by type, when by so doing much useless labour was necessitated. It was not that Aldus did not know about old Greek or the best current Humanistic manuscripts; but he did not think his problem out. He appears to have been seduced by the amusing trickery of reproducing current handwriting by type; and that is the reason that in his italic, and still more in his Greek fonts, he was about nine times too clever!

With the Aldine italic, *originality of idea* in type-forms ceases. The *civilité* introduced by Granjon at Lyons a few years later was very different in form from italic type, but the idea was the same — it was a type based on a cursive handwriting used in a particular class of documents and of a certain period and locality. The script shown by typefounders now is *our* version of such types as the Aldine italic and *civilité*. It is supposed to imitate our best handwriting, though usually it reproduces the impossibly perfect letters of a writing-book, which if children followed absolutely and persistently we should invoke the aid of the rod!

Of every class of type there are many forms, but one or two forms only that are the best. We can learn what these best forms are by knowing what early handwriting and early type was, and what early printers meant to do. Only when we understand their problem can we justly judge how well they solved it. To see what the manuscripts were that they tried to reproduce in type is a step to this knowledge; to see how forms produced by a pen were changed when rendered in metal is another. A third step is the realization of the influence of history, nationality, scholarship, and custom upon type-forms. We must also have a comprehension of the evolution of economic problems — how cheaper books were demanded, how that want was met, and what its effect was on types and their use. The ability to recognize all this can be arrived at only by that historical perspective and that training of the eye which is gained by study and observation.

And, too, by examining early types with all these factors in mind, we can finally arrive at some approximation of a canon of taste in types. No person or group of persons can be so opinionated as to assert that their conclusions represent learning and taste, or expect them to be so considered. But any one may arrive at sound conclusions as to types, if he knows thoroughly the history of type-forms, has an eye sensitive to their variations, and has familiarized himself with the ways in which they have been employed by masters of typography.

Fifteenth century types are the classics of type history. We can know very little about the best types if we are not familiar with them. But types of this class can be used only in accordance with certain conventions that often unfit them for the work of to-day. It is for this reason that we must glean from types used in different countries in the sixteenth, seventeenth, and eighteenth centuries, a knowledge of those more modern typographical forms which, in a minor way, are also classic, and yet more related to the printing we have to do. A man may admit that Horace and Virgil are classics, and yet feel the need of other books in his library. So it is with type-forms. We cannot always use "classical" types, but we can always use good types. While it may be necessary at times to choose types for printing the *Æneid*, it is quite as important to know what types to select for the kinds of books we print so much oftener nowadays. To this end we must make some study of the best fonts in use in various countries from the end of the fifteenth to the beginning of the nineteenth century.

CHAPTER XI

A WORD ON TYPE SPECIMENS

IN describing fifteenth century types it has been necessary to consider their manuscript sources; and in order to find out what types were used, to examine fifteenth century books; so that up to this point, the printer and his book have been much in evidence rather than his specimen-sheet or specimen-book, although as we know, Ratdolt issued a specimen-sheet at Augsburg in 1486.[1] Up to 1480 or thereabouts the early printer was his own type-founder, and not only cast the fonts for his own work, but designed them. The exchange or sale of types between different printer type-founders was not very common. Their collections were usually augmented by the work of their own hands. A printer's foundry was merely an appanage to his printing-office, and the workman in it was socially of a lower class than the printer. But in the last two decades of the fifteenth century we begin to find type-cutters — and perhaps sometimes type-founders — whose abilities were at the service of any one who wished to pay for them. These men, however, probably worked — at first, in any case — to order, and if they had types for sale, put out no "specimens" of them. It was at this period, too, that the division between printer and publisher first appears.

For knowledge of type in use in the sixteenth century one is still chiefly occupied with the printer and the books he made, although a few "type specimens" were issued by founders, and some by printers; such as the sheet of 1525

---

[1] See Burger's *Monumenta Germaniæ et Italiæ Typographica,* pl. 5, or Redgrave's *Erhard Ratdolt, and his Work at Venice* (Bibliographical Society's Monographs, No. I, London, 1894), pl. 9. This specimen was discovered about 1884 at Munich, in the binding of an old book.

showing the types used by Joh. Petri of Basle[1] and the Nuremberg specimen-sheet of 1561 put forth by Valentine Geyssler that Burger alludes to as existing in the Borsenverein library at Leipsic. Plantin issued in 1567 an *Index, sive Specimen Characterum Christophori Plantini*, containing in all forty-one varieties of letter—seven Hebrew, six Greek, twelve roman and ten italic, three scripts and three gothic. Later, one of larger *format*, but without a title or date, appeared. J. Van Hout of Leyden also published a specimen in 1593. The Typographia Medicea (founded by Cardinal Ferdinand de' Medici to print the Gospels for Oriental peoples) published in 1592 an Arabic alphabet and instructions for the use of Arabic type, though this could hardly be considered a "specimen."[2] Raphelengius, who was in charge of the Plantin office at Leyden, issued a somewhat similar *Specimen Characterum Arabicorum* in 1595. In the sixteenth century there were also men who cut types to the order of printers.

As to seventeenth century specimens, that of the printer Fuhrmann[3] was brought out at Nuremberg in 1616, and the interesting specimen-book issued by the Vatican printing-office in 1628,[4] portions of which, containing the supposed alphabets of Adam and an inscription in unknown characters found at the foot of Mt. Horeb (suppressed in the Specimen of 1628), may have been published by the Propaganda Fide a little earlier. The Propaganda Fide issued, however, throughout the seventeenth century, gram-

---

[1] See Burger's *Ein Schriftprobe vom Jahre* MDXXV. Leipsic, 1895.

[2] *Alphabetum Arabicum. In Typographia Medicea* [Rome], 1592.

[3] *Typorum et Characterum officinæ Chalcographiæ Georgii Leopoldi Fuhrmanni . . . designatio.* Nuremberg, 1616.

[4] *Indice de Caratteri, con l'Inventori, & nomi di essi, essistenti nella Stampa Vaticana & Camerale.* Rome, 1628.

mar specimens of its various alphabets for use in missionary work, the *Alphabetum Ibericum* appearing in 1629, and other alphabets in 1631, 1634, 1636, 1637, and 1673. These were continued in the eighteenth and nineteenth centuries.[1] Elzevir at Leyden brought out a specimen in 1658, and Luther of Frankfort, another in 1670. The widow of Daniel Elzevir published a specimen-sheet in 1681, and Joseph Athias, who bought the Elzevir foundry, issued his about 1686. The first English specimen was the tiny sheet of Nicholas Nicholls, produced in 1665. Joseph Moxon's specimen of 1669[2] (the first English specimen that is dated) and the University of Oxford's specimens of 1693[3] and 1695 are among the most notable English seventeenth century examples.

In the eighteenth century, we begin to find men who merely furnished types in stock or cut them to order— not artisans so much as business men who employed artisans—just as later we find publishers who merely employed printers. When the trades of printer and founder became distinct, and their interests separate, specimen-sheets of types became more common. In a few instances the types in a given printing-house were shown in specimen-books—which exhibited its equipment for customers to choose from. But almost all type-founders put forth specimen-books and specimen-sheets showing what types they had to sell to *their* customers, who were the printers. During the eighteenth century, therefore, these were very

[1] See *Catalogus Librorum qui ex Typographio Sacræ Congreg. de Propaganda Fide variis linguis prodierunt*, etc. Rome, 1773.

[2] *Proves of Several Sorts of Letters Cast by Joseph Moxon. Westminster. Printed by Joseph Moxon in Russel Street at the signe of the Atlas.* 1669.

[3] *A Specimen of the Several Sorts of Letter Given to the University by Dr. John Fell, late Lord Bishop of Oxford. To which is Added the Letter Given by Mr. F. Junius. Oxford. Printed at the Theater A.D.* 1693.

often met with—especially in its later years. But although common then, these early books and sheets are now rare. Blades in his interesting little tractate on specimen-books laments their scarcity. "Books such as soon become obsolete," he says, "have to pass through what, with literal truth, may be called a *fiery* ordeal. That is when they become too antiquated to be of any value to the current generation and yet require a century to pass over their heads before they have any merit in the eyes of the antiquarian. Perhaps no class of books is more subject to this unkind destiny than the specimens issued by Type-founders, which soon become so worthless in the very eyes of their own parents, that large editions entirely disappear and 'leave no track behind' even in the very foundries which gave birth to them. I imagine it to be as true of the Continental as it is of the old English foundries, that not one of them can show a copy of their first specimen books."[1]

These specimens are among the important "sources" which must be consulted in studying the types of the sixteenth, seventeenth, and eighteenth centuries.

After the middle of the sixteenth century there seems to be a general and sudden decline in all European countries not alone in the excellence of the types themselves, but also in the way they are used—both suddenly falling away from the high standards of earlier printing. This is because it took, perhaps, a century for the printed book to outgrow the influence of the manuscript; and this hundred years was over. As a century covers, roughly speaking, the lives of three generations, it is clear that a father, a son, and a grand-

---

[1] *Some Early Type Specimen Books of England, Holland, France, Italy and Germany. Catalogued by William Blades, with explanatory remarks.* London, 1875.

son might very well be influenced by the tradition of the manuscript, while to the fourth generation manuscripts would be simply out-of-date affairs with little direct influence on printing. Furthermore, the class of men who had by this time become interested in printing did not include so many people of education as in the first century of typography. The early printers—more or less educated men—endeavoured to copy manuscripts (and generally fine manuscripts) not alone in letter-form, but in arrangement, in order to make the printed book as nearly identical with the manuscript as they could. Soon the spread of literature, through the medium of the press, led to a demand for more and smaller and cheaper books, and printers were obliged, also, to deal with entirely fresh typographical problems, for which the early manuscript was no guide. Then too (as Pollard very truly says), "the enthusiasm with which the new art had at first been received had died out. Printers were no longer lodged in palaces, monasteries, and colleges; Church and State, which had at first fostered and protected them, were now jealous and suspicious, even actively hostile. Thriving members of other occupations and professions had at one time taken to the craft. A little later great scholars had been willing to give their help and advice, and at least a few printers had themselves been men of learning. All this had passed, or was passing. Printing had sunk to the level of a mere craft, and a craft in which the hours appear to have been cruelly long and work uncertain and badly paid." Thus more books, cheaper books, less cultivated men, new problems which they were not always capable of solving, and forgetfulness of the standards which for three generations had influenced printing, were some of the elements causing this change in typography. It became, indeed, as important for the printer of the latter part of the sixteenth

century to realize what the great models in types and printing are, as it is for us; and if his printing then became
worse, it is for precisely the same reason that our own is
to-day no better.

CHAPTER XII

GERMAN TYPES: 1500–1800[1]

IN fifteenth century German gothic or black-letter fonts, a differentiation of type-faces began to show itself, as we have seen, in the last twenty years of the century, between types that were somewhat pointed — like *lettre de forme* — and a rounder, more cursive gothic letter, with certain peculiarities — the closed a, looped b, d, h, and l, and a tailed f and s. The first type was called "fraktur." The second — in its original intention a kind of vernacular type, which became very popular from 1490 to 1500 — was ultimately known as "schwabacher." Although there were many variants of these two type-forms, they are the ancestors of the two varieties of gothic character shown today in German specimen-books under the same names. Of these two type-families, the first developed with extreme rapidity, while the second retained more or less its primitive features. We are so accustomed to identify styles with periods, that we forget that there is no sharp distinction between the end of one style and the beginning of another; and that the tendency which brings about a change of style exists for a long time before it comes to its hey-day, and survives a long time after it has gone out of fashion.

§1

Fraktur — the pointed form of these two types — is the first to be considered. A *Diurnale*, printed at Nuremberg by Hans Schönsperger in 1514 (*fig.* 73), is a splendid example of early fraktur, though the type has too much variety of

---

[1] This chapter, with others which treat of types from 1500 to 1800, is a guide to a course of exercises in training the eye. The text, however much it abounds in dates, names, or historical facts, is of little importance compared with the study of the facsimiles or examples to which it directs attention.

form. The descending f's dwindle to the form of pegs; flourishes on capital letters and the tails to the g's and h's are all
too restless, and the eccentric curves in rounded portions of
capital letters are in form particularly disagreeable and vulgar. Special characters were cut for this font, intended for
use in the last line of a page, so that their "curly-cues" could
project into its lower margin, just as there was a set of letters with friskings, intended to gambol over the margin at
the top. The classical example of this kind of type is that
shown in the same printer's Story of the Knight of Teuerdanck (a poem of chivalry of very indifferent merit), composed in honour of the marriage of Maximilian and printed
at the Emperor's expense at Nuremberg in 1517 (*fig.* 74).
It took five years to prepare, and in some cases punches were
cut for seven or eight varieties of a single letter, and when
proofs were first shown, printers could not believe that it was
composed from movable characters. Ingenious and splendid
as is the effort of the type-cutter to imitate the work of the
pen, the result scarcely seems worth the trouble. It was a
tour de force, and cannot be considered an example of normal
type-work.[1]

In the pages of the *Teuerdanck* the style of gothic type
changed entirely, and the simpler forms of the older fraktur were twisted into less agreeable shapes. These types are
characteristically German—which is, artistically, seldom a
compliment! An idea of sixteenth century fraktur can be
had from the *Thurnier Buch*, printed at Frankfort in 1566

[1] Vincenz Rockner, court calligrapher, designed the type for the *Teuerdanck*,
and is supposed to have copied it from a manuscript attributed to Johann Neu-
dörfer. At first thought to be printed from wood-blocks, an inverted i in the
edition of 1517 disposed of this theory. The type (also used in the seventeenth
century) was probably cut by Hieronymus Andrae, who had other sizes in
his own printing-house, where he executed books for Dürer. (For whole
upper and lower case alphabet, and figures, see *Druckschriften*, pl. 3). The
Teuerdanck was reprinted by Schönsperger at Augsburg in 1519.

DEus ppicius esto mihi peccatori·Et sis mihi cu
stos oīnibus diebus vite mee·
Deus Abrahā·Deus Ysaac·
Deus Jacob miserere mei Et
mitte in adiutoriū meum pro-
prium angelū gloriosissimū:
qui defendat me hodie:et pte-
gat ab oīnibus inimicis meis
Sctē Mihael archangele·De-
fende me in plio:vt non pereā
in tremendo iuditio·Archan-
gele christi· Per gratiā quam

73. *Type used in Diurnale: Schönsperger, Nuremberg*, **1514**

Nicht lanng darnach kam Neydelhart
Vnnd klagt dem Helden Er wer hart
Durch teglich arbeyt worden schwach
Pat Jn darauf das Er all sach
Die nacht wolt han in guter acht
Vnnd nach notturfft bestellen die wacht
Allennthalb in dem ganntzen heer
Besetzen die thor vnnd die weer

74. *Type used in Teuerdanck: Schönsperger, Nuremberg,* 1517

by Sigmund Feyerabend,[1] a page of Löneissen's *Von Zeumen* of 1588[2] (without place or printer), and the title-page from the Strassburg *Fundamentbuch* of 1579, printed by Bernhard Jobin (*fig.* 75). On this page the third to sixth and eighth to tenth lines are printed from type, the form of which is nearer to German types used three hundred years later, than to those of a hundred years before. It is a distinct decline from the purer gothic letter. In this title-page the decorated letters are cut on wood, but their tormented forms are really what the typographer would have been glad to find in type. Later this ambition was fulfilled. These types commended themselves to the rank and file of German printers, and became the ancestors of the modern German fraktur. The difference between fifteenth and sixteenth century German fraktur may be seen in our illustration (*figs.* 76 a *and* 76 b).

For the fraktur of the first half of the sixteenth century a good example is shown in *Lied auf die Schlacht von Pavia,* printed in 1525.[3] By the seventeenth century the fraktur type-form had practically crystallized, and the changes that occur in it are not sufficiently marked to make it worth while to pursue its history very carefully. Almost any German seventeenth century book shows its usual style. Here we shall leave it, for the moment, to consider the character called schwabacher.

There were many kinds of schwabacher type. We find a form of schwabacher used in 1509 by Johann Schoeffer at Mainz in his *Reformacion der Stat Franckenfort.*[4] Much the same sort of type—perhaps a little more pronounced in

[1] *Druckschriften*, pl. 45.   [2] *Ibid.*, pl. 73.

[3] Gustav Könnecke's *Bilderatlas zur Geschichte der deutschen Nationallitteratur. Eine Ergänzung zu jeder deutschen Litteraturgeschichte.* Marburg, 1895 (second edition, illustrated), p. 125.

[4] *Druckschriften*, pl. 27, smaller text.

its schwabacher form — was employed by Chrystoph Froschauer at Zurich in 1567 in his *Kunstrich Buch* (*fig.* 77).
The paragraph in a cursive type imitated the German
handwriting of that period — a fussy, restless kind of character, which is distracting to the eye and has somewhat
the appearance of ravelled carpet-threads.[1] In Leonhardt
Thurneysser zum Thurn's *Historia . . . aller . . . Erdge-
wechssen*, printed at Berlin by Michael Hentzsken (*fig.* 78),
a schwabacher type is used. This last book shows the rate
at which both type and composition went downhill after
the middle of the sixteenth century — very far from the simplicity of a hundred years before. Pages composed in schwabacher have head-lines set in tortured forms of fraktur, and
words in italic capitals are introduced into lines of black-
letter. Then again, italic is employed for Latin terms and
names in the midst of black-letter text, and the notes are a
muddle of roman and black-letter characters. Paragraphs
are indented, and yet paragraph marks are used. Even the
hands and asterisks which mark the paragraphs are ugly
in form. Everything about the composition is bad !

As to the sixteenth century roman types used in Germany, Johann Schoeffer of Mainz printed in 1520 Ulrich
Hutten's *De Unitate Ecclesiæ Conservanda* in a heavy roman
type of a kind very common at that period, a page of which
is reproduced (*fig.* 79). The same printer in 1525 issued
the *Canones Apostolorum* in a larger and better roman character, accompanied by a charming italic. While the composition of the page was too fanciful for so solid a letter,
it is an elegant piece of work, and the types are finer than
most contemporary roman fonts.[2]

One city that stands out splendidly in the work of the
sixteenth century German press is Basle. The great figure

[1] *Paléographie Latine*, pls. 118, 121.   [2] *Druckschriften*, pl. 94.

75. Title-page of *Fundamentbuch*: Jobin, Strassburg, 1579 (reduced)

76. (a) *Alphabet of Fifteenth Century Fraktur used by Neumeister, Mainz, 1479*

76. (b) *Alphabet of Sixteenth Century Fraktur used by Feyerabend, Frankfort, 1566*

Dann wenn man die Jonica kürtzer dann von acht teilen der dicke deß schafft macht/ so wirdt sy seer klothächtig scheynen: dann sy nit so vil auff dem postement verjüngt ist als die Dorica: vnd ye schmeler ein postement ist/ye breiter vnd dicker die Columm scheynt. Aber damit das postement breit scheyne/habend sy die gesimps am postement alle gevierdt außgeladen/welcher doch gar nit zů der Jonica dienet: dann das schafftgesimps nur den fünfften teil von der saul dicke dick ist / vnnd aber die postementgesimps vast noch als dick sind. Auff das ich aber bescheidenlich in diser ordnung fortfare / wil ich hie zůzeygen ein Columnen als der fürnemsten fürgerissen haben/wie sy der hocherfaren meister der Architectur Bramante zů Rom in seinem werck gebraucht hat: welcher Bramante ist gewesen das liecht der rechten Architectur/wie das seine gebeüw vnd bůcher außwisend.

DIse Jonische Colum̃ wirt gezogen auff den weybischen Cörper einer dapfferen frauwẽ: wie dañ in meinen ersten Bůchle gnůgsam anzeigt ist. In welchem yetzgemeldtẽ Bůchle zweyerley Jonische Colum̃en beschriben sind: eine zů den vnderen wercken: vnd eine zů den obern: als zů den außzügen/oder der gleychen/da man keiner postemẽt bedarff. So wil es sich aber offt zůtragen/ daß die selbig Colum̃ vnderweylen auch ein postemẽt můß haben/so sol der Werckmeister zů diser nachuolgenden ordnung greyffen. Welche man also sol zůrichten. Jr gantze höhe sol in eilff teil geteilt werden. Der selben eilff teilen anderthalben sol das postement hoch seyn. Die selben anderthalben teil in acht teil geteilt/ ist ein teil das vnder fůßgesimps/vnd ein teil das ober gesimps am postement. Die überige sechs teil in drey geteilt/der selben drey teilen zwen/ist die breite deß postements.

Das vnder fůßgesimps werde zům ersten in drey teil geteilt/der selben teilen einer ist die vnder fůß=

77. *Cursive and Schwabacher used by Froschauer, Zurich*, 1567

Das Saltz ist

Der Lungen/den Humoribus Radicalibus, vnnd allen theilen des Leibs / so dise feuchtigkeiten jhr Habitation vnd Wohnunge habendt

¶ Paracelsus stimbt mit den Alten Philosophen in disem Gewechs / fast aller Krefften / die sie gegen den innerlichen Gliedern erzeigen sollen / zu / Allein daß er für die Corporalische Materien / die Geistliche substantzen / als der Wurtz / Krauts / Blüfts / vnd Sohmens Subtiliteten derselbigen appliciren

lert / vnnd weil dieselbigen vil treffliger / ein geringere / vnnd der Natur gemessere Potion / brauchen heisset.

¶ Wider die Apostemata vnd Hitz der Lungen vnd Leber / Also wider den Hüsten / vnd wider die Strangulariam oder das ersteckendt Halswehe der Kinder / das Oel teglich dreymahl ⁊c eines Lots gebraucht / ist sehr nützlich eingenommen.

¶ Ein halbes Quintlein inn Milch genossen / treibt die Würm ab / vnd vertreibt das Krimmen.

Art / Eigenschafft vnnd Gebrauch deß
Gewächß FOENICVLI HORTENSIS, nach Paracelsischer
weis / welche Leiplich / Materialisch / vnd Complexionalisch ist /
Aussterhalben deß Kindtlichen Leibs.

¶ Das Antidotum mit Chamillen Oel vermischt / vnd mit dem die Gliedlein der Kinder geschmiret / vertreibt jnen den Krampf.

¶ Die Leiblein einer handt breit vnd den Nabel damit gesalbet / vertreibt jhn das Bauchkrimmen / vnd treibt die Würm ab / macht Windt / vnd öffnet jnen das Leiblein / Es reinigt den Magen vnd das

Gedern / vnd öffnet die Poros darmit die bösen Tunst so zwischen Fell vnd Fleisch ligen / vnnd vil böser Feuchtigkeit verursachen / darauß geriben werden.

¶ Das Saltz mit Meyenbutter zu einem Selblein gemacht / vnnd die bösen Kauden deß Grindts auff dem Haupt oder am Leiblein damit gesalbet / machet die dörren vnd heylen.

G ij   Wirckende

Margin notes (left group):
Paracel. stimbt mit den Alten vberein.
Apostema.
Hitz der Lungen.
Hitz der Leber.
Hüsten.
Strangularia.
Subtiliteit Kercter dann das darauß sie gezogen.
Wurm.
Krimmen.

Margin notes (right group):
Antidotum.
Krampff.
Bauchkrimmen
Würm.
Winst machen.
Magen reinigen.
Poros öffnen.
Böse Kawen.

78. Types used by Hentzsken, Berlin, 1578

DE VNITATE EC

CLESIAE CONSERVANDA, ET SCHI SMATE, QVOD FVIT INTER HENRI CHVM QVARTVM IMP. RO. ET GREGORIVM SEPT. PONT. MAX. CVIVSDAM EIVS TEMPORIS THEOLOGI LIBER AB HVT- TENO INVENTVS.

NEMO ASCENDIT IN CAELVM, niſi qui deſcēdit de cælo filius hominis, qui eſt in cælo. Per hæc ſancti euangelij uerba cōmen-dat dominus unitatem eccleſiæ, quæ per carita tem concordans membrorum unitate colligit ſe in cælum in ipſo redēptore, qui eſt caput ec-cleſiæ. Sic enim ipſe orat ad patrem pro fideli-bus ſuis, quos prædeſtinauit cōcordes fore in uinculo caritatis, &pacis, Rogo inquiēs, ut omes unum ſint, ſicut tu pater in me, & ego in te, ut & ipſi in nobis unum ſint. &dilectio, qua dilexiſti me, in ipſis ſit, &ego in eis. Vnde ſanctus Auguſtinus in ipſius e-uangelij expoſitione, in uno inquit eſtote, unū eſtote, unus eſto-te, & uæ illis, qui oderūt unitatem eccleſiæ, preſumentes in homi nibus partes facere. Vtinam uoluerint hoc attendere, qui partes in hominibus fecerunt, ut faciunt ſcindentes unitatem eccleſiæ, quale flagitiū ſchiſmatis cōſtat grauius eſſe, quàm ſcelus idólola triæ, quoniam legitur in ueteri teſtamento idololatria gladio pu nita eſſe, ſchiſma autem hiatu terræ. Quapropter neceſſarium du ximus ſcribere aliqua de ſtatu huius tēporis eccleſiæ. quia quiſ-quis ſenſerit ſe eſſe intra materna uiſcera ipſius eccleſiæ, non po-terit ei quando doluerit, nō condolere. Diu enim eſt quod in re-gno Romani imperij bella ubiqʒ, & ſeditiones aguntur, quod fi-lij à matris eccleſiæ gremio diſtrahuntur, & cum ſuperet in plu-

A   rimis

79. *Roman Type used by Schoeffer, Mainz,* 1520

DES. ERASMI ROTERO-
DAMI PROVERBIORVM CHILIADIS QVARTAE
CENTVRIA PRIMA.

ſ

Dulce bellum inexpertis.

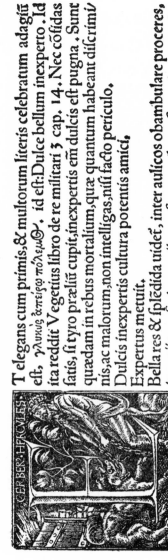

ET elegans cum primis, & multorum literis celebratum adagiũ
eſt, γλυκὺς ἀπείρῳ πόλεμος, id eſt:Dulce bellum inexperto.Id
ita reddit Vegetius libro de re militari ʒ cap. 14. Nec cõfidas
fatis, ſi tyro præl.iũ cupit,inexpertis eñ dulcis eſt pugna, Sunt
quædam in rebus mortalium,quæ quantum habeant diſcrimi/
nis,ac malorum,non intelligas,niſi facto periculo.
Dulcis inexpertis cultura potentis amici,
Expertus metuit.
Bella res & ſplẽdida uideſ, inter aulicos obambulare proceres,
in regijs uerſari negocijs : at ſenes,quibus uſu penitus cognita
res eſt,ab ea felicitate libenter abſtinent.Suaue uidetur,amare puellas, ſed rijs qui nondum
ſenſerunt,quãtum amori inſit amari.Ad eundem item modum accommodari poterit, ad
quoduis negocium multo cũ periculo,multisɋ cõiunctum malis,quod nemo uelit capeſ
fere,niſi iuuenis,& rerum imperitus. Siquidem Ariſtoteles in rhetoricis hanc adfert cau/

80. Roman Type used by Froben, Basle, 1526

in printing there was Froben (1460–1527), who set up his printing-house as early as 1491; but who is now chiefly remembered by his association with Erasmus after 1514. Erasmus lived with Froben while some of his books were in the press, and this was the great period of the office. Among Froben's foremost achievements were the first published edition of the New Testament in Greek, with a new Latin translation by Erasmus, issued in 1516, and the editions of Jerome, Ambrose, Tertullian, and Cyprian which Erasmus supervised. Erasmus's own books were also printed by Froben; and a portion of a page from *Adagiorum Opus D. Erasmi Roterodami* is reproduced (*fig.* 80). The massive and monumental sort of roman type which Froben used, often combined with splendid, rich borders and initials in close harmony with it, made books of great dignity and style, which scarcely miss—but none the less do lack—real beauty.

In the group of distinguished printers there, were Oporinus, printer for Luther; Petri, Episcopius, Cratander, Curio, and Bebel. Their editions, especially the folios embellished by brilliant decorations and initials by the Holbeins, Urse Graf, and other designers, will repay study. It is easy to recognize most Basle books of this period by their heavy roman type, very solidly set, and by certain typographical peculiarities of arrangement. There are of course exceptions, such as the magnificent folio *De Humani Corporis Fabrica*, of Andreas Vesalius, printed by Oporinus in 1543 —a volume not at all of the Froben order, but reminiscent rather of Plantin or some Italian printer. Its noble old style type and delicate italic, delightful initial letters and the careful anatomical engravings and famous title-page "The Anatomical Chamber" (attributed to Titian but by Jan Stephan van Calcar), make up a remarkable volume. The closeness of the type-setting is noteworthy and recalls much earlier books, and its presswork is uniformly good.

Erasmus's Latin translation of the New Testament, printed in italic by Froben in 1521, in a square 12mo, is an interesting example of one of Froben's small *formats*, and its brilliant decorations make its little pages almost "sing." The divisions are usually marked by captions in spaced capitals used in Froben's characteristic way. This edition was dedicated by Erasmus to Leo X (*fig.* 81). Erasmus's tractate, *Antibarbarorum*—a small quarto issued by Froben in 1520, printed from roman fonts, with decorations by Holbein—is another example of Froben's smaller books.[1]

The *Officina Isingriniana* at Basle was responsible, in 1542, for a wonderful botanical book—Leonhard Fuchs's *De Historia Stirpium*—which has various features worth notice. For the preface it employs a brilliant Venetian italic (*for example, see fig.* 104), which on these folio pages is most effectively displayed. The indexes of plants in Greek, Latin, and German are set respectively in Greek, roman, and fraktur types, four columns to a page. The text-pages follow, composed in the characteristic heavy, squarish roman type affected by Basle printers; the divisions of name, genera, form, place, time, etc., under each plant being set in lines of small spaced capitals. The glory of the book is its delightful outline plates of plants, cut on wood by Veit Rudolph Specklin, which in freedom and truthfulness are beyond praise. In some copies these are carefully coloured. A full-length portrait of the author backs the title-page, and a pleasant touch is given at the end by representations of the two designers, Füllmaurer and Meyer, at work, with

---

[1] For some fine titles, etc., from his books, see Butsch's *Bücher Ornamentik der Renaissance*, I, pls. 40, 41 (Holbein's design), 46 (A. Holbein), 48, 52, 53, and 59 (Holbein's initials).

EPISTOLA PAVLI AD CO,
RINTHIOS PRIMA.

AVLVS uocatus apoſtolus Ieſu
Chriſti, per uoluntatem dei , & Soſthe
nes frater, eccleſiæ dei , quæ eſt Corin,
thi , ſanctificatis per Chriſtum Ieſum,
uocatis ſanctis , unà cum omnibus qui
inuocant nomē domini noſtri Ieſu Chri
ſti, in quouis loco , uel ſuo , uel noſtro.
Gratia uobis & pax à deo patre no,
ſtro, & domino Ieſu Chriſto. Gratias ago deo meo ſemper pro
uobis de gratia dei, quæ data eſt uobis per Chriſtū Ieſum , quod
in omnibus ditati eſtis per ipſum, in omni ſermone, & omni co,
gnitione (quibus rebus teſtimonium Ieſu Chriſti confirmatū fuit
in uobis) adeo , ut nō deſtituamini in ullo dono, expectātes reue
latiōne domini noſtri Ieſu Chriſti , q & cōfirmabit uos uſq; ad
finē , inculpatos in die domini noſtri Ieſu Chriſti. Fidelis deus, p I. Theſſ. 5.
quē uocati eſtis ī cōſortiū filij ipſius Ieſu Chriſti domini noſtri.

Obſecro autem uos fratres , per nomen domini noſtri Ieſu
Chriſti, ut idem loquamini omnes, & non ſint inter uos diſſidia,
ſed ſitis integrum corpus eadem mente , & eadem ſententia.

Significatum eſt enim mihi de uobis fratres mei, à familiari
bus Chloæ, quod contentiones ſint inter uos. Dico autem illud,
quod unuſquiſq; ueſtrum dicit: Ego quidem ſum Pauli, ego uero
Apollo, ego uero Cephæ, ego uero Chriſti. Num diuiſus eſt Chri
ſtus? Num Paulus crucifixus eſt pro uobis? aut in nomine Pauli

R 3   *bapti,*

81. *Italic in Erasmus's New Testament*
Froben, Basle, 1521

Sapientes ubi audierint promo=
uebunt, & cordati industriam confe
quentur, ut intelligant sententias, in
terpretationem, sapientum consilia
& exempla.

Prae omnibus fructibus sapientû com
para sapientiam, & praeter facultates tu
as intelligentiam posside. Quod si eam
magnifeceris, te uicissim exaltabit.

Olomon Dauidis filius, rex Israelitarum, sententias
côscripsit, unde discanf sapientia, castigatio, intelligentia, prudentia, iustitia, ius & rectû, unde & callidi
tarê imperiti, & pueri scientiam & consilia petant:
Sapientia foris clamitat, in plateis uocê edit, mul-
titudini prati, pro portis clamitans, & in urbe concionatur.
Quousqp tandem imperiti amabitis imperitiam, & stulti amaro-
res animis delectamini, & fatui scientiam odistis? Aduertite animû
ad increpationem meam. Ecce spiritum meum uobis effabo, sententiam meâ exponam.   De meus scientiae initium.

Deus enim ex ore suo sapientiam & scientiam, & in
telligentiam largitur, rectis dat successum. Protegit pro=
bos. Ius tuetur, & iter sanctorum suorum custodit. Ita de
mû intelliges iusticiam, ius, recta & bonas uias omnes.

Penes me consiliû & successus est. Ego intelligentia sum,
penes me est potentia. Per me reges regnau, & principes
constituunt iusta. Per me domini dominantur, & regnant
omnes indices terrae.

ἐ μὲν ᾗ τὸ σε κεῆιοδρ ὦ ἀξεσον,
ᾗ δὲ ὁ προφονεοντες νοήρεαδρ ἀικαμ ἔχυτορ
ἀνίρ ᾗ δὲ χωὶ , τώλ᾽ ἔλγεα δυομευίεδsι·
κέφραπα δ᾽ ἐψιείηδι.

[Hebrew text]

Ir solt das
heiltumb nit den hunden gebê/Vnd
eüwere perlê solt ir nit für die sew wer
ffen/auff das sie die selbigen nit zur
tretten mit iren füssen/vnd sich wen
den/vñ euch zerreissen. ꝛc.

Alles das ir wöllent/das euch die leüt thûn sollt/das
thunt yn auch ir/Das ist das gesetz vñ die propheten.
Des herrn aug sihet auff die vn fröichten.
                                          Jo.Petreius

82. Specimen of J. Petri, Basle, 1525

flowers before them, while a conceited-looking gentleman
—the "sculptor" Specklin—appears to be impatiently wait-
ing for them to get through!

A beautiful edition from Henric Petri's press is a work
by Henricus Loritus (called Glareanus from his birthplace,
Canton Glarus), entitled *Dodecachordon.* This was written to
prove that there were twelve ecclesiastical modes identical
with the ancient Greek modes in music. To illustrate this
the printer employs some very interesting music types. At
the top of the massive pages the title is arranged in a condensed lower-case Italian letter which gives great elegance
to the work. This book (of its kind one of the most distinguished that I know) was printed in 1547.

The rough specimen of Joh. Petri (*fig.* 82) shows the
kind of roman and italic used in Basle printing-houses, but
the successful manner of its use can be realized only by seeing such books as I have mentioned. Besides three sizes of
roman and two of italic (the largest size of each much like
Schoeffer's), the sheet displays a Greek font and some Hebrew type. The fraktur at the bottom is very characteristic
in its ugliness. Published in 1525, it is, except for Ratdolt's,
the earliest specimen-sheet known.

At the end of the sixteenth century, the use of roman
letter, or "antiqua" as it was, and is, called in Germany, became less frequent, and in the seventeenth century it was
comparatively little used. By the beginning of the eighteenth
century it succumbed to the popular taste for fraktur—
though to be revived a little later.

By about 1550, both fraktur and schwabacher types had
taken on very much the general appearance of their modern German equivalents, except that they were heavier and
more masculine in appearance. Luther's German Bible of
1534 shows a title-page set in a heavy, vulgar sort of frak-

tur,[1] and its opening page of the Psalter is set in schwabacher types of characteristic form. The *Fabeln* of Burk-
hard Waldis, printed in 1550, shows again a typical form of
fraktur,[2] as does the text of the same writer's *Ursprung und
Herkumen der zwölf ersten alten König und Fürsten Deutscher
Nation.*[3]

The German books of this period are discouraging typographical productions. Their general character may be seen
by glancing at the rank and file of German folios in any
library which owns a collection of sixteenth century German books. The curious may investigate perhaps with
some profit (but with little pleasure) the Hohenzollern Collection illustrative of German history given to the library
of Harvard University by Mr. Archibald Cary Coolidge in
1902. But for most people, a glance at the pages devoted to
this period in Könnecke's *Bilderatlas* will be enough. The
title-pages in which red is so unsparingly introduced are
typographically as tasteless and bad as they can be, and exhibit a "frightfulness" which leaves nothing to be said.[4] As
the century went on, the work seems even worse. The *Historia von D. Johann Fausten* printed at Frankfort in 1587[5]
and other editions of the same work are very ugly and very
obviously Teutonic.

§ 2

The elaborate specimen of George Leopold Fuhrmann of
Nuremberg shows the types in use in the early years of
the seventeenth century in a well-known German printing-
house. This book was published in 1616. Its introduction
gives an account of the origin of printing and its chief promoters. The fonts which are shown comprise six sizes of
black-letter, ten of roman and italic, two of Greek, and four

[1] *Bilderatlas*, p. 141.   [2] *Ibid.*, p. 144.   [3] *Ibid.*, p. 143.
[4] *Ibid.*, pp. 151, 153, 154, 156.   [5] *Ibid.*, p. 160.

fonts of music with initials and ornaments. Copies are so rare that I have never had an opportunity to examine one.

German seventeenth century printing was not helped by pompous and overcharged copper-plate title-pages, and portraits in elaborate frameworks. These copper-plate title-pages, which took the place of the older red and black titles, were often imposing. There were typographical title-pages as well, but comparatively unimportant affairs, supplementary to the engraved title. The title-pages in Zeigler's *Asiatische Banise*, Leipsic, 1689,[1] show how badly things were going typographically by the end of the seventeenth century.[2]

§ 3

In the eighteenth century, the first fifty years show but little change or improvement. Look, for instance, at such a title-page as is shown in the first volume of Broctes's *Irdisches Vergnügen in Gott*, Hamburg, 1721,[3] Gottsched's *Critischer Dichtkunst*, published by Breitkopf in 1730,[4] or Breitinger's *Dichtkunst*,[5] issued at Zurich in 1740 — as tasteless and muddled printing as one can conceive.

By the middle of the eighteenth century, a change of fashions in German printing began. Vignettes were introduced and a little less matter was put upon title-pages. Anaemic roman types were also occasionally used. The *Messias* of Klopstock is an example of a book with text printed in vulgar, overblown fraktur types, with very few

[1] *Bilderatlas*, 196.

[2] " The introduction of the copper-plate marked a new epoch in book illustration, and wood-engraving declined with its increased adoption. . . . Woodcuts, headings, initials, tail-pieces, and printers' ornaments continued to be used [in books of the seventeenth century], but greatly inferior in design and beauty of effect to those of the sixteenth century." Crane's *Decorative Illustration of Books*, London, 1896, pp. 129, 130.

[3] *Bilderatlas*, p. 207.   [4] *Ibid.*, p. 209.   [5] *Ibid.*, p. 211.

words on the title-page (*fig.* 83). Such an aesthetic writer
as Winckelmann allowed his *Geschichte der Kunst des Alterthums* to appear (at Dresden in 1764) in a very hideous
and typical German character (*fig.* 84). If a well-known
printer wrote and printed a book about printing, one would
certainly expect *him* to execute it as well as he knew how;
and perhaps Breitkopf did, but his quarto volume *Ueber die
Geschichte der Erfindung der Buchdruckerkunst,* published
at Leipsic in 1779, is printed on miserable paper, in ugly
fraktur type, poorly composed — a volume such

> As to be hated needs but to be seen.

At the end of the century, still lighter and weaker types
and styles were in vogue. Lessing's *Nathan der Weise* in
1779 [1] shows the general feebleness of taste. Herder's *Briefe*,
published in 1793, shows the fraktur types which had come
to be the fashion. [2] As early as 1775 a general desire for light
types had influenced the forms of fraktur itself, as in J. G.
Jacobi's *Iris*, evidently imitating — very unsuccessfully —
contemporary French printing (*fig.* 85). Some of the pale,
condensed fraktur used at this period was probably influenced by those French condensed *poétique* types made fashionable by Fournier and Luce. The attempt to imitate French
work was also owing, in some degree, to that fashion for
things French encouraged by Frederick the Great, who —
after those earlier tentative plans mentioned by Fournier
had come to nothing — established about 1767, through
his court printer, Decker, a foundry and printing-house,
fashioned after the Imprimerie Royale de France. The Parisian founders Gillé, Fournier, and Didot, and Bodoni of
Parma were among those who supplied, either then or later,
much of its material.

[1] *Bilderatlas*, p. 238.   [2] *Ibid.*, p. 251.

Der
Meßias

ein

Heldengedicht.

LABORVM DVLCE LENIMEN

CHH

HALLE,
bey Carl Herrmann Hemmerde.
1749.

83. Title-page of Klopstock's Messias: Halle, 1749

Johann Winckelmanns,

Präsidentens der Alterthümer zu Rom, und Scrittore der Vaticanischen Bibliothek,
Mitglieds der Königl. Englischen Societät der Alterthümer zu London, der Maleracademie
von St. Luca zu Rom, und der Hetrurischen zu Cortona,

Geschichte der Kunst des Alterthums.

Erster Theil.

Mit Königl. Pohlnisch- und Churfürstl. Sächs. allergnädigsten Privilegio.

Dresden, 1764.
In der Waltherischen Hof-Buchhandlung.

84. *Title-page of Winckelmann's Kunst des Alterthums: Dresden*, 1764
(reduced)

Mir schlug das Herz; geschwind zu Pferde,
Und fort, wild, wie ein Held zur Schlacht!
Der Abend wiegte schon die Erde,
Und an den Bergen hieng die Nacht;
Schon stund im Nebelkleid die Eiche,
Ein aufgethürmter Riese, da,
Wo Finsterniß aus dem Gesträuche
Mit hundert schwarzen Augen sah.

Der Mond von seinem Wolkenhügel,
Schien kläglich aus dem Duft hervor;
Die Winde schwangen leise Flügel,
Umsausten schauerlich mein Ohr;
Die Nacht schuf tausend Ungeheuer—
Doch tausendfacher war mein Muth;
Mein Geist war ein verzehrend Feuer,
Mein ganzes Herz zerfloß in Gluth.

Ich

Ich sah dich, und die milde Freude
Floß aus dem süßen Blick auf mich.
Ganz war mein Herz an deiner Seite,
Und jeder Athemzug für dich.
Ein rosenfarbes Frühlings Wetter
Lag auf dem lieblichen Gesicht,
Und Zärtlichkeit für mich, ihr Götter!
Ich hofft' es, ich verdient' es nicht.

Der Abschied, wie bedrängt, wie trübe!
Aus deinen Blicken sprach dein Herz.
In deinen Küßen, welche Liebe,
O welche Wonne, welcher Schmerz!
Du giengst, ich stund, und sah zur Erden,
Und sah dir nach mit naßem Blick;
Und doch, welch Glück! geliebt zu werden,
Und lieben, Götter, welch ein Glück!

Q 3   Politik.

85. Pages of Jacobi's Iris, Düsseldorf, 1775

Fauſt.

Ein Fragment.

Von

Goethe.

Ächte Ausgabe.

Leipzig,
bey Georg Joachim Göſchen,
1790.

The printers and publishers who took a principal rôle in fostering the incoming taste for lighter types and more open composition which marked the beginning of the nineteenth century were Goschen and Unger, and perhaps the publisher Cotta of Tübingen, whose imprints figure on many publications of the period. Georg Joachim Goschen (1752–1828) was the publisher of the first edition of Goethe's *Faust*, the title-page of which is reproduced (*fig*. 86), and which speaks—or "whispers"—for itself. Goschen was a painstaking printer and a learned man; but he is not much remembered nowadays, though he took an important part in the revival of fine printing as then understood —notably in his editions of Wieland. On such title-pages as his *Faust* or Unger's *Wilhelm Meister* (*fig*. 87) we see how little was put on the title-page, how poorly that little was placed there, and in what dejected looking characters it was printed—all that remained of fifteenth century German fonts after the repeated whittlings of these enlightened gentlemen!

As will be noted, almost all the letter-forms employed in these later title-pages and books were fraktur, the schwabacher seeming to be displaced by its less attractive rival, which in turn was giving way before the fashion for Didot roman types, which were carrying everything before them.

II

WE have a contemporary account of type-founding in Germany and Prussia by Fournier, who in the year 1766 wrote:

"Germany, the cradle of Printing, has successfully cultivated the art, by establishing several celebrated foundries, which are usually richer in material than those of other countries, because, in addition to the ordinary types common to other foundries, those have been added which are peculiar to that particular country, like the German characters called Fracture [sic] and Schwabacher, which it is necessary to have in all sizes (*fig*. 88).

"At Vienna there are two foundries, of which one brought from Venice belongs to M. Trattener [sic], founder and printer to the Emperor.

"At Frankfort-on-the-Main, there are also two; the most important, which is very amply provided with ancient and modern characters, is known under the name of the Lutheran Foundry. It belongs to M. Luther, descendant of the famous Luther, so well known to the Christian world. It is furnished with sets of matrices by French artists.[1] The other, according to the specimens issued in 1714, belonged to Jean Henry Stubenvoll.

"At Leipsic there are three foundries; the first and the most considerable is that of M. Jean Gottlob Emmanuel Breitkopf, type-founder and printer. It is the most interesting foundry that I know of in Germany, on account of the number and variety of its ancient and modern types, its music types and its ornaments. The better of the two others belongs to M. Hr. Erhardt; it is fairly well equipped with both Latin and German characters.

"At Basle there are two foundries; the first, which is very noted for the number and variety of its types, of which

---

[1] The so-called Lutheran Foundry at Frankfort was the representative of the first printing-office established at Frankfort-on-the-Main in 1531, to which a foundry was added. This foundry and printing-office descended through various hands to Erasmus Luther, a relative of Martin, under whom it acquired a very great reputation. It supplied many German and Dutch printing-offices with their types. Enschedé thinks that the Elzevirs of Leyden procured several of their Greek fonts from this foundry; and that Daniel Elzevir and other celebrated printers bought its types and punches. Toward the end of the eighteenth century, much of its material went into the Berlin foundry directed by Unger.

Wilhelm Meisters

Lehrjahre.

Ein Roman.

Herausgegeben

von

Goethe.

Erster Band.

Berlin.
Bey Johann Friedrich Unger.
1795.

87. *Title-page of Wilhelm Meister: Unger, Berlin,* **1795**

Wäre es möglich, daß die
vor dreyhundert Jah=
ren verstorbene Gelehrte wie=
der in die Welt kämen, und
in die Palläste geführet wür=
den, welche die ruhmwürdig=
ste Käyser, Könige, Fürsten,
Herren und Obere der Re=
publiken und Städte zum
Sammelplatz und Aufent=
halt der gelehrten Werke er=
richtet haben: so würden sie
sich über alle in einer so kurzen
Zeit geschehene grosse Verän=
derungen nicht satt wundern
können.

Der ausnehmende Vor=
zug des Nutzens von
der Buchdruckerey ist: Daß
sie den Namen dessen, der
was lobens= und lesenswür=
diges geschrieben hat, der
Vergessenheit entreissen, und
die etwas sauberes und nütz=
liches abgedruckt haben, be=
halten selbst ein immerwäh=
rendes Andenken. Andere
Fabriken und Manufactu=
rien arbeiten der Vergäng=
lichkeit begierig in die Hän=
de. Die Früchte der edeln
Buchdruckerey aber geben
von einer Hand in die ande=
re, und bleiben gute Waare.

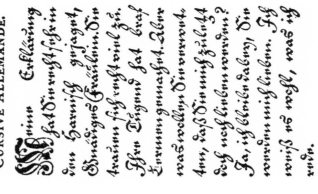

88. *Fraktur, Schwabacher, and Cursive, as shown by Fournier le jeune*

some came from French masters, and of which new specimens were issued in 1721, belonged at that date to M. Jean
Pistorius, founder and printer. The other, the stock of which
is made up of types more modern in cut, belongs to M.
Haas, a very celebrated type-cutter. The other German foundries are as follows: to wit, two at Halle, two at Nuremberg, one at Wittenberg, one at Dona, one at Erfurt, one at
Brunswick, one at Lüneburg, one at Cologne, one at Augsburg, one at Prague, one at Stuttgart in Wurtemburg."

"Prussia had no type-foundry until 1743, when one was
brought from Brunswick. It was of little value and was established in Berlin. This foundry not succeeding, a man
named Kanter started another in the same city, equipped
with fonts from the Breitkopf foundry at Leipsic and the
Zinche foundry at Wittenberg; its stock has since been
increased by other types made by a certain Gallner, a rather
tasteless and unintelligent type-cutter.

"The King of Prussia, wishing to establish a Royal Printing-House at Berlin modelled on that of the King of France,
gave orders to procure at Paris the punches, moulds, and
matrices necessary for a foundry, which was to form the
nucleus of such an establishment. M. Simon, printer to the
Archbishop [of Paris], being consulted about this undertaking, wrote and printed in 1741 a *Projet d'établissement
d'une Imprimerie Royale à Berlin,* which was sent to the
King, with a *recueil* of my types, intended to equip this
foundry. This scheme having fallen through, the King
brought to Berlin a celebrated type-cutter of the Hague,
named Jean-Michel Schmidt, giving him orders to set up
a Royal Foundry; but the wars which have since broken
out, and the death of this type-cutter in 1750, have sus-
pended its establishment."[1]

[1] Fournier's *Manuel Typographique,* Tome II, pp. xxix–xxxiv.

For the types produced we have the "Specimens" shown in works on typography by Pater (1710), Ernesti (1733), and Gessner (1740–45); and the specimen-books of Trattner (1759–60) and Unger (c. 1791).

The first, a small quarto book in Latin by Paul Pater about printing and printing types, was published at Leipsic in 1710 by J. F. Gleditsch and Son under the title of *De Germaniæ Miraculo Optimo Maximo, Typis Literarum, earumque differentiis, Dissertatio.* The third chapter treats of the different types then in use in Germany and their names, and shows specimens of capitals and lower-case in roman and italic, in various weights, and in sizes from Grosse Missal-Versal to Nonpareil. These are followed by a variety of fraktur and schwabacher types, Greek, Hebrew, Samaritan, Chaldaic, etc. The book is probably one of the earliest tractates on the typographical material of a nation, and gives a characteristic collection of fonts in use in German printing-houses at the end of the seventeenth and beginning of the eighteenth century. Its title-page (*fig.* 89) indicates what could be done when a German printer took the bit in his teeth. A page of roman and italic types, still retaining some good qualities, and another showing fraktur, schwabacher, and roman, are reproduced (*figs.* 90 *and* 91).

The second book, in which types and printing of the same period are covered even more fully, is J. H. G. Ernesti's book *Die Wol-eingerichtete Buchdruckerey,*[1] a treatise on printing, published at Nuremberg by the heirs of Johann

---

[1] *Die Wol-eingerichtete Buchdruckerey, mit hundert und ein und zwanzig Teutsch, Lateinisch, Griechisch, und Hebräischen Schrifften, vieler fremden Sprachen Alphabeten, musicalischen Noten, Kalender-Zeichen, und Medicinischen Characteren, Ingleichen allen üblichen Formaten bestellet und mit accurater Abbildung der Erfinder der löblichen Kunst, nebst einer summarischen Nachricht von den Buchdruckern in Nürnberg. . . . Nürnberg, gedruckt und zu finden bey Johann Andreä Endters seel. Erben. 1733.* An earlier edition appeared in 1721.

DE
GERMANIÆ MIRACVLO
OPTIMO, MAXIMO,

literarum,
EARVMQVE DIFFERENTIIS,
DISSERTATIO,
QVA SIMVL
ARTIS TYPOGRAPHICÆ
VNIVERSAM RATIONEM EXPLICAT
PAVLVS PATER, PP.

Multiplicetur scientia.   Non alio munere.   fortissimus conatibus.

Proſtat *LIPSIÆ*,
Apud JO. FRIDER. GLEDITSCH ET FILIVM.
Anno M.DCC.X.

89. *Title-page of Pater's Dissertatio, Leipsic,* 1710 (*reduced*)

Textualis quadratus: Text Verſal Antiqua und **Capitälgen.**

LABORE MONACHORUM MANUALI, TYPIS LITERARUM, NOSTRA ÆTATE, MULTA QUO-TIDIE LIBRORUM VOLUMINA IN LUCEM PRODEUNT:

Eiusdem

Eiusdem Curſivus : Text Verſal Curſiv.

HABEMUS ABUNDANTIAM BONORUM LIBRORUM, EOS-QVE PER MANUS IGNORAN-TIUM SCRIPTORUM, NEQVE TAMEN VITIATOS. Trithemius.

Textualis antiqvus barbar. Text antiqva:

Stant & augentur commerciis artibus-que Mechanicis regna, quæ ire in peius & minui certum eſt, ubi quilibet e po-pulo ſcitatur literas: raro mercatorem ſe ferat, qui ex literis gloriatur. *Gramond. hiſt. Gall.*

Idem Curſivus barbaricus: Text Curſiv.

Qvod ſi clarisſimorum inventorum ſoler-tia divinitatem olim quibusdam mortali-bus, communi gentium conſenſione conci-liavit; qvo honoris titulo dignos cenſebis,

90. *Types from Pater's Dissertatio, Leipsic,* 1710

bracht; hingegen nehmen sie ab, und müssen vergehen, wo ein jeder aus dem Pöbel wil dem Studiren nachgehen : Denn wer sich rühmet, daß er studiret habe, der wird nicht leicht einen Kauffmann abgeben, schreibet und urtheilet Gramond, ein Frantzösischer Historicus.

Mittel Schwabacher.

Außer dem ist des Königs ernster und gnädiger Wille, auch allen weltlichen Obrigkeiten und Geistlichen inclusivè, kund gemacht, per Mandatum, acht zu haben auf die Schulen, die ingenia stupida, oder tölpische Köpffe, die Halßstarrige und Faule nicht zu toleriren, oder zu dulten ; sondern zu andern Handthierungen und Manufacturen anzuweisen, damit die Fleißigen nicht gehindert, die Seminaria nicht beschweret, noch die beneficia nichtswürdigen Leuten möchten conferiret werden, und also dem Publico kein Schade oder Schande von ihnen erwachse. Berlin vom 8 September des 1708. Jahres.

Neue Leipziger grobe Mittel Fractur.

Lob der Buchdruckerey.

O Kunst ! der nichts zu gleichen ist,
Die Kirche kan zu keiner Frist
   Hier ohne dich bestehen:
Was acht ich Rath=Hauß, Canceley,
Was Schöppenstuhl, was Schreiberey,
   Wo du dich nicht läst sehen?
Du bist der Künste Königin,
Ja selbst der Weißheit Meisterin:
   Daß Advocaten sind gelehrt,
   Daß man den Artzt hält hoch und werth,
   Daß man die Lehrer liebet:

Daß

91. *Fraktur and Schwabacher Types: Pater's Dissertatio, Leipsic,* 1710

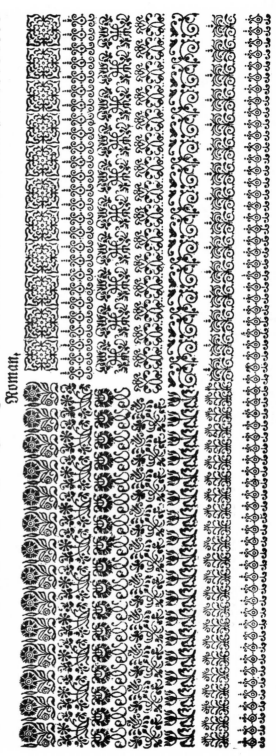

92. *Typographical Ornaments, probably from the Enders Printing-house, Nuremberg, 1721*

Canon.

Roman.

Andrea Endters—a well-known "printing family"—in 1733. After about fifty introductory pages the specimen-sheet begins, probably from the Endters printing-office, and showing its types in 1721. Here we have ten pages of frak-tur, starting with the shaded "Imperial" letters and ending with pearl—forty-seven varieties of every degree of taste-lessness and, in the smaller sizes, every variety of illegibil-ity, though a few of the latter have some distinction. In cer-tain cases larger types are introduced in lines of another font, quite in the manner of the lining system to-day. The schwabacher letters are fairly good characters and retain their sturdy traditional forms.

Twenty-two sizes and varieties of roman and fourteen varieties of italic are shown. In the larger sizes of roman, the letters are narrow and condensed and there are exces-sive contrasts between the thick and thin lines, but as sizes become smaller, the Roman letter becomes rounder and more monotonous in colour. Awkward in shape and arranged in lamentable fashion, books printed in it were easier to read, but scarcely less ugly than when printed in fraktur.

The italic type displayed has the same faults as the ro-man—round, open, but awkward in shape and quite with-out charm. It is supplied in a light and a heavy face, the latter to be used, probably, with fraktur. One reason why the effect of these italic types is so faulty is their miserable fitting and the wretched composition, and it is only fair to say that on such yellowing, spongy paper no character could be given a lively, sharp impression. This specimen also shows Greek, Hebrew, and exotic types, characters for music, the calendar, medicine, etc. At the end of the book is a garden of type-flowers or "Röslein," which displays many of the good old traditional patterns which have never been bettered (*fig.* 92).

A third "source-book" is Christian Friedrich Gessner's *Buchdruckerkunst und Schriftgiesserey*,[1] published in four volumes at Leipsic, between 1740 and 1745. Apparently this work was to an eighteenth century German printer and amateur, what Fournier's *Manuel Typographique* was at that date to Frenchmen of similar tastes. The first volume contains an account of the invention of printing, lives of printers (especially those of Leipsic), portraits of all degrees of interest and excellence, printers' marks, plans for imposition, and alphabets—Greek, Hebrew, Syriac, Turkish, Arabic, Coptic, Armenian, etc. There are chapters on orthography; and plates showing the ancient cases for Latin, Greek, Hebrew, Arabic, and other languages. Typefounding is accurately illustrated, and there are pictures of presses, the case, and compositor's material, tools, and appliances down to the diminutive candle which gave him light. But it is the *Schrift-Probe* or specimen of types in Bernhard Christoph Breitkopf's (1695–1777) foundry which is interesting to us.[2]

Of the German eighteenth century type-founders, Breitkopf is easily the most important. He began life as a journeyman printer, started as a type-founder in 1719, and published this specimen-sheet of his foundry at Leipsic in 1739. He apparently cut most of his own punches. He was also a musician, and the name is familiar in connection with music printing. When Goethe went to Leipsic in 1765 he met Breitkopf, and some of the poet's earliest poems were

[1] *Die so nöthig als nützliche Buchdruckerkunst und Schriftgiesserey, mit ihren Schriften, Formaten und allen dazu gehörigen Instrumenten abgebildet auch klärlich beschrieben, und nebst einer kurzgefassten Erzählung vom Ursprung und Fortgang der Buchdruckerkunst, überhaupt, insonderheit von den vornehmsten Buchdruckern in Leipzig und andern Orten Teutschlandes im* 300 *Jahre nach Erfindung derselben ans Licht gestellet.* . . . *Leipzig, ben Christian Friedrich Gessner,* 1749. 4 vols.

[2] Vol. I, p. 145, second series of folios.

Text Fractur.

Wiſſet, daß ihr nicht mit ver= gänglichem Silber oder Golde er= löſet ſeyd von eurem eiteln Wan= del, nach väterlicher Weiſe; ſon= dern mit dem theuren Blute Chriſti.

Tertia Fractur.

Da aber Juda gen Mizpe kam, an der Wüſten, wandten ſie ſich gegen den Hau= fen, und ſiehe, da lagen die todten Leich= name auf der Erden, daß keiner entrunen war. Und Joſaphat kam mit ſeinem Volk, ihren Raub aus zutheilen.

Von Chriſtian Zingk, in Wittenberg, in Stahl.

Grobe Mittel Fractur.

Singet Gott, lobſinget ſeinem Nahmen, ma= chet bahn, dem, der da ſanft herfähret; Er hei= ßet Herr und freuet euch vor ihm. Der ein Vater iſt der Wäyſen, und ein Richter der Wittwen; Er iſt Gott in ſeiner heiligen Woh= nung. Ein Gott, der den Einſamen das Haus voll Kinder giebet.

K 3 Schwa=

93. *Fraktur Types from Breitkopf's Schrift-Probe*
Leipsic, 1739

Tertia Antiqua.

Jova, noli in me iracunde animad-
vertere : noli me atrociter punire.
Miferere mei ægrotantis, Iova: fane
me, Iova.

Tertia Curfiv.

*Jovam mihi jugiter habeo propofi-
tum, quo mihi dextro non labe fiam.
Itaque non tantum animo & mente lætor & exalto.*

Grobe Mittel Antiqua.

Sed me vitæ viam docebis tu, apud quem
plene gaudiorum ad eft copia, cujus in dex-
tra perennes funt voluptates.

Vorftehende 3 von Chr. Zingk, in Stahl.

Kleine Mittel Antiqua.

Itaque non tantum animo & mente lætor &
exalto, verum etiam ipfum corpus meum tuto
degit, quoniam tu nos es animam meam relictu-
ras oreo, nos es paffurus.

Mittel Curfiv.

*Quum Jovæ confidam, cur animæ fic dicitis?
faceffe in veftrum montem volucris. Ecce autem
arcus in tendunt impii adaptatis ad nervum fuis
fagittis, ut clam in homines frugi jaculentur.*

Grobe

94. *Roman and Italic Types: Breitkopf's Schrift-Probe*
Leipsic, 1739

set to music by the son, Johann Gottlob Immanuel, who succeeded his father in the conduct of the foundry, and was also
a bookseller and printer. The latter was a contemporary of
Fournier, and they corresponded on the subject of music-
printing. His own improvements in music types were introduced about 1754. Another idea of Breitkopf's was map-
printing from types, and he also did something toward re-
forming the shape of German characters, a field in which
there was illimitable opportunity. When he died, his printing-house was one of the largest and most important in the
country. He was, it is said, the purchaser of some of Baskerville's matrices. The house he founded is still extant.

Fournier said Breitkopf's foundry was "the first and most
considerable of those at Leipsic, and the most interesting
foundry that I am familiar with in Germany, on account
of the number and variety of its ancient and modern types,
its music types, and its type ornaments." The first four
pages of Breitkopf's specimen show eighteenth century
fraktur (*fig*. 93), and the next four pages fraktur and schwabacher together — the latter the better of the two, especially
in larger sizes.[1] Nothing good can be said about the fraktur
letters. The roman and italic types in this specimen are
unattractive, too. The capital letters are very condensed and
show excessive contrasts of thick and thin lines, and compare unfavourably with those in Pater's volume. The lower-
case roman in the medium sizes is square and blocky in
effect (*fig*. 94). As the sizes grow smaller, the effect becomes more and more monotonous and "airless." The italic
is somewhat condensed and ungainly in design. Some of

---

[1] Fournier says that schwabacher "has been very much used in Germany —
where it took the place of italic when employed with the German character,
or to indicate some other text than those which were represented by the
German, roman, and italic characters employed in the same work."

these types were cut by Christian Zingk of Wittenberg, no doubt the foundry "*de Zinche à Wittemberg*" of which Fournier speaks, and others by Johann Caspar Muller and Joh. Peter Artofao, of Leipsic, Andr. Koler of Nuremberg, and Pancr. Lobinger of Vienna. The folding plates following this specimen of Breitkopf's show *Dutch* xvii century types which came from the foundry of Erhardt (*figs.* 217 *and* 218) at Leipsic, which Fournier says was, after Breitkopf's, the best establishment there. For tastelessness of composition no example could be more to the point than this book, which was, nevertheless, published in the interests of typography.

The specimen of Johann Thomas Trattner of Vienna may properly come under German specimen-books of this period. Its various parts devoted to roman, German, and exotic types and ornaments were published in 1759 and 1760.[1] The roman types are mostly beneath contempt; and the models for them seem to have been gathered from the four quarters of the earth. Some show Dutch influence, others French, and a few of a very round, colourless roman and italic are so bad that they could have originated nowhere except in Trattner's own foundry! A condensed and irregular Dutch italic is one of the features of the Latin types. To German text types some ornamented letters add a touch of horror hitherto unachieved by any Teutonic type-cutter; but the entire vulgarity of the fraktur displayed is relieved by some very good schwabacher fonts. In Trattner's fraktur, as in his roman fonts, there seems to be a taste for a thin condensed letter, modelled on the condensed types then popular in France. A great many ornaments, mostly copied or derived from French work of the period, are displayed in

[1] The title-page of the first part reads: *Specimen Characterum Latinorum existentium in Cæsarea ac Regio-Aulica Typorum Fusura apud Joannem Thomam Trattner*, etc. Vienna, 1759. A second edition, enlarged, appeared in 1769, sometimes to be found with a supplement dated 1782.

XXI. Cicero Schwabacher.

Sie sind hinweg! Sie sind verschwunden! Doch nein! Kein leeres Schattenbild hat Augen und Gehör gefüllt: Ein lehrender Betrug hielt meinen Sinn gebunden. Durch sie, durch ihre Hülf allein hast du, Vernunft! den Feind bezwungen. Ihm wird nur Schimpf. Der Sieg wird dein. Ihn hat dein Licht und sie verdrungen.

XXII. Garmond Fractur.

Die List, die dir den Fall gedroht, Schlägt auf sein stolzes Haupt zurücke. Die Welt, die ihm den Hals zur Knechtschaft willig both, Sieht itzt mit aufgeklärterm Blicke. Die Künste flohn von unsren Hütten, Da Barbarey für Andacht galt, Da man Vernunft für Frechheit schalt; Itzt hat die neue Kunst den wüsten Geist bestritten. Du lägst noch itzt, o Alterthum! In unbekannter Nacht begraben. Wo wär Unsterblichkeit und Ruhm, Die dir die treuen Söhne gaben? Sie wären noch der Motten Raub, Des frechen Ungeziefers Speise.

XXIII. Eine andere Garmond Fractur.

Umhüllte nicht noch jetzt, Virgil, ein ewger Staub Die Frucht von deinem langen Fleisse? Entzückt uns wohl, was Rom entzückte, Da deinen Mund, mein Cicero, Ein frecher Catilina floh? Wofern es nicht der Druck dem Geiz der Zeit entrückte. Umsonst hätt euch des Glückes Gunst Vor longobardscher Wuth verstecket; Hätt euch nicht itzt die Druckerkunst Vom Tode wieder aufgewecket. Wem säng Homer? Wen rührtet ihr? Vom Epheulaub umschlungne Stirnen? Kein Leser würde jetzt, Demothenes! mit dir Auf des Philippus Herrschsucht zürnen. Wie oft hat euch der Tod bedrohet, Der euren Fall durch Krieg gesucht? Der Krieg zwang euch zu neuer Flucht, Ihr Künste, da ihr noch den ersten Wuth entflohet!

XXIV. Eine andere Garmond Fractur.

Vergnüge dich mein Sinn, und laß dein Schicksal walten. Es weiß, worauf du warten sollt: Das wahre Glücke hat verschiedene Gestalten, Und kleidet sich nicht nur in Gold. Dein Geist würkt ja noch frey in ungekränkten Gliedern, Du hast noch Haus und Vaterland: Worüber klagst du denn? Nur Stolz schämt sich im Niedern Und Uebermuth im Mittelstand.

95. *Schwabacher and Fraktur: Trattner's Abdruck dererjenigen Deutschen Schriften, etc., Vienna,* 1760

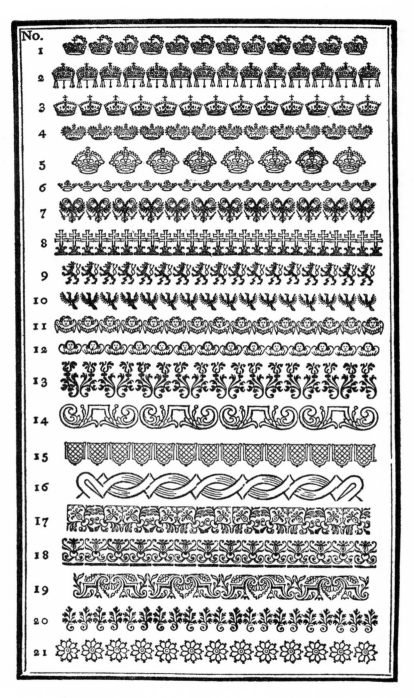

96. *Ornaments: Trattner's Abdruck von denjenigen Röslein, etc.*
Vienna, 1760

Mit Königl. Privilegium

1
2.
3.
4.
5.
6.
7.
8.
9.
10.
11.

Cicero Fractur. Erſter Verſuch.

Der Edelmuth iſt durch ſeine Bennenung ſchon erklärt, dennoch könte man ſagen, er ſey der geſunde Verſtand des Stolzes und das edelſte Mittel Lob zu erwerben.

Corpus Fractur von Didot.

Man könnte ſagen: die Laſter erwarteten uns auf dem Wege des Lebens wie Gaſtwirthe, bey denen man nach und nach einkehren muß; und ich zweifle, daß uns die Erfahrung vorüber drängen könnte, wenn wir den Weg zweymal machen dürften.

Bourgeois Fractur auf Corpus Regel.

Der Ruhm großer Männer muß beſtändig nach den Mitteln abgemeſſen werden, wodurch ſie ihn errangen. Die Könige ſtempeln Menſchen, wie Münzen: ſie geben ihnen den Werth, welchen ſie wollen; und man iſt gezwungen, ſie nach ihrem Kours, nicht aber nach ihrem Schrot zu nehmen

Petit Fractur.

Nichts iſt ſo anſteckend als Beyſpiel, und wir ſtiften niemal Gutes oder viel Böſes, was nicht ähnliches Gute oder Böſe hervorbrächte. Gute Handlungen ahmen wir aus Wetteifer, und böſe, aus der natürlichen Verkehrtheit nach, die von der Scham gefangen gehalten und durch das Beyſpiel in Freyheit geſetzt wurde.

97. (a) Neue Deutsche Lettern and (b) Ornaments: Unger's Schriftproben, Berlin, c. 1791

Beim Ausgange der Kirche gegen die andre Seite der Stadt hin, überrascht von dem Hügel herab, auf welchem Loretto liegt, der Anblick einer der reizendsten Naturscenen. Ein weites, reich bebautes, mit Reihen von Fruchtbäumen durchschnittenes Thal, senkt sich an dem Fuß der Berge; darüber hin, und seitwärts hinaus schweift der Blick auf die gränzenlose Fläche des Adriatischen Meeres. Diese Segen und Freiheit athmende Aussicht gibt beßre Empfindungen wieder, und verdrängt jene, die der Anblick der Priestergewalt über des Volkes Blödsinn erregte. Sie verschwinden ganz, diese widrigen Eindrücke, je weiter man sich von Loretto entfernt und auf dem Wege nach Rom die hohen Appeninen ersteigt.

gen Gelehrten zufallen möge, deren Geschmack zugleich geübt genug ist, den rechten Gesichtspunkt, aus welchem dieser Versuch dieser Art angesehen werden muß, zu fassen. Das Urtheil solcher Männer wird für mich sehr bedeutend und unterrichtend seyn. Schlimm wäre es, wenn sie einem Recensenten in die Hände fiele, der so darüber abspräche und so ohne Kunstkenntniß davon urtheilte, wie vor einiger Zeit der in der Hallischen gelehrten Zeitung über meine kleine in Holz geschnittene Landkarte. Fast eben so ging es meinem Versuch in einer andern gelehrten Zeitung, die ich aus Achtung für die gelehrten und mit Recht geschätzten Herausgeber nicht nennen will. —

Daß bei diesen Lettern noch hier und da verbessernde Abänderungen möglich sind, gebe ich gern zu, und ich werde meinen ganzen Fleiß darauf verwenden, sie noch vollkommener zu machen.

98. *Unger's and Didot's Modifications of German Fraktur, 1793*

combinations which have much of the ingenuity of current French work and few of its agreeable qualities. We reproduce a page of schwabacher and fraktur, the latter in the condensed form alluded to (*fig.* 95), and a page of these *vignettes de fonte* (*fig.* 96).

Johann Frederic Unger (1750–1804) of Berlin was the individual who figured as the chief representative in Germany of the Didot and Bodoni influence. He was a really learned and distinguished man, a friend of Goethe and a correspondent of Schiller. His foundry and printing-house contained the chief part of the ancient material of the old Lutheran foundry at Frankfort-on-the-Main, which, toward the end of the eighteenth century, Unger acquired for his Berlin establishment.

Unger's *Schriftproben der Didotschen und gewöhnlichen Lettern*, issued about 1791 at Berlin, clearly exhibits the sort of thing he was introducing into German typography, and some of the pared-down fraktur types 'and a page of the new decorations (so called) which Unger introduced are shown (*figs.* 97a *and* 97b). The hair-like serifs and light strokes in the roman letters, and, under the heading *Neue Deutsche Lettern*, the anaemic italic, the condensed and fantastic fraktur fonts, show what he desired to popularize in German typography. Relegated to the back of this prim little book are the *Ordinaire Deutsche Lettern*, both in schwabacher (some of them excellent) and fraktur, which at least have the merit of a certain robustness. Cursive letters, a repertoire of colourless, starved-looking borders, and a folding-sheet of forlorn-looking music types, complete the collection. The *Neue Deutsche Lettern* in this specimen were cut by Unger and his engraver Gubitz, except the Corpus Fractur, which Firmin Didot engraved. Didot's types may be contrasted with Unger's modifications of German fraktur (*fig.* 98), where I think Unger went Didot one better— or worse!

At this period German typography sunk to its lowest ebb. Up to that time German fonts had some strength and the composition some character; but by the year 1800 the boldest and noblest typography in Europe had degenerated to the weakest and poorest. What happened to it later— in the early part of the nineteenth century—is "not worth forgetting." Of its connection with the modern English revival of printing, I have later to speak.

CHAPTER XIII

ITALIAN TYPES: 1500–1800

ITALIAN printing during the first half of the sixteenth century retained a certain elegance. The tradition of monumental work had not died out, and we see, as late as 1560, some very noble books in a fine form of roman letter either reminiscent of, or printed in, fifteenth century fonts, such as were sometimes called the *carattere Veneto*. There was still, in the types and their use, the grand manner. From the middle of the sixteenth century, Italian printing sharply declined in excellence. The roman and italic letter had some time before this become generally popular, so that the types used were not very often of Gothic form. But while Italian roman type did not possess all its early elegance, the great declension came in its use. By looking at a few books which are average specimens of Italian sixteenth, seventeenth, and eighteenth century printing, it is easy to see by what route it ran downhill.

§ 1

Ovid's *Metamorphoses* with commentary by R. Regi, published at Milan in 1509 by Nicolas Gorgonzola, is a book which at first sight might have been printed in the fifteenth rather than the sixteenth century. The text, in large roman type, runs at the right of left-hand pages and the left of right-hand pages, and the outside of the page is filled (as in manuscripts) by wide columns of notes, set in smaller roman characters. These columns of notes, much infested by a family of very black paragraph marks, are allowed to come just as they will—sometimes extending to the bottom of the page, sometimes not, and here and there surrounding three sides of the text. At the beginning of each Book, an unattractive initial is usually inserted, to take the place of those before painted in by hand; for spaces were still sometimes left for an illuminator's work. This detail indicates a beginning of the decline in Italian book-making; but this book maintains something of the grand manner (*fig.* 99).

Boccaccio's *Decamerone*, issued in the name of the heirs of Filippo di Giunta at Florence in 1527, like so many Giunta books, very closely imitates the Aldine style. It is printed entirely in one font of italic type, with the exception of its title-page, headings, and running-titles, which are in roman capitals. Small roman capitals are used with the italic letter, and spaces are left for initials to be filled in by hand. Its use of italic makes it a sixteenth century book, but it would be a very creditable and beautiful volume for any century. An imitation of this edition was made at Venice in 1729, which may be consulted if the edition of 1527 is not available.

Books were still printed in gothic types, and a Venice edition of the *Opera* of Boethius, printed by Luc Antonio Giunta in 1536, is, in its arrangement and its black-letter type, completely Gothic, and, in its way, very handsome. It is set chiefly in two sizes of Italian gothic characters, arranged in double column. The running-titles are in a large size of much the same letter. Marginal notes set in small black-letter and arabic numerals for folios are perhaps not quite in the style; nor is the title-page, which shows signs of "display" lines. Yet the book is a reminder of the persistence of black-letter volumes in the home of the roman letter (*fig.* 100).

Alessandro Vellutello's edition of Dante's *Commedia*,[1] printed by F. Marcolini at Venice in 1544, shows the Al-

---

[1] Students of Italian printing may consult the Dante collections at Harvard and Cornell Universities, which furnish a great number of editions interesting for purposes of comparison.

Nde per immenſum:Totum hūc librum undécimíque partem Orphei geſtis carminibuſque ita díca uit poeta:ut ab inſtituto non diſcedat:uariaſque tranſfigurationes exponit :nam orpheus Apollinis: uel ut alii ſcribunt:Oeagri fluuii & Calliopes muſæ filius:ſcientia ac cantus ſuauitate mortales omnes dicitur ſuperaſſe:citharamque ad ſimilitudinem teſtudinis a Mercurio confectam:donoque Apolliuſ datam a patre accepiſſe:cuius modulatione non homines ſolum:ſed feras ſiluaſque ac ſaxa mota ſuiſ ſe.Is enim ut ſcribit Dio.doctrinæ deditus cū theologiæ operam impendiſſet:in ægyptum tranſiit : plurimatúque ibi rerum percepta ſcientia:Græcorum doctiſſi-

Orphei nuptiæ. mus:tum in deorum cerimoniis:tum in theolo gía tum in poematis cantuque eſt habitus .nauſ gauit ſiuper cum argonautis obque uxoris amo rem ad inferos cū deſcendiſſet:a Proſerpina ſua uitate cātus alllecta impetrauit:ut defuncā uxo rem ab inferis excitaret,nam eurydice q̄ i fauſto ómine ſibi copularat dum per prata ſimul cum aliis nymphis uagaretur:a ſerpente percuſſa inte riit:tantoque dolore morſens affecit maritum: ut non ſatis eē duxerſt lugeſ ſed ad inferos quo que ad eam repetetendam deſcendere nihil du bitarit.eo igitur cum peruenſſet:tantum carmi nis ſuauitate affecit:ut uxorem a Plutone ea acci peret conditione:ne illam prius:q̄ ad ſuperos re

Orpheꝰ ad iſeros uerſus eēt reſpiceret:ſed Orpheus ueriꝛ ne uxor ſequeretur cūm iam fere ad ſuperos peruenſſet. eam reſpexit:;quæ illico ad inferos retracta Or pheum in maximis cruciatibus reliquit:qui cum deſperaret ſe iterſ ea potiri poſſe : omnes aſper natus mulieres dicitur:primuſque apud Thracef puerorum amoribus indulſiſſe.id uero ægre fere tes thraciæ mulieres ſacra Bacchi celebrantes il

Serpēs I ſaxum Cicones lum cithara canentem feraſque mulcentē diſcer pſerunt:cuius caput úna cum cithara in Hebrū͂ iectum:cum Leſbū uſque peruenſſet : ſidque ſer pens laniare uelletꞏin ſaxum ab Apolliine dicit fuiſſe transformatus:⸿ Ad oras Ciconum .Cico nies populi ſunt Thraciæ iuxta Hebrum fluuiū habitantes.⸿ Et orphea uoce . adiectiuum ē et phea.Vnde etiam penultimam producit quæ a græcis per.ꜹ.ſcribitur. ⸿Nequicquam fruſtra. neque enim felices illæ nuptiæ fuerunt. ⸿Sed nec ſolemnia uerba:qualia hæc eſſent : ſauſtæ ſe liceſque hæ ſint nuptiæ.⸿ Vſque:ſemp. ⸿ Rho

Tænari us. dopeius uates Orpheus poeta Thracius cuius hymii in pleroſque deorum etiam nū extant. Rhodope autem mons eſt Thraciæ altiſſimus. ⸿ Tænaria porta. Tænarus Laconiæ promóto rium eſt:in quo ſpecus eſſe dicitur per quem ad inferos deſcenditur. ⸿ Perque leues populos:cor poribus carentes. ⸿ Perſephonem:Proſerpinam ⸿ Vmbrarum dominum Plutonem. ⸿ Oppoſi ti.Hac oratione Orpheus perſuadere Plu toni atque Proſerpinæ:ut ſibi Euridicem uxorē reſtituant:ac per aliquot adhuc ános uiueſ apud ſuperos permittant. ⸿ Mundi poſiti ſub terra.

Augu ror. Auguro Periphraſis eſt infeſorum. ⸿Opaca tartara:ob ſcura:tenebroſa.eſt enim tarrarus inferorū locus ꝓfundiſſimus. ⸿Meduſæi mōſtri.cerberi canis I ſeroꞃ tricipitis:q̄ ut meduſa ꝑ capillis:itaꝑ pilis colubros ac ſerpeſtes habet.Merito āt ſe excuſat Orpheus:ne ut Hercules credaſ ād extrahendū Cerberū illuc deſcendiſſe. ⸿ Auguror .cōiecto & ſignis colligo:auguror āt & auguriā i'eadē ſigni ficatiōe dicius. ⸿ Veteris rapinæ.nā pluto ꝑperpinæ amore captus eā rapuit.⸿ Per chaos hoc igēs. ⸿ Per hias ſmen

Nde per imenſum crocco ue latus amictu
Aethera dígreditur ciconum que hymenæus ad horas
Tendit:& orphea nequicquā uoce uocatur.
Affuit ille quidem, ſed nec ſo lemnía uerba.

Nec lætos uultus:nec fœlíx attulit omen:
Fax quoꝗ quā tenuít lachrymoſo ſtridula ſūo
Vſque fuit:nulloſque inuenit motibus ignes.
Exítus auſpicio grauior:nam nupta per herbas
Dum noua naíadum turba comitata agatur
Occidit in talum ſerpentis dente recepto,
Quam ſatis ad ſupas poſtꝗ rhodopeius auras
Defleuit uates:ne non temptaret & umbras.
Ad ſtyga tenaría eſt auſus deſcendere porta:
Perꝗ leues populos:ſimlacraꝗ ſūcta ſepulchro
Perſephonen adiit,inamataque regna tenentem
Vmbrarum.dominū:pulſiſꝗ ad carmía neruís
Sic ait:o poſiti ſub terra numina mundi
In quem decidimus quicquid mortale creamur
Si licet:& falſi poſitis ambagibus oris
Vera loqui ſinitis:non huc ut operta uiderem
Tartara deſcendi:nec uti uilloſa colubris
Terna meduſæi uincirem guttura monſtri.
Cauſa uiæ eſt coniunx in quā calcata uenenum
Vipera diffudit:creſcenteſque abſtulit annos.
Poſſe pati uolui:nec me temptaſſe negabo.
Vicit amor ſupera deus híc bene notus i ora ē.
An ſit & híc dubito:ſed & híc tñ auguror eſſe
Famaque ſi ueteris non eſt mentita rapínæ:
Vos quoꝗ iūxit amor:ꝑ ego hæꞇ loca plēa ꞇioríſ
Per chaos hoc ingens uaſtiꝗ ſilentía regni:
Eurydíces oro properata retexite fata.
Omnía debentur uobis:paulūmque morati

❧Finitij Manilij Seuerini Boetij viri clariſſi
mi editio prima in Categorias Ariſto.

Xpeditis ble q̃ ad pꝛe
dicamenta Ariſto. Poꝛ
phyrij ſñoe oigeſta ſūt
bos quoꝗ̃ cõmentarios
in pꝛedicameta ſcribens
mediocris ſtili ſerie pꝛe
cutus: nihil ve altioꝛum
qõnum tractatione pꝛni
ſcruſ ſed viluciandi:imo
veratione ſeruata nec an
gere lectoꝛe bꝛeuitate vo
lui, nec vilatatione õfun
dere. Quare ꝑus bꝛeui
ter buiꝰ operis aperieda videꝰ intentio: que eſt buiꝰ. Re
bus placetibus:ꞇ in pꝛeia ꝑncipaliter nãe õſtrutiõe ma
netibus humanu ſolũ genue extitit:q̃ reb꞊ noia poſſet
iponere. Uñ factum eſt: vt vt ſingulatim oïa ꝑſecutus bois
aiue ſingulis, vocabula reb꞊ apparet. Et hoc q̃dem Ꝟbi gra
tia, cõpus boiem vocauit illa:ꝰ No lapide:aliud lignuꝰ,
aliud No coloꝛe. Et rurſus qꝯuꝗ̃ ex ſe aliū genuiſſet: pꝛis
vocabulo nũcupauit. Deſuꝛa quoꝗ̃ magnitudinis pꝛo

Hoiuꝰ poð
vuplex ſit:ꝰ
ſolꝰ reb꞊ pꝛi
cðoꝰ noiaꝰ,
di dit ac nꝯ
minum nõu
veſignauit.

❧Eñ oñ ꝑpriu:ſempꝰ adeſt ſpðꝰ:nec eas vllo mõ relinquit:
qñuꝗ̃ inſepabile accñs a ſubõ nõ pñt ſegregari Ɜ illis:ter
ſe videꝰ eꝰ cõe ꝗ̃ ea in qbꝰ inſunt ꝑter ꝑpꝛia vel inſepabilia
accñtia eꞗ nõ pñt. Inſepabilia No accñtia cõparat ꝑpꝛio:
q̃ñ vt in ſpe oḿ eſt rariſſime ſūt ſpéi atꝗ̃ accñtie ſilitudi
nee. Quo circa multo magis ꝑꝑij atꝗ̃ accidétis cõtates
difficile reperiunꝰ, accñs.ñ.ñ pꝛu õtu vt viuidi ſolet in inſepabi
le. accñs atꝗ̃ ſepabile:ꝗ̃ No ſub gñe in pꝛñuꝗ̃ viuidumꝰ:ea
nullo alio niſi tñi genere ꝑdicatione ꝑticipaꝰ. Quod ſi
ꝑpꝛiu inſeparabile qꝯda accñse a ſepabili accñti pluri/
mũ viffertat:ꝗ̃ jõ nullas ꝑpꝛij ꞟ ſepabilis accñtis ſilitu
dines qꝛit. Sed qñ iſ̃m certis quibuſda cauſis ab inſepa/
rabilibus accidétibus viffert:hoꝛ ꞟ cõtates inueniri pñt
ꞟ iter ſe õſequarñ vna q̃dē ac eſt q̃ſ
ꞟ iter ſe õſequarñ vna q̃dē ac eſt q̃ſ ſuꝑꝰ expoſuimus,
ſõa No qñ ſicut ꝑpꝛiu ſemꝓ ꞟ oïſ pñt adeſt:ita ꞟ inſepabi
le accñs. Ɜa ſicut riſibile omni hominiꝰ ꞟ ſemꝓ adeſt:
ita etiam nigredo omni coꝛuo ꞟ ſemper adiunctaeſt.

❧Diffart auteꝰ qñ pꝛopꝛium vni ſoli ſpéi adeſt
quéadmodũ riſibile hominiꝰ inſeparabile vero ac
cidés, vt nigrũ nõ ſoli ethiopi, ſed ꞟ coꝛuo adeſt
ꞟ carboni ꞟ hebeno, ꞟ quibuſda alijs. quare pꝛo/
pꝛiũ conuerſim ve eo citius eſt ꝑpꝛiũ pꝛedicatur
ꞟ equaliter. inſeparabile vero accidés conuerſim
non predicatur, ꞟ pꝛopꝛioꝛ quidem equalis eſt

Pꝛopꝛũ ꞟ
inſeparabile
accñs:ocbit
ꝗ̃ fine ꝟie
nãꝗ̃ õſiſtit
ea ꝗ̃ eoꝰ ꝑ/
eticipat:ꞟ iꝗ̃
bus tpã cõſñ.
derantur.

100. Gothic Type in Opera of Boethius: Giunta, Venice, 1536

CANTO XVIII.

Che mi fa souenir del mondo antico.
Io fui colui; che la Ghisola bella
Condussi a far la uoglia del Marchese,
Come che suoni la sconcia. nouella.
E non pur io qui piango Bolognese:
Anzi nè questo luogo tanto pieno;
Che tante lingue non son hora apprese
A dicer; Sippa, tra Sauena el Rheno:
E se di cio uuoi fede, o testimonio;
Recati a mente il nostro auaro seno.
Cosi parlando, il percosse un demonio
De la sua scuriata, e disse; Via
Ruffian, qui non son femine da conio.

mente credere, chel Marchese la torrebbe
per moglie. COme che suoni la sconcia
nouella, In qual altro modo si publichi di
tal cosa la corrotta fama, perche dicano,
che alcuni diceuano, non esser uero, che
Messer Venetico fesse di tal cosa conscret
uole, Et altri, che nulla ne era seguito,
auenga chel Marchese lhouesse fatta, per
altri mezi, molto sollecitare, E dice che
costui credette celarsi bassandol uiso, Pers
che nessun uitio è piu degno dessor uatus
perato, dispiacendo non solamente a buos
ni, ma è ancora in abominatione a rei.
E Non pur io qui piango Bolognese, Mos
stra che molti Bolognesi per auaritia sino

macchiati di questo uitio, come fu lui, E tanti dice esserne in quel luogo, che tante lingue NON
sen hora apprese, Non son hora apparecchiate, A dicer Sipa, A dir si, perche sipa dicano a Bologna
in luogo di si, TRa Sauena fiume che corre presso di Bologna da la parte di Romagna, EL Reno,
medesimamente fiume, che corre presso ad essa città da la parte di Lombardia talmente, che Bolo
gna, oue si dice Sipa, uien ad esser tra luno e laltro di questi due fiumi. Qui non son FEmine da
conio, cio è, Femine da moneta coniata e stampata, mediante laquale, legiermente si corronpe
la pudicitia de le femine, & infiniti ne sono gliessempi, Onde Ouid. in quel de arte, Aura sunt
uere nunc secula plurimus auro Venit, honos, auro conciliatur amor. Et altroue, Munera, cre
de mihi placant hominesq; deosq;. Et altroue ancora, Dummodo sit diues barbarus ille placet.

Io mi raggiunsi con la scorta mia:
Poscia con pochi passi diuenimmo
La, doue un scoglio de la ripa uscia.
Assai legiermente quel salimmo;
E uolti a destra su per la sua scheggia,
Da quelle cerchie eterne ci partimmo.
Quando noi fummo la, douei uaneggia
Di sotto, per dar luogo a glisferzati,
Lo duca disse; Attienti; e fa che seggia
Lo uiso in te di questi altri mal nati;
A quali anchor non uedesti la faccia,
Però che son con noi insieme andati.
Dal uecchio ponte guardauam la traccia;
Che uenia uerso noi da laltra banda,
E che la ferza similmente schiaccia.

Di sepra, il poeta mostrò che Virg. haueu
assentito chegli tornasse alquanto a dietro
con Venetico, che al contrario di lui pro
cedeua per la bolgia, a cio che lo conoscess
se. Laqual cosa significa, che la ragio
ne uuol chel senso habbia cognitiõe de par
ticolari in quel miglior modo che glie con
ceduto, & hauutala, che ritorni, onde di
ce, che si raggiunse a lei, che era la sua
scorta, e che poi con pochi passi diuenero
la, doue uno scoglio di quelli, che di so
pra ha detto, che in forma di poni riciidie
noi fossi e gliargini, Ilqual usciua fuori
dal piede de lalta ripa, o uogliamola dir
roccia, che dogni tiorno cingeual cerchio.
Ilquale scoglio dice, el essi si liron assai le
giermente, perche la salita non era molto

aspera, E moralmente, perchel uitio, chein questa prima bolgia si punisce, essendo de men grati
del cerchio, legiermente se ne può hauer la cognitione. E Volti a destra su per la sua scheggia, Se
prima serano lungo la riua uolti a sinistra, come di sopra ha dimostrato, uolendo hora su per questo
scoglio, che haueano saliti, attrauersar la prima bolgia desso cerchio, era necessario, che uolgessero

101. *Italic in Dante's Commedia: Marcolini, Venice, 1544*

PAVLI IOVII NOVO
COMENSIS EPISCOPI NVCERINI
Historiarum sui temporis

LIBER PRIMVS.

VIESCEBAT TERRARVM ORBIS NVLLIS bellorum procellis agitatus, ac in primis Italia quassata paulo ante intestinis malis, opima pace florebat, quum bellum opinione hominum maius ac atrocius in Italia exarsit: quod postea Europam non modo omnem, uerum Asiæ atque Aphricæ longinquas partes concussis ubique uel euersis clarissimarum gentium imperiis, pau corum annorum curriculo perturbauit. Quin et perua gata quoque est eadem fatalis bellorum lues quicquid terrarum Oceano alluitur, incognitósque antea populos nobis aperuit, ad quos neque Romana uirtus, neque ullæ priscorum literæ penetrarant. Ita ut his quinqua-

102. *Opening of Paolo Giovio's Historiarum sui Temporis: Torrentino, Florence, 1550*
(reduced)

dine manner still surviving. The book, it is true, is printed in *two* sizes of italic, the larger for the verse, the smaller for the notes; still these notes surround the text in very fifteenth century style (*fig.* 101). Spaces are, in a few instances, left for painted initials. The first page bears a title in large spaced capitals, but otherwise it remains pretty faithful to an earlier typographic model. The illustrations from woodblocks are vivid and effective—and famous. In this edition the rectification of an omission in the second canto of the *Purgatorio*, of lines 64–66, seems to have been made by stamping the needed matter on the margin with a woodblock.

A folio edition of Paolo Giovio's *Historiarum sui Temporis* in two volumes, printed at Florence in 1550–52 by Lorenzo Torrentino, Ducal Typographer (to Cosimo de' Medici), is a very different and very imposing work. Its great pages of roman types are splendid, and the type-setting (although not so solid as in earlier volumes) is still careful. We notice, however, that the dedication to Cosimo de' Medici is printed in larger type than the opening address or the text of the book itself, and on the first page, too, we find a large block initial. The title-page is arranged in six sizes of roman capitals combined with some striking lower-case roman, and also italic, letters. The composition of chapter headings in three sizes of capitals, with a woodcut initial below, also shows the beginning of that mixture of different sizes of letter which was soon to end in typography which was very debased indeed (*fig.* 102). The prefatory and final matter shows the beginnings of the arrangement of a book as we know it now—and is very well managed; though these were the parts which gave opportunity for great abuses in the unskilful hands into which printing later fell.

That famous work Giorgio Vasari's "Lives"— *Le Vite*

de' più Eccellenti Architetti, Pittori, et Scultori Italiani—published at Florence in 1550, is also very well printed for this period, and its octavo volumes show a remarkably good handling, typographically, of rather a complicated text, in a manner perfectly practical and readable to-day. In this respect it is very modern in arrangement. Chiefly composed in a handsome, solid, roman old style font, each notice begins with a title in spaced roman capitals, and a seven-line decorative initial. The chapter headings of the opening discourses on Architecture, Sculpture, etc., appear in a beautiful and masculine italic, and their text begins with plain but distinguished two-line initials. Poetry is set in italic, and inscriptions in small capitals, spaced. This *editio princeps* was also printed by Lorenzo Torrentino (*fig.* 103), though the revised and enlarged work on which subsequent editions were based, was printed by the Giunti and issued in three volumes in 1568.

Some Venetian books of the middle of the sixteenth century were printed entirely in an interesting form of italic, a page of which is reproduced (*fig.* 104) from L. Nogarola's *Dialogus qui inscribitur Timotheus, sive de Nilo,* printed by J. Gryphius for Vincenzo Valgrisi at Venice in 1552. Its calligraphic quality is remarkable, and it is also interesting because it employs italic capitals, and shows how far type-founders had departed from the Aldine character. The roman type used in the introductory address is neither better nor worse than most current old style roman fonts.

An edition of Dante with notes by Landino and Vellutello, edited by Sansovino, issued in Venice by the Sessas in 1564, is an example of what next came to pass in Italian printing. The text is set in italic surrounded by masses of notes in *roman* type. The beginning of the book, with its miscellaneous introductory paraphernalia, shows all the

in San Clemente fua badia. Et tanto fono ftate ftima-
te fempre le cofe fue in detta città:che egli ne ha auu-
to quefto epitaffio.

Pingebat docte Zeufis ; condebat & ædes
Nicon; Pan capripes fiftula prima tua eft.
Non tamen ex uobis mecum certauerit ullus:
Quæ tres feciftis, unicus hæc facio.

Mori nel MCCCCLXI. Aggiunfe all'arte della pittu-
ra nella miniatura quella bellezza che fuor nella maniera vecchia s'è vifto poi nell'opre di GIEROLAMO
PADOVANO fatte in Santa Maria nuoua di Fioren-
za ne libri da lui miniati, & in quegli di GHERAR-
DO MINIATORE fuo creato, come ancora fi vide
per vn VANTE MINIATOR FIORENTINO, &
GIEROLAMO MILANESE, che mirabilifsime opre
fece in Milano fua patria.

DOMENICO GHIR
LANDAIO PITTORE
FIORENTINO.

Olte volte fi truouano, ingegni ele-
uati & fottili, che volentieri fi dareb
bono alle arti & alle fcienze, & ec-
cellentemente le eferciterebbono;fe
i Padri loro gli indirizzaffero nel
principio a quelle ftefse a le quali na
turalmente fono inclinati. Ma fpeffo
auuiene che chi gli gouerna non conofcédo forfe piu
OO

103. *Types of Vasari's Vite: Torrentino, Florence,* 1550

recitat, uel potius referentem inducit Aegyptium,
nec illam refellit. eandem itaq; Platonem secutū suſ
spicari facilè possumus. FR A. Quonam modo
istud conijcis? cum de Nili incremento nullibi Pla
to locutus sit, quin potius ter ad summum Nili memi
nit, nec tamen affert quippiam, quod ad hanc sentenſ
tiam attinere uideatur. quod tum maxime in Timæo
debebat facere, cum quandam narrauit esse Aegyſ
pti regionem Delta nomine, propè cuius uerticē scin
ditur Nilus, ubi Saitica sunt pascua. TIM. A bū
de huic rei eo in loco satisfecit Plato, quem modo re
tuli. Nam si in Aegypto aquis pluuijs non crescunt
flumina, sed illis, quæ è terra scaturiunt; Nilus autē
augescit, nec ullam suis accolis calamitatem imporſ
tat, quemadmodum reliqui amnes aliarum prouincia
rum. Ergo & ipse scaturientibus aquis augebitur.
FR A. Verum est, sed istud, quod dicis, Socraſ
tis persona non agit Plato, uerum Solonis, qui sacer
dotis Aegyptij sermonem recenset. TIM. Vide
q̄ minime sim pertinax in disputando. Do tibi istud,
hanc non esse Platonis sententiam. At habebo salſ
tem hanc eandem Aegyptijs adscribendam, quibus
etiam cū melius sua scire, quàm alios uerisimile sit, ma
gis esse credendū existimauerim. FR A. Quasi ue
ro desint, qui scribāt Aegyptios de hac re aliter sen

104. *Italic used in Nogarola's Dialogus*
Gryphius, Venice, 1552

N O VE- sto canto decimo- settimo, pone l'aut tore la for ma di Ge- rione, la quale intende che sia in figu- ra di fraude, perche ha a trat tare de' fraudolenti, & prima dimostra quella che in essa può da si aguzza, che con essa può trapassare i monti, & rompe- re muri, & armi. Et certamen te la fraude non dimostra no- cumento se non nella coda, cioè nel fine, perciochè il frau dolente cela, & asconde il pen siero, & consiglio suo, & for- to couerta d'alcun bene t'in- ganna, & sempre il fine della fraude è noceuole, nè ti puoi accorgere dell'inganno, se nõ nel fine. Onde è nato il pro- uerbio, che nella coda stà il ue leno, & è tanto potente la fraude, che passa monti, cioè, uince ogni gran potenza. E t rompe mura, & armi. Il che dinota che nessun riparo uale contra di quella, nè difesa. E c c o co lei, che tutt'ol mõdo appuzza. E 'l mondo in buono odore, & incorrotto, quando gli huomini osseruano la fede, & amano la uerità, e di questi dice il Salmista. Innocens manibus, & mũdo

ARGOMENTO.

D Ante descriue la forma di Gerione, che significa la fraude. Discesi su la riua che diuide il settimo cerchio dall'ottauo, & giunti da Gerione, Dante uà più innanzi per conoscer la ter za maniera de' uiolenti contra l'arte. Tornato poi a Virgi- lio, discende per aria sul dosso di Gerione nell'ottauo cerchio.

E c c o la fiera con la coda aguz-
za,
Che passa monti, & rompe mura, &
armi:
Ecco colei, che tutt'ol mondo ap-
puzza.
Sì cominciò lo mi Duca a parlarmi,
Et accennolle, che uenisse a proda,
Vicin al fin de' passeggiati marmi.
Et quella sozza imagine di froda
Sen uenne, & arriuò la testa e'l busto:
Mà'n su la riua non trasse la coda.

per ingannar i Troiani comin cia la narration sua dalle co- se uere, dimostrando l'in- ganno d'Vlisse nella morte di Palamede, dopo sotto questa uerità, occulta la sua bugia, fingendo l'odio ch'egli por- taua a Vlisse, & molte altre cose. Adunque le prime parti nella fraude, sono in sul fasso, cioè in cosa soda, & uera, & la coda rimane nell'aria, cosa mobile. L A faccia sua era faccia d'huom giusto. Haueª questo mostro la faccia d'huo- mo, il resto del corpo di ser- pente, & la coda di scorpio- ne, il che alcuni dicono signi- ficare tre spetie di fraude. Vna nelle parole, & questa si dino ta per la faccia humana, per- che solo l'huomo usa il fermo ne. La seconda nelle cose, cioè nell'arti, & nelle merci, & questa dinota pe'l serpente, il quale è astuto animale, & di uarij colori, come tali fraude son uarie, & diuerse. La terza nel fatto, sì come son ladroni, & assassini, i quali, come'l scorpione, dánno punte auelenate. Ma giudico esser più uera allegoria, che ogni fraude sia cõposta di queste tre forme, se rettamēte si cõ- sidera la fraude hà faccia, cioè la prima sua apparēza d'huomo giusto, perche il fraudolente dà principio dimostra humanità, beac-

COMINCIA LA

PRIMA GIORNATA DEL
Decameron,

NELLA QVALE DOPO LA DIMOSTRA-
TIONE FATTA DALL' AVTORE, PERCHE
cagione auueniffe di douerfi quelle perfone, che
appreffo fi moftrano, ragunare a ragionare
infieme, fotto il reggiméto di Pampi-
nea fi ragiona di quello, che piu
aggrada a ciafcheduno.

 V ANTVNQVE *Volte Gratiofiffime
Donne meco penfando riguardo quan-
to voi naturalmente tutte fiete pieto-
fe, tante conofco, che la prefente opera
al voftro iudicio haurà graue, & no-
iofo principio, fi come è la dolorofa ri-
cordatione della peftifera mortalita
trapaffata, vniuerfalmente a ciafcuno,
che quella vide, o altramenti conobbe,
dannofa, la quale effa porta nella fua
fronte. Ma non voglio percio, che que-*
sto di piu auanti leggere vi fpauenti, quafi fempre tra fofpiri, & tra le
lagrime leggendo dobbiate trapaffare. Queſto horrido cominciamen-
to vi fia non altramenti, che a' camminanti vna montagna afpra, &
erta, preffo alla quale vn belliffimo piano, & dilettevole fia ripoſto; ilquale tanto piu viene lor piaceuole, quanto maggiore è ſtata del fali-
re, & dello fmontare la granezza. Et fi come la eſtremità della alle-
grezza il dolore occupa, cofi le miferie da foprauegnente letitia fono
a terminate.

106. *Page from Decamerone: Giunta, Florence,* 1573

"prefatory confusion" of Italian editing and printing in the last half of the sixteenth century. Initials are introduced (sometimes "block" and sometimes "free") both in text and notes, so that the eye is constantly distracted by spots in unexpected places. In spite of remarkable woodcuts reprinted from earlier editions, the book is discouraging to the reader through the typographical mismanagement of its text, which is overpowered by the notes (*fig.* 105). The title-page is execrable—turgid and vulgar.

What Italian printers, who could copy great pieces of printing, did when left more to themselves, is shown in a Florence *Decamerone* of 1573, brought out by the Giunti. This is still printed wholly in italic like earlier editions— or at least its text is—but—and it is such a big BUT— the title-page is set in capitals of three sizes, capitals and small capitals of three sizes, lower-case roman of two sizes, and to this are added two sizes of italic, and a woodcut of Boccaccio! The publisher's preface follows in a large and very handsome spirited italic,—notice the double z's and the &'s,—and then follow four "licenses," set respectively in three sizes of roman and one of italic type. Nor is this all. There is a list of the stories, an address to the reader, these set in italic; and then comes the proem in roman. And after all this interminable muddle of types, we arrive at the *First Day*. Furthermore, a good deal of "displayed matter" in various sizes of roman and italic characters is used to start these latter divisions, and ornamental initials, large and small, begin each of them. In the *Decamerone* type ornaments head each Day, which begins with an eleven-line initial (*fig.* 106). Now without counting the annotations at the end,—which form a little book by themselves,—we have an object lesson in the decay of Italian composition, and we can see just how it declined and from what it declined. This edition was published, corrected, and emended according to the regulations of the Holy Council of Trent, and when a Pope, a King, a Grand Duke and a Duke less grand, and the Inquisition too, say an edition of Boccaccio is "purged"—well, it ought to be![1]

Such loosely constructed little volumes as Bocchi's *Symbolicarum Quæstionum,* issued at Bologna in 1574 with copper-plates by Bonasone of Bologna, a pupil of Raimondi; or Nannini's *Considerationi Civili* on Guicciardini's *Istoria,* published in Venice in 1582 (a very congested piece of work), also show how tasteless a book printed in italic had become when compared with similar early Italian books (*fig.* 107). The italic *capitals* introduced in these later editions with italic lower-case by no means helped their effect, though those used in the Bocchi, as well as the lower-case italic, are interesting, lively letter-forms. Thus while the type effects in Italian books of the sixteenth century—for its first fifty years—retained more or less the manner of the fifteenth century, even the best of them showed a decline by their mixture of varying sizes of type. These tendencies became more marked as the century went on—partly because the actual literary arrangement had become much more complicated, and also because printers did not know (and it was difficult to know) how to manage a superabundance of new literary features and still maintain the former severity of style. They took refuge, as second-rate typographers have always done, in using more sizes and kinds of type. This, together with a lack of the restraining influence of older models, made books less simple and therefore less good.

---

[1] The "purgation" did not concern itself with the freedom of the stories, but chiefly consisted in transforming the clergy figuring in them to lay persons!

CONSIDERATIONI
CIVILI
SOPRA L'HISTORIE
di M. Francesco Guicciardini, &
d'altri Historici,

Trattate per modo di Discorso da M.
Remigio Fiorentino.

Ch'il negar con efficacia di far una cosa che tu
faccia, mette il ceruello a partito a chi crede
il contrario. Consideratione Prima.

OLORO che si mettono a far qualche impresa, & hanno desiderio per
qualche lor disegno, ch'ella non si sap-
pia, anzi vorrebbon pure che si credes-
se il contrario, per condurla meglio, &
per tenere addormentate le persone,
contra lequali tentano di fare quella
impresa, non hanno miglior modo, che
lauorando (come si dice) sott'acqua, negar manifestamente,
& con molta efficacia di far quel che fanno · & la ragione è
questa, perche non potendo esser conuinti nè riprouati con sì
manifesti indizij, che non si possino scusare, ò coprire, ò inter-
pretare altrimenti di quel che sono : & non bastando ancora
il creder che sia così, per conuincerli, è forza che l'animo di
chi ha qualche sospetto di loro, vedendo quella gagliarda & ef
ficace negatione resti ambiguo, & gli si metta il ceruello a par
tito, & che gl'indizij & la credenza ch'egli ha del contrario

A   non

A tanque naualem rem spectarent, ciuium virtute, ac disciplina administrarentur, quam, veluti propriam, cum Republica ortam, atque ab illius incunabulis exceptam maiores nostri per varias temporum successiones posteris transmisere, nullamq. maris oram, vel procellis infestam, vel Piratis infamem formidandam vspiam censuerunt: opes, atque Imperium à paruis initijs ad summam amplitudinem perduxere. Neque verò dubium videtur, ita si tempestates tulissent, quin plurimi bellica virtute, rerumque gestarum fama noti ciues terrestribus pugnis praeesse, neq. minoribus terra, quàm mari praeclaris facinoribus Rempublicam illustrare potuerint: verùm ea, quae arduis rerum maritimarum casibus, periculis, ac laboribus probata virtus enituit, ad continentis Imperium adipiscendum, aut augendum Veneti minimè vtendum rati, à veteri instituto nunquam recessere, neque decurru temporum confirmatum immutari voluerunt. Quo fit, vt vani illi metus penitus à Venetorum magnanimitate alieni existimandi sint, quibus plerique permotos exteris magis, quàm ciuibus terrestres copias committere solitos fuisse sibi persuaserunt, cùm ingentes classes milite refertas eisdem B tradiderint, atque in triumphi morem è praelijs redeuntes in ciuitatis sinum hostium manubijs onustos exceperint. Verùm, vt ad institutum reuertar, Metaurensium Duce Imperatore declarato, Ioanni Fulgosio Genuensi, qui Principatum in patria adeptus antea fuerat, centum cataphractorum equitum Praefectura à Senatu tributa est; horum quinquaginta sub Alexandro; totidem sub Caesare fratribus stipendia publica mererent. Aloysius Gonzaga Rodulphi filius militiae Venetae est ascriptus, annuum stipendium pacis tempore sexcenti aurei, bello mille decretum, quo centum cataphractis, aut ducentis leuioris armaturae equitibus Reipublicae militaret. Hoc anno de munienda Iadera vrbe, quae Illyrici caput est, varijs consultationibus in Senatu agitatum, cùm Suleimanus Turcarum

108. *Roman Types of Morosini's Historia Veneta: Pinelli, Venice, 1623*

§2

In the seventeenth century, the type, and still more the composition and presswork of Italian books, often became a very fearful thing! Take, for instance, a small folio Tasso — *Gerusalemme Liberata* — printed by Giuseppe Pavoni at Genoa in 1617. In this very badly planned volume, the poem is set entirely in a nervous old style italic printed in double column; but poorly designed italic in larger sizes is utilized for its prefatory matter, which is most confused in arrangement. Each canto starts with overloaded, tasteless headings and ornaments, and, as if this were not enough, is burdened by a block-letter initial. Opposite each canto a full-page copper-plate illustration is introduced. The dedication and title-page are also engraved. These copper-plate title-pages were common in Europe during the seventeenth century, and, as before suggested, had a wretched effect on printing. It was the short and easy method of making a book beautiful. And as they were generally over-elaborate in design, they made the slovenly typography all the more ridiculous. Furthermore, as Walter Crane writes,[1] "while the surface-printed block, whether woodcut or metal engraving (by which method many of the early book illustrations were rendered), accorded well with the conditions of the letter-press printing, as they were set up with the type and printed by the same pressure in the same press, with copper-plate quite other conditions came in, as the paper has to be pressed into the etched or engraved lines of the plate, instead of being impressed by the lines in relief of the wood or the metal. Thus, with the use of copper-plate illustrations in printed books, that mechanical relation which exists between a surface-printed block and the letter-

[1] *Decorative Illustration of Books,* p. 116.

press was at once broken, as a different method of printing had to be used." Although the first book decorated with copper-plates was printed as early as 1477, they did not come into general use before the middle or end of the sixteenth century.

Here and there a fine seventeenth century book appears, like Morosini's *Historia Veneta*—an imposing folio of seven hundred pages, reminiscent in style of the early sixteenth century. The types are, in general effect, handsome—that of the preface being an irregular old style of coarse cut, while the text is set in a somewhat thin roman letter. As here employed they make massive pages, very solidly and well set (*fig.* 108). Notes in small italic appear in the margin. Running-titles are arranged in a large, old style lower-case letter. The engraved title-page and overloaded head-pieces which, with several sizes of roman capitals, begin each Book, are very much "of the period." This volume was printed by Antonio Pinelli, "Ducal Printer," at Venice in 1623.

Another seventeenth century work, on navigation, etc., which is a fine piece of typography and a still more wonderful piece of book-making, is *Dell' Arcano del Mare di D. Roberto Dudleo*—that romantic figure Robert Dudley, son of Elizabeth's favourite, Dudley, Earl of Leicester. These enormous folios were printed at Florence, where Dudley then lived, in three volumes, in 1646 and 1647, and dedicated to Ferdinand II, Grand Duke of Tuscany. The typographical decorations are ingenious and the typography most effective, the engraved plates magnificent; and, as a whole, it is a superb production, showing great vigour of conception and style in execution.

For late sixteenth century and early seventeenth century types we have a valuable source-book in the 1628 specimen

Al Lettore.

O hò sempre stimato atto degno di biasmo, il tener nascoste quelle cose, che vtili e diletteuoli insieme esser possono con la publicatione. questa cagione mi hà mosso à dar' in luce, ò più tosto à far mostra à gl' occhi altrui de' Caratteri della Stampa Vaticana, da me in gran parte accresciuti e rinouati, per commun benefitio, e di chi particolarmente è solito di ricorrer' per l'impressione dell' Opere, all' aiuto delle straniere Nationi; Di questi si può godere la bellezza, accompagnata alla varietà che maggiormente dee stimarsi, per hauer dato l'esempio, e la norma all'altre più celebri Stamperie; E perche non si hauesse nel diletto à desiderar qualche parte di vtile, hò voluto che gli medesimi Caratteri, illustrati con la cognitione dell'antichità, portino scolpiti nella fronte i Nomi di coloro, che ne furono gl'Inuentori. Resta che gl'Huomini Letterati spetialmente, al nome de' quali è riserbata per mezzo delle Stampe l'immortalità, honorandogli delle lor fatiche, mi diano occasione di potere con gli effetti mostrar' verso di loro più certo segno della mia osseruanza.

A iiij

109. *Address to the Reader: Stamperia Vaticana Specimen Rome*, 1628

qual' è nella Stampa Vaticana .

In nomine Patris , &
Filij, & Spiritus ſancti.
Amen .

Benedicta ſit
ſancta & indiui-
dua Trinitas ,
nunc, & ſemper
& per infinita
ſeculorũ ſecula.
Aue Maria.

G iiij

110. *Canon Grosso: Stamperia Vaticana Specimen*
Rome, 1628

qual' è nella Stampa Vaticana .

Te Deum laudamus :
te Dominum cõfitemur.
Te æternum Patrẽ : om-
nis terra veneratur . Tibi
omnes Angeli : tibi cæli,
& vniuerſæ poteſtates .
Tibi Cherubim & Sera-
phim : inceſſabili voce
proclamant . Sanctus ,
Sanctus, Sanctus : Domi-
nus Deus ſabaoth . Pleni
ſunt cæli, & terra : maie-
ſtatis gloriæ tuæ . Te glo-
rioſus Apoſtoloru̅ cho-
rus . Te Prophetaru̅ lau-
dabilis numerus. Te mar

H iij

111. *Ascendonica: Stamperia Vaticana Specimen*
Rome, 1628

CARATTERE
detto Corsiuo grosso.

Che è nella STAMPA VATICANA.

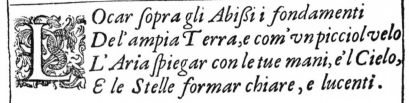

Ocar sopra gli Abißi i fondamenti
Del'ampia Terra, e com'vn picciol velo
L'Aria spiegar con le tue mani, e'l Cielo,
E le Stelle formar chiare, e lucenti.

Por legge à i Mari, à le tempeste, à i venti,
L'humido vnir' co'l suo contrario, e'l gelo
Con infinita prouidenza, e Zelo,
E crear', e nodrir' tutti i viuenti.

Signor fù poco à la tua gran possanza:
Ma che tu DIO, tu Creator voleßi
Nascer' huom', e morir' per chi t'offese.

Cotanto l'opra de' sei giorni auanza,
Ch'io no'l sò dir, no l'san' gli Angioli steßi,
Dicalo il Verbo tuo, che sol' l'intese.

I iij

112. *Corsivo Grosso: Stamperia Vaticana Specimen, Rome,* 1628

of the Stamperia Vaticana and Camerale, founded at Rome in 1587.[1] It is entitled *Indice de Caratteri, con l'Inventori, & nomi di essi, esistenti nella Stampa Vaticana, & Camerale*, issued at Rome and dedicated to Francesco, Cardinal Barberini, whose symbolic bees figure on the title-page, beneath an enormous red cardinal's hat. The dedicatory epistle is printed in a fine old style roman font, and the address *Al Lettore* (in which Brogiotti says that he has been the chief agent in collecting and renovating these fonts) is set in an italic which has a few striking characters—the z and final e, for example (*fig.* 109). Then follows a collection of exotic types with astonishing attributions—in which Adam is called the first inventor of science and letters; Moses is made to father the Hebrew alphabet; Abraham obligingly devises letters for the Syrians and Chaldeans; Esdras is found improving the Hebrew alphabet; and Phœnix gives letters to the Phœnicians! St. Jerome and St. Cyril also had a hand in alphabet-making; and Pythagoras added to the joy of life by presenting the world with a Y. There are a good many more curious inscriptions. The serious part of the work begins on leaf 27, where some heavy roman capitals of the oldest form of old style are shown. The character called *canon grosso* (*fig.* 110) is a fine letter, with exceedingly long ascenders and descenders, resembling types cut by G. Le Bé I and some roman types used in Spain. This is followed by descending sizes of fine old style fonts—such as the *ascendonica* (*fig.* 111). The italic *corsivo grosso* (*fig.* 112) is an interesting and varied character, full of movement and style, and was probably cut by Robert Granjon for this printing-house, and may be the font which the Pope of that day desired to restrict to its private use. In this *corsivo*, the lower-case z's and the final e's, the double s

[1] A further account of it is given on a later page.

and the "swash" C and D, are to be looked at. The smaller
sizes of roman, and especially the italic — varied by series of
capital letters for titles, etc. (*fig.* 113)—show a fine, even
collection of old style fonts of which any printing-house
might be proud. Specimens of Hebrew, of some distinguished Greek capitals (*fig.* 114) and Greek lower-case
(which accord very nicely with the roman fonts), and four
extraordinarily interesting specimens of plain-song music
types, marked *Ex Bibliotheca Vaticana* (*figs.* 115 *and* 116),
follow, and the book closes with two sizes of a large old
style letter, used no doubt with music or for the Canon of
the Mass (*fig.* 117). Restricted to such fine, severe types,
it would be difficult to go wrong. The *Indice* is among the
most interesting "specimens" in the history of printing,
and shows the material of a seventeenth century Italian
printing-office at its simplest and best.

When poorer types were poorly used at this epoch, we
have such wretched little affairs as *La Clori*, a pastoral
tragi-comedy, by Camillo Lenzoni, issued at Florence by
Z. Pignoni in 1626 (*fig.* 118). Its text is set entirely in
italic, but in different sizes and with some roman head-lines.
Furthermore, its prefatory matter is adorned with badly
printed typographical ornaments, which add to its woeful
appearance. The size of italic used for the text, and the
roman capitals used in running head-lines, are too large for
the page — a common fault in Italian printing as the seventeenth century went on. In a similar, loosely built volume of
the period — Alessandro Adimari's *La Clio*, Florence, 1639
—the publishers, Massi and Landi, lazily observe: "Errors
in printing are confided to the discretion of the kind and
careful reader"—so it appears that the scholarly part of
such books was not looked after any better than was their
typography!

VATICANA.   45

FRANCISCVS
CARDINALIS
BARBERINVS

M

113. *Roman Capitals: Stamperia Vaticana Specimen, Rome, 1628*

GRÆCORVM LITTERAE

Prima claſſis

a	b	g	d	e
Alpha	Vita	Gãma	Delta	Epſilòn

A B Γ Δ E

z	j	th	i	c
Zita	Ita	Thita	Iota	Kappa

Z H Θ I K

l	m	n	x
Lambda	My	Ny	Xi

Λ M N Ξ

o	p	r	s
Omicròn	Pi	Rho	Sigma

O Π P Σ

t	y	ph	ch
Tau	Ypſilòn	Phi	Chi

T Y Φ X

pf	o
Pſi	Omega

Ψ Ω.

114. *Alphabet of Greek Capitals: Stamperia Vaticana Specimen, Rome, 1628*

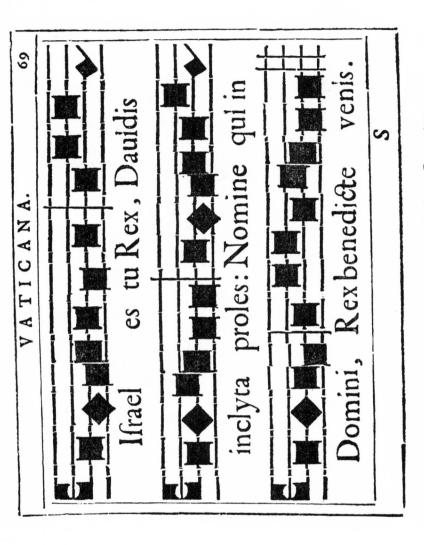

115. *Plain-Song: Stamperia Vaticana Specimen, Rome, 1628*

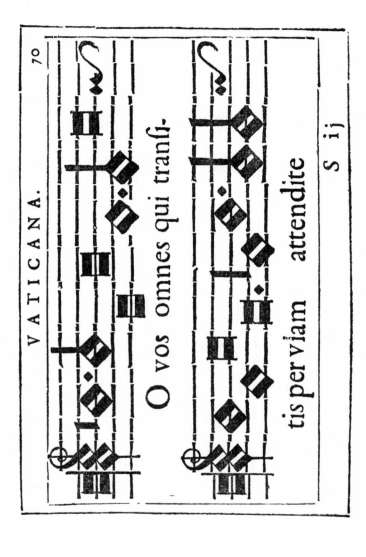

116. Plain-Song: *Stamperia Vaticana Specimen, Rome, 1628*

Leuaui oculos meos in montes : vnde veniet au-xilium mihi. Auxilium me-um a Domino: qui fecit cę-lum & terram.

T

117. *Type used for Missals: Stamperia Vaticana Specimen, Rome, 1628*

ATTO PRIMO
SCENA PRIMA.

Teandro. Tirinto.

Tea. DEH mira o mio Tirinto,
L'adombrato splendore? a pena in Cielo
L'Alba nunzia del giorno
Scote l'ali del sonno, e i venticelli
Messaggieri di lei spiegano à pena
Tra i sentieri de i fior le fresche piume.

Tir. Dolce conforto è il preuenir l'Aurora,
Che noiosa e la notte,
A chi graue pensier la mente adombra;
O che spietato, o che dolore eterno,
Mentre l'aura godrò, fido Teandro
M'apporterà dolente
Della notte l'orrore: ò me infelice,
Forza è pur ch'io'l rimembri;
Notte crudel che or empie il terzo Lustro,
Che à me l'alma rapiro onde spietate,
Che dico l'alma mia? quel che più caro
M'era assai più, fanciullo auuolto in fascie;
Ma

118. *Page from La Clori: Pignoni, Florence, 1626*

The edition of Vittorio Zonca's *Novo Teatro di Machine et Edificii*, published by F. Bertelli at Padua in 1656, well known for its interesting plates,[1] is extraordinarily careless in execution, though simple in composition. Here, rough old style fonts, closely set and very, very badly printed, are used. For so ambitious a folio and such careful illustrations, its technique is inconceivably slovenly; yet this book had already gone through three editions. Another work of a more scientific character was the second edition of Magalotti's *Saggi di Naturali Esperienze fatte nell' Accademia del Cimento*, Florence, a folio printed at the end of the seventeenth century (1691), and a fine example of its kind. The type shows a distinctly modern note (*fig.* 119). As for decoration, effective initials and tail-pieces coarsely engraved on wood are mixed with a series of grotesque headings and scientific plates cut on copper. It was really an important book, and was also intended to be a handsome piece of typography. It came from the Florentine printing-house of Giovanni Filippo Cecchi.

By this time an entire change in Italian book-making is evident. The elements of the old fifteenth century volumes have almost wholly disappeared, and the pretentious, overladen styles of the seventeenth century are in full swing. Neither very careful in detail nor delicate in execution, these more elaborate volumes of the seventeenth and early eighteenth century became like stage properties; the folios seemed as if they were meant to "carry across the footlights." Just as, in a sober Italian palace of the Renaissance, the earliest Italian books looked their part, so these big folios seemed to be at home in the tormented architecture of Bibiena, or amid the audacious magnificences of Ber-

[1] Those at pages 64 and 77 represent presses for printing books and engravings.

nini. The true grand manner of Italian printing, like much
else in Italy at that time, had turned into the false grand
manner in which everything was exaggerated. And as
typography reflected the state of the Fine Arts, we have the
pompous seventeenth century folios of the Italian press.
Books began with Thrones, Principalities, and Powers, displayed and praised in types and terms equally grandiose.
In great Italian houses of that period, filled with gigantic
furniture, pictures, and folios, the only object that must
have appeared inadequate in scale was Man!

This overblown effect was true of the details of types.
The late Italian italic, for instance, developed into a much
more generous, opulent, and careless sort of letter than the
demure little character introduced by Aldus. It had an ex-
uberant "kick" about it that belonged very much to the
art of the day. It was at this time that the italic letter, used
through the sixteenth and sometimes in the seventeenth
century for the text of entire books, began to be employed
for preliminary matter only, or for poetry.

Roman types also were coarse in form. They, like the
italic, were what we should now call "old style." They were
often disagreeable in effect because, as we have seen, sizes
too large for a page were employed; and this, and poor,
rough paper, made these roman characters look coarser
than they were, though the simple capitals were often good
letters. Still, such type had "a way with it." As to composition, it was a little rakish, too — nothing was very correct.
Yet it was almost forgivable because taking its place so well
in the picture.

§ 3

In an eighteenth century edition of Tasso's *Gerusalemme
Liberata*, edited by Gentili and Gustavini, and printed at
Urbino in 1735 (at the Stamperia della Cappilla del SS.

119. *Roman and Italic Types showing "modern" tendency: Cecchi, Florence, 1691*

E S P E R I E N Z A

*Del sollevamento de' fluidi nel vano de' cannellini sotti-
lissimi dentr' al voto.*

*Opinione d'al-
cuni,che il sol
levarsi quasi
tutti i liquori
ne'cânelli stret
tissimi di vano
sia effetto del-
la natural
pressione dell'
aria.
Come segua,
secondo loro,
tal solleva-
mento.*

TRA GLI altri effetti della pressione dell'aria è
stato da alcuni annoverato anche quello del
sollevarsi, che fanno quasi tutti i fluidi dentro a'can-
nelli strettissimi, che in essi s'immergono. Dubitano
questi, che quel sottilissimo cilindro d'aria, che giù
pel cannello preme, verbigrazia, in sull'acqua, operi
più debolmente la sua pressione, per lo contrasto, che
gli fa nel discendere il gran toccamento, ch' egli à col-
la superficie interna dell'angustissimo vaso. Dove per
lo contrario, a giudizio loro, quell'aria,che liberamen-

DEFLUERET· RIPΛQ· ΛESTUS UIRIDΛNTE LEUΛRET·
IPSE ETIΛM EXIMIΛE LΛUDIS SUCCENSUS ΛMORE
ΛSCΛNIUS· CURUO DIREXIT SPICULΛ CORNU·
NEC DEXTRΛE ERRΛNTI DEUS ΛFUIT· ΛCTΛQ· MULTO·
PERQ· UTERUM SONITU· PERQ· ILLΛ UENIT HΛRUNDO·
SΛUCIUS ΛD QUΛDRUPES· NOTΛ INTRΛ TECTΛ REFUGIT
SUCCESSITQ· GEMENS STΛBULIS, QUESTUQ· CRUENTUS·
ΛTQ· IMPLORΛNTE SIMILIS. TECTUM OMNE REPLEBΛT·
SILUIΛ PRIMΛ SOROR· PΛLMIS PERCUSSΛ LΛCERTOS·
ΛUXILIUM UOCΛT· ET DUROS CONCLΛMΛT ΛGRESTIS·
OLLI· PESTIS ENIM TΛCITIS LΛTET ΛSPERΛ SILUIS·
INPROUISI ΛDSUNT. HIC TORRE ΛRMΛTUS OBUSTO·
STIPITIS HIC GRΛUIDI NODIS· QUOD CUIQ· REPERTU̅
RIMΛNTI· TELUM IRΛ FΛCIT' UOCΛT ΛGMINΛ TYRRUS·
QUΛDRIFIDΛMQ UERCUM. CUNEIS UT FORTE COΛCTIS
SCINDEBΛNT· RΛPTΛ SPIRΛNS IMMΛNE SECURI·
ΛD SΛEUΛ·É· SPECULIS. TEMPUS DEΛ NΛCTΛ NOCENDI·
ΛRDUΛ TECTΛ PETIT STΛBULI· ET DE CULMINE SUMMO·
PΛSTORΛLE CΛNIT SIGNUM· CORNUQ· RECURUO·
TΛRTΛREΛM INCENDIT UOCEM· QUΛ PROTINUS OMNE
CONTREMUIT NEMUS· ÈT ET SILUΛE INSONUERE PROFUNDΛE
ΛUDIIT ET TRIUIΛE LONGE LΛCUS· ΛUDIIT ΛMNIS·
SULPUREΛ NΛR ΛLBUS ΛQUΛ· FONTESQ· UELINI·
ET TREPIDΛÈ MΛTRES· PRΛESSERE ΛD PECTORΛ NΛTOS·

120. *Type imitating ancient Manuscript: Manni, Florence*, 1741

Sacramento, a famous eighteenth century office which still survives), we have much less excellent type, but the poetry is printed in roman instead of italic. There are, happily, no decorations except the inevitable copper-plates, which in this case are even relied on for initial letters. The title-page is printed in red and black, in all sorts of sizes of italic capitals and lower-case characters; the prefatory matter is exaggerated in composition; the final notes are unattractive. The edition is interesting only in comparison with a Tasso already referred to. [1]

A curious piece of Italian typography, very characteristic of the eighteenth century, is an edition of Virgil (*P. Vergilii Maronis, Codex Antiquissimus, A Rufio Turcio Aproniano V. C. Distinctus et Emendatus . . . Florentiæ. Typis Mannianis*), published in 1741 at Florence, and printed by Joseph Manni, a person of scholarly tastes. It is set entirely in old style capitals with a few characters imitating those of an ancient and famous manuscript Virgil in rustic characters, in the Laurentian Library, Florence. The preface exhibits a fairly accurate engraved reproduction of a few lines of the model on which the book was based, and in the text the ingenious introduction of but three specially cut letters gives the general effect of a font of "rustic" type (*fig.* 120). Thus the work displays that amazing audacity in arriving at a striking effect, notwithstanding inaccurate details and economy of method, which was typical of Italian printing at that time. Issued at a place and period which appears unfavourable to such a venture, and dedicated to Lovers of the Fine Arts, it also indicates there has always been a public sufficiently sympathetic to encourage such publications. The volume is enlivened by occasional rubrication, which gives it a distinguished air.

[1] See page 165.

Besides the press just mentioned, the Italian printing-houses of reputation outside of Venice at that period were those of Volpi-Comino at Padua, Della Volpe at Bologna, Soliani at Modena, and a few others. To rightly place the work of the Venetian press, or to understand the reputation of Bodoni, we ought to be familiar with the current work of these presses. Space is lacking for this here, but we may say a word about the Padua edition of Arrighi's Latin life of Francisco Morosini (*De Vita et Rebus Gestis Francisci Mauroceni*), a volume brought out by Comino in 1749 (*fig.* 121). It is set in a rather handsome old style character, a good deal leaded. Each Book begins with a tasteless wood-cut head-band, with several lines of capitals in various sizes and variously spaced beneath it, and a large woodcut initial. The italic introduced in the text is unduly small in proportion to the roman letter and far too much spaced. The type-setting is irregular, the presswork very uneven. The imposition is, however, fine, the margins ample, and the paper in texture charming. The prefatory matter is neither attractive in its separate types nor harmonious in relation to the rest of the book. The title-page, with a copper-plate embellishment, is chiefly set in handsome roman capitals of various sizes, with some lines or words rubricated. It is not a bad piece of work, nor yet a good one: but it has a certain modern air.

Many luxurious Italian books of this period, while versions of eighteenth century French work, were freer and more interesting, and they were "embellished" (and really embellished) with many attractive copper-plates which pictured eighteenth century Italian — and especially Venetian — life, with great truth, gaiety, and charm. A volume quite in the French manner is the *Versi Sciolti di Tre Eccellenti Moderni Autori*. This is set in a delicate old style character,

ANTONII ARRIGHII
DE VITA ET REBUS GESTIS
FRANCISCI MAUROCENI
PELOPONNESIACI
PRINCIPIS VENETORUM
LIBER III.

Nterim Picus, de quo supra dictum est, cum classe venit, in
qua tres & triginta variæ for-
mæ naves fuere: eaque nostrorum animi sunt vehementer
recreati. Nam vulneribus ac labore attriti, quem
diu, noctuque propter homicum penuriam suf-
cipere cogebantur, vix vim hostium, atque
impetum sustinebant: vixque in opere versa-
bantur. Militum copia aliquanta allata est: ple-
raque item bello utilia, quæ Achomatem, plu-

121. *Types of Arrighi's Life of Morosini: Comino, Padua,* 1749

AL P. FEDERIGO SANVITALI

DELLA COMPAGNIA DI GESU

Sopra gli studj Poetici di esso dottissimo Padre ; e commenda il Signor Conte JACOPO SANVITALI *pel favore che presta alle belle arti , e per le altre sue rare doti.*

PErche si tarda, qual più so, ti vergo
Umil risposta da le tacit' ombre
De l' amena Vigatto, ove la bionda
Cerere, e il buon Leneo vestono i Campi,
De i celebrati Terzi estivo albergo?
Forse i bei versi tuoi scordar potei,
Inclito Federigo, e ognor la mente
Anzi non ebbi, quante mai nel Cielo
Sorsero da quel dì candide lune
Ebbra, e gioconda del lor dolce suono?
Quando quel foglio tuo, come tentata
Indica vena i suoi tesor dischiude,
Agli occhi miei non aspettato aperse
Occulti sensi, e le parole adorne,
Per soverchio piacer qual mi restassi,
Per me tel dica la faconda Euterpe,

K 2 Che,

122. *Page showing light types, openly set: Fenzo, Venice,* 1758

very much leaded, and though the presswork is careless, the light effect of its type and the use of fanciful copper-plate decorations make it quite attractive — if it be not too critically examined. This open style of composition fore-shadowed the coming fashion for lighter types; but the book was printed at Venice by Modesto Fenzo as early as 1758 (*fig.* 122).

Venetian typography always had a certain individuality. In the fifteenth century — the period of Aldus, Ratdolt, the De Spires, and Jenson — this was surely so; Venetian books in the sixteenth century were rather in a class by themselves, and had a delicate and tasteful quality which was interesting. In some instances an Aldine italic with roman capitals was employed for the text, and spaced capitals for head-lines, in loyalty to the Aldine fashion. An early irregular and very characteristic italic (*fig.* 104) was now and then introduced for prefaces and chapter-headings, and this, too, gave Venetian work a distinguished note. Two-line initial letters were used at the beginnings of new sections, and large capital pictorial initials, cut on wood, sometimes marked chief divisions. Although such typography clearly showed the general decline, it was sufficiently reminiscent of earlier and better work to command respect,[1] and sixteenth century Venetian books had (as in the eighteenth century) an element of taste about them, which made them somewhat charming and more individual than printing of the period in other parts of Italy.

The eighteenth century illustrated books printed in Venice are comparatively little known. The chief Venetian pub-

[1] Two books taken at random — both printed in 1554 — embody these features; namely, Ovid's *Heroides* with commentaries printed by Francesco Bindoni, and Mattioli's commentaries on the *Materia Medica* of Dioscorides — a famous Italian herbal, with excellent woodcuts of plants, etc., published by Valgrisi.

lishers of this class of volume were J. B. Pasquali, the Albrizzi, and Zatta. In 1745 a most imposing edition of Tasso's
Gerusalemme Liberata, in folio, was printed at Venice by Albrizzi (*figs.* 123 *and* 124). This edition—dedicated to Maria
Theresa—owes its chief splendour to Piazzetta's illustrations and ornaments, which are delightful. But it is, too, an
effective piece of printing. In spite of employing types which,
on examination, are terribly coarse, they "play up" manfully
to the gorgeous designs! In spite of presswork at times careless and muddy, the pages have a great air! We may pull
the book to pieces and condemn every detail; but it lives—
insolently careless of what one thinks of it! And another
illustrated edition of the same poem, in two quarto volumes
printed by Antonio Groppo at Venice in 1760, though a
somewhat heavy example of this style, is also a spirited and
pleasure-giving performance. It was no doubt meant for a
luxurious edition,—a gift-book, perhaps,—for its critical
apparatus by Gentili is given so little importance, and its
innumerable illustrations so much, that the latter were apparently its "feature." As such books go, it is a fine edition,
rough and slipshod in execution, but telling and full-blooded.
The types are a series of rough old style fonts, displayed
lines of capitals being much spaced.

An annotated Dante was published by Zatta in 1757 in
a similarly lively style—the title-page to Volume I being
printed in red and black, with a delightful copper-plate
vignette in bright blue! This, too, is printed on agreeable
paper (but not *well* printed) from light old style roman types.
The book is decorated with rather futile copper-plate illustrations and ornaments; the prettiest feature of the latter
being the engraved framework at the beginning of cantos,
around the arguments, themselves engraved. This was a
very common ornamental treatment of similar matter in all

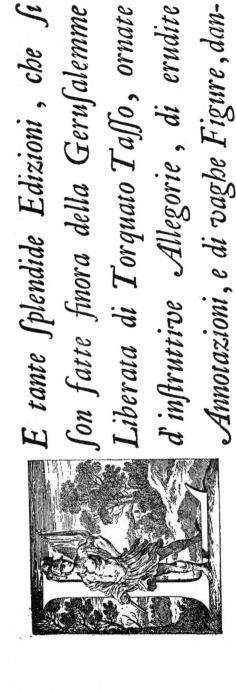

E tante Splendide Edizioni, che si son fatte finora della Gerusalemme Liberata di Torquato Tasso, ornate d'instruttive Allegorie, di erudite Annotazioni, e di vaghe Figure, danno ben a conoscere il gran merito del Poeta, e l' eccellente dignità del Poema ; non essendo ancora stanca la Fama di celebrare i pregj dell'uno , e

123. Italic in Dedication of Gerusalemme Liberata: Albrizzi, Venice, 1745

ARGOMENTO

Manda a Tortosa Dio l'Angelo; u'poi
Goffredo aduna i Principi Cristiani.
Quivi concordi que' famosi Eroi
Lui Duce fan degli altri Capitani.
Quinci egli pria vuol rivedere i suoi
Sotto l'insegne; e poi gl'invia ne'piani
Ch'a Sion vanno: in tanto di Giudea
Il Re si turba alla novella rea.

CANTO PRIMO.

I.

Canto l'armi pietose, e'l Capitano,
Che 'l gran sepolcro liberò di
CRISTO.
Molto egli oprò col senno e con
la mano;
Molto soffrì nel glorioso acquisto:
E invan l'Inferno a lui s'oppose; e invano
S'armò d'Asia e di Libia il popol misto:
Che 'l Ciel gli diè favore, e sotto ai santi
Segni ridusse i suoi compagni erranti.

(1)

124. *Page of Gerusalemme Liberata: Albrizzi, Venice,* 1745
(much reduced)

these books. The remaining volumes are treated in a more sober style. But it is a very Venetian performance — perfectly irrelevant to Dante — and one cares as little about that as the publisher did! This edition, in five quarto volumes, was dedicated to the Empress Elizabeth of Russia.

Zatta's 1772–73 edition of Ariosto's *Orlando Furioso* is a typical late eighteenth century Venetian quarto. It is in four volumes, carelessly printed from rough old style types — the Life in italic, the text and notes in roman. But it is such a large, easy, gay book! — ample margins, attractive, thin paper, full of engraved illustrations and fanciful, lively *encadrements*. It is a very good specimen of the Venetian printing of its time, and perfectly readable.

Another characteristic work which shows the arrival of the fashion for lighter type effects is Carlo Goldoni's *Opere Teatrale* in forty-four 16mo volumes, brought out between 1788 and 1795 in a delightful little *format*, and adorned with amusing copper-plates of scenes from the plays — *rami allusivi*, as they are called by the publishers; though in his letter to the printer (dated Paris, 1788), Goldoni says that he desires no decorations for this edition, but depends on Zatta's reputation for exactness. The type is old style, but very light in cut and very openly set — quite modern in effect, through the composition rather than the type. Another fascinating little book, printed by Zatta in 1787, is a two-volume edition of Tasso's *Gerusalemme Liberata* in 16mo — an example of his more intimate style, and much better printed than the Goldoni. It is set in a workmanlike eighteenth century roman face, slightly leaded, with three verses to a page, and each canto begins with a clever little vignette (*fig.* 125). The presswork, though careless, is respectable for its period. The Tasso appears to have been part of a collection of *Opere* of Italian poets, and was a sort of decorated Italian "Pickering edition," to be read in the grotto of an eighteenth century Italian garden.

Such books—particularly editions like Zatta's Dante or Albrizzi's Tasso—were often entirely inappropriate to their subject in treatment, and just as often wholly delightful! The reason we like them so much—or that I do—is that they reflect so perfectly the Venetian life of which they were accessories — that *vie galante*, painted by Guardi, described by President de Brosses, and mirrored in the theatre of Goldoni;[1] and we cannot judge such pieces of printing, or any printing, justly, unless we know something about the life in which they played a part. Of course one cannot imagine wanting much to read these Venetian eighteenth century editions now; but then one would not now read *Sabbath Bells chimed by the Poets*, illustrated by Birket Foster, and published in the 'sixties. Our parents, however, did. And that was a very good book, too, no doubt, for it belonged not merely with black walnut furniture and Landseer's engravings, but with the gentle manners, decent reticences, and old loyalties that were matters of course then!

In the last quarter of the eighteenth century the great figure in Italian printing was Giambattista Bodoni, Court Printer to the Duke of Parma. Although the change in type-fashions at the end of the eighteenth century was fostered by Bodoni (who with the Didots had more to do in bringing it about than any one else), it must be remembered that he was at work at Parma as early as 1770. At first he used Fournier's old style types, and later he made copies of Fournier's fonts. The splendour of his early decorated work has not been praised enough; for his later work (done be-

[1] For an account of decorated Venetian books the reader may consult Bertarelli's *I libri illustrati a Venezia nei secoli XVII e XVIII*, in *Revista della Biblioteche e degli Archivi*, March–April, 1903.

Ove si gran vestigio è del tuo scorno,
Tu neghittoso aspetti il novo giorno?
Tasso. C.10.

GERUSALEMME LIBERATA.

CANTO DECIMO.

I.

COsì dicendo ancor, vicino scorse
Un destrier ch'a lui volse errante il passo.
Tosto al libero fren la mano ei porse,
E su vi salse, ancorch'afflitto e lasso.
Già caduto è il cimier ch'orribil sorse,
Lasciando l'elmo inonorato e basso:
Rotta è la sopravvesta; e di superba
Pompa regal vestigio alcun non serba.

A' SUOI AMICI

ANDREA RUBBI.

IL secolo decimosesto fu il centro della poesia italiana. Il grand'epico storico ed eroico, corresi amici, sorge ora in Torquato Tasso. Di quest'uomo io vi ho parlato nelle mie lettere proemiali all'Ariosto; ivi ho scritto sull'indole della poesia d'ambidue. Qui dirò soltanto, e, come spero, con felice ardimento, che il Tasso afferrò l'epica con minori difetti de' suoi emoli antichi e nuovi, e vuol dire con maggior perfezione di tutti. Il solo Virgilio l'avria superato, se avesse ricorretto quel gran poema dell'Eneide. Il nostro Torquato non ha le puerilità, nè le lungherie vuote d'Omero, non l'inugaglianza e la troppa facilità di Camoens, non gli ambiziosi ornamenti di Lucano, non il diabolico di Milton, non l'irreligiosa affetazion di Voltaire, non la cristiana miologia di Klopstock. Senza tante irregolarità degli altri epici egli ha mantenuto tutto l'ottimo qua e là sparso nei lor poemi. La scelta dell'argomento, l'intreccio de' relativi episodi, i ca-

125. Pages from Gerusalemme Liberata: Zatta, Venice, 1787

CAPO VI.

Non può giudicarsi lo Jenson il primo imprimitor di libri in Italia.

COnciossiachè si adunassero per noi fin quì molte parti, aggruppandole a disegnare il semplice schizzo d'una tela assai vasta, già s'incominciò a vedere la frequenza in Italia di tedeschi non meno quanto di francesi, ad animarvi in domicilj diversi, l'arte moguntina, e vedemmo altresì come cautamente s'inoltrarono. Se i due Giovani di Subiaco vantavano d'aver agli altri dato l'esempio, come testè abbiamo accennato, si esprimevano con le precedenti parole in modo, che potrebbe soltanto intendersi d'esser i medesimi stati i primi tedeschi presso la romana Corte: *Nos de Germanis primi*

126. *Types showing "modern" feeling: Bonsignori, Lucca, c. 1796*

tween 1800 and 1813), which is "nineteenth century" in feeling, is that by which he is best remembered. Didot of Paris and Ibarra of Madrid both worked in a style akin to that of Bodoni in the early part of his career. It is because both the Didots and Bodoni later adopted the rather academic and frigid style by which we now remember them, that we forget that they worked earlier just as successfully (perhaps more so) with old style types in an eighteenth century manner. In any case, Bodoni had a very special sort of press, and his editions were too luxurious and individual to be representative of Italian printing;[1] but one cannot appreciate *what he was trying to do*, or understand his success, unless one sees the rank and file of books of his time.

Finally, for two very late eighteenth century books, which are of the file if not of the rank, we may look, first, at Sardini's *Storia Critica di Nicolao Jenson*, printed at Lucca between 1796 and 1798. In this the roman and italic type, though still old style, shows a distinct tendency toward what we now call a "modern face," and also a certain narrowing of the character in the interests of condensation — a bad feature, but one increasingly followed in the next century (*fig.* 126); secondly, we may examine Cristoforo Poggiali's *Memorie per la Storia Letteraria di Piacenza*— printed at Piacenza in two quarto volumes by Niccolò Orcesi in 1789. This work is set in type of an even more "modern" cut, much more spaced and leaded than any we have hitherto seen. It is not an attractive type; still less the italic, which is mean and poor in cut; and the effect of the book is frigid and mechanical. Yet such type is a forecast of the later manner of much Italian printing (*fig.* 127). Not only the types themselves became lighter and lighter, but

---

[1] Bodoni's books are described in the pages devoted to early nineteenth century Italian types.

they were set in a more open way; and some of the late
eighteenth century Italian books were almost as anaemic as
German work of the same period. By the end of the eighteenth century, Italian typography was following those fashions which influenced printers throughout Europe.

In looking back over this three hundred years of Italian
printing,[1] it appears that, for the first fifty or sixty years of the
sixteenth century, books retained something of the "noble
manner," though in details they showed a lack of the simplicity of older work; that this survival of an earlier style
slowly disappeared because (1) the generation had passed to
whom the style of manuscipt books acted as a restraining
influence; (2) more complicated literary apparatus came
into use for which there was no early precedent; and (3) the
class of men interested or employed in printing were neither
as educated nor as skilful as formerly. Gothic type was soon
driven out by roman; and this roman type, which was
all of old style cut, as time went on was used in a larger
variety of sizes and employed with less care. The popularity
of copper-plate engraving for illustration increased confusion, while it did not improve typography; and the pompous architecture and decoration of the seventeenth century
was reflected in the use of types and even in the types themselves. Toward the end of the seventeenth century, books
were printed in a slightly more modern style of letter, and
all through the eighteenth century types became lighter and

[1] *Le Livre en Italie à travers les Siècles*, an illustrated catalogue of a collection of books exhibited by Leo S. Olschki of Florence at the Leipsic Book Exhibition of 1914, may be consulted for titles of some remarkable Italian books
printed from the fifteenth to the eighteenth century. For illustrated Italian
books, many of which are interesting specimens of printing, see Pollard's
*Italian Book-Illustration and Early Printing. A Catalogue of Early Italian
Books in the Library of C. W. Dyson Perrins*. London, 1914. The earliest
work described is dated 1467 — the latest, 1645.

beni (Commentar. Vol. II. par. II. Lib. III. num.70.), e dal Cuasco nella Storia Letteraria dell' Accademia di Reggio (pag. 42.), e *in Milano per Gottardo da Ponte , ad istanza di Giovan Jacopo , e fratelli da Legnano , nel 1519. adì 24. di Gennajo in 8.*

Il giudicio, che formarono gli Eruditi circa questi componimenti del CORNAZZANO, è conforme al datone già dal Zilioli, e per me poc' anzi registrato. Dicono, che, ancorchè non sieno dettate su lo stile de' migliori seguaci del Petrarca, ma su la novella maniera, e secondo il gusto alquanto corrotto, di cui fu introduttore il celebre Poeta Antonio Tibaldeo, seguitato poscia da Pamfilo Sasso, da Antonio Fregoso, e da altri; non è però, che le Poesìe del CORNAZZANO, benchè poco note, e benchè da alcuni disprezzate, come umili , e barbare, non abbiano il loro pregio, trovandosi in esse facilità di rima, giustezza di pensieri, e chiarezza d'espressione. Il Quadrio, giudice in tali materie assai autorevole, dice, che *le Rime Liriche del CORNAZZANO sono delle migliori , che abbia la volgar Poesia , come che paragonare si possano a quelle gioje , che*

TESTO

Nella decadenza dell' Impero Romano paffarono le Scienze tra gli *Arabi*, e fiorirono allora gli *Abufaragj*, gli *Abufeldi*, gli *Avicenj*, gli *Averoi*, e cent' altri, de' quali vedi *Jacopo Kettero*.

PALESTINA

Il Pontefice *Leone X.* fece rifiorire in *Italia* le Lettere, che da lungo tempo languivano in un miferabile oblìo.

198. *Testo* and *Palestina* from Bodoni's *Fregi e Maiuscole* Parma, 1771

sometimes more modelled, until both through cut of character and open composition, the ground was prepared for that entire change of style in type-forms which in the nineteenth century took place.

II

FOURNIER in his account of Italian foundries says: "This country, which aided the initial steps of printing by the establishment of the celebrated Venetian foundries, preserves scarcely anything of its first renown in this respect. There are still some foundries at Venice, but they are not much esteemed. In the last century one existed which was very valuable on account of the beauty of its Latin and Greek characters by French masters. It belonged to Deucheni.

"The City of Rome, formerly the centre of the fine arts, has only one foundry which is worth knowing about, namely, that of the Vatican. It was commenced about 1578 by the celebrated French type-cutter Robert Granjon, who was called to Rome by Gregory XIII. He worked under the orders of Cardinal de' Medici on different Latin, Arabic, Syrian, Armenian, Illyrian, and Muscovite types.[1] This foundry, which has been since somewhat neglected, forms part of the typographical establishment of the Vatican.

"Piedmont, like Savoy, is not rich in foundries. One alone, established towards 1742 at Turin, and for which I have furnished some sets of matrices of my types, suffices for both these territories. It belongs to a society of individuals attached to the Royal Printing House.

[1] Oriental typography was developed at Rome under the protection of Cardinal de' Medici. Some Greek, roman, and Oriental types cut by Robert Granjon for Basa were bought for the Medici establishment; and Granjon was employed there to engrave others. The first book published by the Stamperia Medicea was an Arabic edition of the Gospels in 1590. Its tractate on the use of Arabic types, brought out in 1592 under the title *Alphabetum Arabicum*, has already been mentioned.

"At Milan there is only one foundry and that a poor one, established in 1719 by a printer named Bellagata, who bought the punches and matrices belonging to Ignace Antoine Keblin, a wandering type-cutter and founder who travelled from city to city. This foundry has since passed to three brothers named Sangiusti, of whom one is an ecclesiastic and the other two clock-makers. These last being dead, it now remains in the hands of the ecclesiastic.

"About twenty years since, an individual named Legrand, a type-founder and a very poor type-cutter, established his foundry at Avignon. It has passed into the hands of M. Pernot, who has added to its collection some matrices of other types."

A few Italian specimen-books may be examined as documents on Italian type-forms. As two of them came from printing-houses of a particular character, something must first be said about the printer "by special appointment," and of the press which was founded for some particular purpose.

The first *privileged* printing-house in Rome or elsewhere was that of the printer-publisher, Antonio Blado, who worked there between 1515 and 1567. He was given, in 1549, the title of *Tipografo Camerale,* or printer to the Apostolic Chamber. Blado had some good fonts of type — gothic, semi-gothic, and roman — and was one of the first printers to follow the Aldine office in its use of italic. He also, by the way, printed the first *Index Expurgatorius,* in 1557. His work was continued by his heirs until 1593.

A *special* printing-house for the use of the Holy See was the idea of Pius IV, in 1560 — the year of the assembling of the Council of Trent. Paul Manutius was chosen to take charge of it, and the first book it issued, in 1562, was a work on the council — *De Concilio* — by the English cardinal,

Reginald Pole, to which Manutius contributed a preface. Its output was very largely devoted to the affairs and decrees of the Council. Because its expenses were in part defrayed by a wine-tax levied on the citizens of Rome, it was called *Tipografia del Popolo Romano*. Its work came to an end not many years after the retirement of Manutius to Venice in 1570.

Meanwhile, the Stamperia Vaticana had been founded by Sixtus V in 1587, and, as its name implies, it was housed in the Vatican, next to the Vatican Library, looking out upon the Cortile di Belvidere. Domenico Basa of Venice was its director, and Aldus Manutius the younger was associated with him in its affairs for some ten years, until his death in 1597. A magnificent example of Basa's work is the folio *Della Trasportazione dell' Obelisco Vaticano*, etc. (recording Fontana's feat in setting up the obelisk in the Piazza of St. Peter's), printed at Rome in 1590. Apart from the splendid architectural plates, the beautiful roman and italic (*corsivo grosso*) fonts, and Basa's bold, clever management of them, produce a volume very sumptuous in its effect.

In connection with this printing-house a foundry was set up—the only one at Rome which Fournier thought worth consideration. A good deal of its material was the handiwork of Granjon, whose italic letter was particularly admired, and who also cut many fonts of Oriental alphabets. In 1610 the Tipografia Camerale and the Stamperia Vaticana were united.

The specimen-book of this office was published in 1628, and was compiled by its director, Brogiotti. An account of its types and some reproductions of them have been given under Italian seventeenth century printing.

We now come to the press and foundry of the Congregation of the Propaganda, also at Rome, which was established in 1626 in a "polyglot" printing-office for missionary purposes. It was started through the gift, by Ferdinand II, of Illyrian types for a Missal, and the exotic types of the Vatican printing-office were added to its stock. Some of the Medici Oriental types were also in use there; others were engraved for it by Stefano Paolini. In a year or two it possessed punches and matrices for the alphabets of twenty-three languages. The best period of this office was during the last half of the eighteenth century under the directorship of Ruggeri and Amaduzzi. Bodoni received his early training from Ruggeri, cut some of the types for this office, and always retained an attachment for it. Under Ruggeri's successor, Amaduzzi, the establishment had fonts for forty-four languages. Specimens of these, accompanied by learned tractates on their composition — generally found nowadays bound together — are important documents in the history of the founding and use of "exotic" fonts. What the office accomplished is recorded in the tasteful little *Catalogus Librorum qui ex Typographio Sacræ Congreg. de Propaganda Fide variis linguis prodierunt*, published at Rome in 1773. Sixteen specimens of alphabets are among its entries, and then follow lists of books published in each language. Since the publication of this catalogue, other alphabets have occasionally appeared up to the present day.

An interesting use of some of these exotic types is shown in an effective folio volume, printed from fonts in this office, and issued at Rome in 1736, in commemoration of the death of Maria Clementina Sobieski, wife of the Old Pretender — entitled *Parentalia in Anniversario Funere Mariæ Clementinæ Magnæ Britanniæ &c. Reginæ.* Hebrew, Greek, Arabic, Syriac, Armenian, Chaldaic, Coptic, Ruthenian, German, and even the tongue of Malabar — every language except

English —celebrates the virtues of the unfortunate titular Queen of England!

Toward the end of the eighteenth century the printing-house of the Propaganda was despoiled unmercifully. Under the French Directory, "the government commissioners being charged with selecting in Italy *the monuments of art with which it is important to enrich France*, proceeded to take the necessary steps to procure for the Republic's printing-office a set of matrices of all the foreign characters in the Propaganda office in Rome." This was in 1798. In the next year, the "necessary steps" were taken and the French commissioners confiscated much of its material — not merely punches and types, but almost everything else they could lay their hands on.

Although beyond the limits of the eighteenth century, its later history may be recorded here. After 1800 the office began to recover; but presently Napoleon took a hand in its affairs. Pius VII, when in France for Napoleon's coronation in 1805, was taken by the Emperor to visit the Imprimerie Imperiale; where were printed, in honour of the Pope, a Latin address[1] and also a volume containing the Lord's Prayer in one hundred and fifty languages[2]—the Imprimerie being filled with fonts which, though styled *typis imperialibus*, were stolen from the Propaganda printing-office!

[1] *Adlocutio et Encomia Variis Linguis Expressa, quæ Summo Pontifici Pio VII, Typographiæ Imperiale Musæum Invisenti, Obtulit Joannes Josephus Marcel, Typographæi Imperialis administer generalis, Lutetiæ Parisiorum, Typis Imperialibus. Anno Reparatæ Salutis* 1805, *Imperiique Napoleonis Primo*—in which NAPOLEON always appeared in capitals, and Pius in capitals and small capitals!

[2] *Oratio Dominica CL Linguis Versa, Et Propriis Cujusque Linguæ Characteribus Plerumque Expressa ; Edente J. J. Marcel*, etc. The last page bears the inscription, "Hic opus Polyglotticum coram Supremo Pontifice impressum est." One hundred and fifty presses are said to have been simultaneously in use to effect this; and at the end of the Pope's visit, a bound copy of the completed book was given him.

However, Bodoni in 1808 made it a present of types; but in July, 1812, the office was suppressed, and in November the Prefect of Rome ordered that all matrices stored there should be sent to Paris. Some of Bodoni's characters were hidden and some other material was kept back. Nevertheless, by this and former pillage, the greater part of the punches, matrices, and types were lost to it.

On the return of the Bourbons to France, the Imprimerie Royale was confided to one of the Anissons, a family which had held control of the French national printing-house for a hundred years before the Revolution, when the last director, Anisson du Perron, "*périt révolutionnairement*" in 1794. Pius VII demanded the return of the confiscated material, which was essential for use in books for Catholic missions. Anisson replied that it was at the Pope's disposal, but nothing was done. Apparently there were "reasons," and they were such forcible ones that the types remain in the Imprimerie Nationale to-day. The Propaganda Office has been revived under later Popes, and still exists, though its glories are decayed and it has to-day mainly an historical interest.

Our next Italian specimen is Bodoni's *Fregi e Majuscole* of 1771.[1] In this we are able to see what types and ornaments Bodoni used in the earlier part of his career. They are (as he says in his very "worth-while" preface) a derivation from Fournier, but lack that precision which Bodoni embodied so characteristically in his nineteenth century types (*fig.* 131 a). They exhibit, however, his admiration for Fournier, whom he copied in a flattering but barefaced manner. Granted that the most agreeable features of the book *are* copied, this "specimen" of 1771 is one of the most tasteful and charming volumes of its kind in existence. Each page

[1] *Fregi e Majuscole incise e fuse da Giambattista Bodoni, Direttore della Stamperia Reale. A Parma, nella Stamperia Stessa.* 1771.

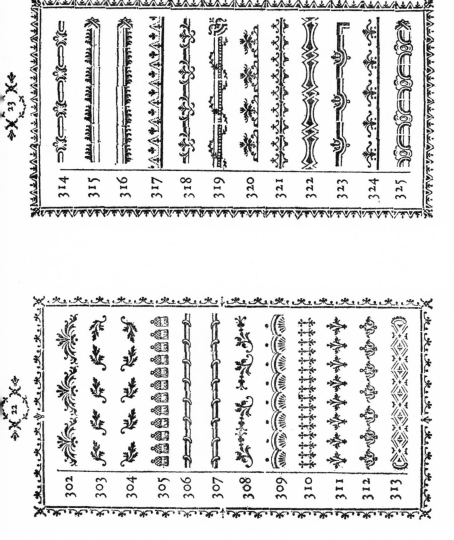

129. *Ornaments from Bodoni's Fregi e Majuscole, Parma, 1771*

Fournier, che spiran forse maggior proporzione di parti. La preferenza che al Fournier fi era data dai re di Svezia, e di Pruffia per provvedere le loro stamperie, giustificava il nostro giudizio.

I caratteri adunque in questo saggio impressi, sono una derivazione dei Fourneriani, e chi vale nella cognizione di queste cose, non ci priverà almeno della tenue lode di una esatta imitazione. Ho detto esser questo, come in effetto egli è, un saggio, non avendo fin'ora fatti i ponzoni, e le matrici che per i caratteri in esso contenuti. Quanto ai caratteri greci, esaminati tutti, que' del secolo XVI, anteporremo d'imitare quelli di Arrigo Stefano, che sono tanto più belli, e ben conformati di que' di Aldo Manuzio, quanto il primo nella greca letteratura superava il secondo. Ebbero

Ut Apes in faltubus omnia libant,
Sic vos . . . . . *Virgil.*

131. (a) *Page from Saggio Tipografico.* (b) *Reverse of half-title of Fregi*
Bodoni's Fregi e Majuscole, Parma, 1771

giungo, che questa fu perfezionata sotto Luigi XIII. situata nelle gallerie del Louvre, e diretta da Sebastiano Cramesi. Egli ebbe in custodia i conj, e le madri, e quanto appartiene all'arte della stampa. Successe ad esso Sebastiano Matrè suo nipote per parte di sorella, che morì nel 1687. La vedova sua moglie continuò nel suo uffizio.

Nel 1690 il ministro de Louvois chiamò da Lione Giovanni Anisson; e nel 1691 venne qualificato direttore e regolatore della stamperia Reale.

Nel 1707 Giovanni Anisson cedè il suo posto a Claudio Rigod suo cognato.

Luigi Lorenzo Anisson nipote di Giovanni ottenne ai 19 Marzo 1723 la concorrenza con Rigod, e la di lui sopravvivenza. Rigod morì nel Luglio seguente. Li 22 Agosto 1735 Giacomo Anisson di Peîron entrò in uffizio unitamente a suo fratello Luigi Lorenzo. Quest'ultimo è quello che presiede, se più esiste, alla stamperia

GARAMONCIN IIᵒ.

Reale, una delle meglio ordinate, e più ricche, vaste e belle che si trovino. Ivi si stampano quasi tutti i pubblici fogli, ch'escono dal ministero. Vi si fanno ancora delle edizioni pregiatissime di celebri autori in tutte le lingue e caratteri.

Altro non mi resta, che nominare alcuni stampatori più celebri a mia cognizione. Li divido in due classi; Oltramontani e Italiani. Lascio i già nominati di sopra.

Oltramontani.

Froben, Schover, Tournes, Revager, Gesner, Bade, Turnebi, Vascosani, Westfalia, Huguetani, Treijel, Martini, Collines, Dizj, Morelli, Griffi, Rovilli, Oporini, Benenati, Scheleichj, Schureri, Seceri, Stephani, Plantini, Elzevirj, Kurner, Gurmond, Leonard, Wechel, Commelj, Virrè, Vaillant, Hackii, Mugnet, Micballet, Coignard, Desprex, Egmond, Anissonj, Jansonj ec.

is surrounded with borders, of which scarcely one is bad, or scarcely two alike. The types are old style, but their delicacy shows current tendencies; and this is specially true of the italic (*fig.* 128). The Greek character is condensed and very ugly, and but one font is shown as against the twenty-eight varieties exhibited in Bodoni's Greek specimen of 1788.[1] Bodoni's ornamented letters (*fig.* 130 a) are modelled on those of Fournier. The 377 *vignettes* or ornaments (exactly the number shown in the *Manuel*) are mostly recut after Fournier's designs, but Bodoni's versions have less colour and warmth and a certain Italian twist to them — of those shown (*fig.* 129), all but two (305 and 325) are copies or adaptations. Their arrangement as borders for initials (*fig.* 130 b) and as head-pieces, etc., is ingenious. Bodoni's title-page, half-title to the specimen of types, and some minor decorations — for instance, the type "bees" surrounding type "flowers," to which he has added the familiar motto from Virgil (*fig.* 131 b) — are neatly "lifted" from Fournier's *Manuel*. All the same, the book is enormously instructive to compare with Bodoni's great, chilly masterpieces, the *Oratio Dominica* and the *Manuale Tipografico* of 1818. And there are two other books of Bodoni's early period which appeal specially to students of types — his *Iscrizioni esotiche*, composed by J. B. Rossi and issued in 1774, and his folio *Epithalamia Exoticis Linguis Reddita* of 1775, employing alphabets of some twenty-five languages and exquisitely decorated. These, with his *Manuale Tipografico* of 1788, and his less known folio collection of Latin, Greek, and Russian types of the same year, show Bodoni's original material and incidentally his first way of working, and are discussed in another chapter in connection with his later work.

[1] *Serie de' Caratteri Greci di Giambatista Bodoni*, 1788.

Our last type-specimen book is that of Zatta of Venice of 1794,[1] apparently a second and enlarged edition of an earlier book. The Zattas were printers, publishers, and type-founders — *Tipografi, Calcografi e Libraj Veneti* — and their establishment was the largest and among the most esteemed in Venice. Their specimen opens with a *résumé* of the history of typography, and among contemporary printers mentioned are Comino of Padua, the brothers Foulis of Glasgow, Baskerville of Birmingham, Ibarra of Madrid, Didot of Paris, and Bodoni. The definition of a typographer shows that they had read Fournier's *Manuel* to advantage. A statement about the knowledge necessary to proper cutting and casting of type, with occasional details as to their own practice, is followed by a table of types in stock, weight per page, etc. In the types shown, smaller sizes have the prevailing tendency to lightness which was coming into fashion; as in the *Garamoncin II°* (*fig.* 132). These fonts are not very well cut, and the italic, especially in mass, is gray and uninteresting. *Testo d'Aldo I°* is, however, a fine letter, and appears to be a survival of an earlier period — as does *Canoncin I°* and *Canoncin II°*, and *Canon* in both its sizes. The reproduction of the *Filosofia II^a* shows in the roman, but particularly in the italic, that an approach to a modern face type had been made in Italy (*fig.* 133). The borders — in some cases interesting as showing Italianized derivations from Fournier (*fig.* 134) — are effective but coarse. The specimen is (naturally enough) to French specimens, what Italian eighteenth century volumes are to the more finished French books then current.

---

[1] *Saggi dei Caratteri, Vignette e Fregi della Nuova Fonderia de Antonio Zatta e figli, Tipografi, Calcografi e Libraj Veneti.* Venice, 1794. As has been said, the chief Italian printing-houses at the time of Bodoni's *début* were the Tipografia del Santissimo Sacramento at Urbino, the Volpi-Cominiana Press at Padua, and those of Soliani and Zatta respectively at Modena and Venice.

Gli *Elzeviri*; molti riguardano gli Elzeviri, come i più abili stampatori non solo in Olanda, ma in tutta l'Europa. Bonaventura, Abramo, Luigi e Daniele Elzeviri sonosi distinti nella loro arte. In verità sono stati molto inferiori ai Stefani tanto per l'erudizione, quanto per le edizioni Greche ed Ebraiche, ma non sono stati ad essi inferiori nella scielta dei buoni libri che hanno stampato e nell'intelligenza del mestiere, ed anzi gli sono stati superiori nella scielta, e delicatezza dei buoni caratteri. Il loro Virgilio, Teren-

zio, nuovo *Testamento Greco*, ed altri libri dei loro torchj, dove trovansi dei caratteri rossi sono capi d'opera nella loro arte. Più volte hanno stampato il catalogo delle loro edizioni che fra le altre comprendono tutti gli autori classici, i di cui piccoli caratteri sono belli tanto, quanto nocevoli alla vista.

I Stefani si riguardano come i regi della stampa, tanto per l'erudizione, che per le edizioni Greche ed Ebraiche. Otto sono gli Stefani che si distinsero nella loro carriera, ma Roberto ed Enrico suo secondo genito si re-

133. "*Modern*" *Types from Zatta's Saggi dei Caratteri, Venice, 1794*

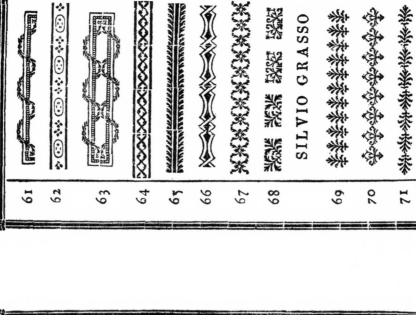

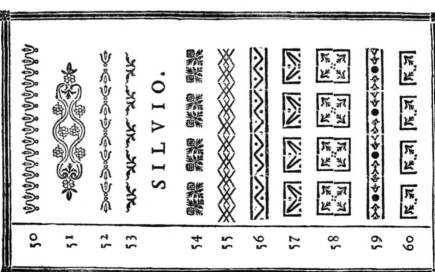

124. Borders from Zatta's Saggi dei Caratteri, Venice 1794

Besides describing a few specimen-books, I have devoted some space to the history of the offices themselves, because it is one more evidence of the antiquity of much that we think of as modern. The "privileged press," which had certain rights (analogous to those of the King's Printers in English Bibles and Prayer-Books), and the "special press," founded to promote the needs of some particular department of knowledge, are neither of them new projects. Many types in the two or three great presses and foundries of the world came originally from old offices of this second class, which did not survive, either because the motive power which carried them on ceased with the death of the founder; or a special work which they were intended to do was accomplished; or because they lacked that fundamental necessity to the foundation of all great presses — a certain vision backed by permanent endowment. A large number of private presses existed in Italy at the time of which I am writing. Indeed, the earliest of them was founded in 1491. There were, in the sixteenth century, fifteen private presses in different parts of the Italian peninsula; and in the seventeenth and eighteenth centuries a dozen different private ventures of this sort, sometimes presided over by authors or book-lovers, sometimes by religious communities. And they exist to-day. For neither the privileged press, the institutional press, nor the private press are things new under the sun!

CHAPTER XIV

FRENCH TYPES: 1500–1800

ALTHOUGH the first press set up in Paris in 1470 employed roman types, French printing for some years thereafter was executed from gothic fonts — *lettre de forme, lettre de somme,* and *lettre batarde* (*fig.* 135). This press — a private venture of two scholars — could not, at the moment of its foundation, exert sufficient influence by its use of roman fonts to overcome the custom of employing, and the prejudice in favour of, gothic types. In the first half of the sixteenth century, the roman letter again asserted itself, and gothic characters were no longer the exclusive use of French printing-houses. This was due largely to the influence of that singular genius, Geofroy Tory of Bourges, "who was at the forefront of all progress made in books, in the second quarter of the sixteenth century." He was at once poet, translator and critic, artist and workman, dreamer and reformer. He had been a traveller in Italy and was deeply moved by the Renaissance spirit. He wrote, printed, and published books; he designed type in which to print them, and ornaments with which to adorn them. He reformed French orthography. He was a prime mover in introducing roman types and made innovations in the arrangement of title-pages. In short, he was a kind of divine jack-of-all-trades. His famous *Champfleury,* begun in 1523, was published in 1529. It is one of the important books in the history of letter design; and Tory was rewarded in 1530 for its production with the title of *imprimeur du roi.* Almost every one of his publications was charming, and his decorations for them, and for the books of other printers, the last word in distinction. Tory is important to *us* because of his part in fostering the fashion

Quesitũ ē ex parte
tua st cõmutationes
fieri valeant pzeben=
daꝛ: cũ commutatio
dignitatum in tuꝛoñ
concilio fuerit inter=
dicta. Geneꝛaliter i=
taꝗ teneas ꝗ cõmu=
tationes pzebendaꝛ
de iure fieri nõ pũt
ꝑserti cũ pacxiõe ꝑm=
issa : ꝗcirca spũalia
bl cõnexa spũalibus

En telle mesuꝛe que
bous mesureꝛes, on bo°
mesureꝛa. Et pourquoy
regarde tu le festu en
loeil de ton fꝛere ꝗ tu ne
bois point bne poultꝛe
qui est en ton oeil. Du
cõment dis tu a ton fꝛere,
frere permetz que ie tire
hoꝛs de tõ oeil bng festu
ꝗ boicy bne poultre est
en ton oeil. Hypocrite,
iecte premieꝛement la
poultre hoꝛs de ton oeil
ꝗ adoncques tu berras a
tirer le festu hoꝛs d loeil
de ton frere.

Ad nostram noueꝛis audientiam peꝛ=
ueniſſe quod cum.R.laicus lator pꝛeſen=
tium ab. XD. mutuum recipeꝛe voluiſ=
ſet: crediroꝛ ne per canonẽ cõrra vſura=
ꝛios ediꝛum poſſet in poſterum cõueniꝛi
domos ꝛ oliuas recepit ab eodẽ titulo
emptionis': cum reueꝛa cunctus vſura=
ꝛi° ageꝛet: quo patet ex eo quod crediroꝛ
debiroꝛi promiſit quod quicumque a ſep=
tẽnio vſque ad nouẽnium daret. Iꝛ. vn=
ciaꝺ raꝛeoꝛum quẽ vix dimidiã iuſti pꝛe=
ꝛii contingebãt domos eivꝺ reſtirueret
ꝛ olivas.

135. *Lettres de Forme*, Lettres de Somme, *and Ancienne Batarde*
shown by Fournier le jeune

Vant que ie commence a enseigner nostre ꝑmiere lettre A. deuoir estre faicte Choses
dele. I. Ie veulx cy prier le bon estudiãt requises
quil sache premieremẽt que cest que le a bien fai
Point, q̃ cest que la Ligne tant droitte re lettres
que nõ droitte, quõ dit corbee en rond Attiques
ou en angle. Que cest que Rond, Que
Quarre, que Triangle, et cõsequamẽt
quil sache les figures plus generales
de Geometrie. Car nosdittes lettres At
tiques en font toutes faictes & figurees
comme ie le mõstreray aidãt nostre sei=
gneur. Et afin quon n'aye cause digno=
rãce, Ien escripray cy les diffinitiõs de
lune apres lautre, & les figureray selõ

que Euclides les nous a iadis laissees par escript.

    P Vnctus, dit Il, est cuius pars nõ est. Cest a dire. Le point est vng signe qui   *Euclides*
ne peut estre diuise. Et cõme dit messire Charles Bouille en sa Geometrie   *Charles*
en Francois. Le point ne sapelle ne quantite ne mesure, mais le terme de tou=   *Bouille.*
te quantite, Ie quel na longueur ne largeur, ne parfond.   *Le point*

for roman letters, thereby displacing gothic types, and because he introduced in French printing the accent, apos-
trophe, and cedilla. Epitaphs are notoriously untrustworthy,
but even making due allowance for that, we may well stand
abashed at a person who was recorded as an "accomplished
Scholar in both Latin and Greek, most devoted Lover of
Letters, very expert Printer and learned Author, inasmuch as he wrote elegant Distichs on the Parts of the
House, composed some humorous Epitaphs in Latin in
very ancient Style, translated Treatises of Xenophon, Lu-
cian, and Plutarch from Greek into French, taught Philosophy at Paris in the College of Burgundy, was the first
Man to discuss seriously the Art of Printing, described the
Forms of the Letters, or Characters, of the Alphabet, taught
Garamond, Chief of Engravers, and always performed the
Duties of a good Man." Tory was born about 1480, and died
in 1533.[1]

The first sixty years of the sixteenth century may be
considered the Golden Age of French typography. The
reign of François I—from 1515 to 1547—contributed to
the quickening of intellectual progress and brought greater
refinement into daily life. The Italian campaigns of his

[1] Tory's *Champfleury* is not readily accessible, but the translation of Auguste Bernard's *Geofroy Tory*, issued by Houghton Mifflin Company, in
1909, has delightful reproductions of Tory's designs and initials, redrawn
by Mr. Bruce Rogers. A charming series of borders to Books of Hours on
pp. 101–117, two sets of magnificent decorative initials (pp. 186, 187, 188,
190, and 191), and the Greek and roman alphabets (shown on pp. 194 and
195) should be noted. While not a complete collection of Tory's designs, the
book gives a good idea of the scope of his work.

The original French edition of Bernard's book — *Geofroy Tory, Peintre
et Graveur, Premier Imprimeur Royal, Réformateur de l' Orthographe et
de la Typographie sous François 1ᵉʳ* — was published in Paris in 1857. Its
author was formerly an employee of the Didots, and the expense of its publication was borne by Ambroise Firmin Didot. An excellent notice of Tory
is given in Lepreux's *Gallia Typographica, Série Parisienne I, Imprimeurs
du Roi*, Pt. 1, pp. 505 *et seq.*

reign, and of previous reigns, had much to do with this. For though the military operations of France in Italy between 1494 and 1525 were of slight political or territorial value, the influence of Italy on the Gallic mind — the impression of its beauty and art and science on the one hand, and the conviction of its spiritual and social rottenness on the other — was of immense and lasting value in bracing the morals and stimulating the artistic faculties of the French. Like some of his predecessors, François loved Italian art, and imported Primaticcio, Da Vinci, Del Sarto, and Cellini to adorn Fontainebleau. Things Italian were fashionable at court, and the court in turn set fashions for the cultivated world of France. It was natural enough that books should reflect the prevailing mode — and this is one reason why French books of the earlier sixteenth century show so much Italian feeling. They were more decorative than Italian work, and more delicate and elegant in effect; and in this they showed themselves French. But the Italian influence was there; and "this invasion of foreign germs produced a marvellous blossoming of native genius."

Henri Estienne, head of the famous Estienne family, — "the Eternal Honour of French Typography," — who worked in the last years of the fifteenth century (but who between 1502 and his death in 1520 produced over a hundred books), and his son, the great scholar-printer Robert Estienne, husband of Perette Badius, carried over into the sixteenth century the great tradition in typography. After Henri Estienne's death, his widow (like widows of many French printers, for reasons perhaps economic as well as sentimental) speedily married Simon de Colines, who had been associated with her husband. De Colines' beautiful books also show Italian feeling, but always tempered by a delicacy of execution and *netteté* of effect characteristic of the French artist. They were less direct, tolerant, and ample than Italian books of the same period, and "tighter"—more consciously workmanlike.

Another printer, to-day less remembered, who did beautiful work, was Michel Vascosan. He, too, was a son-in-law of Badius. It is to De Colines, to Robert Estienne, and to Vascosan that the Parisian press of that period owed the introduction of the chief reforms which the Aldine press had already adopted, namely, disuse of gothic types, adoption of handy *formats*, and cheap books for students. To De Colines in particular is attributed the use of italic types for entire books, and the execution of the first really good Greek font with accents, a decade before the appearance of the *grecs du roi*. Both the italic and Greek fonts appeared in 1528, and tradition has it that De Colines was himself their designer. At first the best printers were often type-founders too, although Garamond merely cut and cast type for the use of others.

Roman and italic fonts were increasingly employed for all parts of a book by progressive French printers of this epoch; as in Geofroy Tory's *Champfleury* of 1529;[1] Charles Estienne's work, *De Dissectione Partium Corporis Humani*, printed at Paris by Simon de Colines in 1545;[2] and Kerver's *Hypnerotomachie ou Songe de Poliphile* of 1546.[3] Of course, black-letter books modelled on Gothic manuscripts were still produced in France in the early sixteenth century—such Gothic volumes as the *Horæ Beatæ Virginis ad usum Parisiensem*, printed at Paris by Gering and Rembolt in 1502,[4] or Hopyl's magnificent *Missale Diocesis Coloniensis*, printed at Paris in 1514,[5] being examples; though Books of Hours were printed by Kerver in roman type in the earliest years of the century. Then again, books in a style transitional between

---

[1] *Druckschriften*, pl. 19.   [2] *Ibid.*, pl. 98.   [3] *Ibid.*, pl. 90.
[4] *Ibid.*, pl. 68.   [5] *Ibid.*, pl. 4.

pure "Gothic" and "Roman" were common — such as a Josephus of 1514 (mentioned later) — set in roman letter, touched up with lines of bold *lettre de forme*. For many years vernacular romances continued to be set in a *lettre batarde*, and such work was not much influenced by current fashions. Limits of space compel me to speak chiefly of work by "advanced" men; but old styles of printing persisted along with it.

§1

Sixteenth century examples of French printing have been selected from several points of view. I have wished to show a certain chronological progression in typographic styles from the beginning to the end of the century; to mention particularly famous books like *Champfleury*, or the *Songe de Poliphile;* and to exemplify as fully as possible the beautiful printing of men like the Estiennes, Badius, De Colines, Vascosan, Le Royer, and the two De Tournes, although these books do not show, in a strict sense, progression so much as various ways of utilizing the same style.

The quarto *Quincuplex Psalterium*, printed by Henri Estienne at Paris in 1509, is an example of a sixteenth century book composed entirely in roman fonts. In it a difficult problem in typography has been cleverly solved. Three versions of the Psalms in Latin are presented side by side, printed in a roman letter, and with copious notes — the two remaining versions placed in a sort of appendix and printed in double column. It is a book somewhat Italian in effect, but has elements of delicacy which are purely French; for instance, the charming little ornaments in red, which fill out broken lines in the columns of each version, a device also employed in the Complutensian Polyglot. The Psalms are set in a very handsome old style roman font, a little more modelled than Italian characters of the same kind and period. The notes are composed in a smaller size of much the same sort of roman. The work is printed in red and black throughout.

In the same year that Estienne printed this Psalter, Thielman Kerver issued at Paris, in 16mo, a *Psalterium . . . Virginis Marie* [*sic*], arranged by St. Bonaventura. This beautiful book is a splendid example of the *manière criblée*. The text is printed in *lettre batarde* in red and black. It has ten full-page metal cuts, and every page has borders, many "historiated." The descriptive legends in these borders are, however, printed in *lettre de forme*, and some opening verses in a roman letter. Furthermore, some blocks for the outer margins of pages contain no "scenes" at all, but are pieces of distinctly Renaissance decoration. At first sight the book appears Gothic; but here and there the "Roman invasion" is evident. This Gothic plan with Renaissance details was precisely analogous to that of a Parisian church of the period — St. Eustache, built in 1532; just as French Books of Hours, printed in roman type with borders of open Renaissance design (such as Tory's), had their counterpart in Italian "classical" churches — of which, in French classical style, Paris later on had various examples.

A good instance of a book transitional between Gothic and Roman is a Latin edition of Flavius Josephus, published in quarto at Paris by François Regnault and Jean Petit in 1514. The printers employed for the text a roman type of regular cut, and marginal notes are set in this same size of roman. Displayed lines on the title-page, and titles of principal divisions and running-titles, are, however, in a bold *lettre de forme*. The many initials used are mostly of Gothic design, and the continuous text is broken by gothic paragraph marks. In short, all the details are Gothic in feeling. The excellent workmanship and consistent plan make this book, in spite of the mixture of types, a much handsomer volume than, theoretically, it has any right to be.

Tory's *Champfleury* (a small quarto) was printed at Paris in 1529. It is divided into three books. The first is a disquisition on language; the second, illustrated with wood engravings, treats of the origin and design of roman letters, and institutes a comparison between their proportions and those of the human face and figure; the third contains Tory's magnificent roman capital letters, in alphabetical order, designed on a geometrical framework of squares and circles — on the order of similar schemes for drawing letters by Albert Dürer and others.[1] At the end is a series of alphabets — Hebrew, Greek capitals, roman capitals, a "Cadeaulx" alphabet (a sort of free Gothic hand), and a free rendering of alphabets of *lettre de forme* and *lettre batarde* — with a few words in each. Of the remaining alphabets, the *Lettres Tourneures* and *Lettres Fleuries* are the only ones that need detain us. The title-page and decorations are very distinguished. The book is printed in heavy, early, unattractive roman type, rough in design and execution, and solidly set, without much attention to clearness of arrangement (*fig.* 136). Here and there a rather crabbed Greek letter is introduced. *Champfleury* is a famous volume, but it is full of learned affectations, and it is difficult to read, both as to its matter and the manner of its printing.

[1] As in Dürer's *Vnderweysung der Messung* (1525) and Pacioli's *De Divina Proportione* (1509), both of which Tory criticizes. For an analysis of Renaissance roman capital letters, see the publication of the K. K. Österreichisches Museum für Kunst und Industrie — *Die Initialen der Renaissance. Nach den Constructionen von Albrecht Dürer herausgegeben von Camillo Sitte. . . . Unter Mitwirkung von Josef Salb*. Vienna, 1882. It is illustrated with examples of lettering described.

An edition of *Les Commentaires de Jules César,* translated into French by Estienne De Laigue and Robert Gaguin, was printed in 1531 at Paris by "Maistre Pierre Vidoue . . . pour honnestes personnes Poncet le Preux,[1] et Galiot du Pré," which, though set in one font of roman type throughout, except for notes and the headings to each book of the *Commentaires,* is, none the less, a very archaic affair. This is because its roman type is so rough in cut, the block initials are so heavy in design, and because its text is not broken up, paragraphs being indicated by florets, which are also used at the beginning and end of display lines, running-titles, etc. Some of the illustrations are earlier in style than the book itself, having already been used in other volumes. Apart from the pictures, the book reminds one of Basle rather than of Paris, and in spite of the roman type the pages have an antique air.

Sixteenth century music printing owes its beginnings in France to the talents of Pierre Hautin. He was able to improve upon earlier Italian music printing by doing away with a second impression, which up to that time was necessary. This invention was taken advantage of by Pierre Attaingnant, son-in-law to Philippe Pigouchet, and "printer to the King for music" from 1538 to 1552. He issued in 1532 a collection of twenty Masses, published in seven divisions, the first of which is entitled *Primus Liber viginti Missarum Musicalium tres Missas continens,* the music being by De Manchicourt, Claudin, and Gascoigne. Its title-page, repeated for each division, is printed in four sizes of *lettre de forme* beneath an elaborate representation of the celebration of High Mass, and surrounded with woodcut borders. This is followed by a dedication by Attaingnant to Cardinal de Tournon, chapel-master to François I, faced by a privilege,

[1] Ancestor of Georges Lepreux, author of *Gallia Typographica.*

printed in *lettre batarde*, giving Attaingnant the sole right to print and sell books musically noted or in tablature, for a term of six years from June 18, 1531. The masses which follow are printed in one impression, with the words beneath in *lettre de forme*, the notes being lozenge shaped, sometimes closed, sometimes open. The music types are so large and bold that the effect of these great pages is extremely imposing. The volume is a folio of 530 pages and of considerable rarity[1] (*fig.* 137).

The *De Philologia et De Studio Litterarum* of Guillaume Budé is a quarto book printed in a rough roman font, and with head-lines in small capitals, the folios — in roman numerals — being *capitals* of the same font. The first two lines in the titles of both tractates appear to be cut on wood. The initials — or at least some of them — belong to a famous alphabet, but are coarsely cut and badly printed. It is very Italian in manner, but not a handsome book, though it was printed by Josse Bade of Asch (better known as Jodocus Badius Ascensius) at Paris in 1532. Now in 1535, Robert Estienne printed another quarto book by the same author — *De Transitu Hellenismi ad Christianismum*. The improvement is remarkable. The type is a suaver, more rounded font, better aligned and better set. Tory's famous initials are used and are very brilliantly printed. The head-lines of dedications, and of Books I, II, and III, are composed in a beautiful attenuated roman letter, in a line of capitals and two lines of lower case. The title-page is, like those of many Estienne titles, badly managed and unattractive, largely because of the sprawling Estienne device. Yet the book is much more workmanlike, and shows an immense improvement over Badius' edition of Budé's *De Philologia*. Robert Estienne printed many books in small *format*, sometimes in italic and

[1] A copy of this book is in the Boston Athenaeum.

137. *Music Types combined with Lettre de Forme, used by Attaingnant, Paris, 1532 (reduced)*

Ioannis Ruellij Canonici Parisiensis

ET MEDICI, DE NATVRA STIRPIVM LIBER TERTIVS.

Agaricum.

Cap. I.

Garicum vt fungus nascitur in arboribus Galliarum. glandiferæ præfertim arbores hoc ferunt. Circa Bos=phorum quoq; prouenit colore candido. Est autē fun=gus albus, odoratus, antidotis efficax, in summis arbo=ribus nascens, nocte relucens. Signum hoc eius, ꝙ in te=nebris decerpitur. Dioscorides author est in arborum caudicibus nasci, quadam putrilagine. Sunt qui radicē esse stirpis cuiusdam existiment. Quibusdam radix in=telligitur similis laserpitio, textu raro ac soluto, super=ficie minus compacta. Duo genera constituunt. fœminam, quam & præferunt mari, recto venarum discursu, pectinatim digesto: mas rotundus, conuolutior quaquoqueuorsum, & cōcretu suo spissior. Vtriq; gustus initio dulcis, mox ex dis=

138. *Roman of Ruel's De Natura Stirpium: De Colines, Paris, 1536*

sometimes in roman. In his nine-volume edition of Cicero's *Opera*, published in 1543, he first makes use of the fine italic which he had cut in imitation of the Aldine character.

In the King's Library at the British Museum, Jean Ruel's *De Natura Stirpium Libri Tres* is exhibited as typical of Simon de Colines' work, and of the style of printing that he made popular in France. A beautiful, mellow, Italianate roman font, in a large size, is used for the table of contents and text. A clear and charming font of the same character serves for the index, in which notice the interesting shapes of arabic numerals. Tory's fine *criblé* initials begin the three great divisions of the book. Each chapter, headed by its title in italic and its number in the same line (at the right), also begins with a block-initial, the letter appearing in white on a *criblé* background (*fig.* 138). Running-titles are set in spaced capitals, and the exquisite, refined lower-case roman letter, much used by De Colines, appears on the title-page and at the beginning of each book. A word should be said about the italic used in the preface. Though condensed, it is very distinguished, and with it roman capitals are employed in the Aldine manner (*fig.* 139). I know few books more satisfying throughout than this noble folio volume— one of the finest of sixteenth century French books. It was printed at Paris in 1536.

This italic type was used by De Colines for entire books in small *format* — such as his pretty 16mo editions of the *Odes* and *Epistles* of Horace of 1539, and of Martial's *Epigrams* of 1544. Very fine in folio pages, in small books the italic appears a much cruder character. De Colines' editions of Jean Fernel's *Monalosphærium* (1526), the same author's *Cosmo Theoria* (1527), and Sacrobosco's (Holywood's) *Textus de Sphæra* (1521 or 1527), are interesting examples of his treatment of scientific books, and contain

some famous decorative borders, diagrams, and initials —
some of the latter by Tory.[1]

A fine book by Robert Estienne that recalls the Italian
manner, although the title-page is disfigured by Estienne's
enormous printer's mark, is the monumental Cicero, published in four folio volumes at Paris in 1538–39. The work
has just that quality of delicacy in its running head-lines
of large lower-case roman which makes it French rather
than Italian, though the type is almost an Italian fifteenth
century character.

Michel Vascosan, a rival to the Estiennes in perfection
of work, brought out at Paris in 1543 a Latin edition of
Caesar's *Commentaries*—a distinct advance over Vidoue's
edition of 1531. Very Italian in composition, the types,
both roman and italic, are more modelled and easier to the
eye than those of De Colines —more French, in fact, and
less Italian. A title-page, arranged simply in roman upper-
case and lower-case letters, in one or two sizes, and without
the usual printer's mark (Vascosan did not employ one);
titles of various books, as well as running-titles, set in
spaced capitals; marginal notes composed in a small and
condensed italic ; — all these details are arranged in an Italian way, but the types have a markedly French look. Some
eleven-line initials designed by Oronce Finé are worth examination, as well as the prefatory matter, which, set in
italic, contains interesting maps and some illustrations.

On an earlier page I contrasted Italian and French printing by describing the former as simpler, ampler, and more
monumental, and the latter as more conscious, elaborate,
and elegant. This difference cannot be better shown than

---

[1] De Colines' printing is always worth study, and M. Ph. Renouard's *Bibliographie des Éditions de Simon de Colines* (Paris, 1894) is an excellent guide
for this purpose.

Chriſtianiſſimo Galliarum Regi

FRANCISCO, HVIVS NOMINIS PRIMO, IOANNES

Ruellius S. D.

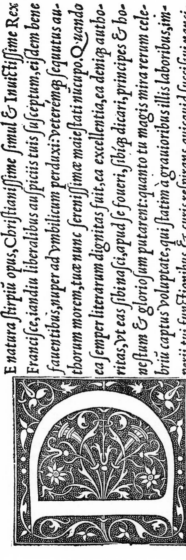

E natura ſtirpiũ opus, Chriſtianiſſime ſimul & Inuictiſſime Rex Franciſce, iandiu liberalibus auſpiciis tuis ſuſceptum, eiſdem bene fauentibus, ſuper ad vmbilicum perduxi: veteremḡ ſequutus au-thorum morem, tuæ nunc ſereniſſimæ maieſtati nucupo. Quando ea ſemper litrarum dignitas fuit, ea excellentia, ea demīḡ autho-ritas, vt eas ſibi naſci, apud ſe foueri, ſibiḡ dicari, principes & ho-neſtum & glorioſum putarent: quanto tu magis mira rerum cele-briũ captus voluptate, qui ſtatim à grauioribus illis laboribus, im-perii tui functionibus, & curis reſpirans, quicquid ſucciſui nanci-ſceris otii, id totum auſcultandis inſignium ſcriptorum lucubrationibus nauiter impendis: eaſḡ poſtea tam præſenti memoria recitas, tam culto ſermone perornas, vt quæ loqueris omnia, mul-to locupletiora, multóḡ meliora reddas, meram ſal, meram ſapĩetiam. Quare citra ſuſpicionem

139. *Italic of Preface of Ruel's De Natura Stirpium: De Colines, Paris, 1536*

Auquel Polia & luy, l'vn apres l'autre, racomptent les eſtranges auantures.
& diuers ſuccez de leurs amours.

En ce premier chapitre Polia declaire de
QVELE RACE ELLE EST DESCENDVE, ET
*comme la uille de Treuiz fut edifiee par ſes anceſtres. Puis en
quele maniere Poliphile deuint amoureux d'elle.*

E peu de grace que vous trouuerez en mon parler (nobles Nymphes & ſingulieres) vous ſera
perdre grande partie du plaiſir qui pouroit eſtre
en l'hiſtoire que vous demādez a ouyr: car ie ſuis
ſeure que ma voix ſemblera en ceſte compagnie
diuine le cry d'vn Cormorant entre le chant des
Roſſignolz. Neantmoins le deſir que i'ay d'o-
beyr a voz requeſtes gracieuſes , que ie tien
pour commandemens, me fera prendre vne hū-
ble hardieſſe de deuiſer en voz preſences ſans
auoir reſpect a mon inſuffiſance: car certainement vous meritez d'entendre ce
diſcours par vne langue plus eloquēte que la mienne, pour peruenir a l'effect
de voſtre intention. Tant y a, que ie ſeray grandement contente & ſatisfaicte
en mon eſprit, ſi par mon parler (combien qu'il ſoit lourd & mal apris) ie vous
puis donner aucune recreation: & eſpere que ma promptitude a vous obeyr,
pourra bien effacer toutes les faultes qui me pourroient interuenir en ce faiſant. Puis qu'il vous plaiſt (donques) entēdre l'origine de mes anceſtres, & ma
deſtinee en amours, laquelle au moyen de ma baſſe condition, n'a peu peruenir a la haulteur de voſtre cognoiſſance, pource que petite chandelle ne peult
rendre grande lumiere: ie m'en acquicteray le plus brief qu'il me ſera poſſi-
ble, vous ſupliant que ſi ce n'eſt ſi proprement comme il eſt requis pour voz
preſences, il vous plaiſe excuſer l'imbecillité d'vne femme terreſtre, peu exer-
citee en telz affaires. Et toy ſaincte fontaine ou repoſent les ſacrees oidon-
nances des ſecretz de la grand deeſſe noſtre maiſtreſſe, ſur les riues de laquelle ie ſuis preſentement aſſiſe, entre tant de Nymphes & Deeſſes Heroiques,
les viſages deſquelles ie veoy nayuement figurez dedans tes clairesvndes, dōt
tu es plus a hōnorer: pardōne moy ſi ie ne te puis regarder ny autres tes ſem-
blables en liqueur, que mes yeux ne fondent en larmes, pource qu'entre mes
predeceſſeurs ſ'en eſt trouuē de telz, qui par diſpoſition diuine ont eſté muez
en pareilles ſources, comme iadiz aduint a la miſerable Dircé, premierement
attache e a la queue d'vn Toreau ſauuage par Zethus & Amphion, en ven-
geāce de leur mere Antiopé, que le Roy Lycus leur pere auoit repudiee pour

Z

in French and Italian editions of Colonna's *Hypnerotoma-chia Poliphili*. The Italian edition was printed by Aldus in 1499, and is one of the finest early Italian illustrated books. A French edition was published by Jacques Kerver, and printed by Louis Baübloom (called Cyaneus), at Paris in 1546, entitled *Hypnerotomachie ou Discours du Songe de Poli-phile*. Aldus's edition is the better book of the two, because so much more direct and simple (*fig.* 28). Kerver's edition is fine in its way—a more ambitious piece of book-making, put together with a more modern feeling (*fig.* 140). Not only of type and its arrangement—for instance, the management of title-pages and chapter headings—is this true; in the French version of the Italian illustrations we find the same tendency to complication and over-refinement. The initials in the French edition are exceedingly distinguished—a famous series, often reproduced.

A French scientific book that has great charm is Jacques Focard's *Paraphrase de l'Astrolabe*, printed at Lyons in 1546 by Jean de Tournes I, in a charming italic, with side-notes in roman, and full of attractively rendered illustrative draw-ings and diagrams. The prefatory address is composed in a delicate roman letter. It is followed by an alphabetic table set in italic, a table of chapters, etc. Then the book proper begins with a fine initial. The subject of each chap-ter is displayed in roman, the text is in italic. Each defini-tion is set in spaced small capitals, and when necessary elucidated by a marginal diagram. Elaborate and exquisite illustrations of the astrolabe and its parts are supplied. They are the work of Bernard Salomon—his earliest asso-ciation with the printer De Tournes. The book is beauti-fully complete in plan, and the plan beautifully achieved.[1]

In 1556, Vascosan printed a mathematical book by

[1] A copy is in the Bowditch Collection, Boston Public Library.

Oronce Finé, *De Rebus Mathematicis, hactenus desideratis,* in four books. The title-page shows some splendid lower-case letters. An opening address is set in a noble font of roman, followed by verses in a smaller size of the same font, and in a well-cut Greek character. The various propositions are composed in roman, with explanations set in an exquisitely clear italic. The diagrams are a charming feature of the book. They are drawn to the width of the page, and blanks within them often contain fanciful little florets of solid black, or with cross-hatched leaves — probably with the practical aim of saving the diagrams from too heavy impression. The book is a masterpiece of restrained style, through the beauty of its types and the elegance of their arrangement. The readability of its italic comes about through its evenness of line (*fig.* 141).

A Paris edition of a book on the same subject as Focard's work, *L'Usage de l'Astrolabe,* by Dominicque Jacquinot (second edition), printed by Guillaume Cavellat in 1558, and *Les Principes d'Astronomie et Cosmographie,* translated from the Latin of Gemma Frisius, issued at Paris by the same printer in 1557, are examples of like books in small *format.* The first is printed in roman, the second in italic. Both are agreeable little volumes — especially the latter — and show an attractive way of printing scientific handbooks.

Estienne Groulleau's French edition of *Les Sept Livres de Flavius Josephus de la Guerre et Captivité des Juifz,* translated by D'Herberay, was printed in Paris in 1557. It is a great contrast to Regnault and Petit's edition of Josephus, and a much more modern volume, though it falls short in style of books by De Colines and Vascosan. A roman type, less classical and more "old style" than we have seen hitherto, is used for the text, which is unbroken by para-

PROPOSITIO I.

Blatis duabus lineis rectis inæqualibus: duas medias lineas rectas, sub eadem ratione continuè proportionales, in primis reddere notas.

¶QVA RATIONE MATHEMATICA
hoc dignißimum ac utile problema dissoluatur, nemo hactenus sufficienter tradidisse uidetur: tametsi Græcorum quamplurimi, nõ aspernandi philosophi atque mathematici, ut illud explicarẽt problema, quod cubi duplicatio dicitur, uariis ac subtilibus admodum inuentis, easdem lineas proportionales tentarint exprimere. Quemadmodum ex Eutocio Ascalonita Archimedis interprete, & Georgio Valla Placentino, qui singulorum exposuerunt adinuentiones, colligere haud difficile est. Nullus siquidem eorundem Græcorum authorum offendetur, qui in disquirendis eiuscemodi lineis proportionalibus, uiam aliquam certam obtinuerit: utpote, qui regulamentorum quorundam adminiculo, tentando, uel potius hinc inde palpitando, totiésque conceptas iterando descriptiones, proprias adinuentionum traditiones suspectas, inexplicabilésque reddiderint. Nos igitur præfatas lineas rectas, inter datas extremas continuè proportionales (ne mathematica simulatque suscepti negotij uioletur integritas) uia hactenus à nemine tentata, ex fidißimis Geometricorum elementorum rudimentis, multifariam, ac prima fronte conabimur reddere notas: idque p otißimum illius diuinæ proportionis adminiculo, quâ data linea recta sic diuiditur, ut in illa medium & extrema continuæ proportionis (quæ in tribus ad minus uidetur consistere terminis) inueniatur. Huius præterea diuinæ proportionis beneficio, ut quinque regularium corporum ab Euclide conciliata est harmonia: sic & nos bonam partem eorum, quæ in ipsis desiderabantur Mathema-

a

141. *Types used by Vascosan*, Paris, 1556

Les singularitez des seize
premiers Liures de Pline,
historien naturel.

Pline naturel historien
fut nay souz l'Empereur Tyberien, et
mourut souz l'Empereur Tite, qui
destruit Hierusalem apres la passion de
nostre Seigneur, auquel il attribua ses
œuures.

Au premier Liure qui est bref il fait seulement ses preambules.

Au second il traite du monde, e des
autres chposes. Il descrit que le monde est
seul et rond, immobile naturellement, combien
qu'il y ayt aucunes parties mobiles, et qui se
peuuent mouuoir, par concauitez de la terre,
pleines de vent. Il y ha quatre Elements,
la terre, l'air, l'eau, et le feu en hault, par
dessus l'air prochain au premier Ciel, qui
est feu naturel, parquoy ny fault point de
bois pour le continuer. Au dessouz de la
terre, sont les planettes (que l'on dit erran-

A ij

142. *Granjon's Civilité: Breton, Paris,* 1559

graphs. Running head-lines are arranged in capitals, not quite enough spaced. The chapter headings, while employing the handsome, large upper and lower-case letters then the fashion, drop dizzily to a minute italic for a second line. Titles of chapters occur at the foot of pages where there is not room for a single line of text, the chapter itself beginning on the facing page or even over-leaf. The title-page decoration is attributed to Tory, and the book has many attractive illustrations within cleverly designed *encadrements* made up of separate pieces. Ill-considered in detail, and carelessly thrown together, it is none the less a somewhat charming book.

Robert Granjon of Paris, publisher, printer, type-cutter, and founder, introduced at Lyons about 1557 his *civilité* types, an ingenious rendering of a Gothic cursive handwriting in vogue at the time.[1] These types attracted attention, and Granjon obtained from Henri II a "privilege" of ten years' duration for what he called *lettre françoyse d'art de main.* Its first use was in *Dialogue de la Vie et de la Mort*, a French translation by J. Louveau of an Italian book by Innocent Ringhier. Such types were commonly called *caractères de civilité*, because early employed in two popular books for children — Louveau's translation from Erasmus, *La Civilité Puérile distribuée par petitz chapitres et sommaires*, and Gilbert de Calviac's *Civile Honesteté pour les Enfants, avec la manière d'apprendre à bien lire, prononcer et escrire*, etc. This latter book was printed at Paris in 1559 by Philippe Danfrie and Richard Breton, to whom Granjon allowed the use of these fonts. An example of a book printed in *civilité* is *Sommaire des Singularitez de Pline*, a thin 16mo, printed by Richard Breton at Paris in 1559, in two sizes of this type. Though beautifully arranged in the style of a manuscript

[1] Steffens's *Paléographie Latine*, pl. 119 a.

of that date, it is exceedingly hard to read (*fig.* 142). There were many forms of *civilité* types, and an interesting one is reproduced (*fig.* 143), though obviously of a much earlier date than the 1742 specimen of the Paris founder, Claude Lamesle, from which it is taken.

An exquisite book is the folio *Livre de Perspective de Jehan Cousin Senonois, Maistre Painctre à Paris*,[1] printed at Paris in 1560 by Jean Le Royer, originally an engraver, but appointed by Henri II *Imprimeur du Roy ès Mathématiques.* Its title-page with an elaborate and sumptuous printer's mark is followed by a great decorative engraving, present-ing the five *Corps Réguliers de Géométrie* in a magnificent *encadrement.* This folio is printed chiefly from a mellow roman font, with running-titles set in a large lower-case letter (*fig.* 144). The preface and the author's and printer's addresses to the reader are composed in a beautiful, lively italic (*fig.* 145). Le Royer's address indicates that this book was his first venture—which perhaps accounts for the misfit of the initial in the passage we reproduce. But these decorations and initials are by Cousin, and in tone blend delightfully with the type; and the diagrams of perspec-tive, chiefly engraved by Le Royer, are exquisitely ren-dered. The book is beyond praise for its simplicity and ele-gance—one of the handsomest volumes of its time. The reader should examine, if possible, Le Royer's edition of Ambroise Paré's *Méthode Curative des Playes et Fractures de la Teste Humaine*, 1561.

The Lyons Press at this period did work of great dis-tinction. Claude Paradin's *Alliances Généalogiques des Rois de France* is an example—and a book where an enor-mously difficult problem is successfully surmounted. In this

---

[1] There is a copy in the Boston Public Library. Cousin was a painter, sculp-tor, and painter of glass, besides being the author of two books on design.

Civilité au Corps de Gros Romain, Numero XLIX.

L'heure de vous lever étant venue, faites d'abord le signe de la Croix, et donnez aussitost votre cœur à Dieu, et ne soyez pas du nombre de ceux qu'on a bien de la peine à faire lever; mesme si vous avez la prudence et l'honneur en recommandation, vous ne souffriez pas qu'aucune personne d'autre sexe entre en votre chambre, pendant que vous y estes; ainsi vous la tiendrez fermée de votre costé.

Levez-vous donc avec tant de circonspection, qu'aucune partie de vostre corps ne paroisse nue, quand mesme vous seriez seul dans la chambre, et que vous ayez quelqu'un qui fasse votre lit, ne le laissez pas néanmoins découvert, quand vous en sortez; remettez au moins la couverture.

Prenez d'abord les habits qui vous couvrent le plus, pour cacher ce que la nature ne veut pas qui paroisse, et faites cela pour le respect de la Majesté d'un Dieu qui vous regarde; ne sortez iamais de la chambre à demi vestu.

Accoutumez-vous à garder le silence, ou à parler de quelque chose de bon en vous habillant :

M   Hebreu

143. *Old Civilité from Lamesle's Épreuves Générales des Caractères Paris, 1742*

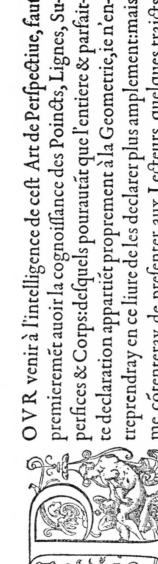

POVR venir à l'intelligence de cest Art de Perspectiue, faut premieremét auoir la cognoissance des Poincts, Lignes, Superfices & Corps:desquels pourauutât que l'entiere & parfaite declaration appartiét proprement à la Geometrie,ie n'entreprendray en ce liure de les declarer plus amplement:mais me côtenteray de presenter aux Lecteurs quelques traicts & figures des plus necessaires à l'intelligence & execution de cest Art:plus tost pour les faire resouuenir de telles choses, que pour les-en instruire entieremét, renuoyant à la Geometrie ceux qui ne les auroient par cy deuant apprises, pour en estre plus amplement informez. Quant à presentil me suffira de vous proposer ce que dit est, & vous declarer les noms, vsages, & accidéts d'aucunes lignes, poincts & figures appartenants particulieremét à la Perspectiue.Donques (pour

A iiij

144. *Roman of Cousin's Livre de Perspective: Le Royer, Paris, 1560*

folio of over one thousand pages, every page bears a coat of arms—sometimes two and three. The text below them varies from one line to almost a full page—except where broken by half-titles separating the different Royal Houses. Unity of effect—the problem in this case—is arrived at by placing the arms always at the same point at the top of the page, immediately beneath a running-title of roman capitals, and by beginning the text always at a given point below them, leaving the lower part of the page blank or not, according to the amount of matter. The result is that a book containing great variety of text, of unequal amount to a page, appears perfectly "natural" and harmonious because unified by this reiteration of position. Practically but one font of a robust old style roman is used for the text. The heraldic bearings, which avoid monotony by being designed with great reserve and frugality of line, are brilliantly printed from very well engraved wood-blocks. Jean de Tournes I printed this book in 1561. His work always deserves study. In 1558 he produced a beautiful little 16mo *Biblia Sacra*. The text is arranged in double column and employs a clear and delicate roman font; a very exquisite italic—no doubt Granjon's—being used for the prologue to each book. Decorations and initials are brilliantly designed in arabesque, and the illustrations are delightful and distinguished.

La Vita et Metamorfoseo d' Ovidio, edited by Simeoni and printed by Jean de Tournes II at Lyons in 1584, was a re-impression in Italian of a French book printed in 1557[1] by Jean de Tournes I, and dedicated by its author to Diane de Poitiers. It is adorned with exquisite decorative borders. The delicate illustrations are by Bernard Salomon—*le petit Bernard*—one of the most distinguished designers of the French-Italian school. The type beneath its pictures is the

[1] I have been unable to see a copy of this edition.

point to notice, however — the delicate, silvery italic of Robert Granjon (designer of the *civilité* character), who worked at Lyons in connection with Jean de Tournes and Sebastian Gryphius, and there married Antoinette Salomon, daughter of the designer. From 1570 almost all Lyons printers used this kind of italic type.[1] This volume shows the delicacy and charm of French workmanship in a fanciful kind of book — a veritable gem of book-making. Some of the decorations used by De Tournes were like goldsmith's work, and often had a niello-like quality which was characteristic of much Lyons typographic ornament (*fig.* 146).

This closes our consideration of the books of an unsurpassed epoch in French printing.

I know of no specimen of types issued by any sixteenth century French founder,[2] but a celebrated foundry — according to Fournier the oldest private foundry in France — was begun in the sixteenth century by the Le Bé family, "the first masters of which," Fournier adds, "being of an investigating as well as intelligent turn of mind, collected and preserved many matrices of old characters which were in use since the very beginning of printing."

Guillaume Le Bé I was born at Troyes in 1525. Between 1545 and 1550 he was a pupil of Garamond and Estienne. He, too, was under the spell of Italy, for he had been both at Rome and at Venice to perfect himself in his work. He cut Oriental fonts with ability. Hebrew was his specialty, and, but twenty-one years old when he cut his first Hebrew types, in a period of fifty years he had engraved some seventeen varieties of this character. He perfected Hebrew fonts for

[1] Delacolonge specimen, pp. 108, 109, and 111.

[2] Many Greek and Hebrew "Alphabets" were published at Paris in the sixteenth century; but these were not "specimens" of Greek and Hebrew types, as might appear, but little elementary grammars for students.

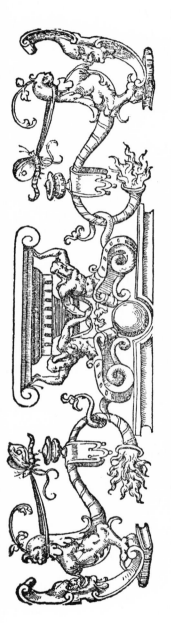

IEHAN COVSIN AV LECTEVR.

AMY Lecteur tu as icy en mon œuvre, contenant les premieres Reigles de l'art de Perspectiue, que i'eusse voluntiers dedié et adressé au Roy ou à quelques Princes et grans Seigneurs, selon que coustumierement il se faict, si i'eusse senty de l'eloquence et sçavoir assez en moy pour n'y oser adresser. Ie l'eusse semblablement voluntiers laissé aller avecq ses figures simples, s'il n'eust esté question qu'es mains des experts, et exercez en l'art, qui d'eux mesmes et à la simple veue de la figure eussent peu cognoistre et voir ce qui en est. Mais i'ay vou-lu servir aux rudes et ignorans qui voudront en cognoistre quelque chose, et satisfaire à l'insta-

145. Italic in Cousin's *Livre de Perspective: Le Royer, Paris,* 1560

Fanciullo nel paniere co i piedi
di Dragone.   29.

Poi ch'ha Palla il Ceston posto da banda
Con il figliuol, che senza madre è nato:
Alle figlie di Cecrope comanda
Custodir, nè scoprir ciò ch'hà celato.
Aglaura, intenta all'opera nefanda,
Sol'al dir della Dea non hà mirato,
Scuopre la cesta, & , fuor di sua intentione,
Troua vn fanciul co i piedi di Dragone.

C 5

146. *Robert Granjon's Italic: De Tournes, Lyons,* 1584

Robert Estienne, and was engaged to cut that needed for the Plantin Polyglot Bible. Le Bé also engraved music for Leroy and Ballard, the earliest privileged Parisian music printers. Besides the accumulation of his own handiwork, Le Bé bought in 1561, the year of Garamond's death, most of the punches, matrices, etc., of Garamond's types, and almost all the material of his foundry, of which he was named appraiser. At his death in 1598, Le Bé was the first engraver of Oriental characters in the world.

Le Bé had a son of the same name and business (the correspondent of Moretus), who added to the collection of types through his efforts and researches; and he in turn had a son of like name and occupation, who continued the foundry with credit. The third Le Bé died in 1685, and the foundry was managed by Claude Faure until Madame Le Bé's death in 1707, and then for her four daughters by Jean Claude Fournier, *père*, its director for over twenty-five years. About 1730 it was bought by his eldest son, Fournier *l'aîné*, who, his younger brother tells us, "sustained by his talents the reputation of this celebrated foundry, combining the art of type-cutting with that of type-founding."

Of the Le Bé foundry I know of no specimen; nor did Fournier *l'aîné* apparently issue any after he acquired it. This is surprising, for he was very proud of his ancient punches, strikes, and matrices of types by Garamond, Granjon, Le Bé, Sanlecque, and others. The list of them that he gave in 1757 showed that it was a collection in which any man would take pride.

§ 2

In the seventeenth century, French types became less Italian and more what we now call an "old style" letter — by no means so fine a character. Some of the larger volumes were splendid in their way, such as *Courses de Testes et de Bague faites par le Roy . . . en l'année* 1662, printed in 1670 by Sébastien Mabre-Cramoisy,[1] or L. J. de Boullencourt's *Description Générale de l'Hostel Royal des Invalides,* printed at Paris by Desprez in 1683.[2] The best of these books were perhaps printed from types in the Imprimerie Royale; and were imposing rather than tasteful—grandiose, and as uncomfortable as grandiose things have a habit of being. Smaller French books of this epoch were also somewhat discouraging in effect. Many of them were copies — and not very good ones — of the compact volumes of the Elzevirs. While quite modern in make-up, there is nothing about such books of much interest to a printer. French seventeenth century printing — heavy in type and in decoration — was indeed precisely like the art of the time; in short, belonged to the pompous period of Louis XIV. As the century closed, types became more "modelled," but were still somewhat archaic in their general effect.

An early seventeenth century folio which possesses considerable style, composed in type something like characters used by Plantin, is the *Civitas Veri sive Morum* of Delbene. This is printed in a large and very effective roman character. Italic of the period is employed for its prefatory verses, this italic having all the characteristic swash letters. Tailpieces and head-pieces are introduced, cut on wood, but the handsome title-page and large illustrations are engraved on copper. In form of type, in type-setting, and in imposition, the book has distinction. It was printed at Paris by Ambrose and Jerome Drouart, in 1609.

Sébastien Cramoisy of Paris was a great figure among printers of his day, and his name appears on the *Obser-*

[1] *Druckschriften,* pl. 39.   [2] *Ibid.,* pl. 40.

vatio Apologetica, etc., of Gabriel Trivorius,—royal histori-
ographer to Louis XIII,—printed in 1631. Cramoisy was
afterwards appointed first director of the Imprimerie Royale du Louvre; but he also printed on his own account, and
employed other men to print for him. This book is a good
specimen of an early seventeenth century quarto. The rubricated title-page and prefatory Address to the King are
printed in very heavy, roughly cut types, and an Address to
the Reader in a smaller size of unattractive italic, also used
elsewhere. Chapter heads and running-titles are in spaced
capitals and small capitals. The index to the contents of the
chapters is set in an italic, and the text of the book is composed in roman old style—fine fonts which appear like
those of Garamond. In spite of these types, fine paper, ample margins, many initial letters, and distinguished imposition made more attractive by red hand-ruling, the effect
of the typography is antique and tasteless, owing to presswork that is very poor indeed.

"In 1640 a Parisian writing-master named Pierre Moreau," says Fournier, "endeavoured to make punches and
matrices of some new types, in the style of handwriting.
Of these he made four kinds, *grosse* and *petite batarde, lettres
rondes,* and another *batarde brisée.* He dedicated the first
proofs of them, in 1642, to Louis XIII, who encouraged the
talents of this new typographer by giving him the post of
Printer in Ordinary to the King, which he enjoyed for some
time; and he printed several works with the aforesaid characters. The taste for this kind of printing having gone by,
as it was of no general typographical utility, Moreau was
obliged to give up his occupation." Moreau's types are cleverly shown in J. Baudoin's *Les Saintes Métamorphoses ou Les
Changemens miraculeux de quelques grands Saints. . . . À
Paris, en l'Imprimerie des nouveaux Caractheres* [sic] *de P.*

Moreau, Me Escrivain Juré à Paris, & Imprimeur ord^re du Roy. . . . 1644. In this book the type (for once) really appears to be writing — a careful and lively copy of the agreeable calligraphy of the period. The ornaments used with it are reproductions of writing-masters' scrolls and whimsical figures, and here and there heavy flourishes are added to words to produce a further illusion of penmanship (*fig.* 147). The clever arrangement of notes, the verse in a smaller size of type, the black-letter introduced in the dedication, and the interesting figures used for folios should be noticed. Six different fonts are used in the volume. It is a "trick book," but so well done that one enjoys being fooled. An edition of Virgil's *Æneid* of 1648 contains examples of all Moreau's fonts. Moreau has the distinction of having designed raised letters for the use of the blind, but his plans are said to have failed through lack of money to develop them.

The great Paris Polyglot of Gui Michel Le Jay, published in ten enormous folio volumes in 1645, falls into this period. Its chequered history and that of some of its exotic types neither belongs, nor can be told, here; but its typography should be examined as an example of what could be done then and what we should not dare to attempt now! Taking seventeen years to complete, it was nearly the ruin of Le Jay — Polyglot Bibles being an expensive business for their promoters. It was printed by Antoine Vitré,[1] *imprimeur du roi pour les langues orientales,* and one of the most distinguished seventeenth century printers, ranking with Cramoisy and the later Estiennes. Apart from the printing of the Le Jay Polyglot, Vitré is now chiefly remembered for his purchase of the collection of Oriental types formed by Savary de Brèves, French Ambassador to Constantinople

---

[1] The magnificent engraving, by Morin, of Philippe de Champaigne's portrait of Vitré is familiar to lovers of fine prints. Vitré died in 1674.

visible fait apres sa mort, en la
personne, tant de luy-mesme, que
de sa femme & de ses enfans.

ADVIS
Aux personnes de condition,
diuersement affligées.

Vous, dont la condition est chan-
gée, & qui des plus hautes pros-
peritez de la vie, vous voyez tombez
en des disgraces qui vous la font
haïr; Au lieu de vous fâcher de ces
pertes, consolez-vous-en plustost,
& les tenez pour de purs effets

147. *Moreau's Calligraphic Types, Paris, 1644*

Petit Parangon Italique.

Jule Cesar naquit le douzième jour du cinquième mois, qui de son nom fut depuis appellé Juillet, l'an 654 de Rome, quatre-vingt dix-huit ans avant JESUS-CHRIST. A l'âge de seize ans il perdit son pere, & l'année d'après il fut désigné grand Prêtre de Jupiter.

Italique de Saint Augustin.

Monsieur, le commencement de votre derniere Lettre m'a extrèmement affligé; mais le milieu & la fin m'ont fait passer de la tristesse à une joie qui m'a pensé faire mourir. Jamais mort n'eut été plus douce que la mienne.

Italique de gros Romain.

CHARLES II. dit le Chauve, Roi de France, & depuis Empereur, étoit le dernier des enfants de Louis le Débonnaire, qui l'avoit eu seul de Judith, fille de Velfe Comte de Baviere sa seconde femme. Il nâquit à Francfort sur le Mein le 13 Juin de l'an 822.

148. Old Italics from Sanlecque's Epreuves des Caractères, Paris, 1757

and Rome. This purchase, made for Louis XIII by Richelieu's direction, involved Vitré in serious monetary troubles, as he was not reimbursed for twenty years. These types form the basis of the collection of Oriental types now in the Imprimerie Nationale.

Among seventeenth century architectural folios, one of the most beautiful is Roland Fréart's *Parallèle de l'Architecture Antique et de la Moderne*, printed by Edme Martin at Paris, in 1650. The types used, though of a somewhat archaic design, are picturesque and full of movement; and they are arranged with great sense of style. The full pages of italic and roman are specially good, and the typography is really aided by beautifully engraved architectural and decorative copper-plates. It is a very superb book in the best manner of a poor typographical period. A later edition, published by Emery and others at Paris in 1702, is by no means so well printed. It was translated into English by John Evelyn.

Pierre Le Petit, who was printer to the French Academy in 1643, and produced its first dictionary, was son-in-law to Jean Camusat, first printer to the Academy ; and married his daughter Denise, the original of one of the most delightful engraved portraits in the iconography of printing. An excellent example of good mid-seventeenth century work is Le Petit's edition of *Vies de Plusieurs Saints Illustres de Divers Siècles; Choisies & traduites . . . par Monsieur Arnauld d'Andilly*, one of the celebrated group connected with Port-Royal. It is a folio, printed from very handsome, delicate old style type, more elegant and *maigre* in effect than is usually found in books of this period. The title-page is set in the usual seventeenth century massive old style capitals in lines alternately red and black, and bears Le Petit's printer's mark, a relief engraving on metal. The ornaments

and large floriated initials occurring at the beginning of each
new Life are cut on wood. The type-setting of the book is
very simple. The title of the Life of each saint is set in various sizes of displayed old style capital letters like those
on the title-page, and chapter headings and running-titles
are arranged in roman capitals, much spaced. The arguments to each chapter employ a clear and handsome italic
—a very elegant font used with great effect in the Table of
Chapters. This well-printed book appeared at Paris in 1664.
Le Petit also printed a splendid edition of Arnauld d'Andilly's *Œuvres Diverses* in three folio volumes in 1675.

All the faults—there were not many virtues—of the
period are exhibited in *Le Théâtre de P. Corneille*, published
in two folio volumes printed at Rouen, but sold in Paris by
(Vol. I) T. Jolly and (Vol. II) G. de Luyne in 1664. Cumbrous in form, with ungainly decorations from wood-blocks,
—among which the eternal *corbeille de fleurs* appears in
swollen shapes,—with displayed lines set in spaced capitals
in all kinds of sizes, and with text in a heavy old style type,
it is as awkward and archaic a work as can be conceived.
There were quantities of like books, and one need not linger
over them.

In 1667, Claude Barbin of Paris published Michel Le
Clerc's French metrical translation of Tasso's *Gerusalemme
Liberata* under the title of *La Hierusalem Delivrée*. It is not
a beautiful book, but the italic used for the text of the translation is a characteristic lively French font of the period,
though much less fine than sixteenth century italic. What
appear to be marginal notes set in roman type on the outer
margins of each page are really the Italian text of the poem.
The introductory type matter is tasteless and heavy, and
engraved plates and rough woodcut decorations, considered an embellishment, do not much embellish.

Bossuet's *Discours sur l'Histoire Universelle*, written for the Dauphin, and printed at Paris in 1681 by Sébastien Mabre-Cramoisy, a learned man and an excellent printer, is a good specimen of a luxurious seventeenth century book. It has a typographical title, but a copper-plate head-piece is introduced on the first page showing Time bearing a shield on which are the Dauphin's arms, and the text begins with an engraved initial Q supported by a symbolic dolphin. The text-pages are set in handsome old style type, with wide margins, on which notes appear in italic (sometimes in double column). Running-titles are arranged in capitals and small capitals. The volume ends with a fine copper-plate tail-piece. Mabre-Cramoisy was grandson of Cramoisy, first director of the Imprimerie Royale; was first his associate and then became sole director from 1669 to his death in 1687. Like his grandfather, he printed books on his own account, of which this is an example.[1]

The first edition of Racine's *Athalie* was issued at Paris by Denys Thierry in quarto, in 1691. A title set in the oldest of old style capitals, an enormous woodcut of the customary vase of flowers beneath, and an imprint make up the opening page. A preface is set in a handsome roman letter, and the play follows, entirely composed in a large and very irregular but spirited italic font. Names of characters are arranged in spaced capitals, and stage directions in a minute roman, also used for side-notes. "Scenes" are separated from each other by crowded rows of "flowers." The whole performance is very antique in style, and, though imposing, tasteless.

Finally, for an example of ambitious book-making at the

[1] Reproductions of the characteristic title-pages of Bossuet's celebrated funeral orations, most of which Mabre-Cramoisy published, are shown in Le Petit's *Bibliographie des Principales Éditions Originales d'Écrivains Français*, etc., pp. 401–415.

end of the century, look at the folio *Veterum Mathematicorum*—Athenæus, Apollodorus, and others—printed in 1693 at the Imprimerie Royale (then under the direction of Jean Anisson) from manuscripts in the Bibliothèque Royale. I mention it merely to contrast it with the much finer books on similar subjects printed in the preceding century. Employing all the aids known to luxurious book-making at that day, it utterly fails in elegance and simplicity, and by the same token belongs to its epoch.

The second important foundry in France, set up in 1596 by Jacques de Sanlecque, may be accounted a seventeenth century establishment, although no specimen was issued from it until the middle of the next century. The first Sanlecque was a pupil of Le Bé, and like him made a specialty of Oriental fonts, cutting those needed for the Paris Polyglot. He was succeeded by a son, Jacques II, who died in 1659, the widow carrying on the business until it passed to their son, Jean. The foundry was inherited in the next generation by Jean's son, Jean Eustache Louis de Sanlecque, who issued a specimen—*Épreuves des Caractères du fond des Sanlecques*—at Paris in 1757, printed by A. M. Lottin. The *Avis au Lecteur* says: "The learned and discerning have so many times stated that the greater part of the Sanlecque types were engraved by the best masters, that I do not think it necessary to add anything here to what has already been said. It suffices to tell those who are ignorant of the fact, that these characters have served in such esteemed and sought-after editions as those of Cramoisy, Vitré, Le Petit, Savreux, Leonard, the Elzevirs, and others." The book therefore contains fonts of a much earlier period than its date would indicate. It is full of charming type, some of it no doubt special productions of the first Sanlecques, and other characters by old type-cutters. In larger sizes the italic

149. Seventeenth Century Types for Liturgical Books, from Sanlecque's Épreuves des Caractères, Paris, 1757

Gros Canon.

Memor esto
verbi tui fer-
vo tuo , *
in quo mihi
spem dedisti.
Hæc me
consólata est

Petit Canon.

Asperges me ,
Dómine, hyssópo
& mundábor: la-
vábis me, & super
nivem dealbábor.
Pſ. Miférere mei,
Deus, secundùm
magnam miferi-
córdiam tuam.
Glória Patri, &c.

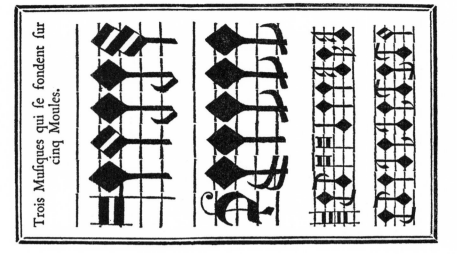

Trois Musiques qui se fondent sur cinq Moules.

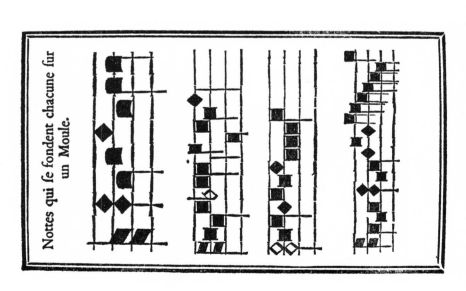

Nottes qui se fondent chacune sur un Moule.

150. *Old Music Types from Sanlecque's Épreuves des Caractères, Paris, 1757*

is especially interesting; apparently very old forms being shown in the *Saint Augustin, gros romain*, and *petit parangon italique* (*fig.* 148). Some roman types which follow seem to have been cut for Church office-books to be used with music (*fig.* 149). The plates of music types are extremely curious (*fig.* 150). They resemble those engraved by Hautin about 1525 for Attaingnant—the first Parisian printer to use movable music types. Louis de Sanlecque died in 1778, and the subsequent history of the foundry is given on a later page.

We also reproduce here some ornaments that appear to belong to the seventeenth century, from the eighteenth century specimen of the Parisian printer Lamesle (*fig.* 151); and some roman and italic types which appear to be of early date, from the 1773 specimen of the Lyons foundry of Delacolonge (*figs.* 152 *and* 153). The last are early examples of the same size of type in different weights of face.

<h2 style="text-align:center">§ 3</h2>

In the eighteenth century a few classes of books stand out among the vast production of French printers and publishers—the official folio and *livre de gala*, the history or memoir in quarto, the illustrated book in octavo, 16mo, and 32mo. There were, of course, an endless number of books in all sizes which were not illustrated, and volumes in quarto which were; but these divisions are characteristic of the century. The great official folios were very magnificent indeed, such as *Description des Fêtes données par la Ville de Paris* of 1740, printed by Le Mercier.[1] The *Voyage Pittoresque* of the Abbé de Saint-Non and the folio La Fontaine's *Fables Choisies*, illustrated by Oudry, are examples of similar work, though private ventures. A few of these that are

[1] *Druckschriften*, pl. 99.

interesting from a printer's point of view, I briefly describe. The type employed for such work in the early eighteenth century was an imposing sort of old style, except where it was a specially designed "Royal" font. In later books of this class, type followed that fashion for lighter forms which came in at the end of the eighteenth century, but which is more reminiscent, to us, of nineteenth century fonts. These great books show but one aspect of the French press.

The rank and file of eighteenth century quartos and octavos were more legible than the similar seventeenth century book had been. A reader's comfort was better looked after. Their arrangement, too, seems modern to us — they are no longer antique and unappetizing, but merely quaint or old-fashioned. A very modern page, in lightness of effect, is Watelet's *L'Art de Peindre*,[1] printed by the Parisian establishment of Guérin and Delatour in 1760. As elsewhere in Europe, as the century advanced, books — or the best editions — became more open in composition, and therefore far easier to the eye. Then, too, books were smaller and in consequence the types themselves became lighter, partly owing, no doubt, to improvements in paper-making which encouraged type-founders to make more delicate characters, and printers to employ them. Finally, at the end of the century, the movement culminated in fonts which were not old style at all.

Illustrated books — and there were quantities of them — depended with a few exceptions upon their copper-plate illustrations and decorations, more than upon typography, for their reputation. In some books, with plates, head-pieces, and tail-pieces by Eisen, Choffard, Marillier, or Moreau *le jeune* that are often superb of their kind, the typography is indescribably poor. One cannot comprehend how the public

[1] *Druckschriften*, pl. 80.

Suite des Vignettes de gros romain.

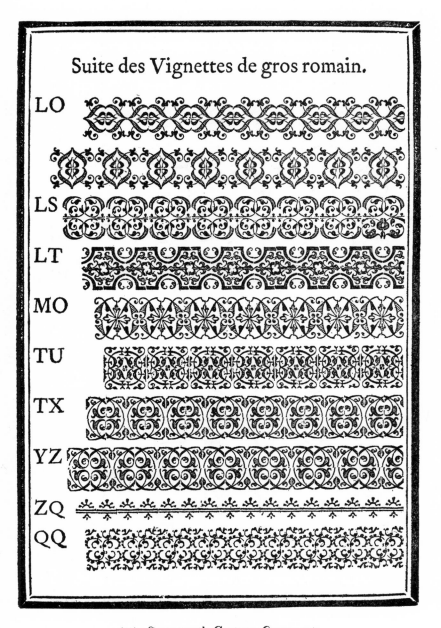

LO

LS

LT

MO

TU

TX

YZ

ZQ

QQ

151. *Seventeenth Century Ornaments*
Lamesle's Épreuves Générales des Caractères, Paris, 1742

Il faut crain-
dre, dit M. l'ab-
bé de Condillac,
d'étouffer la cu-
riosité des enfans
en n'y répondant
pas.

L'innocence
est cet état de
l'enfance, qui ne
fait pas encore
ce que c'est que
le bien & le
mal.

152. *Early Types (œil maigre): Delacolonge's Caractères et Vignettes, Lyons, 1773*

L'invention

eft l'art de

rapprocher les

idées qui paroi-

ffoient les plus

éloignées, d'en

faire fentir le

La jouiffance

eft le fentiment

réfléchi de la

poffeffion.

Combien eft-il

de perfonnes

qui poffedent

153. *Early Types (œil gras): Delacolonge's Caractères et Vignettes, Lyons, 1773*

LIVRE IV.

Je mene au grand trefor qu'un Dieu voulut cacher ;
Il eft gardé par maint obftacle ;
Et d'abord, pour premier miracle,
C'eft par mon fein qu'il faut marcher.

Perçons-le, dit le Prince. On affemble mille hommes,

Travaillant jour & nuit, bien nouris, bien paiez ;
Et moiennant de groffes fommes,
En peu de jours les chemins font fraiez.
Le rocher traverfé, fe prefente un abîme.
Le Tréfor eft plus loin, dit un autre écriteau ;
Comble-moi. Soit ; comblons ; dit l'Amadis nouveau ;
Le Tréfor, à ce que j'eftime
Sur ces précautions, doit être un bon morceau.
Nouveau travail & nouvelles dépenfes.
Mais l'abîme comblé, les belles efperances
Se reculent encor. D'une épaiffe forêt
Un pin gravé lui dit : *Le Tréfor eft tout prêt ;*
Mais pour aller jufqu'à fa niche,
Il faut abattre bien du bois.

154. *Old Style Types used by Coignard, Paris,* 1719

could endure such meanly printed text as an accompaniment to such beautiful ornamentation. But works like La Fontaine's *Fables Choisies* with Oudry's illustrations were splendid exceptions; and there were some printers — the Praults and Barbous, for instance — whose beautifully decorated books were well executed from the typographic point of view.

As the century advanced, volumes in small *format* became increasingly popular for luxurious editions of works of a lighter class, and in them delicately engraved plates and coquettish, fanciful head and tail-pieces could be used to better advantage than on a quarto or folio page. The celebrated *édition des fermiers-généraux* of La Fontaine's *Contes*, published by Barbou at Paris (dated Amsterdam) in 1762, in two octavo volumes, is a famous example of such a book.

Among volumes in small 16mo, Barbou's well-edited *Collection des Auteurs Latines* were from a mechanical point of view very attractive and workmanlike books. They were sought after, too, for their engraved decorations by Cochin, Eisen, and other artists *à la mode*, their pretty woodcut tail-pieces by J. B. Papillon, and the agreeable typographic decorations which, with the types employed, were from the foundry of Fournier *le jeune*. After the year 1755, many volumes of the *Auteurs Latines* bore the inscription, "Litteræ quibus impressus est hic liber a P. S. Fournier juniore incisæ sunt."[1] The Barbous (printers at Limoges, from the sixteenth century) founded their Paris house in 1704, which was at the height of its reputation between 1750 and 1790. It was then under the direction of Joseph

[1] The *Collection* was completed in 1780, by which time it comprised thirty-four works in sixty-eight volumes. For list of these, see Paul Ducourtieux: *Les Barbou, Imprimeurs, Lyon-Limoges-Paris*, 1524–1820, Limoges, 1896, pp. 277 *et seq.*

Gérard Barbou, the most distinguished member of the family, promoter of the *Collection* just spoken of, and patron of Fournier *le jeune*. He published all Fournier's books — except the *Modèles*, which was printed by his predecessor, an uncle, Jean Joseph Barbou, in 1742.

In the last quarter of the century, the editions brought out by the Didots were often splendid productions. This family was very important in the history of French late eighteenth century printing, though it played its great part in the development of French type-forms, after 1800. The first of the Didot family was a certain Denis Didot, a printer and publisher, whose son, François Didot, — generally considered the "founder" of this family, — a printer and bookseller, was born at Paris in 1689, where he began his work in 1713. He is chiefly remembered nowadays for the publication of a collection of travels in twenty volumes by his friend the Abbé Prévost, which was issued in 1747, and was considered a good piece of printing in its time. He died in 1757.[1] Two of his sons, François Ambroise (1730–1804) and Pierre François (1732–1793), were the heads of branches of the family, each of which contributed largely to the perfection of the many industries connected with bookmaking.

François Ambroise was a clever type-founder, and the first of the family to give to types "the Didot touch," in fonts brought out about 1775 that were cut by Waflard. Didot was the printer of a famous collection of French classic authors, published by order of Louis XVI in 1783; and a series of finely executed books brought out at the instance of the King's brother, the Comte d'Artois, to whom he was printer by appointment. He so greatly perfected

[1] Or according to some authorities in 1759.

the point system inaugurated by Fournier, that the Didot point superseded its older rival and remains to-day the basis of French typographical measurement. He introduced in France in 1780 the making of *papier vélin de France* (a highly finished wove paper modelled on that used by Baskerville) at the Johannot mills at Annonay. It was with François Ambroise Didot that Franklin placed his grandson, Benjamin Franklin Bache, in 1785. In his diary, the lad writes: "My grandpapa has prevailed upon Mr. Didot, the best printer of this age and even the best that has ever been seen, to consent to take me into his house for some time in order to teach me his art. I take my meals at his house and sleep at the house of Mrs. Le Roy, a friend of my grandpapa; I went thither today with my cousin and I became acquainted with his family and something more. He combines in his house engraving, the forge, the foundry and the printing-office; it is a very amiable family, as it seems to me; the meals are frugal." On April 7, he adds, "Today I have engraved my first punch with Mr. Didot's younger son. It was an o. They assert that I have not succeeded badly."

This François Ambroise had two sons, Pierre *l'aîné* (1761–1853), who succeeded to the printing-office, and Firmin (born 1764), who took over his father's type-foundry. Pierre is remembered as the publisher of the magnificent *éditions du Louvre*[1] of Virgil, Horace, La Fontaine, and Racine, the latter being considered, at the beginning of the last century, one of the most splendid books ever printed. He was at the forefront of the neo-classical movement in printing, and with his brother Firmin's chilly types and the dry

---

[1] Called so because the Government, in tribute to his abilities, gave his printing-office the rooms in the Louvre formerly tenanted by the Imprimerie Royale, which in 1795 removed to the Hôtel de Penthièvre.

designs of a chosen group of artists, produced editions of arctic frigidity. Pierre and Firmin Didot in 1784 issued jointly an *Épître sur les Progrès de l'Imprimerie*, later mentioned. Firmin was most eminent as a type-founder, and in his hands the *type Didot* crystallized into those forms familiar to us now. He was also interested in stereotyping, by which he popularized low-priced editions of standard French, English, and Italian books. He was a very cultivated and learned person — translating (among other works) Virgil's *Bucolics*, printed from type that he himself designed and cast. Napoleon made him director of the foundry of the Imprimerie Impériale, and he was offered its full direction in 1830. He died full of years and honours in 1836.

Ambroise Firmin Didot (1790–1876), son of Firmin, and grandson of François Ambroise, with his brother Hyacinthe, succeeded to the publishing business of this branch of the family, since styled Firmin-Didot. They belong, however, to the nineteenth century.

Pierre François Didot (1732–1793), head of the younger branch of the Didot family, and the son of the original François, was a type-founder and publisher, and also interested himself in paper-making at Essonne. Henri Didot, (1765–1852), son of Pierre, is remembered for his "microscopic" types, a *tour de force* executed at an advanced age. The *assignats* issued by the Convention were engraved by him, and their production played a very important part in the revival of stereotyping. Another son, Léger Didot (1767–1829), invented a successful "endless roll" paper-making machine, and was also employed in type-founding. A third son, Didot *le jeune*, succeeded his brother Henri as a successful type-founder. A daughter, Félicie, married Bernardin de St. Pierre. These are the chief members of a learned race of printers, publishers, type-founders, paper-makers, authors, and inventors—whose family reunions must have resembled a meeting of the Royal Society!

None of the Didots had — typographically — the originality of Bodoni, but as able, industrious, and far more scholarly men, they had immense influence on French typographic usage. Familiar with the work of Baskerville, rivals and critics of Bodoni and Ibarra, they stood in France for the tendencies that were fashionable in England, Italy, and Spain; and thus all their typographic innovations were in the direction of lighter and more modelled fonts. Late eighteenth century Didot editions were very lucid, readable, elegant volumes, printed from type full of feeling, and just on the turn between "old style" and "modern face" fonts. As in Bodoni's case, too little attention has been paid to the work of the Didots at this period; for we remember them now as chief exponents of that dubious pseudo-classical taste that brought in, with the nineteenth century, the rigid Didot letter, which (not bettered by English fashions then much copied) was, with its still worse derivations, a curse to French typography for more than half a century.

The first example of French eighteenth century printing to be discussed is a quarto volume by Antoine Houdart de la Motte, of the French Academy, entitled *Fables Nouvelles*,[1] published in 1719 at Paris for Grégoire Dupuis, and printed by Coignard. The *Discours sur la Fable* is set "solid," and this part of the book is reminiscent of the seventeenth century, as are the general make-up of preliminary matter, the rows of "flowers" separating the Fables, the heavy tailpieces on wood, etc. But the Fables themselves are set in a delicately cut old style font, very much leaded, and thus the volume is transitional in style between seventeenth and

[1] There is a copy in the Boston Athenaeum.

eighteenth century French printing (*fig.* 154). The engravings at the head of each Fable, especially those designed
and engraved by Gillot (master to Watteau), are interesting in themselves, and because they are surrounded by
simple lines instead of the elaborate frameworks of a subsequent period — such as those in Dorat's *Fables,* and similar
books described later.

Montfaucon's *Monumens de la Monarchie Françoise,* a
great folio edition in five volumes, was printed at Paris in
1729–33 by Claude Simon for the publishers, Gandouin
and Giffart. There is little of interest about it as a whole.
In detail it has one or two points worth notice. The type
employed for the Address to the King in volume first is
one of the old Garamond italic fonts — very beautifully
displayed in spite of the absurd amount of leading. The
ornaments on the title-page, at the head of the preface, and
beneath the "privilege" are the work of J. B. Papillon, a
wood-engraver who had great reputation. The introduction
of bands of type "flowers" is a poor feature of the book, and
the innumerable engraved plates, though no doubt useful,
are another disturbing element. The book is a good example of early eighteenth century printing — in style a little
earlier than its date.

Our next example is A. M. de Ramsay's *Histoire du Vi-
comte de Turenne,* in two quarto volumes, printed at Paris
in 1735 by the Veuve Mazières and J. B. Garnier. The
imposing title-page printed from somewhat seventeenth
century old style types, with lines alternately in red and
black, has an engraved heraldic decoration. Its heavy capitals
scarcely prepare one for the delicacy of the italic fonts of
the preface, or the elegant modelled roman type of the text.
The wide margins bear side-notes in a smaller roman
letter. Running-titles are set in spaced capitals of the font.

Each book begins with an attractive engraving and an initial letter, also engraved. In the second volume the *pièces justificatives* are set in much smaller type, and both its cut and its management—it is much leaded—give these pages a modern effect. It is a good reading edition to-day, and in its time must have been accounted a very "advanced" sort of book.

The *Œuvres de Jean-Baptiste Rousseau* (1671–1741), printed at Paris (dated Brussels) in 1743 by Didot (probably François), in three large quarto volumes, is in its massive qualities almost a seventeenth century edition, but it has an element of taste about it that the seventeenth century did not afford. Printed entirely in a large size of masculine and nervous old style roman type, splendidly placed on ample quarto pages, and really adorned with decorations by Cochin of a delightful suavity of design, it is a superb book. The italic employed for occasional verse is an interesting font. The volumes were printed from type made by Fournier *le jeune*, who is here styled Simon Pierre (*fig.* 155).

For a smaller *format*, the attractive edition of *Œuvres de M. Boileau Despréaux*, edited by Saint-Marc, Paris, 1747, in five 12mo volumes, is an example of a luxurious and convenient edition. Overloaded with introductions, notes, and all sorts of miscellaneous apparatus, it is in general effect advancing toward a more open style of printing. In the first two volumes, which are the ones to be looked at, the poetry is set in a letter for its time noticeably light in cut and uniform in design. Leading and spacing add to the delicate effect. Though in other parts of the volumes this manner is not kept up, none the less the typography strikes a novel note. It was printed by Jean Baptiste Coignard, *imprimeur du roi*, third of his name to be printer to the

French Academy, and the founder of a charity for Parisian printers, which still exists.

Among eighteenth century books in such *format*, I have mentioned the *Collection des Auteurs Latines* published by Barbou, who used in them Fournier *le jeune's* types and ornaments. In this connection, a three-volume edition of the *Comœdiæ* of Plautus (Paris, 1759) may be examined. For a very full showing of Fournier's types and ornaments— though the engraved flowers appear to be by Papillon— see F. J. Desbillons' *Fabularum Æsopiarum Libri Quinque Priores*, very agreeably printed by Barbou in the same year (*fig.* 156).

The magnificent edition (in four volumes, folio) of La Fontaine's *Fables Choisies* with illustrations from paintings by Oudry, redrawn by Cochin *fils*, who, with others, engraved the plates, is one of the landmarks in French decorative book-making. Cochin apparently had the oversight of the whole work, which was published between 1755 and 1759 jointly by Desaint and Saillant and by Durand.[1] It was printed by Jombert, who produced many fine books on military subjects. Of Oudry's famous but frigid full-page designs I shall not speak, except to praise the work of the engravers.

The typography is magnificently adequate for the enormous pages of the work. The *Fables* are set in a very handsome, round, old style font, which is as readable as type can be. Half-titles and titles are finely displayed in roman and italic capitals, much spaced; the serifs of the roman capitals showing, however, a bad tendency towards hair-lines.

---

[1] This edition created considerable noise at the time of its appearance, and the first volume was the subject of an elaborate attack, defence, and rejoinder, in the *Journal des Sçavans* for February, the *Mercure de France* for March, and the *Journal des Sçavans* for September, 1756. The critic, from internal evidence, may have been a type-founder.

LETTRE XLVII.

AU MÊME.

IL eft vrai, Monfieur, que le chagrin a pris le deffus chez moi, & qu'il ne faut pas moins que les marques de fouvenir que vous me donnez, pour me dédommager de tous les ennuis que m'a caufés la fauffe amitié de ceux fur lefquels je comptois le plus. J'ai trouvé à la lettre dans mon voyage de Paris, l'original de ce que Térence a fi bien peint dans l'Andrienne:

Id genus eft hominum peffimum,
In denegando modò queis pudor eft paululum :

155. Fournier le jeune's Types: Didot, Paris, 1743

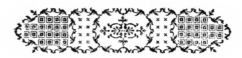

FABULARUM
ÆSOPIARUM
LIBER QUARTUS.

PROLOGUS.

AB illo vetere , simplici , mundo ſtilo
Jam tum receſſit paululùm Latinitas ;
Ubi romana pubes ſemel abhorruit
Ab ſcriptitandis verſibus ſenariis ,
Quales Poetæ veteres omnes comici
Fundere ſolebant. Imò ferme ceteri
Veteres Poetæ , ſi qua præſertim vafræ
Lubido Muſæ ſcriptionem ludicram ,
Menippeamque concinnare juſſerat ,
In metro amabant liberum hunc morem ſequi
Suavem profectò , nec vocabulis minùs ,
Quàm rebus ipsis aptandis idoneum.
Romanorum ille Varro *a* qui doctiſſimus
Ante , & poſt fata dictus eſt , hujusmodi
Senariorum millia multa ſcripſerat ;

a A. Gellius , Lib. III. Cap. X. Varronis de numero ſepten-
nario Librum exponens : *Tum ibi ,* inquit *, addit ſe quoque jam
duodecimam annorum hebdomadam ingreſſum eſſe , & ad eum diem
ſeptuaginta hebdomadas Librorum conſcripſiſſe.*

The composition is splendid, its only weak point being the occasional use of triple rules beneath running-titles. To my mind, the glory of this great work is J. J. Bachelier's floral tail-pieces, etc., cut on wood by J. B. Papillon and Le Sueur, which are among the most splendid woodcut decorations of their kind known. Copied and re-copied in every book on ornamental design, they must be seen on these pages to be appreciated. Great pains were taken with these decorations, which were intended to show the perfection that wood-engraving — then neglected and despised — could attain in competent hands. Bachelier, who "invented" them, was a flower painter and director of design at the Royal Porcelain Manufactory at Vincennes. He adapted them to printing on rough paper by drawings executed in a very open manner, and they were interpreted by the engravers with this in mind. A passage about them in the *Avertissement* to Volume I is worth reading, and the most important are described in a note at the end of Volume IV.[1] I recommend their study to designers wishing to learn how to draw ornaments to be printed with letter-press.

The four 16mo volumes that make up the *Anthologie Françoise, ou Chansons Choisies, depuis le 13e Siècle jusqu'à présent,* edited by Jean Monnet (whose superb portrait by Cochin engraved by A. de St. Aubin faces its title-page), are thoroughly delightful pieces of printing. The preface is set in an italic — *au goût nouveau* (that is to say, a letter very even and monotonous in line), and the introduction by De Querlon, in a respectable old style roman font. The pleasantest part of the book begins with the *Chansons* and their music (printed from Fournier's music types), most beautifully

---

[1] They are the designs on the title-page, at the head of the dedication, and in Vol. I, pp. 10, 14, 34, 44; Vol. II, pp. 26, 48, 54, 64. The comparatively recent so-called "reproduction" of this edition is beneath contempt.

arranged, and touched up with gay little head and tail-pieces on wood, many of which are delightful. It appears to be set in Fournier's types, and some of its typographic head-bands are to be found in his specimen-book. The work was printed at Paris in 1765 by Joseph Gérard Barbou (*fig.* 157).

Claude Joseph Dorat was a fashionable person who wrote as poor poetry as fashionable versifiers generally do. Dorat's books interest a printer because they express the *dernier cri* in typographic modes of their time, and show the kind of printing that then satisfied a "smart" public. The editions best remembered—for nobody nowadays remembers his poems—are those of his *Fables Nouvelles* and *Les Baisers*.

The *Fables Nouvelles* has a Hague imprint, though really published by Delalain of Paris in 1773. Dorat alludes, in his preface to this edition, to the *pompe typographique* of its presentation. There was little pomp about the volume, however, as far as types were concerned. It is composed in a clear old style font of merely respectable cut, and headings to the *Fables* employ decorated capitals and type ornaments to the last degree trivial. The presswork is uneven, the paper none too good, but the engraved decorations by Marillier, though too heavy for so small a page, are—the best of them—quite wonderful, and just miss being wholly charming. At any rate, they are famous.

Les Baisers, also with The Hague as its imprint, but issued at Paris by Delalain in 1770, is another typical edition. Though it was decorated by Eisen, it is very indifferently printed and (as a whole) is a much overrated book.

Jean François de Saint Lambert wrote an insipid poem, *Les Saisons*, somewhat in the manner of Thomson, in four parts—Spring, Summer, Autumn, and Winter. This had

XXVII.

Aimable fil-le de l'A-mour,

Où fuyez-vous, chere Es-pé-ran - ce?

Fe - rez - vous pé-rir en ce jour

Le Dieu dont vous prîtes naiſſan - ce?

Ai-ma-ble fil-le de l'A - mour,

Où fuy-ez-vous, chere Eſpé-ran - ce?

J'étois content de ſouffrir dans ſa Cour,

Je faiſois mon bonheur de ſentir ſa puiſ -

fan - ce ; Mais, vous m'abandonnez

peut-être ſans re - tour, Et ſans vous

il n'eſt plus d'ardeur, ni de conſtan-ce.

Ai - ma-ble fil-le de l'A-mour.

Où fuy-ez-vous,chere Eſpé-ran - ce?

157. *Fournier le jeune's Music Types: Barbou, Paris, 1765*

L'un monte le bélier délivré de sa laine ;
390 L'autre veut effrayer, caché dans les roseaux,
Ses jeunes compagnons se jouants dans les eaux ;
Leurs cris, la cornemuse & le chant des bergères,
Vont apprendre leur joie aux échos solitaires.

Un jour, sous les berceaux d'un verger écarté,
395 Contemplant ces pasteurs, partageant leur gaité,
J'abordai le fermier, qui de l'ombre d'un hêtre,
Observoit, comme moi, cette scène champêtre.
Qu'il est dans votre état d'agréables moments !
Lui dis-je ; & tous nos arts, nos vains amusements
400 Valent-ils ces travaux que la joie accompagne,
Et la simplicité des jeux de la campagne ?
Non, dit-il ; j'ai connu vos plaisirs si vantés,
Ils sont trop peu sentis, ils sont trop achetés ;
Je leur ai comparé les plaisirs du village ;
405 J'y vis, je suis content, & bénis mon partage.
Jeune, & né d'un sang noble, à la guerre entraîné,
Je n'y démentis pas le sang dont j'étois né :
Mais mes fonds dissipés, mes fermes consumées
Par ce luxe sans frein qui corrompt nos armées,
410 Quand la paix couronna les succès de mon Roi,
Je me vis sans fortune ainsi que sans emploi.
Le besoin n'avilit que les cœurs sans courage :
Moi, plein du sentiment des forces de mon âge,

158. *Roman Type of Saint Lambert's Saisons, Paris*, 1775

enormous popularity and was many times reprinted. A seventh edition (still sought after for its beautiful engravings) was published in 1775 at "Amsterdam"—really, I suppose, Paris. To the poem — which with introduction and notes fills the first half of the book — are added two or three short stories, one of which is alluded to by Madame Campan as attracting the attention of Marie Antoinette. Some fugitive verse and "Oriental Fables" complete a volume which (exquisitely illustrated by Moreau *le jeune* and Choffard) had a very fashionable public. The book shows every evidence of employing Fournier's types, and the ornaments are undoubtedly from his foundry. The points about it which are typographically so important are the very modelled old style fonts used for the *Discours Preliminaire* and the poem itself (*fig.* 158), and the new style of italic in the "arguments" to each book of *Les Saisons* (*fig.* 159). This italic is midway between the old style italic previously used and that put forth later by Firmin Didot. It is very easy to read, owing to regularity of line and design; but it is as inferior in style to that which it supplanted as the Didot type was inferior to it. The typographical head-pieces for the stories should be looked at. The book is a very good example of the use of somewhat refined old style types; though it is greatly disfigured by the heavy rules on the title-page and below running-titles.

The celebrated *Voyage Pittoresque, ou Description des Royaumes de Naples et de Sicile* of the Abbé Jean Claude Richard de Saint-Non (1730–1804), is a combination of the great official folio with the illustrated *édition de luxe*. Its five gigantic volumes give an opportunity for the insertion of innumerable plates. Old style types of medium weight, a good deal leaded, are used throughout. The composition is a little confused, and some inadequate type decorations, needlessly introduced, are overwhelmed by the magnificent engraved decorations, unsurpassed of their kind. The *Voyage* has a further interest because it helped on the vogue for classical *motifs* in decoration, through its agreeably rendered plates of classical furniture and utensils. The designs from Greek vases in two colours are admirable pieces of copper-plate printing, and a word should be said about the sumptuous engraved Dedication to Marie Antoinette, in Volume I. Saint-Non, the most distinguished amateur of the second half of the century, was himself a passable engraver as well as an archaeologist and antiquary. A convinced idealist, he dedicated his life to producing this wonderful work, which, begun in 1778, was finished in 1786. It was printed by Clousier and—incidentally—ruined Saint-Non.

A book in small *format* that shows Didot *l'aîné* at his best as a printer, is the Abbé de Lille's *Géorgiques de Virgile, en vers François*. Delightful old style types are used in this pretty little 32mo edition, which was printed for the Paris publisher, Bleuet, in 1782 (*fig.* 160). This should be compared with a volume already alluded to (in a way a "specimen-book") that shows some new Didot characters—the octavo *Épître sur les Progrès de l'Imprimerie* (1784), written by Pierre, eldest son of François Ambroise Didot, and printed in italic types designed by Firmin Didot, his second son. It employs for the poem a very light, monotonous italic (*fig.* 161). The notes are set in a smaller size of it, mingled with a roman letter which is somewhat colourless in effect. The general conception of its type is still old style, but pared down to the last degree. This italic was not an invention "from a clear sky," but merely "developed" the type *au goût nouveau*, of which we have seen examples in mid-eighteenth century French specimen-books. Firmin

ARGUMENT.

*L*E *Soleil & la chaleur font éclore une multitude d'êtres nouveaux qui animent les élémens. Caractère de grandeur & d'opulence que l'Été donne à la nature. Elle est moins variée qu'au Printems ; elle ne doit être vue qu'en grand. Riche & vaste paysage fait pour être vu pendant l'Été ; ses effets sur l'ame. Éloge de l'Agriculture. Combien il est facile de rendre heureux les Laboureurs ; leurs mœurs. L'Été dans sa force. Puissance & majesté de la Nature sous la Zône Torride ; la chûte du Nil ; une forêt. Paysages tels qu'on les désire pendant la chaleur , & leurs effets sur les sens & sur l'ame. Tondaison. Fenaison & gaité des travaux champêtres. Un Gentilhomme que la guerre avoit ruiné prend une ferme. Maturité des bleds. Corvée &*

159. *Italic in Saint Lambert's Saisons, Paris,* 1775

Enfin, malgré cette gêne, l'obſervation des regles de notre poéſie produit de
moins grandes beautés que l'obſervation
des regles de la poéſie latine. Dans celle-ci,
le mélange marqué des ſyllabes breves &
longues amene néceſſairement le rhythme :
dans la nôtre, les regles ne preſcrivent rien
ſur la durée des ſyllabes, mais ſeulement
ſur leur nombre arithmétique; de ſorte
que des vers françois peuvent être réguliers
ſans être nombreux, & ſatisfaire aux loix
de la verſification ſans ſatisfaire à celles de
l'harmonie.

Je n'ai parlé juſqu'à préſent que de cette
harmonie générale qui, par l'heureux
choix, l'enchaînement mélodieux des
mots, flatte agréablement l'oreille. Il eſt
une autre eſpece d'harmonie nommée imitative, harmonie bien ſupérieure à l'autre,
s'il eſt vrai que l'objet de la poéſie ſoit de
peindre. Pope en donne l'exemple & le pré-
cepte à la fois dans des vers imités admi-
rablement par l'abbé Dureſnel, & que j'ai
eſſayé de traduire.

Peins-moi légèrement l'amant léger de Flore;
Qu'un doux ruiſſeau murmure en vers plus doux encore.
Entend-on de la mer les ondes bouillonner?
Le vers, comme un torrent, en roulant doit tonner.
Qu'Ajax ſouleve un roc & le lance avec peine;
Chaque ſyllabe eſt lourde & chaque mot ſe traîne.
Mais vois d'un pied léger Camille effleurer l'eau;
Le vers vole, & la ſuit auſſi prompt que l'oiſeau.

Mais, il faut en convenir, c'eſt peut-être
à cet égard que la langue latine l'emporte
le plus ſur la nôtre. La quantité des ſyllabes,
dont la briéveté ou la longueur précipite
ou ralentit le vers, étoit déterminée chez
les Latins : nous avons auſſi des breves &
des longues, mais beaucoup moins mar-
quées; notre proſodie n'eſt point décidée
comme celle des anciens, & cette déciſion
laiſſe tout le jugement & tout le travail
de l'harmonie à l'oreille & au goût du
poëte.

D'ailleurs, comme je l'ai déjà dit, nous
avons dans notre langue trop peu de ſons
pleins, trop d'E muets, trop de ſyllabes

160. *Roman Types used by Didot l'aîné, Paris,* 1782

Didot's italic types superseded those of Fournier *le jeune*, which until then had been popular, and allusion to this is made in the *Épître*. The *Épître* was reprinted in an exquisite little volume in 18mo — Pierre Didot's *Essai de Fables nouvelles dédiées au Roi; suivies de Poésies diverses et d'une Épître sur les progrès de l'Imprimerie. . . . À Paris, imprimé par Franç. Ambr. Didot l'aîné avec les caractères de Firmin son 2^d fils*, 1786. The same series of types is used in both books, but not in the same sizes. In this small *format* the delicacy of type is warranted — and the composition is very tastefully managed.[1]

Tasso's *Gerusalemme Liberata* was printed at Paris by François Ambroise Didot *l'aîné*, in 1784–88, "by order of Monsieur," — the Comte de Provence (afterwards Louis XVIII), — who chose the subjects for Cochin's illustrations. It is a beautiful example of Didot's printing. The type is a delicate old style, though a little too much influenced by Bodoni in the contrasting weight of line, an effect increased by the vellum-like paper employed. The Didots no doubt believed that the *papier-vélin* improved their books, by enabling them to attenuate the thin strokes of the type — refinements which these highly finished papers were able to "take" only too successfully.

In 1782, the Paris publishers Molini and Lamy issued a prospectus of an edition of a work first brought out in 1757 by the Comte de Caylus and J. B. Mariette — the *Peintures Antiques de Bartoli*, which reproduced frescoes discovered at Herculaneum. This new edition of one hundred copies was to be all that was most distinguished, and for it some

---

[1] For title-pages of books in small *format*, printed in light Didot types much spaced, consult the facsimiles, in Le Petit's *Éditions Originales*, of *Paul et Virginie* of 1789 and *La Chaumière Indienne* of 1791, both by Bernardin de St. Pierre.

new types of Didot *l'aîné* were to be used. The portion of
the prospectus which is reproduced (*fig.* 162) shows this
beautiful transitional font, which retains the charm of old
style letter, but has a touch of grace and delicacy which
makes it very much of its period. It is one of a series of
steps by which the Didots learnedly but foolishly descended
to the types they used about 1800.

In François Ambroise Didot's edition of the *Œuvres de
Fénelon* in nine quarto volumes, begun in 1787 and completed by his son, Pierre Didot, in 1792, the shape of letter
used is still old style, but it is so thin and fragile that it is
scarcely recognizable as old style at all. This results in
faded-looking pages that are perfectly legible, but give an
insecure feeling to the eye (*fig.* 163). This edition should
be compared with Fénelon's *Aventures de Télémaque*, also
printed in quarto in 1787 by Pierre François Didot, brother
to François Ambroise. The preface states that it is set in
"*les nouveaux Caractères de sa Fonderie*," and that the sub-
scribers, allowed to choose between a *caractère gras* and a
caractère maigre for this edition, had given six hundred
votes for the former against two for the latter. The choice
seems justified, for the *gras* employed in *Télémaque* (*fig.* 164)
is *maigre* enough, in all conscience! However, it is a type
with some colour left in it, and it is beautifully imposed
and printed on a rich *papier d'Annonay*, made for the book.

The Kehl editions of Voltaire (with the imprint *Société
Littéraire Typographique*) were printed from Baskerville's
type, purchased by Beaumarchais for the purpose. Three
editions were proposed; but the octavo and 12mo seem to
have been the only ones completed. The octavo is the better
of the two, and its pages have distinction and charm.
Their marked lightness of effect is gained by very open
leading and by titles set in spaced capital letters, much

ÉPÎTRE

SUR LES PROGRÈS

DE L'IMPRIMERIE.

A MON PERE.

Cet art qui tous les jours multiplie avec grace
Et les vers de Virgile et les leçons d'Horace;
Qui, plus sublime encor, plus noble en son emploi,
Donne un texte épuré des livres de la Loi,
Et, parmi nous de Dieu conservant les oracles,
Pour la religion fit ses premiers miracles;
Des grands événements cet art conservateur,
Trop ingrat seulement envers son inventeur,
N'a pas su nous transmettre avec pleine assurance
Le génie étonnant qui lui donna naissance.
Toi qui sus concevoir tant de plans à la fois,
A l'immortalité pourquoi perdre tes droits?

161. *Page employing Firmin Didot's Italic, printed by F. A. Didot*
Paris, 1784

PROSPECTUS.

Le recueil des Peintures antiques de Pietro-Sante Bartoli, dont nous annonçons une seconde édition au public, parut pour la premiere fois in-folio, à Paris, en 1757. Deux illustres savants, le Comte de Caylus et M. Mariette, consacrerent les plus grands soins à l'exécution d'une entreprise aussi intéressante, afin qu'elle répondît à la célébrité dont ils jouissoient dans la république des lettres.

A peine ils en ouvrirent la souscription qu'elle fut remplie ; leurs noms, qui font seuls leur éloge, étoient trop imposants dans le monde littéraire pour ne pas y obtenir un pareil succès. Nous rappellerons ce qu'en a dit M. le Beau, dans l'Éloge de M. le Comte de Caylus : « M. le « Comte de Caylus, dit-il, voyoit avec regret que les ouvrages des anciens « peintres, dont on a fait de nos jours la découverte sous les ruines

162. *Types used by F. A. Didot, Paris, 1782*

VIE DE M. DE FÉNÉLON.

humilier ou nous confondre, ne paroît occupé que de nos intérêts et de notre bonheur.

Fénélon vouloit que toutes les affaires de son diocese lui fussent rapportées, et il les examinoit par lui-même; mais la moindre chose importante dans la discipline ne se décidoit que de concert avec ses vicaires généraux et les autres chanoines de son conseil, qui s'assembloit deux fois la semaine. Jamais il ne s'y est prévalu de son rang ou de ses talents, pour décider par autorité, sans persuasion : il reconnoissoit les prêtres pour ses freres, recevoit leurs avis, et profitoit de leur expérience. *Le pasteur,* disoit-il, *a besoin d'être encore plus docile que le troupeau;* il faut

163. *Caractère Maigre used by F. A. and P. Didot, Paris*, 1787–92

L I V R E   XVIII.

d'un beau prétexte pour contenter leur ambition, et pou
se jouer des hommes crédules : ces hommes, qui avoien
abusé de la vertu même, quoiqu'elle soit le plus grand
don des dieux, étoient punis comme les plus scélérat
de tous les hommes. Les enfans qui avoient égorgé leur
pères et leurs mères, les épouses qui avoient trempé leur
mains dans le sang de leurs époux, les traîtres qui avoien
livré leur patrie après avoir violé tous les sermens, souf
froient des peines moins cruelles que ces hypocrites. Le
trois juges des enfers l'avoient ainsi voulu ; et voici leu
raison : c'est que les hypocrites ne se contentent pa
d'être méchans comme le reste des impies ; ils veulen

164. *Caractère Gras used by Pierre François Didot, Paris*, **1787**

helped by the small sizes of the types employed, which lend themselves readily to this kind of treatment. Some of the tables of contents are particularly interesting in composition. The 12mo edition, planned on the same lines as the octavo, scarcely "arrives," as its type seems rather a misfit for such a small *format*. This work — *de longue haleine* — was printed in seventy volumes octavo, and in ninety-two volumes 12mo, being begun in 1784 and finished in 1789. Artistically a success, it was financially a complete failure. And it is one of the sarcasms of destiny that the Revolution which Voltaire helped bring about, wrecked the "definitive edition" of his works! Pages of *La Pucelle* of 1789 are reproduced (*fig.* 165).

As an indication of changing typography the student should look at Dorat's *Lettres en Vers, et Œuvres Mêlées*, published by Delalain in 1792. It is much the same kind of a book as the *Fables;* but by 1792 types had wholly changed, becoming feeble in colour and modern in shape. Ephemeral volumes like Dorat's are often more "rewarding" typographically than better books, because they depended on luxurious presentation to get themselves read. They are the equivalent of a nineteenth century "gift book." To see the best printing of a century, one must know what books were in fashion — for many volumes, forgotten now, were the ones on which the printer spent most labour.

C. M. Saugrain's octavo edition of the New Testament in Latin and French (translated by De Saci) was begun by Didot *jeune* in 1793. In plan a handsome work, it is wrecked by its chilly "modern" types, excessive leading, and a paper too rough for the fonts employed. It is illustrated by Moreau *le jeune*, who seems very ill at ease in designing Biblical subjects. The edition is inscribed to the *Assemblée Nationale*, which, though pledged to receive no dedications of books, made an exception in its favour, to show — in 1791 — "its attachment and respect for the Christian Religion."

A six-volume edition of *Œuvres de Molière* was printed in 1791–94 at Paris by P. Didot *l'aîné*, in an edition limited to two hundred and fifty copies, set from some new types cut by Firmin Didot. It was part of Pierre Didot's quarto series of *Auteurs Classiques François et Latine.* To understand it typographically, compare it with the six-volume quarto edition of Molière, of 1734, which was intended to be "printed with magnificence" by Pierre Prault, with illustrations and decorations by Boucher, Oppenort, and others. Prault's edition is from old style types, full of warmth and colour, while in the Didot *Molière*, though the types are not absolutely modern face, they have lost their suave quality — they are too regular and lack picturesqueness, and produce very arid pages.

A folio Latin edition of Lucan's *Pharsalia*, published and edited by Antoine Auguste Renouard and printed from the types of Didot *fils aîné* in 1795, is an example of the use of over-modelled late Didot types, and a very hideous piece of work it is! Each letter of these fonts, perfect enough in itself, has too much light and shade, and in mass lacks solidity of effect. The type jumps at you! The arrangement, too, is without much sense of style. It fails just where Bodoni and even the Foulis brothers succeeded; though none the less it is typographically a very instructive volume for the student.

In France the typographic event of the close of the century was the appearance of Pierre Didot's *éditions du Louvre* of Horace and Virgil. The *Opera* of Virgil, in folio, was a limited edition of two hundred and fifty copies, printed in 1798 from types designed and cast by Firmin Didot.

LA PUCELLE

D'ORLEANS.

AVERTISSEMENT

DES EDITEURS.

1784.

CE poëme eft un des ouvrages de M. de *Voltaire* qui ont excité en même tems et le plus d'entoufiafme et les déclamations les plus violentes. Le jour où M. de *Voltaire* fut couronné au téâtre, les fpectateurs, qui l'acompagnèrent en foule jufqu'à fa maifon, criaient également autour de lui : *Vive la Henriade, vive Mahomet, vive la Pucelle.* Nous croyons donc qu'il ne fera pas inutile d'entrer dans quelques détails hiftoriques fur ce poëme.

Il fut commencé vers l'an 1730 : et jufqu'à l'époque où M. de *Voltaire* vint s'établir aux environs de Genève, il ne fut connu que des amis de l'auteur qui avaient des copies de quelques chants, et des fociétés où *Thiriot* en récitait des morceaux détachés.

A 3

CHANT PREMIER.

Amours honnêtes de Charle VII et d'Agnès Sorel. Siége d'Orléans par les Anglais. Aparition de faint Denis, &c.

JE ne fuis né pour célébrer les faints : (*a*)
Ma voix eft faible, et même un peu profane.
Il faut pourtant vous chanter cette Jeane
Qui fit, dit-on, des prodiges divins.
Elle afermit, de fes pucelles mains,
Des fleurs de lis la tige gallicane,
Sauva fon roi de la rage anglicane,
Et le fit oindre au maître-autel de Reims.
Jeane montra fous féminin vifage,
Sous le corfet et fous le cotillon,
D'un vrai Roland le vigoureux courage.
J'aimerais mieux, le foir, pour mon ufage
Une beauté douce comme un mouton ;
Mais Jeane d'Arc eut un cœur de lion :
Vous le verrez, fi lifez cet ouvrage.

C 2

165. *Baskerville's Types as used in Voltaire's La Pucelle, Kehl, 1789*

ODE I.

AD VENEREM.

Intermissa, Venus, diu

Rursus bella moves. Parce, precor, precor!

Non sum qualis eram bonæ

Sub regno Cinaræ. Desine, dulcium

Mater sæva Cupidinum,

Circa lustra decem flectere mollibus

Iam durum imperiis. Abi

166. *Types of folio Horace: Pierre Didot, Paris, 1799*

It was decorated with twenty-three engraved plates after designs by Gérard and Girodet, and was intended to surpass Bodoni's folio Virgil of 1793. This was followed in 1799 by Pierre Didot's folio Latin Horace with decorations by Percier—a companion limited edition. I have some of the "trial" pages of the Horace which belonged to Renouard and were probably given him by Didot. The type is clear to read, but quite without charm. Variations of light and shade are extreme, and the serifs of capital letters such as M and N are literally hair-lines at right angles to the upright strokes (*fig.* 166). The pages as a whole are imposing but lifeless. The decoration to the first ode, designed by Percier and engraved by Girodet, is splendid enough of its kind, but is as hard in feeling and execution as the typography beneath it (*fig.* 167).

From this survey of French books, we see that in the sixteenth century black-letter was at first used, but was slowly driven out by the fashions introduced by Tory and the Italian influence in French art; that during that century, especially in the first half—the great period of French printing — French types were a slightly more delicate form of the best Italian letters of the preceding century. In the seventeenth century, letter-design became less classical and monumental in feeling and inclined more toward what we now know as heavy "old style" types, and of these (as we shall see later) some of the finest were cut only through royal subvention. In the eighteenth century, types, though still rather heavy in the earlier years, became lighter in form and method of composition as time went on, until the type-forms developed into "modern face"— the rigid uniformity of which was then mistaken for classic severity.

It is a wonderful showing that the French printer makes from 1500 to 1800.[1] His best typography — like much else that is French — was all along the centuries characterized by distinction and elegance. And this was not all. Hand in hand with these went lucidity of thought and resultant lucidity of product — that *inspired practicality* which is the fascinating and peculiar possession of the brave sons and daughters of Gaul!

[1] A good list of examples of French printing of various periods is contained in the Catalogue of the *Cercle de la Librarie. Première Exposition. . . . Partie Rétrospective* (*Histoire de la Typographie Française par les Livres, depuis l'origine jusqu'à la fin du XVIIIe siècle*). Paris, 1880. Another volume to be consulted for titles of books typographically interesting, printed in France up to the end of the eighteenth century (*especially* those that were printed at the Imprimerie Royale until the Revolution), is *Rapport du Comité d'Installation : Musée Rétrospectif de la Classe* 11, *Typographie — Impressions Diverses* (*Matériel, procédés et produits*) *À l'Exposition Universelle Internationale de* 1900. Paris. The successive changes in the types and arrangement of title-pages of representative French books of the period we are treating can be seen from the facsimiles in Jules Le Petit's *Bibliographie des Principales Éditions Originales d'Écrivains Français du XVe au XVIIIe siècle*. Paris, 1888. The work of the seventeenth century is particularly well represented under Corneille, Racine, and Molière.

M. F. Thibaudeau's *La Lettre d'Imprimerie — Origine, Développement, Classification ; et* 12 *Notices illustrées sur les Arts du Livre* (2 vols., Paris, 1921) is a study of French printing-types, their development and use. It is valuable for its notices of French type-founding, printing, etc., from the Gothic period to the end of the last century. As the author writes from the historical rather than the critical point of view, the book is not intended to be a guide to the choice of types. It is elaborately illustrated, though many of the examples have been already utilized by Bouchot and Le Petit. M. Marius Audin's *Le Livre : sa Technique, son Architecture* (Lyons, 1921) takes up the different styles of type in vogue since the introduction of printing in France. A line or two of each type — or the nearest equivalent available — begins these notices. An excellent feature is the citation of titles of books that are printed from the types described.

QUINTI
HORATII FLACCI
CARMINUM
LIBER QUARTUS.

~~~~~~

ODE I.

AD VENEREM.

Intermissa, Venus, diu
Rursus bella moves. Parce, precor, precor!
    Non sum qualis eram bonæ
Sub regno Cinaræ. Desine, dulcium
    Mater sæva Cupidinum,
Circa lustra decem flectere mollibus
    Iam durum imperiis. Abi
Quo blandæ iuvenum te revocant preces.

19.

167. *Page of folio Horace: Pierre Didot, Paris,* 1799
(*reduced*)

¶ Quis credidit Auditui nostro: &
uelatum est, Et ascendit sicut virgultum
radix de terra deserti: Non erat forma ei,

Petit Canon de Garamond.

Aspeximus autem eum, & non erat aspectus, & No
ctus fuit & Reiectus inter viros vir dolorum, & expert
faciei Ab eo, despectus inquam, & non putauimus eu
& dolores nostros portauit, nos Autem reputauimus
Deo & HVMILIATVM.

W

168. *Garamond's Canon and Petit Canon Roman Type, from the Egenolff–Sabon–Berner Specimen Issued at Frankfort in 1592*

II

TYPES used in the books described could almost all be purchased from foundries of their respective periods; but there were important types which could not be thus secured, that owed their existence to government subvention. The Crown had paid attention to fine types and printing in the fifteenth century, and there were royal printers as early as 1487, of whom Pierre Le Rouge was the first. Geofroy Tory was an *imprimeur du roi*,[1] and François I, somewhere about 1539, conferred on Robert Estienne the title of Royal Printer for Hebrew and Latin, and in 1538 made Conrad Neobar King's Printer for Greek. After Neobar's death, Robert Estienne united in himself the functions of Latin, Greek, and Hebrew typographer, and there were in later times royal printers for music, mathematics, and Oriental tongues. These royal printers in Hebrew, Greek, and Latin probably owed their posts to the institution of five *lecteurs royaux* (*lectores regii*) by François I in 1530, appointments which were the origin of the Collège de France. This foundation, sometimes known as Collège de Trois-Langues, was to encourage studies in Greek, Hebrew, and the Latin classics, and incidentally to counterbalance the scholastic view of education to which the University of Paris, and particularly the Sorbonne, was committed. There were two readers for Greek, three for Hebrew, and another for " *l'éloquence latine*," and it was natural enough that royal readers in Latin, Greek, and Hebrew should be followed

---

[1] Defined by Lepreux as an officer of the crown, in principle compensated, exclusively entrusted with the printing either of decrees of authority or certain specified works, and therefore enjoying, in order to guarantee authentic and pure texts, as well as rapidity of publication, certain immunities and advantages, as well as special and personal privileges. The term *imprimeur du roi* furthermore particularly denoted marked artistic ability in the practice of typography.

by royal printers (*typographi regii*) in Latin, Greek, and Hebrew; just as the royal types (*typi regii*), such as the *grecs du roi*, followed in due course, and were in turn housed by the Imprimerie Royale (*typographia regia*).

It was at the instance of François I that Claude Garamond, a pupil of Tory, and the first and perhaps most distinguished of French letter-cutters and type-founders, produced his famous Greek fonts called *grecs du roi*. His roman and italic types were cut in several sizes, in 1540–1545, according to some authorities. Garamond is said to have based his roman on Jenson's model, but on comparing the two types, this appears untrue. Jenson, to whom more credit has been given as a type *designer* than is, perhaps, altogether his due, certainly cut (if we suppose he cut the roman types of the De Spires) the most successful roman letter that until then had appeared. As design, however, it was chiefly a clever transcript of a much more beautiful Humanistic manuscript hand. Garamond, in his new roman, was no longer reproducing a manuscript, but creating letters to be considered independently as types. His fonts show this. His mastery of technique, and a certain conscious elegance in design, remove them entirely from the grave simplicity of Jenson's letter. At the time that Garamond's types were cut, Jenson's roman types were famous, and, Jenson being a Frenchman, of course it was natural to have him in mind when preparing new roman types. So in that sense Garamond modelled his type upon Jenson's characters, but this does not mean that he exactly copied their design. His italic he based, he admits, on the Aldine italic, and on examination there is a certain similarity, although it is much freer in effect, owing, among other things, to its sloping capitals. Garamond is nearer to Aldus in his italic than he is to Jenson in his roman.

Garamond's roman fonts were wonderfully beautiful — clear and open. The very small loops to the e's and the narrow a's are characteristic, as are capitals that are large relatively to lower-case letters. The italic capitals slope at different angles, and when composed with the lower-case have a restless quality. On the other hand, both fonts, especially the italic, have a delightful unconventionality of design — free and spirited, yet noble; full of contrast and movement, yet with elegance and precision of line that marks them as French[1] (*fig.* 168). In what appears to be one of these fine roman fonts, Robert Estienne in 1549 printed a most beautiful book — Paolo Giovio's *Vitæ duodecim Vicecomitum Mediolani Principum.* It is composed throughout in one size of roman, except for poetry, which is set in two sizes of italic. The initials are the work of Geofroy Tory, and the ten portraits of the Counts of Milan are reduced copies, by Tory, of those in a manuscript in the Bibliothèque Royale (*fig.* 169). Although it is not stated that the book is printed from Garamond's types, its title-page bears the celebrated mark of the basilisk and the Greek motto which was usually employed by Estienne in his books printed from Garamond's royal Greek fonts.[2]

Garamond's roman and italic gave the gothic character its deathblow. It was very much used in Italy, England, and

---

[1] In the *Avant-Propos* to the first volume of Claudin's *Histoire de l' Imprimerie en France*, it is stated that a modern impression of Garamond's types appears in the Foreword of Volume I, Preface, and pages A, B, C, D, and II to XXIV. They were, indeed, based on the *caractères de l' Université*, but these were not cut by Garamond in the sixteenth century, but by Jannon in the seventeenth century.

[2] The device is composed of a spear around which are twined olive branches and a basilisk with a salamander's head — emblems of wisdom in peace and war. Beneath it appears the punning motto: Βασιλεῖ τ' ἀγαθῷ κρατέρῳ τ'αἰχμήτῃ, "To the wise King and the valiant Warrior," generally accompanied by the words *Typis Regiis.*

Holland, either in fonts sent there, matrices sold there, or by imitations. In Germany his types were also sold as shown in the Egenolff-Frankfort specimen of 1592—merely the German adoption of a French design; for although Garamond died in the year 1561 in poverty, after his death, says Vitré sarcastically, "he was recompensed by tributes without end."

Garamond's famous Greek characters, the *typi regii, grecs du roi*, or royal types, were cut about the same time.[1] Their design was based on the handwriting of a clever calligrapher, Angelos Vergetios — "*notre écrivain en grec*," as François I styled him. Garamond was employed to cut the punches of these types under the direction of Robert Estienne, and they were completed, apparently, by 1541. They were in three sizes. These fonts were intended to reproduce as closely as possible the Greek handwriting of that day as exemplified by Vergetios' fine manuscripts; and although this was not, from a present-day point of view, an advantage, it was thought to be so then. Garamond certainly achieved exactly what he intended, for the calligraphic appearance of the type is striking enough; in fact, rather disagreeably marked in its largest size. Fournier states that no Greek characters save these possessed practically all known ligatures. One of Garamond's reforms was the adoption of larger and more adequate Greek capitals, which replaced the small and unimportant capitals in current use. Robert Proctor said of this Greek type that "it was, and is, by far the best type of its kind that has ever been cut. ... I believe," he adds, "that an English type-founder of to-day would add his testimony to that of the French

---

[1] Greek typography was introduced into France by the Parisian printer Gilles de Gourmont as early as 1507, but his types were superseded by Garamond's *grecs du roi*.

PAVLI IOVII NOVOCOMEN-
sis in Vitas duodecim Vicecomitum Mediolani
Principum Præfatio.

ETVSTATEM nobi-
lissimæ Vicecomitum fami-
liæ qui ambitiosius à præalta
Romanorũ Cæsarum origi-
ne, Longobardísqʒ regibus
deducto stemmate, repete-
re contẽdunt, fabulosis pe-
nè initiis inuoluere viden-
tur. Nos autem recentiora
illustrioráque,vti ab omnibus recepta,sequemur:cõ-
tentíque erimus insigni memoria Heriprandi & Gal-
uanii nepotis, qui eximia cum laude rei militaris, ci-
uilísque prudentiæ, Mediolani principem locum te-
nuerunt.Incidit Galuanius in id tempus quo Medio-
lanum à Federico AEnobarbo deletũ est, vir summa
rerum gestarum gloria, & quod in fatis fuit, insigni
calamitate memorabilis. Captus enim, & ad trium-
phum in Germaniam ductus fuisse traditur: sed non
multo pòst carceris catenas fregit, ingentíque animi
virtute non semel cæsis Barbaris,vltus iniurias,patriã
restituit.Fuit hic(vt Annales ferunt)Othonis nepos,
eius qui ab insigni pietate magnitudinéque animi,ca
nente illo pernobili classico excitus, ad sacrũ bellum
in Syriam contendit,communicatis scilicet consiliis
atque opibus cũ Guliermo Montisferrati regulo,qui
à proceritate corporis, Longa spatha vocabatur. Vo-
luntariorum enim equitum ac peditum delectæ no-

A.iii.

169. *Roman Type (Garamond?) used by Estienne, Paris, 1549*

ΗΝ Ρωμαϊκὴν ἱστορίαν ἀρχόμενος συγγράφειν, ἀναγκαῖον ἡγησάμην προτάξαι τοὺς ὅρους ὅσων ἐθνῶν ἄρχουσι Ρωμαῖοι. εἰσὶ δ᾽ οἵδε· ἐν μὲν τῷ ὠκεανῷ, Βρεττανῶν τῆς πλείονος μέροις· διὰ δὲ τῶν Ηρακλείων στηλῶν ἐς τήνδε τὴν θάλασσαν ἐσπλέοντε, καὶ ἐπὶ τὰς αὐτὰς στήλας περιπλέοντι, νήσων ἄρχουσι πασῶν, καὶ ἠπείρων ὅσαι καθήκουσιν ἐπὶ τὴν θάλασσαν· ὧν εἰσὶν ἐν δεξιᾷ πρῶτοι Μαυρούσιων ὅσοι περὶ τὴν θά-

τὴν Σικελίαν ἀψιμαχιῶν πολλῶν, ἔργου δὲ μείζονος οὐδενὸς, Ταῦθεν ὁ Καῖσαρ ἔπεμψε τὰς ἀρετὰς τῆς Πομπηίου περικόπτειν, καὶ τὰς πόλεις τὰς χορηγούσας προκαταλαμβάνειν. καὶ τῷ δὲ μάλιστα κάμνων ὁ Πομπήϊος, ἔκρινε μάχη μείζονι κριθῆναι περὶ ἀπάντων· τὰ μὲν δὴ πεζὰ τῷ Καίσαρος ἐδεδίει, ταῖς τε ναυσὶν ἐπαιρόμενος, ἤρετο πέμπων, εἰ δέχοιτο ναυμαχία κριθῆναι, ὁ δὲ, ὠρρώδει μὲν τὰ ἐνάλια πάντα, οὐ σὺν τύχῃ μέχρι δεῦρο κεχρημένος αὐτοῖς, αἰσχρὸν δὲ νομίσας ἀντειπεῖν, ἐδέχετο, καὶ ὡρίζετο αὐτοῖς ἡμέρα, ἐς ἣν τρεῖς καὶ τριακόσιαι νῆες ἑκατέρῳ ἰδία παρεσκευάζοντο, βέλη τε πολλὰ φέρουσαι, καὶ πύργοις καὶ μηχαναῖς ὅσας ἐπενόουν· ἐπενόει δὲ καὶ ὃν καλούμενον ἅρπαγα ὁ Αγρίππας, ξύλον πεντάπηχυ σιδήρῳ περιβεβλημένον, κρίκοις ἔχον περὶ κεραίας ἑκατέρας, τῶν δὲ κρίκων εἴχετο, τοῦ μὲν ὁ ἅρπαξ, σιδήριον καμ-

170. *Garamond's Grecs du Roi* (three sizes)

experts who have treated this subject, that for evenness of colour, for precision of casting, and for the exactness of alignment and justification, these founts are unsurpassable."[1] All three types are shown in the illustration (*fig.* 170).

These Greek types were first employed in an edition of the *Præparatio Evangelica* of Eusebius, issued by Robert Estienne in 1544—a magnificent folio, printed in the second size of type (*gros-romain*), which was the font finished earliest, and, of the three, made the finest books. The largest size (*gros-parangon*) was used in a folio edition of the New Testament issued in 1550 by Robert Estienne. The smallest of them (*cicéro*) had already been employed in a 16mo New Testament (known as "O Mirificam"), printed by Robert Estienne in 1546. He says in his preface: "O the marvellous liberality of our King, that most excellent and noble prince! for feeling that such were needed to bring together into a narrow compass books of large volume, he bade engrave these smaller Greek characters, which in elegance rival the former, though these were of all letters the most beautiful. These having been delivered to me for the good of the world of letters, how could I better inaugurate their use than by a sacred text, and what text is more holy and august than the Gospel?"

One of the most exquisite books printed from these fonts is Charles and Robert Estienne's Greek edition of *Appiani Alexandrini Romanarum Historiarum*, published in 1551. All three sizes of type are used in it. The type in mass, and the proportion and imposition of the type-page, are very splendid, and there is another reason for looking at it. The superb decorations and initials by Tory, which are employed in all the Greek editions mentioned, are wonderful, in their accord with the colour of the Greek text,

[1] Transactions of the Bibliographical Society, Vol. VII, p. 57.

in their printable qualities, and in their grace of design (*fig.* 171). The most brilliant impression of them is found in the Eusebius. They are among the best of the printed decorations used in the sixteenth century.

Jean Jannon's *caractères de l' Université,* in roman and italic, as well as the *grecs du roi* of Claude Garamond, thus became the nucleus of the magnificent collection of types now belonging to the Imprimerie Nationale de France. Up to the date of the foundation of the Imprimerie Royale, under Richelieu and Louis XIII, there had been, as we know, King's Printers, who had charge and use of typographical material belonging to the Crown — such as the particular types just mentioned. This material was held as a sort of deposit, confided to the care of a director, and when type was needed it was cast from the "royal" moulds and matrices by such founders as the director selected. Thus, in a sense, François I was the founder of the Imprimerie Royale, for, as Bernard says, the types and not the structure where they are preserved are the essential part of a printing-house.

Attention had been directed to scholarly typography early in the seventeenth century by three incidents — the acquisition at Geneva in 1619 of the matrices of the Royal Greek types, and in 1632 of the Oriental fonts belonging to Savary de Brèves; and by the publication of the Paris Polyglot of Le Jay — on which Richelieu cast an envious eye. Then, too, about the middle of the century, the Elzevirs were at the height of their reputation, and were printing books in Holland which attracted Richelieu's attention.[1] In

[1] Richelieu took some personal interest in printing, for he set up a private press at the Chateau de Richelieu. The editions produced there had considerable excellence both as to type and presswork. The types imitated in size, style, and compactness the Elzevir fonts, and are said to have come from the Jannon foundry at Sedan, which produced a small type much in vogue in the seventeenth century, called *petite sédanoise.*

ΑΠΠΙΑΝΟΥ ΑΛΕΞΑΝΔΡΕΩΣ ΡΩΜΑΙ-
ΚΩΝ ΚΕΛΤΙΚΗ.

ΕΛΤΟΙ Ρωμαίοις ἐπεχείρησ πρῶτοι, κỳ τ Ρώ-
μην εἷλον διὰ τᾶ Καπιτωλίᾶ, κỳ ἐμπεπρήκασι. Κάμιλλος δ᾽ αὐτοὺς ἐνίκησε, κỳ ἐξήλασε, κỳ μετ᾽ χρόνοις ἐ-
πελθόντας αὖθις ἐνίκησε, καὶ ἐθριάμβευσεν ἀπ᾽ αὐτῶν, ὀγδοήκεντα γεγονὼς ἔτη. κỳ τρίτη δὲ Κελτῶν
ϛρατιὰ ἐμβέβληκεν εἰς τὼ Ἰταλίαν· ἣν κỳ αὐτὼ
οἱ Ρωμαῖοι διέφθαρκασιν, ὑφ᾽ ἡγεμόνι Τίτῳ Κοΐντῳ.
μετ᾽ δὲ ταῦτα Βοῖοὶ, Κελτικὸν ἔθνος θηριωδέϛατον ἐ-
πῆλθε Ρωμαίοις, καὶ αὐτοῖς Γάϊος Σαλπίκιος δικτά-
τωρ μετ᾽ ϛρατιᾶς ἀπήντα, ὅϛις κỳ ϛρατηγήματι τοιούτῳ χρήσασθαι λέγεται· ἐ-
κέλευσε γὰρ τοὺς ἐπὶ τᾶ μετώπου τεταγμένοις ἐξακοντίσαντας ὁμοῦ συγκαθίσαι
τάχιϛα, μέχρι βάλωσιν οἱ δεύτεροι, κỳ τρίτοι κỳ τέταρτοι· τοὺς δ᾽ ἀφιέντας ἀεὶ συνί-
ζειν, ἵνα μὴ κατ᾽ αὐτῶν ἐνεχθείη τὰ δόρατα· βαλόντων δὲ τῶν ὑϛάτων, ἀναπηδᾶν
πάντας ὁμοῦ, κ σὺν βοῇ τάχιϛα εἰς χεῖρας ἰέναι· καταπλήξειν γὰ ὧδε τοὺς πολε-
μίους τοῦ ὧδε δοράτων ἄφεσιν, καὶ ἐπ᾽ αὐτῇ ταχεῖαν ἐπιχείρησιν. Τὰ δὲ δόρατα ᾖν
οὐκ ἐοικότα ἀκοντί, ἃ Ρωμαῖοι καλοῦσι ὑσσούς, ξύλου τετραγώνου τὸ ἥμισυ, κỳ τὸ
ἄλλο σιδήρου τετραγώνου, κỳ τόδε κỳ μαλακοῦ, χωρὶς γε τῆς αἰχμῆς. κỳ οἱ Βοῖοι
οὕτω ὑπὸ Ρωμαίων τότε ἐφθάρησαν πανϛρατιᾶ. ἄλλοις δὲ πάλιν Κελτοὺς ἐνίκα
Ποπίλλιος, καὶ μετ᾽ ἐκεῖνον τοὺς αὐτοῖς Κάμιλλος ὁ τοῦ Καμίλλου υἱός· ἔϛηϛε δ᾽ ἔτι
Κελτῶν κỳ Παῦλος Αἰμίλιος ἐπήγαγε. περὶ δὲ τᾶ τοῦ Μαρίου ὑπατείαν, πλεῖϛόν
τι κỳ μαχιμώτατον, τῇ τε ἡλικίᾳ μάλιϛα φοβερώτατον χρῆμα Κελτῶν εἰς τὴ
Ἰταλίαν κỳ τὼ Γαλατίαν εἰσέβαλε, κỳ τινὰς ὑπάτους Ρωμαίων ἐνίκησε, κỳ ϛρα-
τόπεδα κατέκοψεν, ἐφ᾽ οἷς ὁ Μάριος ἀποσταλεὶς, ἅπαντας διέφθειρε. τελευταῖα δὲ
κỳ μέγιϛτα τῶν ἐς Γαλάτας Ρωμαίοις περιβόητα ὅϛι τὰ ὑπὸ Γαΐῳ Καίσαρι
ϛρατηγηθέντα γενόμενα. μυριάδι τε γὰ ἀνδρῶν ἀγελῶν, ἐν τοῖς δέκα ἔτεσιν ἐν οἷς
ἐϛρατήγησεν, ἐς χεῖρας ἦλθον· εἴτις ὑφ᾽ ἓν τὰ μέρη συναγάγοι, τετρακοσίων πλείο-
σι· κỳ τούτων ἑκατὸν μὲν ἐζώγρησαν, ἑκατὸν δ᾽ ἐν τῷ πόνῳ κατέκανον, ἔθνη δὲ τε-
τρακόσια, κỳ πόλεις ὑπὲρ ὀκτακοσίας· τὰ μὲν ἀφιϛάμενα σφῶν, τὰ δὲ προσπι-
λαμβάνοντες ἐκρατύναντο. περὶ δὲ τᾶ Μαρίου κỳ Φάβιος Μάξιμος ὁ Αἰμιλια-
νὸς ὀλίγην κομιδῇ ϛρατιὰν ἔχων ἐπολέμησε τοῖς Κελτοῖς, κỳ δώδεκα μυριάδας
αὐτῶν ἐν μιᾷ μάχῃ κατέκανε, πεντεκαίδεκα μόνοις τῶν ἰδίων ἀποβαλών. κỳ ταῦτα
μόνοι ἔπραξε πιεζόμενος ὑπὸ τραύματος ὑπουργία, κỳ τὰ τάγματα ὁπλῶν, κỳ
ἀναθαρρύνων, καὶ διδάσκων ὅπως τοῖς βαρβάροις πολεμητέον, τὰ μὲν ἐπ᾽ ἀπη-

171. *Page of Grec du Roi: Estienne, Paris, 1551 (reduced)*

Sur quoy vous me permetrés de vous demander en cette occasion , ce que, comme i'ay des-ja remarqué , [a] S. Augu-ftin demande aux Donatiftes en vne fem-blable occurrence : *Quoy donc ? lors que nous lifons , oublions nous comment nous auons accouftumé de parler? l'efcriture du grand Dieu deuoit-elle vfer auec nous d'autre langage que le noftre?*

Puis que Iefus Chrift dit clairement

172. *Jannon's Roman and Italic Types: Imprimerie Royale, Paris,* 1642

[a] *Aug. lib.* 33. *contra Fauft.c.* 7. Quid er-go? cum legi-mus , obliui-fcimur quem-admodum lo-quifoleamus? An fcriptura Dei aliter no-bifcum fue-rat quam no-ftro more lo-cutura?

a letter written, apparently, at Richelieu's instance, to Brasset, French Ambassador in Holland in 1640, by Sublet de Noyers, he said: "I have had for a long time the design of establishing a royal printing-office at the Louvre, and because I wish to execute everything in it with the greatest possible perfection, and I learn that in Dutch printing-offices they have a secret method of making ink which renders the impression of the letter much more beautiful and distinct, and that it is something which cannot be made in France, and also that there are a large number of printers in the country, at Amsterdam, Leyden, Blaen, and elsewhere, who would perhaps be very glad to come to earn their living here, I beg you will take the trouble to inform yourself if it is possible to find workmen in said printing-offices, at least four pressmen and four compositors, and among them, if possible, one who knows how to make this printing-ink, and to arrange with them at once for the expenses of their journey and their maintenance, as reasonably as possible and as between private persons; for it is not well to mix up, in any way whatever, the name of the King in this business, nor to disclose our plan to foreigners who may wish in some way to hinder it. You can, if you choose, say that it is Monsieur Cramoisy, the Paris publisher, who has undertaken some big piece of work, who has asked you about the matter."

Six months after this, on November 17, 1640, the Imprimerie Royale du Louvre was installed, with the required number of workmen. De Noyers had charge of its administration, but its first director was Sébastien Cramoisy — whom Richelieu originally intended to appoint as printer to the French Academy. John Evelyn, on a visit to Paris in 1644, speaks of seeing "the King's printing-house and that famous letter so much esteemed. Here," he adds, "I bought divers of the classic authors, poets and others." In 1642, a volume appeared from the presses of the Imprimerie Royale in " that famous letter" of which Evelyn speaks. No doubt great pains were taken with the book, for it was written by the founder of the press — Richelieu; its title being, *Les Principaux Poincts de la Foy Catholique Défendus*, etc. This magnificent piece of printing employs Jannon's imposing roman and italic types. The Address to the King, in very bold italic, is specially to be noticed. The very narrow measure of the pages permits notes to be placed in the margin without loss of effect. Although the impression is uneven, its appearance as a whole is sumptuous and imposing. Above all, it is readable — the quality by which a book must finally stand or fall (*fig.* 172).

Publii Terentii Comœdiæ, also printed in 1642 at the Imprimerie, is, like some other classics in folio from this press, cumbrous in style. It is printed from a monotonous old style font, with a heavy impression, and so large a type is used that there are many "turn-over" lines. Its decorations — except for a truly superb engraved title-page — are not remarkable; but the management of massed capitals at the beginning of each play is clever and distinguished. It is an example of the "divers classic authors" that Evelyn bought on his visit to this press two years later.

The first book issued by the Imprimerie Royale (in 1640) was a folio *De Imitatione Christi*. Other fine books of the early period were the *Introduction à la vie dévote* of St. Francis de Sales of 1641; a Greek Testament and a Latin Bible, both folio, published in 1642; the acts of the General Councils, etc., in thirty-seven volumes, the first of which was printed in 1644; Tasso's *Gerusalemme Liberata* (1644), a very heavy performance typographically, but with agreeable decorations; besides folio editions of Virgil, Horace,

Terence, Juvenal, and other authors. During the first ten years of the existence of this press some hundred volumes were printed.

In 1692, Louis XIV ordered a new series of types, to be used exclusively by the Imprimerie Royale and to be produced without any thought of expense. To decide on what this new character should be, a commission was appointed by the Académie des Sciences, of which Jaugeon[1] was the most active member. Grandjean,[2] first accredited royal type-cutter, was chosen to engrave the punches — in which he is said to have been helped by his friend and pupil, and suc-

[1] It was in this connection, no doubt, that Jaugeon, in collaboration with Truchet (a Carmelite and a versatile mechanician), and M. Filleau des Billetes, of Poitou, prepared for the Académie a treatise on typography, which was to be part of a collection entitled *Description et Perfection des Arts et Métiers*. This covered the art of designing letters, of cutting their punches, of letter-press printing, and of book-binding. Though some of the plates illustrating the book were engraved — among them the celebrated diagram of 2023 squares on which letters were to be designed — the manuscript was never published and is now in the Bibliothèque Nationale. Jaugeon's elaborate theory of designing types was, after years of neglect, put into practice, and a series of types called *Caractères Jaugeon* was cut by Hénaffe for the Imprimerie Nationale in 1904.

[2] According to De Fontenai, Philippe Grandjean de Fouchy, of an old family of Mâcon, was born in 1666. When in Paris, early in life, a friend took him to see a printing-office. In examining its types he thought he saw ways of bettering them. Designing some capital letters for amusement, he succeeded so well that his essays were shown to M. De Ponchartrain, who mentioned Grandjean's work to Louis XIV. In consequence, Grandjean was ordered to enter the royal service to occupy himself with printing. Through the influence of the Abbé Bignon, the well-known bibliophile, Grandjean made new models for punches and matrices for the Imprimerie Royale and invented several appliances for shortening and perfecting the work of a type-cutter. The *romain du roi* designed for the Imprimerie made his reputation. "M. Grandjean," says Fournier, "who assisted the progress of this new foundry, also had charge of it; he maintained it always in the different localities in which he lived, the last place being his house near the Estrapade at the entrance to the Rue des Postes, from which it was transported to the Louvre in 1725, to be joined with the offices there, thus forming a complete printing-house."

cessor, Alexandre. The committee worked for several years to get things to its mind. The result of all this cogitation was the *romain du roi*—comprising twenty-one different bodies of roman and italic, and twenty bodies of roman and italic initials: in all, eighty-two complete fonts.

These types, begun in 1693, were only finished in 1745. They were marked as "royal" fonts in an odd way—by a little projection on the left of the shank of the lower-case l at the height of a short lower-case letter. This annoying feature of an otherwise beautiful font has been continued on the l of roman letters cut for the Imprimerie ever since. It has been said that l was selected by order of Louis XIV—who, by the way, esteemed Grandjean's types so highly that he refused the request of Philip V of Spain for a set of the punches. In some early gothic types a similar mark, derived from manuscripts, also appeared on the left of the l. The best of Grandjean's *romain du roi* fonts were employed in a magnificent folio, *Médailles sur les Principaux Événements du Règne de Louis le Grand, avec des Explications Historiques. Par l'Académie Royale des Inscriptions & Médailles* (*fig.* 173). This book was printed at the Imprimerie Royale in 1702.[1] An enlarged folio edition covering the entire reign, with different *explications*, was issued in 1723; but as it is printed on rougher paper, it does not show the peculiarities of the characters so clearly. A good modern impression of these fonts may be seen in the work printed by the Imprimerie Nationale in 1889, entitled *Cuivres de Cochin destinés à l'Histoire de Louis XV par Médailles.* This book, intended to be a continuation of the similar volumes devoted to the reign of Louis XIV, was never completed, but these designs made for it by Cochin

[1] A *quarto* volume, with much the same title, also published in 1702, does not employ these types, and is not to be confused with the *folio* edition.

dans l'Isle de Saint-Amand, & battit encore huit cens chevaux fortis de Doüay. Aprés quoy il se campa entre cette Ville & Bouchain, & porta la terreur dans tout le Pays, qu'il fourragea jusques aux portes de Cambray. Enfin il marcha vers Condé, & ayant pris d'abord le fauxbourg de l'Escauld, il fit faire un logement sur la contrescarpe ; de sorte que le jour mesme, 25 d'Aoust, le Gouverneur se rendit à la seconde sommation. Le Comte demeura aux environs de cette Place jusqu'au mois de Septembre, & cette entreprise n'ayant esté faite que pour amuser les Espagnols, ou pour les attirer à un combat, il abandonna Condé avant la fin de la Campagne, & prit Maubeuge en revenant.

C'est le sujet de cette Médaille. On y voit Pallas, tenant un Javelot prest à lancer ; le fleuve de l'Escauld effrayé s'appuye sur son Urne. La Légende, HISPANIS TRANS SCALDIM PULSIS ET FUGATIS, signifie, *les Espagnols défaits & poussez au-delà de l'Escauld.* L'Exergue, CONDATUM ET MALBODIUM CAPTA. M. DC. XLIX. *prise de Condé & de Maubeuge. 1649.*

173. *Grandjean's Romain du Roi: Imprimerie Royale, Paris, 1702*

Une description historique & allégorique aurait accompagné les desseins, & chaque page de la description devait être entourée d'un cadre différent, également composé & gravé par Cochin. Au bas de chaque description se trouverait un cul-de-lampe allégorique.

Les quatre premières planches de l'Histoire de Louis XV par médailles ont figuré au Salon de 1755; mais l'ouvrage n'a pas été publié. Il existe à la bibliothèque de l'Arsenal une épreuve des neuf pièces que nous publions aujourd'hui, & elles sont accompagnées du texte qui s'y rapportait (H. n° 7031, in-fol.). Les encadrements entourent ce texte, qui remplit vingt pages; il est resté à l'état d'épreuves, toutefois, & son imperfection indique que ces épreuves n'étaient pas encore définitives. Aux Estampes de la Bibliothèque nationale, il ne se trouve que cinq

174. Grandjean's Romain du Roi (italic): Imprimerie Nationale, Paris, 1889

have been published. In its text Grandjean's italic type[1] is beautifully displayed (*fig.* 174).

Grandjean's type was, Bernard says, "a type friendly to the eye"— and at first sight it seems to be. There was about it, however, something that was to prove, in its developments, very *unfriendly* to the eye. That was its serif,[2] which took the form of an almost unbracketed line, and on the tops of b, d, h, i, j, k, and l extended on *both* sides of the upright stroke. A page printed from these types had, owing to the number of fine horizontal serifs, the appearance of being ruled. Jenson's letters had very thick serifs at the bottom, and triangular serifs at the top. Garamond's fonts had much the same kind of serif, but refined. Grandjean's thin horizontal serif was a movement toward that lightness of effect in type that came about later, but which was then very little thought of. It is the appearance of a bad element in French type-design, and is important in the history of some types to be discussed later. This was not all. In the capitals the contrasts of thin and thick strokes are more marked. The italic lower-case—beautiful of its kind—appears engraved. It is a very decorous type, and it looks as if it had been designed in accordance with rules—many rules. It was of the lucubrations of the committee who arranged elaborate diagrams for it that Fournier *le jeune* exclaimed: "Must there be so many squares to make an O that is round, and so many circles to make other letters that are square!"[3] Yet when all is said, Grandjean's open, clear,

[1] They were retouched, it is said, by Luce in the eighteenth century.

[2] A "serif," it must be remembered, is a short cross-line which occurs at the ends of unconnected lines of a letter. It probably originated in a difficulty felt by cutters of inscriptions on stone, who found that if strokes of letters terminated without some curve or line, they appeared unfinished. To correct this, they made serifs.

[3] *Manuel Typographique,* Vol. I, p. xvii.

wide letters, extravagant of space, almost read themselves. It is, *of its kind*, one of the finest types extant.

Grandjean died in 1714, and the work on these fonts was carried on by his pupil, Alexandre; and Alexandre's son-in-law, Louis Luce, completed them in 1745. All these men were royal type-cutters.

The next important type acquired for the Imprimerie Royale was that of Louis Luce, third royal type-cutter, who between 1740 and 1770 designed a series of fonts of a letter of narrower proportions than the characters we have been considering. There were in this series thirty roman bodies and the same number of italic. Luce says in his advertisement to his *Essai d'une Nouvelle Typographie*[1] of 1771 (beautifully printed by Barbou), that he has tried to make a font different from anything which the Imprimerie Royale has employed, and in the *Essai* he shows Grandjean's letters and his own (*fig.* 175). His are taller and narrower, or, as we should say "condensed," giving them a cramped appearance, something like a modern French type called "Elzevier." His serifs are oblique, and on the left of ascending characters only, which was an improvement; for Grandjean's types with their flat tops are dazzling, and their alignment is too perfect for good effect in mass. Luce's adoption of the serif on the left only, he justified on the ground that all types originated from a written letter, and that in forming a letter with a pen, one would start from the left. He says that it is partly by the delicacy of the serif that he has differentiated these types from the *caractères de l'Université* and from Dutch types of his time. Of the italic, he adds that he has purposely simplified its shape;

[1] *Essai d'une Nouvelle Typographie, ornée de Vignettes, Fleurons, Trophées, Filets, Cadres & Cartels, inventés, dessinés, & exécutés par L. Luce, Graveur du Roi, pour son Imprimerie Royale. Dediée au Roi. A Paris. De l'Imprimerie de J. Barbou, rue des Mathurins. 1771.*

Ce modele fuffit pour faire voir la différence de mes caractères romains & italiques d'avec ceux de l'Imprime-rie Royale ; mon attention a toujours été de m'en éloi-gner, en fuivant le goût, qui me portoit à ne rien faire, qui reffemblât aux Caractères connus dans la Typographie.

La variété que j'ai mife dans les préfentes lettres ,

&icſiɡtglojcdeſtanhimiurbi   *fe démontre affez par leur feule*

comparaiſon avec celles qui fuivent &Etglojcdeftanimiurbi

175. *Luce's Types Poétiques compared with Old Style Types of Imprimerie Royale*
From Luce's Essai d'une Nouvelle Typographie, Paris, 1771

GROS-ROMAIN ROMAIN.

LE corps est cette substance étendue, qui compose la seconde partie de nous-mêmes. Si nous n'étions que des substances spirituelles, nous pourrions ne nous occuper que de ce qui regarde l'esprit; mais les besoins de la nature nous font continuellement sentir la nécessité de prendre soin de nos corps

Le corps est l'agent de l'ame, ainsi nous devons l'entretenir comme un serviteur fidele : mais aussi nous devons le tenir toujours dans la dépendance , & prendre garde qu'il ne secoue le joug de la servitude , & n'usurpe l'empire : c'est ce qui arrive , lorsque nous nous livrons aux passions violentes; car encore une fois, nous pouvons résister à leurs efforts.

GROS-ROMAIN ITALIQUE.

LE courage est une ardeur impatiente d'attaquer. Il ne craint, ni le péril, ni les difficultés. Un fait courageux, dit Montagne, ne doit pas conclure un homme vaillant. Celui qui le seroit bien à point, le seroit toujours & à toutes occasions. Si c'étoit habitude de vertu & non une saillie, elle rendroit pareillement un homme résolu à tous accidents, tel seul qu'en compagnie, tel en champ clos qu'en une bataille : car quoi qu'on die, il n'y a pas autre vaillance sur le pavé & autre au camp.

Aussi courageusement porteroit-il une maladie en son lit, qu'une blessure au camp, & ne craindroit non plus la mort en sa maison qu'en un assaut. Nous ne verrions pas un même homme donner dans la brèche, d'une brave assurance, & se tour-

176. *Luce's Types Poétiques (roman and two versions of italic)*
From Essai d'une Nouvelle Typographie, Paris, 1771

177. *Luce's Ornaments, from Essai d'une Nouvelle Typographie, Paris,* 1771
(*reduced*)

TROPHE'

ALLEGORIQUE

AL'AUTOMNE.

L'ÉQUINOXE d'Automne arrivera le 22 Septembre, à 2 heures 41 min. du foir, e Soleil entrant dans le Signe de la Balance. Il entrera dans celui du Scorpion le 22 Octobre à 10 heures 23 min. du foir; dans celui du Sagittaire le 21 Novembre, à 6 h. 23 min. du foir, & il arrivera au Soiftice d'Hyver le 21 Décembre, à 6 h. 39 minutes du matin.

SEPTEMBRE, eft tiré du nombre fept, que l'on exprimoit par le mot September, avant l'Edit de Charles IX. 1564. Il étoit le feptiéme Mois de l'Année Romaine.

LE FLEURON

CI-DESSUS EST COMPOSÉ DE 9 PIECES.

Le Trophé eft compofé de 7 pieces.

C C

178. *Luce's Employment of his Types and Ornaments*
Page from Essai d'une Nouvelle Typographie, Paris, 1771

that connecting lines are lighter and there are fewer tails to the letters. In the *romain du roi* types, the "complimentary" projection on the lower-case l appears on the left of the shank; in Luce's types, on the right. Luce's elongated type, because it was compact, was adapted to poetry, where broken lines are undesirable. So he called it *poétique*. Although Luce was royal type-cutter, he designed these types as an independent venture, and intended them for general use (*fig.* 176).

His *Essai d'une Nouvelle Typographie* shows a superb collection of ornaments and borders made to accompany his types. These are designed with great skill from a decorative point of view, are wonderful in their variety, and yet harmonize with one another. No modern type-foundry has produced a more magnificent suite of appropriate and "printable" ornaments. They were made on all sorts of bodies, and were meant to take the place of engraved borders, which were then the fashion, but which were expensive, and, furthermore, involved two printings (*fig.* 177).

The "approbation" which Luce's book received in 1771 politely says that his fonts "prove to amateurs that the art of Garamond is susceptible of perfection." The Académie des Sciences in 1772 also commended especially the merit and ingenuity of his ornaments, which could be made up into head-bands, allegorical cartouches, and tail-pieces at will; could be printed with the type, and were of even colour with the typography—never the case when borders were engraved on copper, which was, moreover, much more costly (*fig.* 178). In 1773, by order of Louis XV, the whole collection was bought for the Imprimerie, where it is still. Its ornaments were rightly considered more important than its types,[1] which, as they had been sold promiscuously before

[1] The types were recently employed for Chapter VI of Christian's *Débuts de l'Imprimerie en France*.

their purchase by the Crown, were never used for books printed at the Imprimerie itself.

The smallest size of Luce's new type had already been shown in a delightful little volume of eight leaves, called *Épreuve du Premier Alphabeth Droit et Penché*,[1] issued in 1740. Up to that time the type known as *la petite sédanoise* was the smallest extant. But having called that, for some reason or other, alphabet second, French logic demanded that there be a first — and this was it! In the preface to the little book both these types are shown for the purpose of comparison. The *sédanoise* font was used in a 32mo volume printed by the Imprimerie Royale in 1729 — *Phædri Fabulæ, et Publii Syri Sententiæ* — and the interesting Latin preface makes allusion to the types, which are clear though minute; but Luce's *Premier Alphabeth* (also called *perle*) is almost impossible to read. I do not know if it was ever employed, except in the charmingly got up specimen. Luce, who died in 1773, was succeeded by Fagnon, the last of the royal type-cutters.

The Imprimerie Royale (which has changed its name with various changes of government, being *Royale, Impériale, de la République, du Gouvernement, Nationale*, etc.), as we have seen, was aided by royal subventions, and thereby types were produced which never would have existed for commercial reasons.[2] Royalty and the Court often amused themselves with printing. In 1648, Louis XIV, then a child of ten, visited the newly established Imprimerie du Louvre and "helped" (how much, we may imagine) to pro-

---

[1] *Épreuve du Premier Alphabeth Droit et Penché, ornée de Quadres et de Cartouches, gravés par ordre du Roy pour l' Imprimerie Royale par Louis Luce & finis en* 1740.

[2] Up to the Revolution, the punches, matrices, and a certain number of presses and amount of material belonged to the State; the remainder to the director, who managed them for his own profit.

duce the first page of an edition of the *Mémoires* of Philippe de Commines. Louis XV was taught to print by Jacques Collombat, a distinguished Parisian printer mentioned by Fournier; and a miniature printing-house was set up at the Tuileries in 1718, where the little boy — who was then eight years old — printed some lessons in geography entitled *Cours des principaux Fleuves et Rivières de l'Europe. Composé & imprimé par Louis XV Roy de France & de Navarre en 1718. À Paris, dans l'Imprimerie du Cabinet de S. M.* (*fig.* 179). Some forty or more bits of printing came from this office, which existed up to 1730. The mother of Louis XVI had a printing-office at Versailles in 1758, where she set up and printed a book of devotions, and the Duc de Bourgogne also dabbled in typography. Madame de Pompadour occupied herself at Versailles in 1760 with a little press.[1] Louis XVI, as Dauphin, was taught the trade by Augustin Martin Lottin (a name familiar to students of the history of French printing), and in 1766, when he was twelve, produced twenty-five copies of a book — "all himself," as children say — *Maximes Morales et Politiques tirées de Télémaque, imprimées par Louis Auguste, Dauphin*. At court and at little presses set up in country chateaux, many fashionable and idle people played with printing, much as in our time "unemployed" persons of fortune and leisure have played with book-binding and metal-work — which they abandoned after discovering that to be successful demanded more work than play! No doubt, then, as now, professionals concealed from amateurs — who "adored" printing, or were "fascinated" by types — that profound weari-

[1] The Song of Songs and a *Précis* of Ecclesiastes by Voltaire were produced under her supervision; and the King summoned a detachment of workmen from the Imprimerie Royale, who printed for her Corneille's *Rhodogune, Princesse des Parthes*, with the imprint *Au Nord* — as Madame de Pompadour's apartment was situated at the north of the palace.

ness of spirit which the unlearned enthusiast has always produced in "the man who knows how" ever since antediluvian idlers pestered Noah while building the Ark. I can fancy the sigh of relief with which Collombat saw the "Principal Rivers" trickle safely and expensively to the sea —for it was quite an expensive operation! To all these people (as Crapelet says) "the press was only a plaything which they handled, as children do weapons, without foreseeing the misery it would some day cause them."[1] But many of the rulers of France were seriously interested in printing, and particularly in the achievements of the Imprimerie Royale.[2]

III

FOURNIER *l'aîné* and Fournier *le jeune*, so often mentioned in the history of French type-founding, were the sons of Jean Claude Fournier, who received his training in the Parisian foundry of Jean Cot. He later became connected with the Le Bé foundry, which he managed for the daughters of Le Bé for nearly thirty years. By his marriage with Anne Catherine Guyou he had nine children, six boys and three girls. Of the boys, three died in childhood, and the remaining brothers, who lived to mature age, were Jean Pierre Fournier, usually styled *l'aîné;* a second son, possibly named François,[3] who was a printer at Auxerre, his father's birthplace; and Pierre Simon (who occasionally

---

[1] The Louis XIV *romain du roi* was used in 1790 to print Marat's revolutionary pamphlets.

[2] For productions of the Imprimerie Royale up to the end of the eighteenth century, see *Catalogue Chronologique des Éditions* in Bernard's *Histoire de l'Imprimerie Royale du Louvre.* Paris, 1867.

[3] In 1754 there was but one printer in Auxerre: this was François Fournier, established there in 1742: *Rapport Sartine.* In the Anisson collection, there are letters written from Auxerre by a Fournier, printer, in 1765 and 1771.

transposed his Christian names), commonly called Fournier *le jeune.*

The eldest of the three, Jean Pierre Fournier, was born in Paris in 1706. By the purchase in 1730 of the Le Bé establishment, which his father had superintended until his death in 1729, he became possessor of a really splendid foundry. In his hands it had a great reputation, and justly enough — for it was a noble collection of beautiful old types, cut by masters of French type design. In two scholarly letters addressed to the editor of the *Mercure de France,*[1] Fournier *l'aîné* describes its treasures in a way that shows how much he appreciated them. He specifies such an assemblage of punches and matrices by Garamond, Le Bé, Granjon, and Sanlecque, as make it from our point of view nowadays — as it was held by the discriminating then — the most interesting foundry in France.

Fournier *l'aîné,* who was himself both an engraver and founder of types, lived at one time in the Rue St. Jean de Beauvais — a street much affected by his craft. He married Charlotte Madeleine Pichault, who died in 1764. By this marriage he had a son, Jean François Fournier, and three daughters. The son — sometimes styled Fournier *fils* — married Marie Elizabeth, daughter of the type-founder François Gando *le jeune.* A daughter by this marriage (apparently named Sophie) became the wife of the notorious revolutionary printer, Momoro.[2] They had a son, who later assumed the name of Fournier.

[1] See *Mercure de France,* May, 1756, and January, 1757, for his letters giving a list of the types by these ancient type-cutters.

[2] Antoine François Momoro, a turbulent, visionary, unbalanced sort of person, an adherent of the Revolutionary Hébert, and at the end of his life mixed up in the promulgation of the *Culte de la Raison* (1793–94), being at that period a member of the Commune and Département of Paris. A specimen called *Épreuve d'une partie des caractères de la fonderie de Ant. Franç.*

Fournier *l'aîné* died in 1783, at the age of seventy-seven, in the village of Mongé, and after his death the foundry remained in the hands of his three daughters, who managed it successfully for a long time. According to Capelle, who wrote in 1826,[1] on the death of the sister who had taken upon herself the chief direction of its affairs — which must have been later than 1811 — the foundry was dispersed, its punches, matrices, and moulds being sold to different type-founders. It is likely that at least a part of the material of Fournier *l'aîné's* establishment went to his son, Fournier *fils*.

I know of no specimen book of Fournier *l'aîné*, but he supplied types to illustrate an article on printing that appeared in the *Encyclopédie* (Vol. II, p. 662). He also lent many of the types shown in his younger brother's *Manuel*, and fonts from his foundry appear in Pierres' specimen of 1785. His son, Fournier *fils*, however, issued an interesting Greek specimen[2] in 1767, which comprised the work of Granjon, Hautin, Deviliers, and Picart — the first two known to us as ancient and distinguished type-cutters. In the same year he issued a specimen of a more general na-

Momoro was issued at Paris in 1787, and he was the author of a carelessly compiled *Traité Élémentaire de l'Imprimerie* (printed after 1785) and a wretched little *Manuel des Impositions Typographiques*, reprinted in 1789. Momoro, who seems to have lost his head more than once, lost it definitively on the scaffold in 1794, in the tyranny inaugurated by Robespierre. Madame Momoro (*née* Fournier) has sometimes been identified with the woman impersonating the Goddess of Reason in the fête held at Notre Dame on November 10, 1793. But the fact seems to be that Madame Momoro merely took part in a similar fête at Saint-André-des-Arts, which then stood not far from the Rue de la Harpe, where her husband lived between 1789 and 1792. These fêtes, generally considered orgies, appear usually to have been frigid, classical affairs of exceeding propriety and dulness.

[1] *Manuel de la Typographie Française*, Paris, 1826.

[2] *Épreuve de Caractères Grecs de la Taille de quatre Graveurs*, 1767. [*Caractères Grecs de la Taille de Robert Granjon, Nicolas Deviliers, Pierre Hautin & Jean Picart.*]

LA MARNE.

CEtte Riviere a ſa ſource en Champagne , à une demie lieuë au-deſſus de Langres , d'où coulant au Septentrion elle paſſe à Vi-try-le-François & à Chaa-lons ; paſſant à l'Occident par Château-Thierry & par Meaux , elle ſe rend enfin dans la Seine près & au-deſ-ſous de Charenton.

L'OISE.

CEtte Riviere a ſa ſource en Picardie , d'où cou-lant au couchant , & peu après vers le Midy , elle paſſe

179. *Page composed and printed by Louis XV when a Child*
Paris, 1718

MODÈLES
DES CARACTERES
DE L'IMPRIMERIE,

ET DES AUTRES CHOSES NÉCESSAIRES AUDIT ART.

NOUVELLEMENT GRAVÉS

Par SIMON-PIERRE FOURNIER le jeune, Graveur & Fondeur de Caractères.

A PARIS,
Ruë des sept voyes, vis-à-vis le Collége de Reims.

1742

180. Title-page of Fournier le jeune's Modèles des Caractères, Paris, 1742 (reduced)

ture,[1] and in 1769 an advertisement of his material in the *Mercure de France*[2] supports the theory that he inherited some of his father's famous old characters. About 1787, part of his foundry was sold to Henri Haener of Nancy.

I think that Fournier *l'aîné's* remarkable collection caused some heart-burning on the part of his younger and more famous brother. Yet it was to him that Fournier *le jeune* entrusted the completion of his son Simon Pierre's technical education, and to whom on this account he left a bequest; also making him his executor. For he seems to have been, in the words of Lottin, *Homo Antiquæ Fidei*.

Pierre Simon Fournier *le jeune* was born in Paris, September 15, 1712. Although the education of his older brothers had been carefully looked after by their father, he appears to have been the spoilt child of the family: living with his mother in the country until she died, and only returning to Paris shortly before his father's death. He studied drawing under J. B. G. Colson, miniaturist and water-colour painter, and member of the Académie de Saint-Luc. This probably helped him in type-designing. He was at first employed by his elder brother in cutting wood-blocks (possibly head-pieces, etc.), and later on he engraved punches for capital letters, of the kind then known as *grosses et moyennes de fonte*, a size hitherto supplied only in type cut on wood. He continued his work by producing several fonts of type and some tasteful "flowers" or *vignettes de fonte*,[3] as they were

---

[1] *Épreuves des Caractères à l'usage de l'Imprimerie. Avec differentes sortes de Vignettes. À Paris: Chez Fournier Fils, Graveur & Fondeur en Caractères d'Imprimerie, rue du Foin St. Jacques à côté de la Chambre Syndicale des Libraires.* 1767.

[2] *Avis* in *Mercure de France*, March, 1769, p. 208.

[3] The oldest type ornaments usually consisted of a simple *feuille de vigne* = vine-leaf = floret — from which in France the term *vignette de fonte* came to be applied to all decorative designs cast by founders for use with letter-press. In England, they were called *flowers*; in Germany, *röselein*; in Spain, *viñeta*.

called in France. His italic, a modernized form of the handsomer, more irregular early letter, met with success at once.

   Fournier *le jeune* began to formulate his point system in
1737; he amplified it in 1742, and in the *Manuel* of 1764
gave it its final form—as has been said in a former chapter.
His earliest specimen (in oblong folio) is entitled *Modèles
des Caractères de l'Imprimerie et des autres choses nécessaires
audit Art. Nouvellement Gravés par Simon-Pierre* [sic] *Fournier le jeune, Graveur & Fondeur de Caractères. A Paris, Rue
des Sept Voyes, vis-à-vis le Collège de Reims,* 1742[1] (*fig.* 180).
This was printed for Fournier by Jean Joseph Barbou, and
is one of the most effective and elegant books of its kind
ever issued in France. The preface is set in Fournier's brilliant, modelled italic, and then follows a beautiful collection of
types, beautifully presented (*fig.* 181). On folding plates at
the end of the book is a series of head and tail-pieces made
up of *vignettes* most skilfully contrasted in light and shade
(*fig.* 182)—nothing more ingenious and charming of this
sort has ever been produced! A feature of this book is the
display of large, plain letters for initials, which printers of his
day, he says, almost entirely lacked—"with the exception
of the Imprimerie Royale, which is furnished abundantly
with everything which produces perfect printing, and the
types belonging to which contribute so much to the glory
of printing and the honour of those who made them."

   In addition to the well-known *Manuel Typographique*

---

[1] Fournier also issued, with the same date and imprint, a 16mo specimen:
Caractères de l'Imprimerie nouvellement gravés par Simon Pierre [sic]
Fournier le jeune, Graveur & Fondeur de Caractères. Other specimens were:
Nouveau Caractère de Finance (probably by Fournier *le jeune,* 1757?);
and *Épreuves de deux petits Caractères nouvellement gravés par Fournier
le jeune, et exécutés dans toutes les parties typographiques.* Paris, 1757 or
1758. Also *Tableau des Vingt Corps du Caractères, d'usage ordinaire dans
l'Imprimerie . . . fournis par M. Fournier le jeune* in *Bibliothèque des
Artistes,* etc., by De Petity, Tome II, Part II, Paris, 1766 (4to).

AUTRE PETIT PARANGON.

Le cruel Neron fit mourir sa mere, Antonie sa tante, Britannicus, Senecque, Corbulon un de ses Capitaines, & plusieurs autres de ses proches ; & tua lui-même d'un coup de pied Poppée sa seconde femme.

Saint Pierre, Saint Paul, & les autres Chrétiens furent aussi les inno-centes victimes de sa fureur, il leur fit souffrir les plus cruels tourmens & inventa pour cela tout ce que la rage & la cruauté ont de plus ingenieux.

AUTRE GROS ROMAIN.

On revêtit les uns de peaux de bêtes sauvages , & ensuite on lâcha contre eux des chiens affamez ; on en exposa d'autres aux lions dans l'amphi-théatre ; & on attacha les autres à des poteaux, ou ils furent tous brulez vifs.

Peu de tems après les hommes, & le ciel même étant lasseʒ de la cruauté de ce monstre, il fut lui-même son propre bour-reau ; & lorsque le Senat se préparoit à en délivrer la terre , il s'arracha une vie qui étoit en exécration à tout l'univers.

181. *Roman and Italic from Fournier le jeune's Modèles des Caractères, Paris, 1742*

182. *Use of Typographical Ornaments in Fournier le jeune's Modèles des Caractères, Paris,* 174

of 1764, described on a later page, Fournier *le jeune* was the author of a series of papers, written between 1758 and 1763, and collected in his *Traités Historiques et Critiques sur l'Origine et les Progrès de l'Imprimerie*, a 16mo volume charmingly printed by Barbou. Fournier issued in 1756 a specimen entitled *Essai d'un nouveau Caractère de fonte pour l'Impression de la Musique, inventé par Fournier le jeune.* His part in the improvement of music types (which I do not touch upon), in which composers like Rameau supported him, was very considerable, and in spite of bitter opposition by the Ballard family, who held a sort of monopoly as music-printers, the King named him, in 1762, his supernumerary printer for music. His *Traité Historique et Critique sur l'Origine et les Progrès des Caractères de la fonte pour l'Impression de la Musique, avec des épreuves de nouveaux caractères de Musique*, appeared about 1763.

Fournier *le jeune* married, in 1747,[1] Marie Madeleine Couret de Villeneuve, daughter of Louis François Couret de Villeneuve and Marie Madeleine Borde, and sister to a certain Martin Couret de Villeneuve, a printer of reputation at Orléans — as was his son. The Fourniers lived on the *rive gauche*, in that old-world quarter of Paris near the Lycée Henri IV and the picturesque old church of St. Étienne du Mont — to which parish Fournier belonged. In the year of his marriage he dwelt in the Rue des Sept Voies, where his house stood opposite the Collège de Reims — in the *quartier de l'Université*, within the bounds of which printers were then obliged to live.[2]

[1] About this time Fournier was painted by Bichu — a picture delightfully reproduced by Gaucher, one of the best eighteenth century engravers.

[2] For a practical reason, *i.e.*, to facilitate inspection of their output by the authorities or censors of the University, to which they were attached. This would have been inconvenient if they had been allowed to live in remote parts of Paris.

We think of the Paris of those days as a mass of old houses, deprived of light, air, and verdure. But the houses of that time were only a border to the streets. Behind them, between one street and the next, were great open spaces which afforded the sunlight, silence, and greenery which their fronts were denied; and in Fournier's day, one-third of the city was open land. Indeed, until Louis Philippe's reign, the *rive gauche* was full of trees and gardens; and the dramatist Sardou, who in his early years lived near the Place de l'Estrapade, speaks of the view lost in greenery that his windows commanded. It was amid "these gardens, these silent streets so propitious to labour, perfumed by lilacs, and flowering with pink and white chestnuts," that Fournier had his latest habitation. His dwelling stood at that part of the Rue des Postes which formed a side of the Place de l'Estrapade, in a house said to have been formerly occupied by Philippe Grandjean, type-cutter for the Imprimerie Royale, who kept there the matrices of the royal fonts, and cast type from them — and who died there in 1714. Fournier's specimen, issued in 1764, bears the imprint "Place de l'Estrapade, Rue des Postes," and his *Manuel*, "Rue des Postes." The Place and Rue de l'Estrapade exist to-day, though what was the Rue des Postes is now the Rue l'Homond.[1]

There Fournier died on October 8, 1768. He was survived by his wife and two sons, Simon Pierre and Antoine. An

[1] The Fournier family seem to have retained a house or houses there for many years. In 1804, Rue des Postes No. 908, in 1806, No. 45, were occupied by Fournier's grandson, the founder Beaulieu-Fournier; and his nieces, the Demoiselles Fournier, also lived in the Place de l'Estrapade in 1811. The locality seems to have been long consecrated to type-founders and their industry. Besides Grandjean, Hémery, who was for thirty years manager of the foundry of Fournier *l'aîné* and *le jeune*, lived in the Place de l'Estrapade, as did Joseph Gillé, another important Parisian founder, and the type-founder L. Léger, nephew and successor to Pierre François Didot.

éloge by a certain François that appeared in 1775 (from
material furnished, apparently, by one of the family and
Fournier's friend Bejot, of the Bibliothèque Royale), says:
"Fournier's private life was happy, proving that routine
is not always the mother of *ennui*. His calm spirit diffused
about him unruffled and gentle contentment. He fled the
noise of society, to enjoy retirement and friendship, perhaps giving himself up to this too much during his last
years. Refusing suggested amusements, he devoted himself
wholly to work and research. Such obstinate application
was really the source of his illness, and finally rendered the
advice or help of physicians useless."[1] And other authorities
imply that he ruined his health by overwork. Two years
before his death he wrote of his own foundry: "I began it
in 1736, and it is scarcely finished in the present year,
1766; which is to say that by assiduous and almost continuous work, it has taken me twenty-nine years to bring
it to its present condition. I may state that it is entirely the
work of my own hands, I myself having cut the punches,
struck and justified the matrices, and manufactured a number of moulds—among others all those which are of my
own invention; there being no other instance since the invention of printing, of a complete foundry which has been
the work of a single artist." It was Fournier's lifework, and
it cost him his life!

[1] See *Le Nécrologe des Hommes Célèbres de France, Tome Troisième*, 1770,
p. 231. Also *L'Année Littéraire*, 1768, *Tome VII. Éloge de M. Fournier
père*, etc., p. 265, which was used for the text of a specimen of a *Nouveau
caractère d'Écriture dans le goût Anglais. Gravé à Paris en* 1781 *par S.
P. Fournier le jeune*, and printed by Pierres. See also Lottin's *Catalogue
Chronologique des Libraires*, etc., Paris, 1789 (pp. 233–244, devoted to
type-founders). There is also a notice of Fournier in De Fontenai's *Dictionnaire des Artistes*, Paris, 1776. The accounts of printers in it were prepared with the help of *les personnes les plus consommées dans l'art de l'imprimerie*—M. Ph. D. Pierres having been specially interested in this part of
the work.

After Fournier's death his widow carried on his foundry with the help of the older son, Simon Pierre Fournier, — then about eighteen, — and the following letter was sent by her to persons with whom her husband had held business relations:

"I have the honour to inform you," she writes, "that after a long and most cruel malady, God has taken from me my Husband: my only consolation is to have left to me a son, who for several years past has worked under the eye of his father, who spared no pains to instruct him in his calling: on my part I shall make every effort to continue to give satisfaction and to merit the confidence with which you honour your very humble servant."

Madame Fournier survived her husband some seven years, dying in the Rue des Postes, April 3, 1775. A year later, Simon Pierre Fournier married Marguerite Anne, daughter of a certain M. De Beaulieu of Chartres, by whom he had a son and a daughter. His only brother, Antoine, was nine years younger than he. This disparity of age, and no training or liking for his father's trade, — but, we are told, a taste for *une éducation recherchée*, — led, in 1778, to litigation between S. P. Fournier and a certain Barbou de Champourt, who acted in Antoine Fournier's behalf — he being still a minor.[1] What the outcome was of their dispute as to the disposition of the property, I do not know.

The ultimate fate of Fournier *le jeune's* collection of types was like that of his brother's foundry: for the son is said to have added little to its reputation, and by the beginning

---

[1] See *Mémoire pour le Sieur Simon-Pierre Fournier, Graveur & Fondeur de Caractères d'Imprimerie, Majeur. Contre le sieur Antoine Fournier, Mineur émancipé d'âge, procédant sous l'autorité & assistance du sieur Barbou de Champourt, son Tuteur* ad hoc, *& contre ledit sieur Barbou audit nom.* Paris, 1778.

of the last century the collection appears to have been broken up.[1]

Franklin had dealings with various Fourniers during his life at Passy, and alludes, among others, to Fournier *l'aîné* and Fournier *le jeune*, who were respectively uncle and nephew ; the latter being the Simon Pierre (son of Fournier *le jeune*) just spoken of [2] and who also styled himself *le jeune*. The genealogical table of the Fournier family will aid in disentangling their puzzling relationships.

I have devoted several pages to the Fourniers, and in particular to the career of Fournier *le jeune*, because they were of such great importance in the history of type-founding in France in the mid-century. The elder may be described as a man of integrity who was the owner, and very intelligent owner, of a wonderful collection of ancient types, and as one who walked worthy the vocation wherewith he was called. The younger brother was much more in the public eye, and he was so because, having had some artistic education, possessing the enthusiasm of youth, and being unhampered by convention, he saw possibilities unsuspected by others ; and thus he made a concrete contribution to French type-founding by his type, his ornaments, and the books he wrote to describe and popularize his methods.

(1) The types designed by Fournier *le jeune* do not now seem to us very novel. His roman was an old style character sharper in cut than that commonly in use at his period, and

---

[1] Capelle, who wrote in 1826, is my authority for this statement.

[2] It was he who, in 1780, wrote to Franklin asking him to allow an artist of his acquaintance to paint Franklin's portrait. Franklin replied that he would do so, though much against his custom; but added, characteristically, that he was neither rich enough nor vain enough to be at any expense in the matter. Fournier answered that he would feel honoured by being at all charges, and would send to Franklin the painter whom he had selected. We are not told whether the picture was painted or not.

TABLE OF THE FOURNIER FAMILY IN THE EIGHTEENTH CENTURY

Jean Claude Fournier's three Sons who died in childhood, and his three Daughters, of whom we have no record, are omitted from this Table

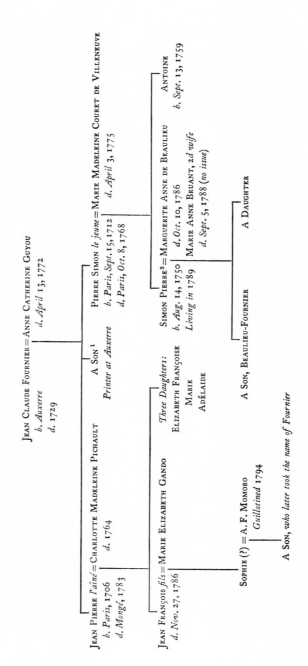

JEAN CLAUDE FOURNIER = ANNE CATHERINE GUYOU
b. Auxerre
d. 1729
d. April 13, 1772

JEAN PIERRE *l'aîné* = CHARLOTTE MADELEINE PICHAULT
b. Paris, 1706
d. Mongé, 1783
d. 1764

A SON [1]
Printer at Auxerre

PIERRE SIMON *le jeune* = MARIE MADELEINE COURET DE VILLENEUVE
b. Paris, Sept. 15, 1712
d. Paris, Oct. 8, 1768
d. April 3, 1775

SIMON PIERRE [2] = MARGUERITE ANNE DE BEAULIEU
b. Aug. 14, 1750
Living in 1789
d. Oct. 10, 1786
MARIE ANNE BRUANT, 2d *wife*
d. Sept. 5, 1788 (*no issue*)

ANTOINE
b. Sept. 13, 1759

JEAN FRANÇOIS *fils* = MARIE ELIZABETH GANDO
d. Nov. 27, 1786

Three Daughters:
ELIZABETH FRANÇOISE
MARIE
ADÉLAIDE

A SON, BEAULIEU-FOURNIER

A DAUGHTER

SOPHIE (?) = A. F. MOMORO
Guillotined 1794

A SON, *who later took the name of Fournier*

[1] *Possibly named François. Jean Claude Fournier, printing at St. Dizier* 1775-1791, *may have been his son.*

[2] *Sometimes called* "*le jeune.*"

of variations in its design which made fonts then known as *ordinaire, approché* or *serré, goût Hollandois, poétique,* etc. The *ordinaire* is that which most clearly shows the changes he made from the "old style" of other foundries. Personally, I do not care much for it. The public of that day were not of my way of thinking, for it had about it a slightly accentuated sharpness which was welcomed. It resembled the types of Garamond more than those of Grandjean. In his italic Fournier abandoned the whimsicalities so agreeable in old style fonts, and made practically a *sloping roman* with a trimmed, mechanical line. In his *Hollandois* types he shortened the descenders, and thus these types had the "rotund" and over-fed appearance that such deformation always gives. His *poétiques*, Luce thought, it appears, were adapted from his — for persons of reputation adopt, adapt, appropriate, and annex, but never ——! And to all these fonts he added series of varied ornamental letters and shaded letters (*lettres grises*), and very delightful they were. Even the rules or *filets* used to separate sections, under Fournier's hand blossomed into something new. Of his ornaments and ornamented initials one may say that he touched nothing that he did not adorn. But these belong to our review of the *vignettes* or *ornements de fonte*, for they were derived from the same sources.

(2) The emblems, ornamental letters, and be-garlanded borders which Fournier made popular in printing were inspired chiefly by the work of men like Cochin, Eisen, St. Aubin, and other French vignettists of the eighteenth century. Seeing what had been done for the book by the engraver and etcher, he attempted to transmute their designs into material for printers. Such typographic ornaments were not new — an immense repertoire of them already existed.

Fournier merely adapted them to the fashion of his day, but he did so with great taste and unity of effect. Thus, to quote Thibaudeau, we have in his *vignettes* "pieces susceptible of forming varied decorative arrangements, of a definite note and style, conceived with such foresight as to their use, that they lent themselves as well to the irregular curves of escutcheons, rosettes, and *culs-de-lampe*, as to form and decorate initials and framework: capable, in a word, of being substituted for the corresponding employments of copper-plate engraving, while presenting the very appreciable advantage, for semi-luxurious editions, of economy of impression."[1]

(3) The remaining work that Fournier did was to popularize the knowledge of his art in a delightful way by his writings — chiefly through the publication of his *Manuel Typographique*[2] — "useful to men of letters and to those who are practitioners in the different branches of the Art of Printing." It contains the most useful information about type[3] and type-founding which could be got together when he wrote. It appeared at Paris in two 16mo volumes, printed by the author in very tasteful fashion and sold by Barbou

[1] *La Lettre d'Imprimerie*, Vol. I, p. 294.

[2] *Manuel Typographique utile aux gens de lettres & à ceux qui exercent les différentes parties de l'Art de l'Imprimerie. Par Fournier, le jeune. À Paris, Imprimé par l'Auteur, rue des Postes & se vend chez Barbou, rue S. Jacques*, 1764–66 (2 vols.). The work was to have comprised two more volumes devoted to the mechanics of printing and biographies of printers, but the author did not live to finish it.

[3] I say "about type" rather than "about printing" advisedly. For Martin Dominique Fertel's *Science Pratique de l'Imprimerie* (St. Omer, 1723) is in some ways a more useful book for a printer who wants to know how to *use* type. It is the first treatise written in French, the aim of which was to show how to arrange a book clearly and attractively. It is admirably done, and should be consulted by any one wishing to reconstitute French typography of the early eighteenth century. Fournier rated Fertel's work very high.

—the first part in 1764, the second in 1768, though dated 1766.[1]

In the *Avertissement Préliminaire* to Volume I, Fournier records in brief what had already been written in France about the history of printing and types, outlines the scheme of his book, and devotes some pages to his new music fonts. "The art of engraving types," he says (forgetful or ignorant of Moxon), "has never been described. Masters of the art have been so rare, that a considerable time has often elapsed without a single one in France, and not one of them has described in writing the processes of his art. It is that fact which obliged me, when I desired to exercise my calling, to define for myself those principles, and to establish those rules, of which I have given an account in the rest of this work." In the text he considers, from a technical point of view, punch-cutting, matrix-making, and type-founding, including under this last head the treatise on his point system quoted in a previous chapter. Then follow *polices* — a series of tables indicating the respective number of each character to be supplied in making up fonts of roman, Hebrew, Greek, music types, etc. A group of plates (preceded by explanatory notes), which show the tools, etc., employed in the various processes described in the text, closes the volume.

In Volume II, in the *Avertissement Préliminaire*, Fournier points out the importance of a more exact knowledge of the kinds and sizes of type in various weights of line, if an intelligent choice is to be made for a given purpose. This is followed by a summary of the books he has consulted and

[1] Fournier was by special decree printer supernumerary to the thirty-six Parisian printers established by law, and this allowed him to print the *Manuel* in a little office set up for the purpose in his house in the Rue des Postes. On his death the press was immediately dismantled by the authorities of the printing-trade.

an account of the principal type-foundries of Europe, most of which I have quoted.

The specimens of types are the most important part of the book. Some of them were lent him by Fournier *l'aîné*, by the Paris founders Cappon and Hérissant, and by Breitkopf of Leipsic. They are grouped under six heads: I. Types in ordinary use. II. Ornaments, *lettres de deux points* (simple and ornamented), rules, etc. III. Types peculiar to particular countries or of special forms. IV. Oriental types. V. Music and plain-song. VI. Types of ancient and modern languages, with explanatory notes.[1]

Fournier's types, in common with those shown in most contemporary French specimens, display varying *nuances* in type-faces of the same body, usually described—to adopt Fournier's enumeration—as *petit œil, œil ordinaire, œil moyen, gros œil, œil Hollandois, œil serré,* and *œil poétique.* "The *petit œil,*" says Fournier, "leaves more space between lines of type, which gives a lighter and more graceful air; but it is more fatiguing to persons of delicate eyesight; *œil ordinaire* holds the middle course between charm and utility; *œil moyen* is a shade stronger in character, which makes it more legible, an advantage still more marked in the *gros œil;* but the lines of this being closer to each other, the pages take on '*un air trop matériel.*' To diminish this weight, the Dutch have thought of making these kinds of *gros œil* types of a thinner face and more elongated shape." Fournier himself added to the variety of faces the *œil serré,* a slightly condensed type that allowed more letters to a line; and his version of *poétique*—smaller and less colourful—has tall

---

[1] Under the title *Les Caractères de l'Imprimerie par Fournier le jeune. À Paris, Place de l'Estrapade, Rue des Postes,* 1764, a specimen similar to that which forms part of the *Manuel* was published separately, but did not contain all the types shown in that work.

No. XXXIV. 32

CICÉRO POÉTIQUE.

Un Général d'armée recevant de toutes parts des plaintes contre un Munitionnaire, le fit venir, & pour premier compliment le menaça de le faire pendre. Monſeigneur, répondit froidement le Munitionnaire, on ne pend pas quelqu'un qui peut diſpoſer de cent mille écus ; & là-deſſus ils paſſerent dans le cabinet. Un inſtant aprés, Monſieur le Général en ſortir perſuadé que c'étoit un fort honnête-homme.

Ceci nous apprend qu'on ne doit pas juger trop précipitamment de la conduite du prochain, ni le condamner ſans l'entendre. Il eſt bien aiſé de dire que certaines gens ſont des fripons, mais il faut le prouver.

No. XXXV. 33

CICÉRO POÉTIQUE.

Vous avez une pièce d'argent, ou même une pièce d'or, ce n'eſt pas aſſez ; c'eſt le nombre qui opère : faites-en, ſi vous pouvez, un amas conſidérable & qui s'élève en pyramide, & je me charge du reſte. Vous n'avez ni connoiſſances, ni eſprit, ni talens, ni expérience ; n'importe : ne diminuez rien de votre monceau, & je vous placerai ſi haut, que vous vous couvrirez devant votre maître, ſi vous en avez : il ſera même fort éminent, ſi avec votre métal qui de jour à autre ſe multiplie, je ne fais en ſorte qu'il ſe découvre devant vous.

La pluspart des gens ne jugent des hommes que par la vogue qu'ils ont, ou par leur fortune.

183. Fournier le jeune's Types Poétiques (cicéro, roman and italic)
Manuel Typographique, Paris, 1764

CICÉRO, GROS ŒIL,
dans le goût Hollandois.

LA pluſpart des hommes de Lettres ne ſe piquent que de doctrine & d'érudition ; ils entaſſent livres ſur livres, ſcience ſur ſcience qui ne perſuadent que de l'obſcurité, de la ſécchereſſe & du travers dans l'eſprit : c'eſt pourquoi il ſe trouve plus de gens de ſavoir que de bon ſens.

Le bon ſens va droit au vrai ; l'éloquence n'eſt que l'interprète, & tout ſon but eſt de lui donner de la force & de la clarté : ſi quelquefois elle s'échappe à y jeter de certains agrémens, c'eſt pour le rendre plus aimable.

CICÉRO, GROS ŒIL.

LA dernière choſe où l'on s'applique, c'eſt à épurer ſon diſcernement : on exerce ſa raiſon à toutes ſortes d'études qui ne ſervent qu'à l'embarraſſer, au lieu qu'il ne faut étudier que pour inſtruire & perfectionner ſa raiſon.

On peut dire que les femmes qui ne s'occupent point de ſciences & de littérature, conſervent plus que les hommes la tranquillité de l'ame : la frivolité de leurs occupations leur tient ordinairement l'eſprit libre & le rend plus aimable.

184. *Fournier le jeune's Types dans le goût Hollandois (cicéro, roman and italic)*
Manuel Typographique, Paris, 1764

capitals, ascenders, etc., that "let in the light" between lines of poetry; and its condensation permitted a long line of poetry to be printed on a comparatively small page, without what is called a "turn-over."

All these variants are shown by Fournier. As I have said, the roman types of the *ordinaire* class became, under Fournier's graver, a trifle sharper and more open in cut than the current old style. In these faces, particularly in italic, one sees the sure advance of a lighter fashion in printing types. The condensed *poétique* types are of the same general character as those of Luce (*fig.* 183), and the series of fonts in *goût Hollandois* (*fig.* 184), a condensed type of large face with short ascenders and descenders, is perhaps modelled on the plan of the serviceable Elzevir types. As the letters grow larger, however, they seem to become disproportionately heavy. Both *poétique* and *Hollandois* types had considerable vogue for books where the printer wished to get as much matter on a page as possible. Of the two, the *poétique* is much more attractive; but the *goût Hollandois* was more used. Its monotonous evenness of line introduced a bad fashion in roman fonts, and its italic[1] was a slanting version of roman rather than a true italic. Fournier had begun to polish the life out of italic letters twenty years earlier, and in his *Modèles des Caractères* of 1742 speaks of a certain air of antiquity in older (or, as he called them, "superannuated") styles of italic that unfortunately he thought it desirable to reform; all the more so, perhaps, because his elder brother had such a wonderful stock of them! In italic characters, he tells us, his improvement was to make type more closely resembling the writing of his day, and to show greater contrast between the thick and thin lines of the let-

[1] This italic was used interchangeably with "old style" and "*Hollandois*" roman.

ters; but to my eye his italic has a rigid and monotonous air that is extremely disagreeable (*fig.* 185 a). It was to be finally superseded by the much worse italic fonts of Didot. But the mischievous influence began, I fear, with Grand-jean's types, which, marvellous as they were, had in them elements that later played havoc with roman as well as with italic characters.

The agreeable shaded letters [1] produced by Fournier may be looked at for the amusing and ingenious manner in which serifs on the shaded italic and roman capitals in large sizes have, by a few strokes of the graver, been made to end in a kind of "spray." This is an example of a delightful effect achieved by the simplest means (*fig.* 185 b). They are not to be confounded with his decorated capital letters,[2] which are, as ornamental type-letters go, simple, and, if sparingly used, most attractive (*fig.* 186). Both had considerable vogue at that day and have been revived in ours. They were inspired by the lettering of engraved title-pages.

Fournier's typograpical ornaments are charming little designs (*fig.* 187) rendered for typographic use just as such things should be. Only close examination reveals their variety and cleverness. At first glance, the larger, more ob-vious decorations, such as those of *gros-romain* size,[3] are the ones that strike us—frameworks with festoons, broken by bunches of flowers or knots. These are not more remark-able than the smallest ornaments—numbers 1 to 93—from which most charming effects were derived. Numbers 4, 5, 6, 7, and 23, 24, when used in mass, gave a field upon which blacker, bolder figures could be built up, with won-derful richness of contrast. Then, again, the bracketed num-bers 138–147, 188–190, and 191–201 show the varieties of

[1] *Manuel Typographique*, Vol. II, pp. 88-93.
[2] *Ibid.*, pp. 88, 89.   [3] *Ibid.*, p. 113.

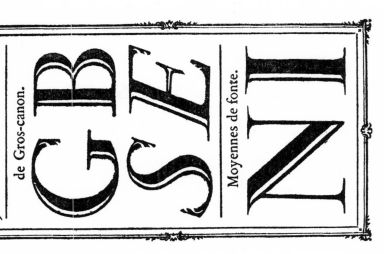

92 *LETTRES*
de Gros-canon.

G B
S Æ

Moyennes de fonte.

N I

188 *ALPHABETS*

2 Italique moderne.

A a B b C c D d E e F f
G g H h I J i J j K k L l M m
N n O o P p Q q R r S ſ s
T t U V u v X x Y y Z ʒ &

3 Italique ancienne.

A A a B B b C C c
D D d E E e F f G G g
H h I f J i j K k L l
M M m N N n
O o P P p Q Q q
R R r S ſ s T T t
V U V u v X x Y y
Z Z z & & fl ſ st nt

185. (a) Fournier le jeune's *Italique moderne* and *Italique ancienne*. (b) *Fournier's Shaded Letters*
Manuel Typographique, Paris, 1764

HISTOIRE

DE

LOUIS DE BOURBON,

SECOND DU NOM,

PRINCE

DE CONDÉ,

PREMIER PRINCE DU SANG,

Surnommé *LE GRAND.*

LIVRE PREMIER.

1621 - 1643.

LOUIS DE BOURBON, second du nom, naquit à Paris 1621. le 7 Septembre 1621 ; il fut titré *Duc d'Enguien,* nom heureux qui rappelloit la mémoire du vain-

186. *Fournier le jeune's Ornamental Capitals*
Lottin, Paris, 1768

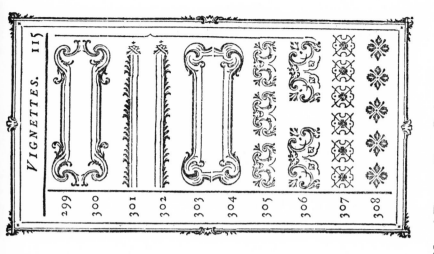

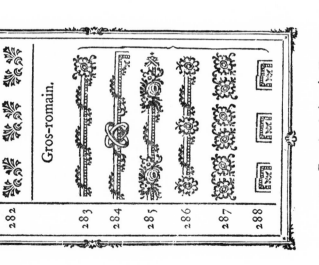

187. *Fournier le jeune's Vignettes de Fonte: Manuel Typographique, Paris, 1764*

ITALIENNE.

Monsieur,

Vous êtes invité, de la part de Monsieur de Briguevillette, de vous trouver mardi prochain, vingt-quatre Juin, à la Fête qu'il donnera chez lui ; à l'occasion du mariage de Mademoiselle de la Frippaudiere avec Monsieur le Baron de Tourponguillet, son fils.

BATARDES ENSEMBLE.

Au Roi,

SIRE,

L'Equité et la bienfaisance de votre Majesté assurent le succès des représentations que les Officiers Municipaux

188. Batarde Types: Fournier's *Manuel Typographique*, Paris, 1764

breaks and endings to rules that could be had.[1] Some characteristic designs are the sunbursts in honour of *le roi Soleil* (339), the medallions (359, 360), the hanging garlands (365), the escutcheons (375), and seven varieties of black butterflies. Even the braces [2] (*crotchets*) are decorated, and the double and triple rules are made interesting. These ornaments became in Fournier's hands something almost as delightful as engraving, and yet wholly new.

The division of the *Manuel* devoted to special characters contains much interesting material [3]—for instance, the *batarde* types (*fig.* 188), the *cursive françoise* or *civilité*, the *ancienne batarde*,[4] and some fine *lettre de forme* and *lettre de somme* which follow.[5] The Flemish and German types are also interesting; and Fournier's much discussed music types [6] should be examined. A final section of the book is given up to alphabets of ancient and modern languages—some of them appear rather apocryphal—gathered from various sources, and to these Fournier has appended little notes full of information. Of these the first sixteen only are of much practical value to the reader of this book.

The *Manuel Typographique* is a work which no student of French typography can afford to be without. The simplicity of the author's style, his naïve pride in his own performances, and its mass of information make a book which will become a favourite with any one who reads it. It is not the work of a scholar, but of an observing, experienced, quick-witted master of his art, who in cultivating that art had cultivated himself. And when we think about the other

---

[1] All the bracketed numbers are full of interesting suggestions. Notice the combination of 203 and 205 with 207, and also the "possibilities" in vignettes 210–215, 234–236, 253–268, 283–288, 296–306, 331–338, 349–355.

[2] *Manuel Typographique*, Vol. II, p. 127.   [3] *Ibid.*, pp. 135–150.

[4] *Ibid.*, p. 142.   [5] *Ibid.*, pp. 143, 144.   [6] *Ibid.*, pp. 172–179.

work that Fournier did — of the types he cut, of the ornaments he designed, of the point system he invented, of the
music he improved — we begin to realize the part he played
in what has been happily called "the renovation of French
typographic material in the eighteenth century." Fournier
was a man typical of a certain class in France, who treat
their work with a respect which dignifies both it and them.
For he was neither a bad workman, a bad pastry-cook, nor
a bad Frenchman, who, being taxed with thinking that ornamental pastry was the one Fine Art in the world, modestly replied, "No: there are *three* Fine Arts — Sculpture,
Painting, and Ornamental Pastry-Making — of which Architecture is a Branch!"

IV

IN the examination of French specimen-books, which con-
cludes this chapter, I shall take Fournier, supplemented
by Lottin,[1] as a guide, and describe when possible the specimens of the founders they name.

The oldest establishment was the Le Bé foundry, which
remained in that family until 1730, and was then purchased
by Jean Pierre Fournier *l'aîné*. It has already been sufficiently treated under the work of the sixteenth century, and
in the notice of the Fourniers.

The second great French foundry was that of Sanlecque.
A specimen of its types was issued in 1757, but so wholly
devoted to *seventeenth* century fonts, that it appears under
the account of that period. In a letter written to Franklin

---

[1] See *Notice Chronologique des Libraires, Imprimeurs & Artistes qui se sont
occupés de la Gravure & de la Fonte des Caractères Typographiques,* contained in Auguste Martin Lottin's *Catalogue Chronologique des Libraires
et des Libraires-Imprimeurs de Paris.* Paris, 1789. It represents the labour
of forty-two years — thirty-six years of preparation and six of revision and
printing.

by Marie, widow of Jean Eustache Louis Sanlecque, in 1779, she says, "I am proprietress of a foundry which I dare assure you is the finest in Europe;" and she continues, "I add, herewith, a little book which contains different impressions of type which will put you in a position to judge of the merit of my foundry by seeing the beauty of its characters."[1] Madame Sanlecque died in 1785, and her daughters sold the foundry to Maurice Prosper Joly, who in turn sold it to Henri Haener of Nancy, the purchaser of some of the material of Fournier *fils.*

The Delacolonge foundry of Lyons is mentioned by Fournier as an ancient and respectable establishment, and its productions up to the year 1773 may be seen in a rare little specimen entitled *Les Caractères et les Vignettes de la Fonderie du Sieur Delacolonge. À Lyon, Montée & près les Carmelites,* 1773. The types in this collection seem to date from so many periods that I hesitate to identify them chronologically. Many in the large sizes are extremely distinguished, especially the *gros canon œil maigre* and *œil gras,* both in roman and italic, which appear to me seventeenth century types, and which are reproduced, therefore, on an earlier page (*figs.* 152 *and* 153). The four *civilité* types[2] are delightful, and the *financière* (*fig.* 189) is a common type-form in French eighteenth century printing. The Greek and Hebrew types are good. A point to be noticed in this book is the difference between the old-fashioned and agreeable italic, such as the *Saint-Augustin,*[3] and the wiry italic in the Dutch taste.[4] The head-pieces are ingenious and interesting and are made up of *vignettes de fonte.* The collection of these

---

[1] Livingston's *Franklin and His Press at Passy,* Grolier Club, New York, 1914, pp. 118, 119.
[2] Delacolonge Specimen, pp. 94 and 98.
[3] *Ibid.,* pp. 32 and 37.   [4] *Ibid.,* pp. 33 and 38.

vignettes is as miscellaneous as the types, and many of them are, I think, very old.[1]

The type-founder Mozet issued a specimen in 1736, but I never have seen it: though I am familiar with the issue of 1743, entitled *Épreuves des Caractères de la Fonderie de Claude Mozet, Fondeur et Graveur de Caractères d'Imprimerie. À Paris, rue de la Parcheminerie, au coin de la rue des Prêtres Saint Séverin.* Mozet's foundry passed to J. F. Hémery, who for thirty years had been director of the Fournier foundries, and who lived in the Place de l'Estrapade.

In 1720, a certain Briquet started a foundry, which on his death he left to his widow. He had as an associate and pupil a Monsieur Loyson, who married the widow, and in 1728 issued a specimen, mentioned by Lottin. Madame Loyson's son by her first marriage — Briquet — associated himself with his stepfather, and with him brought out in 1751 *Épreuve des Caractères de la Fonderie de Loyson & Briquet* (4to), which I have never seen. After Loyson's death, Briquet continued the foundry alone, and produced in 1757 a specimen called *Épreuve des Caractères de la Fonderie de Briquet. À Paris, Cloître Saint Benoît.* This may be properly considered an eighteenth century specimen-book, though not a very good one. The names of the type-cutters who supplied fonts for the collection are given in the preface, and some of the types were imported from Holland. The fonts — except, possibly, those attributed to Garamond — are uninteresting variants of styles found in other specimens. The ornaments are better, and some combinations of them at the end of the book are very beautiful indeed. The way in which they are shown — as units and in various combinations — is useful and clever; the first instance that

---

[1] Delacolonge Specimen, pp. 66–70, Nos. 210, 211, 223, 233, 236, 240, and 249.

FINANCIERE
de deux points de Philofophie.

Nous Syndic & Adjoints de la Librairie & Imprimerie de cette ville., certifions que Mr Delacolonge a déclaré fur les Régistres de notre Chambre Syndicale, vouloir expédier à M Imprimeur-Libraire à caisse contenant caracteres d'imprimerie, à laquelle expédition nous avons

189. *Financière: Delacolonge's Caractères et Vignettes*
Lyons, 1773

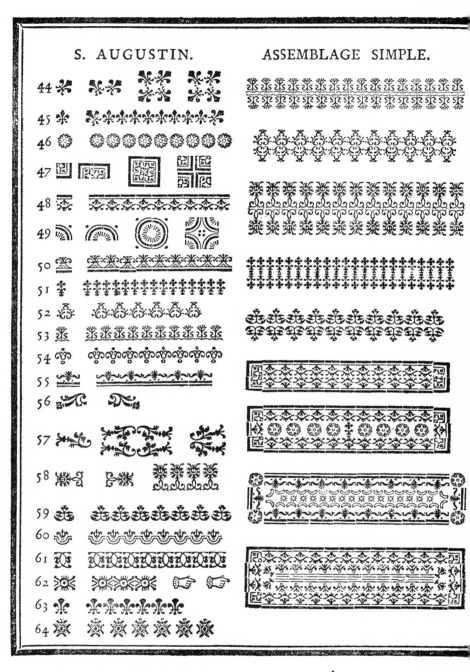

190. *Method of Displaying Ornaments: Briquet's Épreuve des Caractères* Paris, 1757 (*reduced*)

I know of this method of exposition (*fig.* 190). The Loyson-Briquet foundry was sold in 1758 to Vincent Denys Cappon, who had been their *élève*, and after his death in 1783 it was carried on by his widow. It ultimately became part of the stock of the distinguished Parisian printer, Pierres.

The ancient foundry of Denis Thierry was based on Moreau's collection of agreeable and clever cursive types. After two generations it was acquired by the Collombats, father, son, and grandson, and finally passed by sale to Jean Thomas Hérissant, printer and founder, in 1763. A "specimen" was issued by his widow (born Marie Nicole Estienne), dated 1772, entitled *Épreuve des Caractères de la Fonderie de la Veuve Hérissant, Imprimeur ordinaire du Roi, des Cabinet, Maison & Bâtiments de Sa Majesté, Académies des Arts & Manufactures Royales. À Paris, rue Saint-Jacques, au coin de celle de la Parcheminerie.* In the preface to it Madame Hérissant states that part of these types came to her husband by his purchase of the Collombat establishment—which comprised a publishing and printing-house and a foundry. An *Épreuve des Caractères, composant l'Imprimerie de la Veuve Hérissant, rue de la Parcheminerie, No.* 184, of eighteen quarto pages, was issued shortly after the Revolution, but this was, in reality, a sale catalogue. The types shown in it are not noteworthy, except for the three *financières,*—not Moreau's, by the way,—the Greek, Hebrew, Syriac (very fine), and some moderately good fonts of music.

The Thiboust foundry, begun in the seventeenth century, descended from father to son in the Thiboust family—a race of Parisian printers, booksellers, and type-founders—until 1787. I do not know of any specimen issued by it.

The foundry of Jean Cot was assembled by his purchase of a number of small foundries in 1670, and its material passed to a son, Pierre Cot, who, under the title of *Essais de Caractères d'Imprimerie, À Paris*, 1707, issued a 16mo specimen of ornamental characters and announced one to follow with exotic alphabets, ordinary types, music, ornaments, *et autres enjolivements*. He appears to have been a scholarly man, and was the author of a history of letterfounding and printing, which remained unpublished. On his death the establishment reverted to his mother, and finally, through two of her daughters, it came to Claude Lamesle by purchase in 1737. Lamesle issued in 1742 an extremely handsome and dignified specimen called *Épreuves Générales des Caractères qui se trouvent chez Claude Lamesle. . . . À Paris, Rue Galande (au milieu) près la Place Maubert*. This book, both in type and ornaments, I think, presents better than any other the output of French foundries during the last quarter of the seventeenth and the first half of the eighteenth century. The collection of types is remarkably fine. They are purely old style, and after each size the initials and ornaments belonging to that size are introduced. Here and there one finds characters reminiscent of Dutch fonts of the period, and old style fonts which, on account of their leading and light cut, show the approach of a more open style of typography. Titling-letters (in roman, italic, and Greek) and some beautiful *civilité* are worth looking at. The ornaments are, many of them, of thoroughly seventeenth century style. The plates to be consulted (toward the end of the book) are the *lettres de deux points de petit canon, allemande de deux points de gros romain*, and *gros canon maigre ordinaire* in roman and italic[1]—both of them beautiful letters. For the student of French type-forms of the earlier part of the eighteenth century there is scarcely a better book. A second edition with some variations was

[1] Lamesle Specimen, Nos. LVIII and LIX.

brought out in 1758, on the occasion of the sale of Lamesle's foundry to Nicolas Gando *l'aîné*, who in 1736 had exchanged his foundry at Geneva for the Parisian foundry of his uncle, Jean Louis Gando—a native of Basle, who came to Paris on the invitation of Grandjean, about 1705.

Nicolas Gando issued a specimen in 1745, and after the purchase of the Lamesle establishment, he and his son, Pierre François, published, in 1760, *Épreuves des Caractères de la Fonderie de Gando père et fils. À Paris, Cloître Saint Julien le Pauvre, près la rue Galande*, printed by Guérin and Delatour. They were adroit copyists, and very unscrupulous rivals, of Fournier *le jeune*, with whom they had a bitter controversy on the subject of music types. And another Gando, François (a brother of Nicolas), first of Lille, later of Paris, also tormented Fournier *le jeune* by his imitations and trickeries—though after François Gando's death his daughter married Fournier *le jeune's* nephew! The Gando specimen of 1760 contains most of the material which appeared in Lamesle's book, with some rearrangements and additions. The order of the type is reversed, the largest sizes being displayed first. The second type shown is a *gros canon italique nouveau goût*. What this *goût* was, one begins to see in the *gros parangon italique numéro* VII, *petit parangon italique numéro* XI, or the *cicéro italique* engraved by Gando *le jeune* in 1754 (*fig.* 191). These wiry, vulgar types were a new and bad yet popular element in a printer's stock. The *Recueil d'Ornemens* [*sic*] is dated 1745, and was issued by Nicolas Gando—probably a reprint of part of the *Épreuves* of the same date. This *Recueil*, with its rather overcharged head-bands, etc., made up of ornaments, introduces one to a surprising and terrible portico of a temple some ten inches square, constructed entirely of typographical ornaments— a structure which it is hoped will remain unique!—though it is run close by some Austrian and Spanish type-edifices and Italian naval constructions, the whereabouts of which will ever remain (as far as I am concerned) a profound secret.

In all these later eighteenth century French specimen-books three styles of type stand out: (1) The lively, interesting old style roman of earlier periods with its irregular italic. This older italic was less and less shown as the century advanced and the new italic was substituted for it, while the *original old style roman was retained.* (2) *Poétique*, condensed fonts with tall ascenders, or fonts modelled on or suggested by *poétique* type, sometimes called *approché* or *serré*. (3) Fonts in the *goût Hollandois*—a letter of larger body in proportion to its ascenders and descenders, more uniform in colour and monotonous in design.

The "specimens" named hitherto (with the exception perhaps of Fournier's *Manuel*) were practically all put out by type-founders for the use of printers. We now come to the first specimen-book (that I have seen) which appears to be intended by a printer for the use of his customers—an innovation which was to work to the detriment of good typography. The volume has another novel feature, *i.e.*, that with each specimen of type shown, the name of the foundry from which it comes is given.[1] It displays the stock of types that a Paris printer had in 1785.

Philippe Denis Pierres, who issued it, was a man distinguished in his day. Born in Paris in 1741, he was the son of a bookseller, and nephew of Auguste Martin Lottin, whose remarkable book on Parisian printers and booksellers is still an authority, and who was instructor in printing to the Dauphin, afterwards Louis XVI. The first steps in Pierres' career were taken in Lottin's printing-house; but later he assumed charge of the office of his great-uncle,

[1] This was also done in the specimen issued by Pierres in 1770.

CICERO ITALIQUE,

goût nouveau,

Gravée à Paris par *GANDO* le jeune, en juillet M. D C C. L I V.

Après neuf jours entiers, qu'ils passerent à soutenir toutes ces horreurs, Annibal parut enfin au sommet des Alpes, transporté de joïe de voir le pays qu'il se proposoit de conquérir. Il le montroit à ses soldats, pour leur faire oublier les peines passées, & leur disoit qu'ils avoient forcé les murs d'Italie, & que ceux de Rome n'étoient rien en comparaison. Cette flateuse espérance & deux jours de repos, rendirent l'allegresse & la vigueur aux troupes abattues.

Mais voici qu'ils trouvent en s'avançant, une quantité de neige nouvellement tombée, qui engloutit les premiers qui ont la hardiesse de frayer la route aux autres, & qui en s'éboulant, entraîne ceux qui les suivent de près. Alors la frayeur, la consternation, le desespoir se peignirent sur tous les visages. Annibal seul, intrépide & tranquille rassure, console & excite à marcher.

On avance, & on trouve en face un rocher qui traversant le chemin, le ferme d'un côté, & laisse voir de l'autre un ravin de mille pieds de profondeur. Le général, qu'aucun obstacle ne rebute, tente d'autres chemins, mais la neige les ayant tous comblés & rendu impraticables, il revient au rocher, & entreprend de l'applanir. Il ordonne que l'on abatte tous les arbres des environs, & à mesure qu'on les coupe, on range le bois en forme de bucher autour du roc, & quand le monceau est élevé à peu-près au niveau, on met le feu aux arbres, & on l'entretient, jusqu'à ce que l'ardeur de la flamme ait rendu la pierre aussi rouge que le brasier même qui l'environne.

191. *François Gando's Italique, goût nouveau,* cut in 1754
Épreuves des Caractères, Gando, Paris, 1760

CARACTÈRES

DE L'IMPRIMERIE

DE M. PIERRES,

Imprimeur Ordinaire du Roi, du Grand-Conseil de Sa Majesté du Tribunal de MM. les Maréchaux de France, de la Police des Intendance & Administration Générales des Postes, du Collég Royal de France, de la Société Royale de Médecine, des État. de Provence, des Congrégations de France & de Saint-Maur, &c.

COMPOSÉS

Par Honoré-Théodore DE HANSY.

A PARIS.

M. DCC. LXXXV.

192. *Title-page of Caractères de l'Imprimerie de M. Pierres, Paris*, 1785
(*reduced*)

Pierre Gilles Lemercier (of that eminent family of typographers), who retired in Pierres' favour in 1765. Very well educated, a good Latinist, inventor of a press approved by the Académie des Sciences and examined and praised by the King, his work-rooms were a resort of men prominent in the government or belonging to the great learned societies. Baskerville corresponded with him; Franklin was both friend and correspondent; Clement XIV sent him proofs of all types in the Vatican printing-office; the King of Poland gave him a medal for suggestions and help in forming a Royal Public Library; and, in short, Monsieur Pierres was a Very Important Person.

The title of the volume is — *Caractères de l'Imprimerie de M. Pierres, Imprimeur Ordinaire du Roi, du Grand-Conseil de Sa Majesté, du Tribunal de MM. les Maréchaux de France, de la Police, des Intendance & Administration Générales des Postes, du Collège Royal de France, de la Société Royale de Médicine, des États de Provence, des Congrégations de France & de Saint-Maur, &c.,* — merely that! (*fig.* 192). It opens with a dedication dated Paris, New Year's Day, 1785, signed by Honoré Théodore De Hansy, who arranged the book, and who seems to have been employed in Pierres' establishment. The types, printed on one side of the page only, begin with very large sizes of old style roman from Caslon, and as they become smaller, roman and italic of the same size appear on one page. The fonts represented came from Fournier *l'aîné;* Fournier *le jeune;* Cappon; Gando, successor to Lamesle; Joseph Gillé *père,* a distinguished founder (who issued an interesting little specimen in 1778 containing some cursive types, four of which Pierres possessed); and from the old Sanlecque collection. Hebrew and Arabic were supplied by the elder Fournier, and "exotic" types are shown from the office of the Propaganda —

sent to Pierres through Cardinal de Bernis in 1779. Then follow letters for initials; some shaded letters; music, both with round and square notes; and a great number of typographical ornaments. These last show a good many old forms but few novelties, and as the paper of the book is very coarse, they do not seem particularly attractive. At the end of the book are twenty-five sheets preceded by a title reading *Vignettes, Fleurons, Chiffres, Armes, Passe-Partous* [sic], *Cadres, et Autres Ornements. Gravés en Bois*, etc., — an enormous collection of every sort and size of ornament; together with the arms of France and the heraldic bearings employed by the various societies and persons to whom Pierres was accredited printer. The last six sheets are devoted to scenes from the life of our Lord and the saints, intended for calendars. These cuts, from very poor and thin designs by Leclerc, were engraved on wood by "the celebrated Jean Baptiste Michel Papillon."

Pierres' specimen gives an admirable idea of the types and ornaments generally used in France up to the Revolution. It would appear that this collection later went to the printer Pasteur, whose specimen of 1823 displays the seal of the United States of America which Pierres procured for Franklin's use, and which appeared in the specimen-sheet issued by Benjamin Franklin Bache about 1790. Franklin's script types, engraved for him by S. P. Fournier *le jeune* in 1780 and 1781, were displayed on specimen-sheets, at least one of which was printed for him by Pierres.

The official emblems of different régimes shown in many French specimen-books — such as that of Pierres — are a pictorial history of social and political changes in France.[1]

---

[1] See Forestie's *Vignettes Typographiques d'une Imprimerie Montalbanaise.* Montauban, 1900, on which much of the following is based.

The earliest and best of these designs were heraldic, representing the arms of France crowned, surrounded by the collar of the *Ordre du Saint Esprit*. Rendered in line without shading, they were very decorative in quality. In Louis XIV's reign, such head-pieces and emblems became more elaborate in execution; and as the military operations of the period increased, to the royal arms were added drums, flags, laurels, and palms. Toward the end of the reign a sun (emblematic of the glory of Louis XIV— *le roi Soleil*— to protect themselves from which the courtiers, it has been said, carried parasols!) is made use of. In the next reign, armorial bearings reflect the *rocaille* decoration of Louis XV. After the battle of Fontenoy, flags and military ornaments were introduced; and when naval successes were in the public mind, head-pieces became nautical, and sails, ship-lanterns, etc., appeared. In the early part of Louis XVI's reign, the emblems of preceding reigns were used, but at the end of the monarchy we begin to see on shields three fleurs-de-lis and between them the motto *La Loi et le Roi.* Below were attributes of the monarchy and three orders of the body politic—flags, sceptres, shields, roman fasces, as mixed up decoratively as were the antagonistic ideas which they represented in the minds of the people! Later, an ominous Phrygian cap and a sword with the motto *La Liberté ou la Mort* indicates a period when there was a great deal of death and very little liberty! After the storm come more peaceful figures —Minerva between olive branches, Mercury seated on bales of merchandise, or Commerce with cornucopia, anchor, and ships—designs something in the style of Prud'hon's pretty designs for *toiles de Jouy.* In the time of Napoleon I, everything turns to eagles (the best of them designed by Besnard), then to crowned eagles, and finally to eagles on a *cartouche* against the imperial ermine.

Sometimes the eagle is quite an amiable bird and is obligingly holding an olive wreath. The papal arms and tiara in
head-pieces of that date are in allusion to Napoleon's coronation by Pius VII. At the restoration of the Bourbons (not
a particularly good period artistically), there was a return
to the ancient royal arms — three fleurs-de-lis on a shield,
surrounded by flags and sometimes by olive branches and
oak leaves. After the overthrow of Charles X, fleurs-de-lis
were replaced by a tablet (like the "tables of the Law"
in eighteenth century English churches), with the legend
"*Charte de* 1830"; and in the latter part of Louis Philippe's
reign, a Gallic cock sometimes takes the place of a crown.
One head-piece, a vignette of the cocked hat of "the little
Corporal," with sword, field-glasses and gloves, laurel and
palm leaves, and a glory beyond them, was an emblem introduced when Louis Philippe so unwisely revived Napo-
leonic traditions by bringing back the ashes of the Emperor from Saint Helena. At the fall of the monarchy, the
government suppressed the word *Charte* and replaced it by
République Française. On the accession of Napoleon III, a
revival of the designs used by Napoleon I naturally took
place. The eagle, however, became less free in drawing,
and was made to look like Russian and Austrian eagles.
Sometimes the Bonaparte bees and the *Code Napoleon* were
added to the imperial arms. Thus even ornaments in type-
specimens reveal their significance in the light of history
—another proof of the intimate relation of typography to
social and political movements.

SUPPLEMENTARY NOTES

VOLUME I

CHAPTER I. THE INVENTION OF PRINTING, &c.

Page 5, *line* 19. For the latest investigations on Gutenberg and the first printed books, see Otto Fuhrmann's "The Invention of Printing" in *The Dolphin, A Journal of the Making of Books, Number Three,* Limited Editions Club, New York, 1937. This volume, which is called "The History of the Printed Book," is edited by Lawrence C. Wroth, of the John Carter Brown Library, Providence.

Page 6, *line* 9. For the similarity of the first printed books with antecedent MSS, see H. Lehmann-Haupt's paper in *The Dolphin, Number Three,* New York, 1937, "The Heritage of the Manuscript," with illustrations comparing MSS and early printed pages.

Page 9, *add to note* 1. Moxon's only known specimen contained a Great Cannon Romain, Double Pica Romain and a roman Great Primmer, English, Pica, Long Primmer, and Brevier in roman and italic. Reed calls it a sorry performance. See Reed's *Old English Letter Foundries,* Chapter VIII, p. 180 *et seq.*

Page 10, *line* 31. See illustrated article by Paul Koch on "The Making of Printing Types" in *The Dolphin, Number One,* New York, 1933, p. 24 *et seq.* It treats of punch-cutting, justification, and hand-casting.

Page 14, *add to note.* An excellent illustrated paper on the making of English monotype matrices by Beatrice Warde of the Lanston Monotype Corporation, London, entitled "Cutting Types for the Machine. A Layman's Account" appeared in *The Dolphin, Number Two,* New York, 1935, p. 60 *et seq.* The Mergenthaler Linotype Company of Brooklyn, New York, described their process of making matrices in a booklet entitled *Pieces of Brass,* reprinted as the last chapter of their pamphlet *The Legibility of Type.*
See also section on "The Work of the Type-Founder" in Morison's introduction to Berry and Johnson's *Catalogue of Specimens of Printing Types by English and Scottish Printers and Founders,* 1665–1830, p. xviii. But Legros and Grant's comprehensive volume, *Typographical Printing-Surfaces, The Technology and Mechanism of their Production,* London, 1916, already alluded to in my text, is still an authority.

CHAPTER II. A FONT OF TYPE AND ITS CASE, &c.

Page 17, *add to note* 2. For an account of ligatured letters see R. B. McKerrow's admirable book *Introduction to Bibliography for Literary Students,* Appendix III, p. 312 *et seq.*

Page 18, *line* 15. An odd survival in antique (and mock antique) printing or sign painting is the " y " which takes the place of " th " in " the." This " y " is a derivation of the Anglo-Saxon and Middle English letter-form *thorn*, now written " th " and so to be pronounced in the words " ye," " yat," etc. The letter thorn was used in English manuscripts down to the fifteenth century, " y " becoming its common typographical equivalent.

Page 19, *line* 13. Arabic or Indo-Arabic numerals are supposed to have originated in India some centuries before our era, and certain authorities believe that their original forms represented the initial letter of the name of the numeral. They were known to Arabian scholars by the eighth century, and through Arabic influence were introduced into Spain, being found in tenth century Spanish MSS and later in those of France, England, Italy, and Germany. Both in Italy and Germany their use was prohibited in the official transactions of law courts and municipalities which adhered to the use of roman numerals. First used in volumes of mathematics, then for the paging of books, in the fifteenth century they assumed their modern shape and came into general use. Their advantage over the old system of computation lay in the convenience of employing but ten signs (nine units and zero), each possessing an absolute value and a relative value; the last figure on the right expressing its absolute value and the position of each figure towards the left multiplying the unit value of the figure preceding it by ten. See Steffens's *Paléographie Latine*, p. xxxix *et seq*.

Page 22, *in place of note* 2. This statement about Louis Elzevir is incorrect. The earliest instance of a distinction between i and j, u and v being made according to pronunciation, appears in *Dyalogus between Salomon and Marcolphus*, printed at Antwerp by Leeu about 1492. A differentiation between u and v also appeared in Trissino's *Epistola de la vita che dee tenere una Donna vedova*, Rome, 1524, but the printer Vicentino Arrighi did not distinguish between i and j. C. Wechel of Paris in printing Meigret's *Grammere Francoeze*, in 1550, used i for the vowel and j for the consonant. Andreas Wechel, at Paris, in the third edition of *Grammatica* of De la Ramée used both i and j, u aud v, in capitals as well as lower-case letters. In England, John Day in a book printed in 1578 used v and j as we do now. " The practice of the earliest printers, which they presumably took over from the scribes of their time and country, with regard to the letters under discussion was as follows: (1) There was an upper-case letter approximating in shape in Gothic founts rather to the modern J than to I, but serving indifferently for either. (2) An upper-case letter approximating in shape in Gothic founts to U, and serving for U and V. (3) A lower-case i, serving for both i and j. (4) A lower-case j, used for the second of two i's in words like 'perij,' and in Roman numerals as 'viij.' (5) A lower-case u, serving for both u and v, but only used medially or finally. (6) A lower-case v, serving for both u and v, but only used initially. There were no doubt exceptions to the general rule: it has been stated that certain of the German printers used j for the consonantal sound of i from the earliest times, and the two letters were distinguished in Spanish printing [Biel at Burgos, 1485]: but the practice of the great majority of the German, Dutch, and English printers until the end of the sixteenth century was in general as stated — in the case of black-letter printing almost invariably." I am indebted to Mr. R. B. McKerrow for calling my attention to these facts, and refer the reader to his *Introduction to Bibliography*, Appendix III, p. 309 *et seq.*, and his paper in *The Library*, London, July, 1910.

Page 25, *line* 6. These fonts of type, though bought in Holland, were not always of Dutch origin.

CHAPTER IV. Type and Type-Forms of the XV Century in Germany. *In general for fifteenth century.* For a recent volume on fifteenth century printing, see G. A. E. Bogeng's *Geschichte der Buchdruckerkunst. Der Früdruck*, Hellerau bei Dresden, 1930. Besides some 50 illustrations in the text it contains over 100 reproductions of mss and printed pages, etc., magnificently reproduced. It gives a survey of fifteenth century typography in various countries. The second volume was never published. For a fine series of facsimiles of fifteenth century German Gothic types see *German Incunabula in the British Museum. One hundred and fifty-two facsimile plates of fine Book-pages from Presses of Germany, German-Switzerland and Austria-Hungary printed in the Fifteenth Century in Gothic Letter and derived Founts. With an Introduction by Stanley Morison*, London, 1928. Morison divides his plates into 1. Pointed Text (pl. 1–42), 2. Round Text (pl. 43–85), 3. Fere-Humanistica (pl. 86–114), 4. Bastard (pl. 115–143), and 5. Mixed (pl. 144–152). The third, fourth, and fifth divisions are subdivisions of what I call a *batarde* or cursive black-letter, slowly merging into the almost roman type of Holle (*fig.* 23, Morison's pl. 152). Each division of *German Incunabula* is preceded by an explanatory introduction. This book gives in one volume much the same material for the student of fifteenth century German Gothic types that is found in Burger and *Druckschriften*, and is more convenient to use. Since *Printing Types* was written an attempt has been made to establish an exact and adequate terminology for type-design and Morison's and Johnson's classifications are evidences of this — though the first essay was of German origin. This subject is exhaustively — and possibly a trifle exhaustingly — discussed in A. F. Johnson's *Type Designs: Their History and Development*, London, 1934.

For gothic types described in this and other chapters devoted to fifteenth century type, see also Chapter 1, "Gothic Types," of *Type Designs*. The author divides his subject into five categories of types, viz.: — gothic, roman, italic, script, and advertising, and outlines the international development of each class. His numerous facsimiles are, both in interest and execution, of uneven merit.

See also McKerrow's *Introduction to Bibliography*, Appendix II, "Printing Types. General Sketch of their Early Development," etc., p. 288 *et seq.* — an excellent summing up of the subject.

Page 62, *line* 14. Mr. Rudolph Ruzicka, who has thoroughly investigated the ingenious processes employed in printing these coloured initials in the Fust and Schoeffer Psalter, tells me that they were not stamped, as generally supposed, but printed. He writes, "A solid metal block, type high, was made for the filigree work, with a shallow mortise cut in the shape of the initial. The initial itself, also of metal and exactly as thick as the mortise was deep, was inked separately and dropped into the mortise of the filigree block, already inked. The combined blocks were then printed in one impression and in exact register, separately from the type. Of course the initial was a little narrower than the mortise, leaving a fine white line between the letter and its decoration."

CHAPTER V. Type and Type-Forms of the XV Century in Italy. *In general.* In connection with the subject of this chapter, see Johnson's *Type Designs*, Chapter 2, "Roman: The Venetians and the Old Face Group," p. 48 *et seq.*

Page 73, *line* 30; *page* 76, *line* 32; *page* 79, *line* 25. In the light of Mr. Morison's researches I am inclined to give a little less credit to Jenson's types and more to the roman type used by Aldus in the *Hypnerotomachia Poliphili* than formerly. He is right in thinking that the Aldine roman capitals, which are not so tall as the lower-case ascending letters (following the tradition of earlier MSS), give a more harmonious effect to the type in mass than Jenson's capitals from which our modern usage is derived. Morison also contends that the roman types of Aldus represent the beginnings of the old-face group and that Garamond in designing his roman types did not model them on Jenson's roman fonts, but on the Aldine letter. See Morison's paper "Towards an Ideal Type," *The Fleuron*, No. 2, p. 57; and "The Type of the Hypnerotomachia Poliphili" in *Gutenberg Festschrift*, 1925. See also pl. I–XVI in Morison's *Four Centuries of Fine Printing*, London, 1924.

See note to Chapter X, on other forms of italic than that used by Aldus.

CHAPTER VI. Type and Type-Forms of the XV Century in France.
In general. Anatole Claudin's great work, *Histoire de l'Imprimerie en France au XVe et au XVIe siècle* (4 vols.), Paris, 1900–1914, is still the best book to consult on French fifteenth century type-forms, as to text and illustrations.

CHAPTER VII. Type and Type-Forms of the XV Century in the Netherlands.
In general. For fifteenth century Dutch type-forms there is still nothing better than Charles Enschedé's remarkable book, published at Haarlem in 1908, entitled *Fonderies de Caractères et leur Matériel dans les Pays-Bas du XVe au XIXe siècle*. Its upwards of 500 illustrations (many of them printed from the ancient types of the Enschedé foundry) give an unsurpassed documentation of fifteenth century fonts. This book is again referred to in Chapter XV, "Types of the Netherlands: 1500–1800," for which it is also an authority.

CHAPTER VIII. Type and Type-Forms of the XV Century in Spain.
Page 104, *line* 8. For an admirable idea of the decoration of Spanish books, see James P. R. Lyell's *Early Book Illustration in Spain*, London, 1926, with an introduction by Konrad Haebler, and illustrated with nearly 250 reproductions of various kinds. The author states that "as far as I am aware, no book has ever been written in any language dealing with the special subject of early book decoration and illustration in Spain in the fifteenth and sixteenth centuries." Dr. Konrad Haebler, the great authority on the subject of the early Spanish printing press, says that Mr. Lyell "has given us for the first time a comprehensive view of Spanish book illustration from the beginnings up to the time when a change of materials brought with it a change of style. For some unusual reproductions of Spanish printing, see "La Imprenta. Memoria leida ante la Real Academia de la Historia en la Fiesta del Libro Español de 1926" by V. Castañeda, *Boletin de la Real Academia de la Historia*, Madrid, Vol. 89, p. 440.

CHAPTER IX. Type and Type-Forms of the XV Century in England.
Page 114, *line* 13. Among the city archives of Cologne (in a book of applications for permits to visit, or live in, that city), four entries in behalf of Caxton's residence there have been discovered: the first, dated July 17, 1471, and the last, June, 1472 — the latter requesting six months' extension of this privilege. This final period covers the time of publication of *De Proprietatibus Rerum*. Caxton must, therefore, have passed a year or more at Cologne.

Page 116, *line* 26. Mr. S. C. Ratcliff, of the Record Office, London, discovered there in 1928 an Indulgence printed in the second type of Caxton (the first he used in England) and with a few letters of Caxton's third type. This document was the subject of a paper by A. W. Pollard, entitled "The New Caxton Indulgence" in the *Transactions of the Bibliographical Society*, 1928, Vol. IX, No. I, p. 86. "Its supreme importance," says Pollard, "lies in its being in all probability the first piece of printing executed by Caxton after he came to England, and issued at Westminster where he had his press. It also shows that as early as December, 1476, he was not content with the possession of only a single fount of type." Thus the date of the Caxton's introduction of printing in England must be changed from November 18, 1477, to December 13, 1476.

CHAPTER X. THE ALDINE ITALIC.

Page 125, *line* 17. In reference to the Aldine italic, see Johnson's *The Italian Sixteenth Century*, which supplies facsimiles of non-Aldine italic — *i.e.*, that used by Arrighi — his second form of italic — Blado's fine version of it, etc. See also the same author's *Type Designs*, Chapter 5, "Italic: the Old Face."

Page 128, *note* 1. For a treatise on the history of Greek types, see Victor Scholderer's "Historical Introduction" to *Greek Printing Types*, 1465–1927. *Facsimiles from an Exhibition of Books illustrating the Development of Greek Printing shown in the British Museum*, London, 1927 — a fine book invaluable for the study of Greek typography. Sixty facsimiles illustrate the introduction. The last two pages are printed from his own "New Hellenic" Greek font.

Page 129, *line* 22. Mr. Stanley Morison reminds me that italic is the one letter we now have that owes its origin to diplomatic calligraphy, and adds, "It is certainly the fact that more or less close reproductions of Aldine Chancery types were made by many printers in various parts of Italy and elsewhere. Nevertheless, the flowing italics of Garamond, Caslon, and others in use to-day are formed upon very different proportions from those of the cramped design for which Aldus is responsible. There exist in typography at least two independent italics. The first, made by Francesco da Bologna for Aldus dating from 1500 which continued in use for less than one hundred years — secondly, a flowing letter of distinctly calligraphic quality possessing considerable freedom in its line," the work oɪ the scribe Lodovico degli Arrighi of Vicenza, called also Vicentino. Arrighi's type, based on a form of chancery hand had far more movement than the prim Aldine letter. It shows the hand of a writing-master precisely as did Baskerville's type. Arrighi retained a perpendicular though cursive capital and also capitals B, C, D, E, H of the kind called swash letters. Some of his publications were for Trissino of Vicenza, who had a hand in proposed reforms of the alphabet. The few books printed by Arrighi were in the nature of luxurious impressions. Facsimiles of Arrighi's variant italics are shown in figures 1, 3, and 5 in Johnson and Morison's "The Chancery Types of Italy and France," *The Fleuron*, No. 3, London, 1924, p. 23.

Arrighi's types were employed by Janiculo of Vicenza, who also printed for Trissino. A leaflet showing these types, with the additions or changes to the alphabet suggested by Trissino, was lately discovered by one of the students at Columbia University, in the Library of the American Type Founders Company, now deposited there. It shows upper and lower-case letters, ligatured letters, vowels, and diphthongs, a "syllabary" and also the Lord's Prayer and *Ave Maria*, in Italian, with the printer's mark of Janiculo. See Fumagalli's *Dictionnaire Géographique d'Italie*, p. 519. But two other copies of the leaflet appear to be extant. See also *The Calligraphic Models of Ludovico degli Arrighi surnamed Vicentino. A Complete Facsimile and Introduction by Stanley Morison*, Paris, 1926. The most important part of this book is the type designed by Frederic Warde, copying closely Arrighi's cursive type and used in Morison's Introduction. Interesting historically, I think its beauty over-rated, for the curving lines of the f's, g's, and y's give the page a very restless appearance. In the monotype version, with this and other peculiarities modified, it is more satisfactory and a handsome form of italic.

Page 130, *line* 16. A Viennese printer, J. Singrenius, used slanting italic capitals some thirteen years earlier—about 1524. These were also used in Germany at an earlier date than Gryphius of Lyons employed them (in 1537), although his italic was of Basle *provenance*.

CHAPTER XI. A WORD ON TYPE SPECIMENS.
Page 136, *line* 20. Since William Blades issued in 1875 his little annotated catalogue, *Some Early Type Specimen Books of England, Holland, France, Italy, and Germany*, great progress has been made in investigations about type specimens, and after 1922 far more. The few sixteenth century specimens mentioned in this chapter can now be considerably supplemented, and one of great importance, unknown to me, was that of the Egenolff-Sabon-Berner foundry issued at Frankfort in 1592, the significance of which is explained on a later page. Other sixteenth century specimen-sheets not mentioned in my text are those of H. Bauer, *c*. 1509 and L. Thurneysser zum Thurn, 1583. Further discoveries about seventeenth century types have revealed that Anton Janson's types, hitherto classed as Dutch, were the product of a foundry which he owned at Leipsic between 1660 and 1687. In his first specimen-sheet of 1675

some of these types were dated 1672, 1673, and 1674, and Edling, Janson's successor, issued in 1689 a specimen showing Janson's types. Their further history is given in a note to page 156.

The seventeenth century specimen-book of most interest is that of Jean Jannon of Sedan, issued in 1621, and this, too, is also fully described in Chapter XIV, "French Types: 1500–1800." Other seventeenth century specimens can now be recorded: those of G. Baumann, 1604, J. Berner, 1622, A. Vitray, 1636, G. Ritzsch, 1641, G. Hanschen, 1655, P. J. Morsing, 1658, J. P. Fievet, 1664, 1682, J. E. Luther, 1664, 1665, 1666, 1674, 1678, K. Baumann, 1669, R. Voskens and B. Voskens, c. 1670, A. Janson, 1670 (2), 1673–74, 1674, 1678 (2), 1683, 1687 (2), C. Pistor, 1673, J. A. Schmidt, 1674, 1675, 1677, P. Lobinger, 1678, [Nisisch, 1688, A. Chrétien, 1689, J. K. Edling, 1689, J. G. Baumann, 1690, 1699, K. Hartwig, 1690, J. P. Bockenhoffer, 1691, J. Ernst, 1698, and J. Stenglin, 1699. These appear under the caption, "Type Specimens" in R. A. Peddie's *Subject Index of Books published before* 1880. *First Series*, London, 1933, p. 657 *et seq.*, and *Second Series*, London, 1935, p. 766 *et seq.* —a remarkable feat of compilation. Messrs. Birrell & Garnett's annotated *Catalogue of Typefounders' Specimens, Books printed in Founts of Historic Importance*, etc., London, 1928, is not merely a sale catalogue but a really important contribution to this subject. Of the list of English and foreign specimens, in Part I, the earliest is 1592, the latest, 1905 — 103 entries in all. Part II lists books under the types in which they are printed, with a chronological table giving names of cutter or foundry, printer, and place of issue, with comments. For the work of British type-founders consult W. Turner Berry and A. F. Johnson's excellent and comprehensive *Catalogue of Specimens of Printing Types by English and Scottish Printers and Founders*, 1665–1830. *With an Introduction by Stanley Morison*, London, 1935. For the study of French specimen-books and the foundries issuing them, an indispensable book is *Les Livrets Typographiques des Fonderies Françaises créées avant* 1800, by Marius Audin, Paris, 1933. A carefully compiled and useful hand-list of German type-specimens is Herr Gustav Mori's *Schriftproben Deutscher Schriftgiessereien und Buchdruckereien aus den Jahren* 1479 *bis* 1840. Herr Mori's account (alluded to later) of the important Egenolff specimen entitled *Eine Frankfürter Schriftprobe vom Jahre* 1592, published in 1920, his paper *Die Schriftgiesser Bartholomäus Voskens in Hamburg und Reinhard Voskens in Frankfurt a. M.*, illustrated with two broadside specimens dated about 1670, and his illustrated volume, *Die Egenolff-Luthersche Schriftgiesserei in Frankfurt am Main*, published in 1926, were all privately printed, but should be consulted when possible. Herr Mori is also the author of *Das Schrift-giessereien in Süddeutschland und den angrenzenden Ländern*, Stuttgart, 1924, which is interesting because of its reproductions of specimen-sheets, in broadside, etc. of Stenglin (Augsburg) 1708, Pistorius (Basle) 1704, Genath (Basle) 1720, Hartwig, 1690, Baumann, 1699, Köhler, 1710 (all of Nuremberg). The same writer also had a hand in the production of L. W. von Biedermann's *Die Deutsche Schriftgiesserei. Eine Gewerbliche Bibliographie* edited by Dr. Oscar Jolles, Berlin, 1923, of which Part IV, pp. 177–267, is allotted to "Schriftproben." Somewhat more complete in relation to the history of German type-founders is Friedrich Bauer's *Chronik der Schriftgiessereien in Deutschland und den deutschsprachigen Nachbarländern*, published in Offenbach in 1928— a second enlarged edition of the book originally appearing in 1914.

An enormous number of eighteenth and nineteenth century specimen-sheets of all countries, up to and including 1880, are listed in Peddie's *Subject Index. First and Second Series*, already mentioned. Under the entry "Type Specimens," hundreds of examples are given in chronological order, though entries are restricted to date, printer, title, and place. Both volumes must be consulted. Finally, Johnson's *Type Designs* contains a short chapter on type specimens. Since 1880 specimen-books, pamphlets, and sheets have been issued by thousands, but apart from a few showing good modern types, their interest ceased about 1835.

CHAPTER XII. GERMAN TYPES: 1500–1800.

In general. For facsimiles of sixteenth century printing in Germany and Switzerland, see Morison's *Four Centuries of Fine Printing*, pl. 281–306.

Page 139, *line* 7. For the design of fraktur see Konrad F. Bauer's *Leonhard Wagner der Schoepfer der Fraktur*, Frankfort, 1936, with facsimiles of the earliest fraktur types. See also Johnson's *Type Designs*—for Fraktur, p. 37 *et seq.*, for Schwabacher, p. 31 *et seq.*

Page 143, *line* 25. The Basle printers affected type characterized in design by the thickening of round sorts—such as the o—not at the opposite sides of the letter, but obliquely. We meet this peculiarity in types earlier in date than the fonts used by Froben and his contemporaries, and it may have been a derivation from Gothic type design. It gives the Basle type marked liveliness and "a pen quality," in comparison with other contemporary fonts. See also *Periods of Typography. The First Century of Printing at Basle*, by A. F. Johnson, London, 1926, with prefatory essay and 50 plates. Those devoted to Froben and his group are the most interesting.

Page 143, *last line.* Jan Stephan van Calcar was a pupil of Titian and made the anatomical drawings as well as the design for the title-page. The original wood-blocks from his drawings, cut under the direction of Vesalius, were lately re-discovered in the library of the University of Munich. These illustrations, combined with those in the *Epitome* of Vesalius, have been magnificently printed with a descriptive text and were published in folio by the New York Academy of Medicine and the Library of the University of Munich in 1935. It is issued in English and German editions at the Bremer Press, Munich, in types designed by Frederic Warde and Dr. Willi Wiegand. Its title is *Andreae Vesalii Icones Anatomicae.*

Page 145, *line* 22. Mr. Peddie lists a specimen issued by Bauer, *c.* 1509. If correct, Petri's specimen is the third, not the second, earliest known specimen-sheet.

Page 147, *line* 2. For other seventeenth century specimens see list in note to Chapter XI.

Page 150, *add to note.* The so-called Lutheran Foundry would be more correctly styled the Egenolff-Sabon-Berner-Luther foundry. Berner issued at Frankfort, in 1592, one of the most important specimen-sheets extant, which Herr Mori describes in a privately printed paper, *Eine Frankfurter Schriftprobe vom Jahre* 1592 — a contribution to the history of Frankfort type-founding — published in 1920. It contains a reproduction of the only known copy of a *Specimen Caracterum seu Typorum Probatissimorum*, etc., showing a splendid collection of types. To seven or eight sizes of roman the name of Garamond is attached, and to seven sizes of italic and some Greek, that of Granjon, thus disclosing who designed and cut these fonts. At the bottom of the specimen, a paragraph (in the only fraktur shown) surrounded by printers' ornaments, reads: "Specimen of the most distinguished and beautiful styles of type which have ever seen the light of day and by great effort and cost were accumulated, first through the late Christian Egenolff, himself the first printer in Frankfort, and then by his widow and her heirs, namely, Jacob Sabon and Conrad Berner, and which are now issued for the help of all those who use the pen, particularly for the advantage of the authors; in which may be seen what styles of type can be used for their work, and which are also useful for examination by all typefounders and printers, that they may learn what types are suitable and serviceable in their printing-houses and are ready for use. Inasmuch, however, as German [black-letter] and Hebrew types are not much esteemed, they, as well as some other Roman types are not exhibited, although proofs exist of the best of them. All kinds of molds for German, Latin, Greek, and Hebrew are in stock for sale and delivery or are on hand for casting. This sheet is produced by Conrad Berner, in the year 1592.'' This specimen explains the use of these Garamond roman and Granjon italic types in the Netherlands, England, and other countries for some two centuries after Garamond's death by printers to whom either types or strikes were sold, —the Latin specimens (*i.e.*, in roman characters) of this foundry, from 1622 to 1745, exhibiting them. The French artists Fournier mentions were, no doubt, Garamond and Granjon. A fine reproduction of this specimen is given by Berry and Johnson, pl. A. See also Herr Mori's *Die Egenolff-Luthersche Schriftgiesserei in Frankfurt am Main*, with illustrations and genealogical tables. The earliest German type used in the American colonies was procured from this foundry.

Page 152, *line* 1. For German type specimens Herr Gustav Mori accomplishes in a simple way what has been more ambitiously attempted in England and France, in his *Schriftproben Deutscher Schriftgiessereien und Buchdruckereien aus den Jahren 1479 bis 1840*, Frankfurt, 1926. This is a catalogue with an introduction by Herr Mori, of a splendid collection of German specimens, assembled under his direction, comprising 274 items, of which 186 are specimens of type-founders. The exhibition was held at Frankfort under the auspices of the Association of German Type-founders in 1926 and this hand-list should be consulted for a study of German specimen-sheets. For notes on Herr Mori's further contributions to the history of German types and type-founders see the latter part of note to page 136.

Page 156, *line* 9. These types, described as "Dutch" in the Erhardt specimen, were in some, if not all, instances cut by Anton Janson, who may have been a Dutchman, but whose foundry (originally bought from Hahn, a Leipsic printer) was established at Leipsic and in operation there between 1660 and 1687. His first specimen appeared in 1675. He was succeeded by Johann Karl Edling, and Edling's heirs seem to have taken the Janson material to Holland and from them it was bought by Erhardt of Leipsic about 1740, who therefore calls these fonts Dutch types. These types were later acquired by the Leipsic foundry of W. Drugulin, and sold by that house to the Stempel foundry, Frankfort, where they now are. Janson's specimen was apparently shown for the first time at Frankfort in 1926.

Page 157, *line* 5. A facsimile of Trattner's *Abdruck von denjenigen Röslein und Zierrathen*, etc., Vienna, 1760, was issued by Herbert Reichner, Vienna, 1927.

Page 158, *line* 2. An account of Unger's efforts, and Didot's attempts to assist him is supplied in a specimen issued at Berlin in 1793 entitled *Probe einer neuen Art Deutscher Lettern*. Unger's type — on the whole of better design than Didot's—never met with much success; but his account of his various essays is amusing and valuable.

CHAPTER XIII. ITALIAN TYPES: 1500–1800.

In general. In connection with the sixteenth century types treated in this chapter see *Periods of Typography. The Italian Sixteenth Century*, by A. F. Johnson, London, 1926, with 50 facsimiles—interesting for varieties of italic. See also "The Chancery Types of Italy and France," by Johnson and Morison, *The Fleuron*, No. 3, p. 23, already alluded to in note to Chapter X. For interesting facsimiles of sixteenth century title-pages, see Morison's *Four Centuries of Fine Printing*, Italy, 1500–1590, pl. 1–86, devoted chiefly to Venetian, Roman, and Florentine printing.

Page 161, *line* 28. The *gros canon* types used in the first and third lines of the illustration were by Guillaume Le Bé I, who cut them at Venice in 1546–47 and sold "strikes" of them to Torrentino of Florence and Tomaso Giunta at Venice. They resemble closely the *canon grosso* type used in the Vatican office (reproduced in *fig.* 110) but are not identical, and may have been cut by Le Bé or Granjon. Le Bé passed six months at Rome, in the employ of Blado, printer to the Apostolic Chamber, later merged in the Stamperia Vaticana. Blado is chiefly remembered for his fine italic—a modified form of Arrighi's second font.

Page 162, *line* 25. This italic type was used at Lyons in 1546 and at Basle in 1542. I know of no earlier use.

Page 164, *line* 16. But note that in *figs.* 105, 106, and 107 these italic capitals are shorter than the ascenders of the lower-case letter, thus following the Aldine tradition.

Page 167, *line* 6. Barberini was librarian of the Vatican Library. The surprising inscriptions, more decorative than authentic, appear to be transcripts of those on the walls of the library as recorded by Angelo Rocca in his description of the *Bibliotheca Apostolica Vaticana* printed at the Stamperia Vaticana in 1591, which describes and illustrates the building of the Sistine Library. It contains a linguistic appendix, giving the Lord's Prayer in many languages with the appropriate types, thus being one of the earliest collections of type specimens, and shows the surprising efficiency of the Vatican type-foundry at this early date. There is also a brief history of the Vatican Press which completes the book. Apparently the same work is contained in Rocca's *Omnia Opera*, Rome, 1719, Vol. II, p. 210 *et seq.*, and p. 349 *et seq.*

Page 180, *line* 13. Perrenot, not Pernot, was the individual Fournier alluded to. For both Legrand and Perrenot see Marius Audin's *Livrets Typographiques des Fonderies Françaises*, p. 104. (This book is described fully in second note to p. 205, Chapter XIV.) Also L. Morin's paper in *La Fonderie Typographique*, 1899, Nos. 10 and 11.

Page 186, *line* 3. The first edition was issued in 1793 entitled *Caratteri e Vignette o Sieno Fregi della nuova Fonderia di Antonio Zatta*, and what appears to be an enlarged third edition in 1799.

CHAPTER XIV. FRENCH TYPES: 1500–1800.

Page 189, *line* 19. For facsimiles covering French printing (Paris and Lyons) in the sixteenth century, see Morison's *Four Centuries of Fine Printing*, pl. 87–280.

Page 203, *line* 26. The year after the publication of this book, Jean de Tournes II left Lyons for Geneva, where he set up, in 1590, a printing office, ultimately absorbing the material of the brothers Chouet, possessors of types formerly belonging to Paul Estienne. Much of this material, and particularly the woodcuts of *le petit Bernard*, descended to the Imprimerie Fick of Geneva. See third note to Chapter XX.

Page 205, *line* 9. Proofs of Le Bé's types, annotated by him, are now in the Bibliothèque Nationale — the collection containing the Greek, roman, and music types being inscribed in Le Bé's hand: *Éspreuves des lettres que j'ay taillées . . . en divers temps et pour diverses personnes et partie aussy pour moy*. This was not a "specimen" for general use, but in the nature of a private record. In the eighteenth century this book belonged to Fournier *le jeune*, who calls it an *"exemplaire unique."* See Henri Omont's *Spécimens de Caractères Hébreux, gravés à Venise et à Paris par Guillaume Le Bé*, 1546–1574, Paris, 1887, and *Spécimens de Caractères Hébreux, Grecs, Latins et de Musique gravés à Venise et à Paris*, 1545–1592, Paris, 1889. Reproductions of Le Bé's types are given in both.

Page 205, *line* 28. For an account of the Le Bé foundry, see a most useful book entitled *Les Livrets Typographiques des Fonderies Françaises créées avant* 1800. *Étude Historique et Bibliographique* by Marius Audin, Paris, 1933. In this scholarly work the author takes up each French foundry in chronological order and traces, by a kind of "genealogical table," its successive owners from its foundation to its close. This is followed by a bibliography of the specimens of types issued by each foundry, and closes with brief biographical notices of the owner or owners during its successive changes in proprietorship. It is illustrated by reproductions of title-pages and types. This book must be constantly referred to for information about the individual type-founders and their specimens alluded to in this chapter on French types and printing from 1500 to 1800.

Page 231, *line* 15. For eighteenth century typography see facsimiles in Morison's *Four Centuries of Fine Printing*, pl. 324–397.

Page 232, *add to note*. A second enlarged edition of Monsieur Audin's book was issued in Paris, 1924.

Page 234, *line* 10. Garamond's roman and italic types were in common use by the Estiennes (in particular), by Colines, and other Paris printers, and Garamond himself published a few books probably printed in his own fonts. His Canon and Petit Canon types were superior to the Jannon equivalents, so long attributed to him. Mr. Morison (as has been said) believes that his roman was based on the Aldine roman fonts rather than on Jenson's, and this is probable.

Page 236, *line* 7. After Garamond's death an inventory of his material was made by the founders Le Bé and Le Sueur, Andreas Wechel being Garamond's executor in company with his widow. At the ensuing sale Plantin bought some matrices and moulds for his Antwerp establishment, Wechel bought either punches or matrices which he took to Germany, and Le Bé, material for his Paris foundry, ultimately that of Fournier *l'aîné*. Authorities differ, however, in what these various purchases consisted. The Wechels were printers at Frankfort, and it is not surprising to find these types later in the hands of the Egenolff-Sabon-Berner firm, and appearing under Garamond's name in Conrad Berner's Frankfort specimen of 1592.

Page 236, *line* 9. See Scholderer's *Greek Printing Types*, 1465–1927 (p. 10 *et seq.*), already alluded to, on the unfortunate influence of the *grecs du roi* on subsequent Greek printing.

Page 237, *line* 9. This gros romain size was used for the first time in the 1543 *Alphabetum Graecum*—not in the Eusebius.

Page 240, *line* 8. These types, the so-called *caractères de l'Université*, were the work of Jean Jannon of Sedan whose specimen of 1621—the only known copy of the earliest French specimen-book—was found by Mrs. Beatrice Warde in the Collection Anisson in the Bibliothèque Nationale, Paris. Its importance lies in the fact that it proves that Jannon in the seventeenth century cut the types commonly called *caractères de l'Université* hitherto attributed to Garamond. The first book issued by the Imprimerie Royale in 1640, *De Imitatione Christi*, was printed in roman and italic, in a font similar to Garamond's common to French printers. (See facsimiles of these pages in Morison's *Four Centuries of Fine Printing*, pl. 312–314.) The types used in 1642 for a book by Richelieu prove, when examined, to be by a different hand. These latter fonts, however, had always been accepted as Garamond's work, and a modern version recut for present-day use by the Imprimerie Nationale was classed under that attribution; but the Imprimerie does not seem to own any of the original Garamond fonts.

Jean Jannon, born in 1580, type-cutter, type-founder, and printer, came to Paris possibly from Switzerland, where after various vicissitudes he was called by Prince Henry de la Tour to Sedan, then a centre of Protestant activities, as " Printer to his Excellency and the Academy of Sedan," — for such Protestant institutions could not be called universities. Difficulties in procuring material led him, about 1615, to cut and cast his own types, which were finished by 1621. Seemingly things did not go well, so Jannon, leaving his second son (and we assume his types) at Sedan, returned to Paris, after the death of his eldest son, Antipas, in 1639, who was in charge of his father's Paris establishment. In 1642 Sedan (since 1596 an appanage of the house of Turenne) was confiscated by Richelieu; who, knowing, it would appear, of Jannon's type, seized it for use in the Imprimerie Royale then issuing the cardinal's own work *Les Principaux Points de la Foy Catholique Défendus*. This book, by an irony of fate, was printed from types cut by a Protestant at enmity with its author and the Catholic Church. Jannon ultimately returned to Sedan, and died there in 1658, his son Pierre continuing his work as printer but not as type-founder.

The existence of the Jannon specimen was already known, being listed in Bigmore and Wyman's *Bibliography of Printing*, published in 1880; and there described as " Espreuve des Caractères nouvellement taillez," but with this misleading note appended, "A very interesting book on the few (*qy.* seven) but admirable editions in 12mo, printed at Sedan." To Bigmore and Wyman Jannon had only been known for a few miniature books printed in his microscopic roman type called *la Sedanoise* — Virgil (1625), Horace (1627), and, also in Greek, the smallest Testament ever issued (except Pickering's of 1828). Mrs. Warde (Paul Beaujon) has written a valuable introduction to a facsimile of Jannon's specimen entitled *The 1621 Specimen of Jean Jannon, Paris & Sedan, Designer & Engraver of the Caractères de l'Université now owned by the Imprimerie Nationale, Paris*. Paris, 1927. For a further account of Jannon, see Lepreux's *Gallia Typographica. Série Départmentale*, Tome II, p. 18 *et seq.*, and the elaborate paper in *The Fleuron*, No. V, p. 131 *et seq.*, entitled " The 'Garamond' Types, Sixteenth and Seventeenth Century Sources Considered," written by Paul Beaujon.

Page 248, *line* 12. For an admirable series of tables showing the activities of this great establishment from 1540 to 1932, see Audin's *Livrets Typographiques*, pp. 9–34.

Page 249, *line* 16. Fournier *l'aîné's* contention was that merely strikes of Garamond's types were sold and that he retained the matrices, but this is contradicted by other evidence; and in the light of later research, the amount of ancient material in his foundry has, I think, been over-estimated.

Page 250, *line* 14. Some "placards" showing ancient types attributed to Garamond, Sanlecque, Le Bé, etc., were issued before 1788 by the *Fonderie Fournier l'aîné*. See also Audin's *Livrets Typographiques*, pp. 2 and 8.

Page 256, *line* 26. For further information on Fournier *le jeune*, and his types, see illustrated paper by Beatrice Warde (Paul Beaujon) in *Monotype Recorder*, London, March–June, 1926. See also Audin, *Livrets Typographiques*, pp. 89–98.

Page 257, *line* 2. The Grolier Club, New York, possesses a fragment of what appears to be a broadside specimen of the son, who calls himself *le jeune*. The date is preserved and reads *Le 1ᵉʳ Janvier*, 1790, the place being *Paris, rue de* [missing]. This may be the same as No. 38 in Birrell & Garnett's *Catalogue of Typefounders' Specimens*. With it are some impressions of a cover design proved on old sheets of his father's *Manuel*. A version of this same design appears at back and front of a facsimile specimen of Bodoni's first "specimen" *Fregi e Majuscole* of 1771, edited by H. C. Brooks, Florence, 1929 — an example of how Bodoni copied Fournier in his "early manner."

Page 265, *line* 5. In this connection consult Stanley Morison's illustrated paper "Uber die typographischen Ornamente von Granjon, Fournier und Weiss" in *Monatshefte für Bücherfreunde und Graphiksammler*, Leipsic, 1925, No. 10, p. 415, or the English version in the fine volume issued in honor of Herr Weiss entitled *G. R. Weiss zum fünfzigsten Geburtstage*, 12 *Oktober*, 1925, Vienna, 1925. This last volume is a magnificent showing of Herr Weiss's manifold artistic achievements.

Page 268, *line* 2. Another and very rare Lyons specimen of types, *Épreuves des Caractères de la Fonderie de Sr. Marquet*, is seemingly unknown to Audin. It is without date, but shows Fournier *le jeune's* influence, and I should place it between 1765 and 1780. A copy is in the library of the Grolier Club, New York.

Page 270, *line* 3, *third word*. For "ornamental" read "oriental" — for the sub-title of this specimen reads *Épreuves des Caractères Orientaux que se trouvent dans la Fonderie de Pierre Cot, Libraire à Paris*, 1707. This specimen has been re-issued in facsimile by D. C. McMurtrie, Chicago, 1924.